II A

¶ Of the *Shrewsbury Edition* of the Works of Samuel Butler seven hundred and fifty numbered sets only have been printed for sale. Of these, numbers one to three hundred and seventy-five are reserved for the British Empire, and numbers three hundred and seventy-six to seven hundred and fifty are reserved for the United States of America.

¶ Set number ~~686~~ 683

THE SHREWSBURY EDITION OF THE WORKS OF
SAMUEL BUTLER. EDITED BY HENRY FESTING JONES
AND A. T. BARTHOLOMEW. IN TWENTY VOLUMES.
VOLUME ELEVEN: THE LIFE AND LETTERS OF DR.
SAMUEL BUTLER, VOL. II

SHREWSBURY SCHOOL IN 1833
From a sepia drawing by Philip Browne

The
LIFE AND LETTERS OF
DR. SAMUEL BUTLER

by

SAMUEL BUTLER

VOL. II
7TH MARCH 1831–4TH DECEMBER 1839

LONDON: JONATHAN CAPE
NEW YORK: E. P. DUTTON & COMPANY
MCMXXIV

MADE AND PRINTED IN GREAT BRITAIN AT THE CHISWICK
PRESS BY CHARLES WHITTINGHAM & GRIGGS
(PRINTERS), LTD. AT TOOKS COURT
LONDON   MCMXXIV

Contents of Vol. II

	ILLUSTRATIONS	ix
XXIII.	CORRESPONDENCE, 7TH MARCH 1831–21ST OCTOBER 1832	1
XXIV.	A ROYAL VISIT	33
XXV.	CORRESPONDENCE, 29TH APRIL 1833–(?) DECEMBER 1833	63
XXVI.	CORRESPONDENCE, 6TH APRIL 1834–(?) DECEMBER 1834	100
XXVII.	CORRESPONDENCE, 17TH FEBRUARY 1835–28TH NOVEMBER 1835	128
XXVIII.	INTENDED RESIGNATION	147
XXIX.	OFFER OF A BISHOPRIC AND FAREWELL SPEECH-DAY	173
XXX.	APPOINTMENT TO LICHFIELD AND COVENTRY	200
XXXI.	CORRESPONDENCE, 7TH OCTOBER 1836–28TH DECEMBER 1836	227
XXXII.	CORRESPONDENCE, 1ST JANUARY 1837–30TH JUNE 1837	260
XXXIII.	CORRESPONDENCE, 4TH JULY 1837–24TH DECEMBER 1837	292
XXXIV.	CORRESPONDENCE, (?) JANUARY 1838–16TH JUNE 1838	328
XXXV.	CORRESPONDENCE, (?) 4TH JULY 1838–THE END OF 1838	350
XXXVI.	CORRESPONDENCE, 22ND JANUARY 1839–8TH JUNE 1839	384
XXXVII.	CORRESPONDENCE, 12TH JUNE 1839–19TH NOVEMBER 1839	411
XXXVIII.	DEATH, AND FUNERAL SERMONS	426
XXXIX.	CONCLUSION	442
	APPENDIX	
	THE HONOUR BOARDS OF SHREWSBURY SCHOOL	451
	INDEX	475

Illustrations in Vol. II

SHREWSBURY SCHOOL IN 1833. FROM A SEPIA DRAWING
BY PHILIP BROWNE   *Frontispiece*

DR. BUTLER'S HANDWRITING IN 1833   *to face p.* 68

The Life and Letters of Dr. Samuel Butler

CHAPTER TWENTY-THREE: CORRESPONDENCE, 7TH MARCH 1831 —21ST OCTOBER 1832

From the Rev. W. Hildyard

Wiverstead, March 7th, 1831.

"DEAR SIR, WHILST I EXPRESS MY THANKS to you for your kind congratulations on James's success, I must not forget to acknowledge my obligation to you, through whose able instruction my son has attained this highly distinguished honour. I remember to have heard it said, on the election of one of your pupils to an University Scholarship at Oxford, that he was *longe primus*; no one, I think, will deny the just title of *longe longeque primus* to the individual who has produced the three first men at an examination of upwards of fifty candidates for an University Scholarship, a circumstance unparalleled in either University."

*

From the Rev. B. P. Symons

Wadham College, April 8th, 1831.

*

"Your account of the effect which the result of the election at Corpus has had on the school I have read with deep concern. It is too painful to dwell upon, and hopeless thoroughly to explain. All I will say upon it is that I am inclined to attribute very much of it to a faulty but long-established mode of examination, and to an erroneous judgement, rather than to any intentional want of principles. I am, however, much gratified that you allowed my wishes to have any weight in determining you to forbear making the case public, and I beg to offer you my best acknowledgements."

From James Hildyard, Esq.

Christ's College, Monday, June 13th, 1831.

"MY DEAR SIR, You will, I am sure, have no hesitation in believing me when I say that the pleasure I feel in announcing my own success in this letter is considerably enhanced by the share I have in what you also will feel in reading it. All the Browne's medals are this year adjudged to me; the Porson to G. Kennedy, which I am also sincerely glad of.

*

"Believe me, with the most heartfelt gratitude to the person who is the cause of my enjoying my present happiness, yours ever obliged,
JAMES HILDYARD."

From W. Wordsworth, Esq.

(Original in possession of Mrs. G. L. Bridges and Miss Butler)

Rydal Mount, August 3rd, 1831 (?).

"MY DEAR SIR, Mr. Harrison having requested of me a line of introduction, I willingly comply with his wish, both on his and his son's account, as it furnishes me with an occasion of being brought to your recollection.

"Mr. H. is, in a still greater degree than parents ordinarily are, anxious for the well-doing of his son, and is much pleased with the report which, from time to time having examined his son during the last two years, I have been able to make of his progress. He is, however, in point of accuracy and strict attention far from what one would wish to find in a boy of his years; and this I take the liberty of mentioning in order that you may not be disappointed in him. I trust, however, with the benefit of your care that he will in the end do his duty to his teachers, his parents, and himself. Mr. Tillbrook's pretty place remains unoccupied, nor do we hear either of himself or any of his friends coming to it during the remainder of the summer.

"Poor Margaret suffered much in her long, wasting illness. You will be pleased to hear that, through the exertion of this family, she was induced to make a will by which her small property was better disposed of than in strict course of law it would have been. Mr. Carter, my clerk, was so kind as to undertake the office of executor. I am, dear Sir, sincerely yours,
W. WORDSWORTH."

Correspondence

To M. H. J. Klaproth

About August 12th, 1831.

"CHER M. KLAPROTH, Je viens à ce moment de recevoir de M. Cornanusaz [?] votre très obligeante réponse à ma lettre envoyée par lui, et les échantillons de Caucase [?], les intéressans fragmens Buddiques, et le très joli album typographique.

"Je suis très fâché, cher M. Klaproth, d'entendre les tristes nouvelles que vous venez de m'annoncer au sujet de votre perte littéraire. C'est un vrai malheur pour la science qu'un homme de si grand mérite et d'une connaissance si profonde soit la victime des événemens, glorieux pour la nation quoique funestes dans leur suite pour lui-même.

"J'ai mis, mon cher M. Klaproth, la somme de 1,000 francs à votre disposition chez M. N. Carlisle. Daignez, mon cher ami, accepter ce petit legs d'amitié de notre cher Baron: vous ne sauriez pas créer un plus tendre souvenir d'un homme également cher à nous deux, qu'en me permettant de lui succéder dans les devoirs amicals.

"Quant à votre ouvrage inédit, soyez bien sur que j'y prends grand interêt et que je ferai mon possible pour vous servir. J'espère même y réussir, mais il faut du temps. A présent je suis obligé de rester ici jusqu'à Noël; alors je serai à Londres, où je pourrai faire plus qu'en province. Néanmoins je ne tarderai pas à écrire à mes amis littéraires et distingués sur ce sujet. Tout le monde à présent ne s'occupe que d'un seul sujet, la nouvelle loi aux élections au Parlement, mais après quelques semaines j'espère avoir le plaisir de vous annoncer au moins le commencement de mes efforts.

"En attendant voulez-vous avoir la bonté de m'envoyer une courte annonce..."

[The rest of the draft was not found]

From the Rev. S. Tillbrook

Freckenham, November 6th, 1831.

"MY DEAR ARCHDEACON, Hughes has not yet delivered himself of his commission, so I can only say 'thank you' for the charge, which I shall read *when I get it*.

"I have not heard from poor old Holme. I wish he had chosen his asylum here, till the storm abated; he should have had a hearty welcome! My wife and I were struck with your account of the tramps who cross you in your walks. The same thing occurs here. Yesterday two of these shocks of fellows came to our Parsonage and openly said they were 'members of the Birmingham Union out of employ.' I am inclined to believe that there is a plot of some sort brewing, and the more so as I learn from my nephew (who is in the office of the Quartermaster-General) that the clerks are at work day and night in arranging routes, etc., for the troops in case of need. The intended meeting at White Conduit Hill is only one of the links of this disloyal Union. What scenes at Bristol! Bishoprics are at a discount now!

"Touching Peter Spencer, B.A., of Peterhouse College. He was a pupil of mine, and a right funny dog was he. His father is a droll fellow enough, a dealer in feather-beds and bolsters, and, what is better, in choice wines. The son is a great reader, and I believe, indeed I know, that he is an author also. His father told me his book was beautiful, but I never read it. Young Peter is a rhymer and a doggerel wit; on his dog's collar was a distich to this effect:

'My name is Pet, to Pet. Coll. I came.
I'm an honest dog: I hope you're the same?'

He was plucked, I believe once: whether his family bought the goose's feathers I cannot say.

"Though you do not visit Cambridge at Christmas I hope you will come to us, and if I can get to town with you I will. We were all sickening when we left you, and fell ill when we got home. I never was so decidedly ill in my life, and if I had not insisted upon losing blood should have gone raving mad. Wife is well now—so is your jolly godson—so is your faithful friend, Old Till. Kind regards to all!"

I looked out Peter Spencer in the Museum Catalogue, and was referred to "Minimus." The book referred to by Mr. Tillbrook does not seem to have been published till 1863. It is entitled *Parvula, or a few little rhymes, about a few little flowers, a few little birds, and a few little girls, to which are added a few little songs and a few other little things by Minimus* (London: Trübner & Co., 1863).

The unobtrusiveness of this may perhaps be a trifle obtrusive, but the book, so far as I dare pronounce an opinion, is greatly above the average. Dr. Butler has said nothing about Peter Spencer, but Mr. Tillbrook, who knew him well, evidently liked him.

From Robert Scott, Esq.

Oxford, November 28th, 1831.

" DEAR DR. BUTLER, Allow me to thank you for your kindness in remembering me in the case of your prizes, and your doing me the justice to suppose that I should be anxious to see anything of so much importance to Shrewsbury. The Verses themselves of course gratified me very highly, and you may suppose how perfect it seemed to me when I complain of a little inattention in printing and accenting the Greek!!! By the bye, ought not γένοιτ' ἄν in the last line to have been ἐγένετ' ἄν? I take the liberty of surmising that it is not to Bateson that we are indebted for the erudition displayed in the notes to his Latin Verses.

" Payne has got through his examination at last; and you will, I believe, be inclined to think that something is rotten in the state of Denmark, when you know that even his talents and reading ran a risk from the strange bias which the Examiners have taken to Metaphysics: in fact so discursive are their examinations on other points, and so constant in that, that it is literally the only thing which a man can take up with an assurance of advantage. He may take up History, and not be examined in it; the Tragedians, and get nothing but the old questions about ἵνα, ὄφρα, and ὡc. But these moral Metaphysics alone are certain. And this is ' Litterae humaniores.' "

*

To Dr. J. Johnstone
January 2nd, 1832.

"You know my loathing of meanness and humbug. If I were in Parliament I most assuredly would support the Bill, and the whole Bill; that is, I would decidedly vote with the administration. Not that I think the whole Bill is the best of all possible Bills in all its points, but because I know that in such a mighty measure as this it is impossible to have a Bill that is unobjectionable, and I would rather acquiesce in such imperfections as I may think it has, than endanger its efficacy by frittering away parts of it in detail. So much for that matter.

"Now for another. I am, and have been for some time, promoting a scheme for reform in the Church, which I think ought to originate with ourselves rather than with the laity. I wish to sweep away the whole present body of ecclesiastical laws (I have not touched that part of the reform yet), and to have a more enlarged and at the same time a more simplified code—better suited to the enlarged views of mankind in the present age. There is hardly any part of our ecclesiastical law which is not the offspring of the dark ages or of the ancient Roman laws. The house is too ruinous for repair; we ought to pull it down and build a new one. I would sweep away all Bishops' and Archdeacons' Courts and remodel the whole, leaving the common law to take care of the laity, and the ecclesiastical to be wholly concerned with the government of the clergy and inferior officers. Spiritual courts are a monstrous evil."

I have already said that I found no trace of the scheme above referred to among Dr. Butler's papers. It is probable that he gave all papers connected with it to the friend whom he thought most likely to interest himself in the matter.

From the Rev. Thomas Hill
Vicarage, Chesterfield, January 6th, 1832.

"REVEREND AND DEAR SIR, It is not without much apprehension of the appearance of officiousness that I venture to trouble you with this letter, my only apology for which is the desire I feel to do something for our beloved Church in the hour of her peril.

"The confidence with which you honoured me in mentioning to me the admirable scheme you had devised for the augmentation of small livings emboldens me to ask whether it would not be desirable for you, without further delay, to take the sense of your Clergy on that subject, and (if I may presume to suggest such an addition) on the expediency of testifying their willingness to submit to any sacrifices which would contribute to the permanency of the Church by the removal of those abuses which, alas! now render her the object of suspicion and dislike to a large portion of the community. It has long been my persuasion that nothing would be so likely to save her from ruin as a declaration of this kind, bearing the evident marks of sincerity and disinterestedness, from a large body of her Clergy. And I am the more anxious to draw your attention to the subject, because I am persuaded that your name would not only ensure to such declaration the favourable consideration of the Government, but the speedy adoption of a similar course by other members of our body. If it would be more agreeable to you that such a proceeding should be the result of a requisition addressed to you, I would, under your instructions, spare no pains in obtaining the signatures of my brethren in this Deanery to one as consonant as possible to your and their wishes."

From E. Broadhurst, Esq. (a Unitarian)

Cambridge, March 5th, 1832.

"MY DEAR SIR, Accept my warmest thanks for your kind letter. Nothing could be more gratifying to my feelings than the expressions of interest and approbation which it contained from one for whom I feel the highest respect, and to whom I owe many obligations for his uniform kindness and admirable instruction. Moreover I was highly delighted to find that I had not, as I feared, missed the honour of having my name recorded on the Shrewsbury School boards. You must now allow me to apologise, not for an inadvertence, but an error of judgement.

The fear that you would be overburdened, rather than otherwise, with Tripos papers, dissuaded me, almost against my will, from committing what appeared to me likely to be an act of supererogation. Therefore, my dear sir, I must request you to absolve me from this seeming neglect. After much inward deliberation, I have decided not to take my degree, unless, upon unbiassed consideration, I were to find that the doctrines which I have hitherto considered true and unanswerable are both false in themselves and can be proved to be so. I could have wished to hold the title of a Fellow of Magdalene, were it but for a day and unconnected with any pecuniary emolument, but the decided objection which I have to write myself down that which I certainly am not in thought appears to be an insuperable obstacle. If you remember, you said, in speaking to me when at Shrewsbury on this subject, ' that although you knew many in my case who had taken their degrees, you thought from the opinion which you had of my character that I should not add another to the list.' This declaration of yours, thus kindly expressed, has always had the effect of annihilating any symptoms of Jesuitical reasoning which might have obtruded itself on my thoughts."

From the Rev. James Tate

Richmond, Yorks, March 8th, 1832, Thursday Evening.

"MY DEAR SIR, I have great pleasure in giving an immediate answer to your kind letter of the 4th.

*

"Secondly then, of the Greek Grammar. A copy was forwarded to you by my booksellers, Baldwin and Cradock . . . because I desired it. Moor's book in its palmy state, when 2nd Futures Active and Middle were flourishing around with unsuspected Praeterita Media, etc., was the very finest specimen of skill and ingenuity: *materiam superabat opus*. Since I have had to do with it, whatever destruction of false building has been committed might be just in itself, but has made sad havock of the façade. Still, however, as I wanted the book for use in my own school, where for thirty-five years it has been used, and as there was a strong demand for it at Glasgow—in other parts of Scotland also—I have not scrupled to devote a great deal of time and thought to its rectification. Not that I swear to the excellence of everything which Moor originally placed, or which I have since substituted. But it answers my purpose in our way of working at Richmond; and that must plead my excuse for what I have done. I have schemed ... and grown warm upon it; but the chances are very much now against my ever producing a Second Part of Greek Grammar. Dr. Blomfield's minor book from Matthiae, if shortened and cleared of some faults, and on a better type ... might do very well.

"To your objection at p. 7 I have nothing to reply: it is part of the old book, with which I felt no call to intermeddle.

"For *three declensions* and *two conjugations* ... that is marrow and vitals essentially dear to us at Richmond and at Glasgow.

"And now, my dear sir, as you have this little book of grammar in your hand, let me point out to you a few particulars in which the Swale has endeavoured to infuse into the Clyde a stream of more purity and correctness.

"P. 6. 'What of the Greek ablative?' Let nothing be answered till a comparative anatomy of Greek and Sanskrit have taken place: nothing till then.

"P. 15. What vile absurdity it was to say .. мнтερᾰ, not мнтρᾱ, for distinction's sake! No *ear* could possibly make the confusion. Many of these crotchets were manufactured doubtless at Alexandria.

"P. 20. I generally approve of what I have left unchanged; but often, as here on the article, I have altered without any notice.

"P. 35. In *re levi* important errors may be involved; therefore I have said ἀν ... originally privative, before a consonant ἀ.

"P. 47. I have purposely set the neuter next to the masculine, both for clearness and simplicity, and to suggest a principle: what else is the neuter but somehow or other an abortion of the masculine?

"P. 59. In this *monitum* I think much important matter is suggested: my object has been to set masters a-thinking ... where they have only dreamed before.

"P. 65. Here also, to many masters with old books, a startler is given.

"P. 88. The brevity of my book struck me at one time as unhappily deficient in respect of ἵημι. By constantly referring to the parallel forms of τίθημι I rather find advantage gained than difficulty incurred.

"P. 99. I have gladly dismissed '(Attice)' from ἀκήκοα, ἐλήλυθα, etc. There never was any other form in any other dialect. Why could not the Alexandrine Grammarians have said, 'The greater part of verbs *ab initio* pure have the augment so and so—some half-dozen have reduplication'?

"P. 110. On this *monitum quintum* I have been writing largely in the *Gentleman's Magazine*: two numbers are out; a third is ready for next month.

*

"P. 111. My here proceeding with the second class of tenses, and in that process daring to reject for good and all the 2nd Future Active and Middle, has delighted my timid self as a very bold and heroic achievement.

"P. 117. The *Paulo-post-futurum* I had long ago discarded from my grammatical creed: just as good call ἐτετύμμην *Paulo ante praeteritum*.

"I cannot be supposed to make money out of such publications, however much of time, thought, talent, may have been expended upon them.

"To mend the matter, Cameron was insolvent before this last edition came from the press.

"At all events it delights me to contribute to the rectification of Greek Grammar, to the demolition of *Analogica Linguae Graecae*, and to the reformation, on a new extended sound basis, of Greek Etymology.

"So much at a time as scholars may like to read I print once in the *Gent. Mag.* The matter grows under my hand, and I do flatter myself the present generation, which sees a Sanskrit Professorship established at Oxford, will yet be enabled to understand Greek the better, for going to its mother-tongue in search of illustration.

"What could Plato know beyond the obvious composites and derivatives, and why are we to be frightened by any idolatrous 'divine' attached to his name from considering the *Cratylus* as a very mortal and most erroneous piece of bad etymology?

"You will perhaps be surprised when I tell you that if Hemsterhuis, in his grand theory, built on any hypothesis which Schultius's Hebrew speculations suggested to him, he was utterly ignorant of the Hebrew language, and of Schultius the grammarian of it.

"Let me return to the Platonic and Eustathian doctrine. The first verse in the first book of the Iliad contains four most magnificent specimens:

"1. Μῆνις, lasting wrath; Th. μένω, *to remain firm*: but where is the *wrath*? A purely *gratis dictum*! Some man's αὐτὸς ἔφα for it: nothing more.

"2. ἀείδω . . . ab a epitatico, et verbo εἴδω, *scio*, quia haec vox pertinet maxime ad poetas, quibus multarum rerum cognitio attribuitur.

"If Dr. Butler were to tell this to me ten hours together 'by Shrewsbury clock,' with all my love and veneration for him, I would not believe it.

"3. θεά and θεός, à θέω, *curro*, quia planetae qui continuo cursu versantur, apud antiquos dicebantur *dii*,

"Vel a θεάω (which, like κτάω and scores besides, never existed) *intueor, contemplor*, quia Deus omnia intuetur.

"4. Ἀχιλλεύς . . . 'on account of the origin of the name, it is written Ἀχίλευς, being formed from α *intens.* and τὸ χεῖλος, *the lip.*' Ohe! jam satis est.

"Ought not the *proceres* of Greek learning like you to publish the ban of the Greek Empire against the currency of such Brummagem coin?"

From the Rev. S. Tillbrook

Freckenham, Mildenhall, Suffolk, March 29th, 1832.

"MY DEAR ARCHDEACON, Will you be kind enough to answer me the following queries?

"1. Have you in your classical readings of the oldest writers of Greece and Rome met with any allusions to *angling*?

"2. If so, are they confined entirely to ground fishing with rod and line, or have you met with any account of *fly-fishing* or fishing with *artificial baits* of any sort?

"3. Has the practice of angling been in fresh-water rivers or lakes, or in the sea?

"These queries are made in consequence of an application I have just received tempting me (nothing loth) to assist in the publication of a periodical work to be entitled *Museum Piscatorium*, or an account of the British Fish—their natural history, favourite haunts, food, etc., etc., together with the best approved method of catching them with an angle, not forgetting, when caught, to teach our cooks the best way of dressing them, etc., etc., etc.

"The coloured plates, of which I have seen a specimen, are admirable. The work will be scientific, practical, and all that an angler can desire. But it will be expensive, and therefore a safeguard of subscribers must be previously enlisted. The price of each number, large paper, etc., will be 12*s*. every three months; smaller paper, 7*s*. or 8*s*. The whole will be complete, if possible, in twelve numbers. As I have a great deal of leisure time now, I thought the partial superintendence of such a work would be amusing, and occasionally remind my ancient brethren of the angle that 'old Till' was alive and ready, like a true son of St. Peter, 'to go a-fishing,' etc., etc.

"Will you subscribe yourself, and can you, think you, beat me up a recruit or two? George Maddock ought to be a subscriber, and a contributor also. I wish of all things to get a good list of clerical names—Bishops, Archdeacons, etc., etc. —because 'angling' is perhaps the only proper amusement or river-sport of our cloth.

"I shall apply to Bishop Blomfield, who, in his earlier days, was an angler. Would Dr. Dugard subscribe, or Archdeacon Bather, or that jolly fellow Drury? I shall willingly give my best attention, and take care that nothing unseemly or unbecoming the character of an honest angler be admitted into the *Museum*.

"Were you in town this Christmas? I have stayed at home ever since the autumn. My last summer's journey emptied my pockets for one year at least, and I shall not wander again at present. We are all well, thank God, and young master and his mamma unite with me in kind regards to all friends at old Salop, and particularly to yourself and your fireside circle. We have about thirty cases of cholera within ten miles of us. This makes the stoutest of bowels to yearn and quail."

I regret to say that no numbers of the *Museum Piscatorium* were ever published.

Notes for Dr. Butler's Answer to the Foregoing

Fishermen among the ancients were proverbial for their poverty, Lucian, *Dialog. Mort.*, 27, speaking of line-fishing in rivers: Βίον ἄπορον ἀπὸ ποταμοῦ καὶ ὁρμίας ἔχων εἰς ὑπερβολὴν πτωχὸς ὤν. Hence ἁλιέων βίος was a proverb for a life of poverty.

Theocritus, in the only piscatory eclogue of antiquity that has come down to us (a short account of which may be amusing), begins *Idyll* xxi, 1, with reference to it. [That there were other poems on the same subject is clear, *e.g.* the Θυννοθήρα of Sophron.]

He also makes his fishermen so poor that they sleep two in a bed in a wattled hut. He mentions their implements:

καλαθίσκοι—little baskets.
κάλαμοι—rods.
ἄγκιστρα—hooks.
δέλεαρ—the bait wrapped up in sea-weed to keep it fresh.
ὁρμείαι—the line.
κύρτοι—the osier wickerwork for forming a weir.
σχοίνων λαβύρινθος—the labyrinth of rushes, which I take to have been a sort of thing like our eel-traps.
μήρινθοι—stronger cords for pulling the net, or perhaps strong sea-lines.
κῶας—a fleece, as some read it, perhaps for warmth; but others more justly read κώπας, oars.
λέμβος—the boat, which he says was an old one upon the stocks.

φορμός—a mat beneath their heads.

εἵματα πῖλοι—a coarse hair cloth garment, probably such as the Baptist wore of camel's hair, for the scene of the eclogue is thought to be in Egypt.

And so poor were they that, he says, they had neither pot nor pan besides, and were half-starved (verse 40). They angled from a rock, watching their prey and moving the bait about. Then he describes a great fish biting and bending his rod double, which made him afraid of losing the fish, especially as his hook was a bad one. He therefore plays him after he has struck him gently; and when he will not *run* out with the line any longer he pulls him up, and having carefully unhooked him, he *tethers* him, as we sometimes do a pike, for so I interpret

"καὶ τὸν μὲν πειστῆρα κατῆγον ἐπ' ἠπείροιο."

This, however, seems to be sea, not river angling, for the fisherman swears that he will never again ὑπ' ρ πελάγους πόδα θεῖναι, "set a foot over the sea," being enriched with the golden fish that he has caught.

Theocritus i, 40. The fisherman is represented on a smooth *rock* preparing his net (δίκτυον) for a cast.

Theocritus iii. The fisherman is watching tunnies from the top of a rock.

ἠρέμα νύξε, "struck him gently"; ἐχάλαζε, "played him" or "gave him line"; οὐ φεύγοντος, "when he would not run out any longer"; ἔτεινε, "he shortened line."

The ancients seem to have distinguished between eels and other fish: Homer, *Iliad*, xxi, 203, where men are said to be food "for eels and fishes," and xxi, 353, τείροντ' ἐγχέλυές τε καὶ ἰχθύες, where we find the fishes "beginning to sweat."

Fisherman:

ἀσπαλιευτής.
πυρευτής—who used a light at night.
τριοδοντίᾳ χρώμενος—the spearer.
κάλαμος—the cane rod.
ῥάβδος—the staff rod or pole.
λίνον—the line.

τρίχες ἵππειαι—horsehair to tie the hooks to.
ἄγκιστρον—the hook.
φελλοί—the corks to support the net or line.
μολύβδαινα—the lead.

The various kinds of fishing enumerated by Pollux, 96, are ἀγκιστρευτική, with the hook; ἁλιευτική, on the sea; ὑγροθηρική, in marshes; ἑρκοθηρική, with nets (?); πυρευτική, with lights.

Plato, *Sophist.*, i. 220:

κύρτοι—wicker traps.
δίκτυα—nets.
βρόχοι—snares, I suppose, such as to halter pike.
πόρκος—a kind of drag net, or perhaps a flue in which the fish were enclosed in a given space, for Plato includes this in ἑρκοθηρική. Then comes πῦρ ὸς προς φῶς, by firelight; ἀγκιστρευτική τριοδοντία—ἀσπαλιευτική—and ἁλιεύς.

Plato, *De Rep.*, iii, p. 404. B. observes that Homer never makes his heroes feed on fish, though they were on the shores of the Hellespont, but on roast meat as the simplest, most easily prepared, and most invigorating diet.

Fishery was divided into two branches—the ἑρκοθηρική, including net-fishing, weirs, snaring, and spearing, and ἀσπαλιευτική, or line-fishing, Plato, *Sophist.*, *l.c.*

Pollux, x, 132, implements:

φέρνιον—a fishing basket.
σπυρίς—a basket; σπάρτα, σπαρτία, rush baskets.
σπυρίχνιον or καλαθίσκος—rush baskets.
λίνον—the thread of the reel.
δίκτυον—casting net.
ἀμφίβληστρον—casting (?) or drag (?) net.
ἕρκη—the weirs.
πόρκοι—trammels.
κύρτοι } wicker traps or cages—I believe like eel-baskets.
γρῖφος }
γάγγαμον—a seine.

φελλοί—corks to bear up the net; μολύβδαινα, lead to sink it; ῥάβδοι, stiff rods; κάλαμοι, finer ones; κάμαξ, a pole like a trolling-rod.
ὁρμία—the line.
ἄγκιστρον—the hook; the barb was called ἀκίς, whence ἄγκιστρον ἀκιδωτόν, a barbed hook.
θρίξ—the horsehair to which it was tied; often πλεκτή, or plaited.
ἰχθὺς ἐκ ταγήνου—a fish out of the frying-pan; ἐξ ἄλμης, out of the brine or pickle.
τρίγλα—the mullet; σκάρος, a fish said to ruminate and remarkable for breaking from the nets (the ancients said that when a scarus was caught another scarus came and pulled his tail to help him to escape); λάβραξ, perhaps the dogfish; μύραινα, possibly the lot; κεστρεύς, a mullet; χρυσόφρυς, the gilt-head; γόγγρος, the conger; μελανουρίς, (?); ἀνθίας, (?); σφύραινα, (?). Pollux hardly mentions a river fish except the ἔγχελυς, or eel, and the ... or gudgeon.

To the Rev. T. S. Hughes
(Original in possession of Mr. Hughes's representatives)

April 2nd, 1832.

"DEAR HUGHES, In awarding the Pelham prizes I fancy I discover something of the style of the individuals whom I suppose the writers of them. Now as I wish to be quite unbiassed, I shall be very glad if you will look over the copies I send you, and tell me which you think the best; send me word by sending me the motto of that which you think best and second best. None are without some faults, but I have not marked them yet: you may do so if you please.

"If the motto which you send me proves to be that which I also have considered the best, there will be nothing more for you to do than to return me the exercises when I write you my answer. If it turns out to be a different one (and I think there are two whose faults and merits are nearly equal), I will get you to put them into the hands of some other good scholar;

and if you and he come to the same opinion I surrender mine, or in short adopt the opinions of two out of three. I should say they are all inferior to the generality of our Greek verses—indeed considerably so.

"I am now better, but I have suffered cruelly ever since January with inflammatory attacks in head, face, and throat. My face has been very much swelled, and the torture in my teeth almost past bearing.

"With regard to the passage in Shakespeare, it is in *Julius Caesar*, Act II, Scene 1, beginning 'It must be by his death,' to 'And kill him in the shell'; then omit about twenty-six lines, and go on with 'Since Cassius' down to 'the nature of an insurrection.'

"I hope you will not find this very troublesome—an early attention to it will oblige me.

"If Harry Drury and I cannot agree upon the Hexameters, I have requested him to consult B. Kennedy. I have sent them to him because I do not like to give too much trouble to our friend.

"Yours truly, "S. BUTLER.

"P.S. I find old Till is going to publish a fishing-book—perhaps I may help him.

"I see in the *Cambridge Chronicle* for April 6th a Mr. Widnall, a florist at Trumpington, advertises fine dahlias at 18s. a dozen. He advertises about three dozen by name. Will you get him to send me forthwith by the earliest conveyance one root of each sort named in his advertised list, which will come to about £2 15s. 6d., and the [word missing—ED.] may pay carriage to Birmingham by the Rising Sun? I presume the roots are not yet potted, but will come in a mat or hamper: they should be furnished with tickets of their names. I enclose £3. Let them be directed to me, to be forwarded by coach from Birmingham, *i.e.*, provided the package does not exceed half a hundredweight (and I suppose it will not weigh a quarter of a hundredweight), else it should be sent by waggon. My dahlias are almost as fine as my Aldines. I wish you could see them. Pay the carriage of this parcel out of the enclosed, and do not pay the carriage of the dahlias to Birmingham."

From the Rev. W. F. Hook

Coventry, Monday before Easter, 1832.

" MY DEAR MR. ARCHDEACON, . . . As for your humble servant, he has had no attack since you and Mrs. Butler earned his everlasting gratitude by your kindness in nursing him at Beaumaris. Indeed I am well enough to undertake to lecture every day during the holy week. This is both an exercise to myself and profitable to my people. I have always had full congregations and increased my communicants at Easter. I took the hint from the late excellent Bishop of Edinburgh. I see that St. Chrysostom used to preach every day during Lent. The Fathers must have been giants in body as well as mind. Indeed the Patriarch of Constantinople's admirable homilies on St. Matthew and St. John are, in my humble opinion, quite astonishing. He is as plain, simple, and practical as Bishop Wilson, as good a casuist as Bishop Sanderson, as copious in his brevity as Dr. Barrow; and as to his explanation of difficult texts, I find him quite as satisfactory as Grotius or any of the writers in the *Critici Sacri*."

From Robert A. Slaney, Esq., M.P.

Watford, April 16th, 1832.

" DEAR SIR, I have had it in intention several times to trouble you on a subject connected with the comforts and I hope improvement of many of the humbler classes in Shrewsbury. With such an object in view you will excuse my intrusion on your valuable time and my request for your counsel. No man can doubt the policy, in these times, of all proper efforts to bind together the different ranks of Society. We shall double our power to enforce order and discipline on the one hand, if on the other it is seen we are exerting ourselves to encourage industry and forethought. I venture to suggest the adoption of a plan for aiding the working classes in Shrewsbury, which has been found on trial very beneficial elsewhere, though hitherto I believe only adopted in a few country towns or rural districts. Having seen the anxiety with which it is embraced in several places, it seems to me that, with some alterations of the details, the principle would be applicable also to the dwellers in large cities, who more than any other persons require some incitement to prudent habits. I enclose you a printed outline of the plan in question, which I had prepared to explain it to the cottagers in certain townships around us, who have universally become depositors. A limitation of the class of persons would be necessary. Perhaps the bonus given may be too high for a more populous district; and it might probably be better to begin, as a trial, with one parish or division; though after much consideration it seems to me quite practicable (after due arrangements) to embrace a wider range. The more simple the rules are the better, as with these people the least complexity leads to mistake and complaint. The whole would be under the management of a committee of subscribers. Instead of them laying out the amount due to each depositor at the end of the year, a preferable plan would be for each depositor to receive tickets of credit on certain shops (whose prices were cheapest and articles best) where they might lay out the money themselves. This flatters the pride and consequence (not in such a case bad auxiliaries) of these persons. Perhaps one-third or one-fourth the amount deposited would be bonus enough. On the latter supposition, by the outlay of £200 per annum, the beneficial direction of £1,000 per annum would be obtained, and if each family deposited on an average £1 6s., or 6d. per week, we should have above six hundred families each to receive at the most pressing season £1 12s. 6d., or the worth of it, the produce for the most part of their own industry and care. I cannot help thinking the moral effect would also be considerable on their habits.

" It seems to me that if the object was fairly stated a considerable subscription might be raised for this purpose, to which I should be most happy to contribute as I ought to do, and have no doubt Mr. Jenkins would do the same. If half only of what I hope was effected it would still be of some use. There would be very little trouble attendant on this plan, as the rules are laid down; the distribution of tickets of credit would be only once a year and according to ascertained claims. The deposits would be received once a week or fortnight at fixed hours, and perhaps some respectable tradesmen would be found to volunteer in rotation to receive them. If not, some proper person for a small gratuity would easily be found. I cannot help saying I think no party or political feeling (which mars so many things in Salop) could interfere with such an object. Perhaps you will speak on this subject to Archdeacon Bather and Mr. Iliff (to whom I have written), and the other Clergy. Should you approve it I would call on you at any time to consider further arrangements. Whilst invidious remarks are unfairly made on the Clergy (not I hope in Shrewsbury), it would be no bad answer to see them again (as they generally are) engaged in plans to benefit their poorer neighbours. Pray excuse the trouble I have given you, and believe me very truly yours,

"ROBERT A. SLANEY."

From a Rector in the Archdeaconry of Derby

April 27th, 1832.

"REVEREND SIR, A disagreeable circumstance having taken place twice within the last three months, I am under the necessity of applying to you to know whose province it is to notice it, whether mine or the churchwardens, and what the penalty incurred.

"In the parish of Chellaston it is long since there was a resident minister, and the place, from having been neglected, has become full of dissenters. Yet these men, who never enter the church for any other purpose, seem to think that they have a right when they please to ring the bells, without either asking or obtaining leave. Accordingly, little more than two months since, a marriage having taken place in the village, and again on the occasion of the Reform Bill having passed its second reading, without even asking the churchwarden for the key, they broke into the church through the windows, and this last time made it a midnight receptacle for drinking, having sent and got two gallons of ale, which they drank in the church.

"You will oblige me by informing me what the consequences of such conduct would be, and also whose place it is to notice it."

To the Writer of the Foregoing Letter

Shrewsbury, April 30th, 1832.

"REVEREND SIR, Disputes of the kind you mention are certainly disagreeable, not only in themselves, but in their consequences; but if it is possible to come to a good understanding by accepting a promise of abstinence from such conduct in future, it is better than to proceed to litigation.

"If I am rightly informed, the permission to ring the bells depends not on the churchwardens alone, nor on the minister alone, but on their concurrent consent.

"I presume the remedy is by presentation to the Bishop or Archdeacon at his next visitation."

From Robert Scott, Esq. (who had very narrowly missed taking the Ireland)

May 17th, 1832.

"DEAR DR. BUTLER, Many, many thanks for the soothing expressions of your kind letter, which only leaves me room to regret that occasion should ever have been given for it. It was a fond and a long-cherished hope of mine that I might some time or other show myself partly worthy, at least, of my school, and it is bitter indeed, when I had at last the object in my reach, to have it dashed from my grasp for ever. To others it might seem absurd to talk of my being so sure of it, but you will make allowance for my anxiety to set myself right with you, and under the circumstances I think you will not think that it arises entirely from causeless, at least, self-conceit, if I say that I lost it only by ill-fortune. Some of my friends, I see, have informed you that I was ill, and I will leave you to judge of the probable effects of that illness, when you know that it was a violent inflammation of the liver which seized me during Monday night, and it wa raging when I had to go in and strive in the schools; while to make the matter, if possible, worse, we had to compose an argumentative Latin dialogue, so that I was required to carry on in my head and embody in good Latin two conflicting arguments, at a time when positively I was in such a state of pain as ended in actual sickness. In the afternoon I had a little relief, but still was utterly disabled from thinking, and the consequence was that I made several mistakes which the slightest consideration must have rectified. Under all these mischances, the question was at last ' one of great hesitation between us.' I should have been bold to conclude that it was solely by illness that I was beaten, even if Mr. Ellison had not, as I am assured he has, stated it in precise terms.

"With respect to next year, I certainly could stand; but I confess that my pride, true or false, will never submit to risk a fourth discomfiture. And I am persuaded that even you will not wish me to try it next year, when I remind you that my degree will come on within six weeks of that time. And I am not without a presentiment that the end of it would be 2.2.2.2., and 2nd class.

"Be assured, my dear Dr. Butler, that next to the disappointment of my father, who, I am sorry to say, had set his heart very much upon my success, there is nothing in my failure which affects me more than having been the *fainéant* who has sullied the splendour of Shrewsbury and broken the chain of her successes; yet I hope that you will account me rather unfortunate than undeserving, for be assured that few successful candidates have ever read harder than I have done for this object, and it is one of my regrets now that the greater part of my reading was far, very far, deeper and more extensive than anything which I had to apply it to. Perhaps much of the time I devoted to it, if spent in idleness, might have preserved my health and gained my object."

It will gratify the reader to know that on a fourth trial in 1833 Mr. Scott was elected to the Ireland Scholarship.

From the Rev. S. Tillbrook

Freckenham, May 22nd, 1832.

"MY DEAR ARCHDEACON, As the first number of the *Museum Piscatorium* will soon appear, and as we wish to profit by your learned assistance, I must ask you to refer again to your notes, as you have sent me an incorrect reference—who would believe it?

"You say, and truly, I doubt not, that in classic authors the first mention of line-fishing is in Homer, *Iliad*, xii, 253. I have looked in vain and cannot find the passage you refer to. Where is it really?

"Now answer me these queries. Are the terms you quote— δίκτυον,[1] cαγήνη, κάλαμος, ῥάβδος, φελλός, δέλεαρ, κ.τ.λ.—to be found in Homer, or are they taken indiscriminately from Greek writers? Is anything to be gleaned from Hesiod, Moschus, or Bion? Were the fishers of Theocritus anglers or netters? I suppose of the latter kind. Should you infer from 458 of *Georgic II* that Virgil was an angler?

"And now tell me, best and choicest of scholars and wits, have you any objection to be named as one of the occasional contributors to the *Museum Piscatorium*—to be, like myself, a volunteer without pay, but not without honour and glory? The sooner you can answer me these queries the better, and as you are a famous fellow for inscriptions and mottoes, can you remember one fit and appropriate for the *Museum Piscatorium*? If so, pray send it.

"Thank you for subscribing, and for your recruits. I wish we could get George Maddock, because he is so well known in your parts and in N. Wales. I think I must write to E. Morrall to entreat the wit and experience of little Jemmy Lloyd of Pont aber Glas Llyn, and to give us his own, which is very extensive. I had half a mind to ask Dugard as a naturalist, etc., to subscribe, but thought he might think the sum too much. David Jones is a subscriber, as well as John Evans and other worthy Taffies.

"I have been quiet at home for some months and have caught nothing but pike, tench, dace, and so forth. I hope among

---

[1] δίκτυον does not occur in the Iliad. It occurs once for a fisherman's net in the Odyssey, xxii, 386. cαγήνη occurs neither in Iliad nor Odyssey. κάλαμος occurs neither in Iliad nor Odyssey. ῥάβδος occurs in Odyssey, xii, 253, and is there used for a fisherman's, not rod, but spear. φελλός is found neither in Iliad nor Odyssey. Nor yet is δέλεαρ. See Prendergast's Concordance to the Iliad, and Dunbar's Concordance to the Odyssey and Hymns.—ED.

the chances of this world and the chops and chances of Church and State to see you some day a fisher of men with a float (a capital one) and a rod (a crooked one). So good luck to you."

Dr. Butler's reference should have been, not to Iliad, xii, 253, but to Odyssey, xii, 253, etc. If he considered that the writer of the Odyssey referred to line-fishing he was mistaken. The passage runs:

"ὡς δ' ὅτ' ἐπὶ προβόλῳ ἁλιεὺς περιμήκεϊ ῥάβδῳ
ἰχθύσι τοῖς ὀλίγοισι δόλον κατὰ εἴδατα βάλλων
ἐς πόντον προΐησι βοὸς κέρας ἀγραύλοιο
ἀσπαίροντα δ' ἔπειτα λαβὼν ἔρριψε θύραζε
ὣς οἵ γ' ἀσπαίροντες ἀείροντο προτὶ πέτρας."

From a letter of Mr. Tillbrook's dated 22nd June 1832, I gather Chapman to have supposed that the oxhorn held the bait. This is not so: the oxhorn was at the end of the rod, and was to spear the fish with. In the islands of Favognana and Marettimo, off Trapani on the west coast of Sicily, I have seen men fish exactly as described in the Odyssey. A man sits at the extreme end of a jutting rock and chews bread into a paste. He throws this into the water to attract the fish, and then spears them. I never saw this done except in the islands, where old customs survive, and the rod is now shod, not with an ox's horn, but with iron.

The same kind of fishing seems alluded to Iliad, xxiv, 81, but here the oxhorn appears to have been loaded with lead—for Messrs. Liddell & Scott are surely wrong in thinking that line-fishing is referred to, and that the lead was to sink the line. I may perhaps be allowed to say incidentally that the introduction of the identical words κέρας βοὸς ἀγραύλοιο in both the Iliadic and Odysseyan passages that refer to this kind of fishing, suggests the inference, though it does not compel it, that the writer of the Odyssey had the Iliadic passage in, I cannot bring myself to say " his," mind.

As regards the passage from Theocritus, *Idyll* xxi, referred to in the notes that follow Mr. Tillbrook's letter of 29th March 1832, it does not seem possible to doubt that line-fishing is intended by the poet, but the words ἠρέμα νύξα—the fish being hooked—suggest that the fisherman had a spear as well as a rod and line.

From the Rev. S. Tillbrook

Freckenham, June 3rd, 1832.

"MY DEAR ARCHDEACON, Your Homeric references will make the jolly sons of Isaac Walton studious, and the fishes proud. Who would have thought that so many and ancient authorities could have been fished up from Helicon? I asked Greenwood for quotations, and the dull rogue could only call to mind the fishers of Theocritus. We shall be rejoiced to add your treatise as an appendix, or in any shape you like best.

"I have been occupied this week with a strict examination of the change which the May fly undergoes in passing from its first to its second state of existence, and I venture to affirm that there is nothing in Natural History or Natural Theology more wonderful. The change from the chrysalis to the moth is nothing to it. I believe the inhabitants on the shores of the Nile first took their notion of the transmigration of souls from the moth bred among the papyrus and carved at the head of the hieroglyphics in the Pamphylian obelisks; but the moth bursts from the chrysalis in a new form, whereas the May fly literally walks entirely out of *itself*—head, eyes, legs, wings, body, tail, and all. But I cannot describe the phenomenon, though I must attempt it in the pages of the *Museum Piscatorium*.

"I have written, as you suggested, to George Maddock under a frank. I hope something may come of it. I should like to be with you on the Welsh lakes, but cannot.

"Some year let us go to Leintwardine for the last week of your holidays; I am sure you will be delighted with that charming river, the river Teme. Touching flies for the Welsh lakes, I have none. George Maddock knows them well, and so does Shaw and Edward Morrall, and Jemmy Lloyd of Pont aber Glas Llyn still better. Sooty dun hen's hackles, and grouse hackle with olive warping for body, are both excellent. Shaw might make a few whirling duns, with a touch of silver or gold twist round the body; but Maddock will, I daresay, cheerfully supply you. I must stay at home this year; next, D.V., I mean to have a ramble somewhere. If you go to Tall y Llyn fail not for the sake of the nice hot [word illegible] to give that rascal Hugh Morris a ducking and a drubbing. Best regards to Col. Edwards, etc. We are all well here, though a case of cholera happened yesterday within two miles of us.

"I have read Jesse—a nice, unassuming book [*Gleanings in Natural History.*—ED.]. Good hints. Jesse is the intimate friend of the editor of the *Museum Piscatorium*."

From the Rev. S. Tillbrook

Freckenham, June 22nd, 1832.

"MY DEAR ARCHDEACON, I would willingly have sent you Salvianus and Rondeletius, but that I must have them *here* for occasional reference during the publication of the *Museum Piscatorium*. Now a question or two for your consideration.

"Can you give us a nice 'motto' for the *Museum Piscatorium*? such a one as shall embrace the Natural History or Philosophy as well as the practice of Angling? Are you certain as to the tipping or guarding of the hook (by the Greeks) with bone or horn to prevent the fish from biting the line? I suppose you are aware of the passage in the Odyssey where there is a simile—the angler casting. As Chapman translates, he is casting medicine for little fish from his ox's horn—gentles perhaps, or suchlike, to allure the fish. Was the horn at the end of the boats, through which the line ran, the horn of an ox?

"I send you five flies from the redoubtable James Owen of Pont aber Glas Llyn. They are worth any money for the Welsh lakes, and I have but just received them from Liverpool; the dark duns are the best.

"The editor of the *Museum Piscatorium* wishes Shaw of Salop to send him up specimens of the salmon-fry, or sampsons, or skeggers, safely packed in soft flannel, by the Wonder Coach, directed to Mr. William Woods, Publisher, 39, Tavistock Street, Covent Garden. Shaw is referred for payment to Mr. How, the attorney at Shrewsbury; and if Shaw could send me some notes of the best times and places for fishing in the Severn, they would be acceptable.

"I really think I must come and shake hands with you on Monday, so do not be surprised if I drop in at the old Hummum's on Monday or Tuesday. Leave a note to say if you can breakfast at the University Club on Tuesday. Leave it at the U.U.C. I shall be at Mould's (?) in Suffolk Street.

"I am very busy, so God bless you."

From the Rev. T. S. Hughes

September 8th, 1832.

*

"By-the-bye, have you read a novel (though what novel have you not read?) called *Vivian Grey*? Pray do, as I wish to give you the best treat of the kind you ever had in your life."

*

From the Rev. James Williams

"Llanfairynghornwy, September 18th, 1832.

*

"I have lately seen in the papers most honourable allusion made to a plan of tithe commutation by the Venerable Archdeacon of Derby. As this is a subject in which I feel a warm interest, allow me merely to ask whether you have published your sentiments, and if so, where are they to be met with? I am quite sure there is not a moment to be lost in effecting some very considerable reform in Church matters. If you will please to make me Bishop of either Bangor or St. Asaph (no where else), I promise not to be too niggardly in seconding your views.

"There is another subject on which you can perhaps give us some valuable assistance. We are just now establishing a 'Society of Natural History' for the counties of Anglesey, Carnarvon, and Merioneth, the headquarters of which are to be at Carnarvon. It has occurred to me that, with the present liberal sentiments of scientific men, we might occasionally catch a stray lecturer on geology or other subject, who would good-naturedly enlighten our infant understandings with a lecture and give us assistance in forming our museum. As most of the scientific men that visit Wales call on you on their way, you might perhaps give them such a hint. When the plans are a little more matured, I will give you a further account."

*

To Dr. Burton

October 8th, 1832.

"DEAR DR. BURTON, Many thanks for your able pamphlet; you have hit Lord Henley a blow which ought to make him deaf to time, as the pugilists have it.

"I wish I had time to enter into two points only on which we differ.

"You propose to tax livings of £200 a year—I still deprecate this. It would be felt by those who can least afford it, and the produce would be a very pittance according to your own statement in the appendix—only £2,142 out of £75,428.

"Another point is in page 53. 'No two benefices of any kind where there is cure of souls should be held together under any circumstances.' This is utterly impossible to accomplish till you have raised more than one-half the livings in the kingdom. There are much above four thousand under £200 a year, and far above half that number not £150, and a very great proportion not amounting to £100. In my own archdeaconry there are a hundred and fifty-nine livings, of which only forty-eight are of £300 and upwards, ten more of them rather less than £250, and of the remainder

> Nine are above £200 but under £250,
> Leaving ninety-two below £200.

Of these ninety-two,

> Nine do not exceed £20 a year,
> Ten do not exceed £50 a year,
> Sixteen do not exceed £75 a year,
> Fourteen do not exceed £100 a year,
> Thirty-one are from £100 to £150,
> Twelve are from £150 to £200.

Correspondence

"Now surely forty-nine of these can never support separate incumbents till greatly raised, and the remaining forty-three are quite insufficient alone for the maintenance of a minister. You will find this statement different in its details but not different in its aggregate from that published in my charge. But in my charge I was requested by the Bishop, whom I consulted on the occasion, to soften down the appalling insufficiency of the stipend by classifying more generally than I have in this confidential detail to you.

"In fact, according to the data on the result of my archdeaconry, the following may be considered as a rough estimate of the livings in England, amounting to about ten thousand (hardly so much, some being consolidated).

1,450 above	£500	on the average say £800.	
630	,, 400	3,020 above £300.	
940	,, 300		
1,260	,, 200	1,260	
		4,280 ,, £200.	
750	,, £150	5,700 under £200 a year, and on	
1,950	,, 100	the average above half not	
1,800	,, 50	exceeding £100.	
1,200 under	50		

$$9,980$$

"If this be anywhere approaching to the truth—and though it may not be very accurate, it must be not extremely under the mark—there is enough to do with the augmentation fund for many years.

"Perhaps you may put out another pamphlet—if you do, any use you can make of this is very much at your service; it can only afford materials for thinking.

"I would apply half the fund yearly in building decent comfortable houses, such as can be built from £600 to £800 or even £1,000; because then you remove all objection to residence, and you in fact increase the value of the living by the value of the house-rent. I would especially have regard to the population in this.

"In many cases a clergyman would challenge a bounty, and I would be liberal. I would give £200 towards building a house for every £100 of challenge. Thus a man, by laying out £200 of his own, which I would allow him to do by an act like the Gilbert Act, would have £600 towards a house; by laying down £300 of his own he would have £900, which would generally build a house quite good enough for a clergyman on a moderate living.

"You might thus calculate on building at least forty if not more glebe houses annually. The remaining half of the fund I would apply to the augmentation of small livings which have sufficient houses, and I would allow also a portion of such augmentation to be laid out in the improvement of the existing house, and thus you might calculate on making at least twenty houses comfortable residences. And here again I would excite emulation on the Queen Anne's Bounty system, by giving £200 in augmentation for every £100 challenged. Suppose a clergyman had an inconvenient house and wanted to improve it, and at the same time to better his living. Let him offer £100, and he would have £300 to be laid out in the improvement of the house—or, if his house was sufficient, to be laid out in augmentation of the living.

"You will see that I consider a provision for residence as the very first principle to be acted on. But there may be many cases of heavy duty, with great population and small stipend, when it would not be necessary to attend to the house (that being sufficient), but to the augmentation of the living.

"I would consider those cases which challenged a bounty as entitled to first consideration, but I would always set apart a portion for those which did not, and could not. Let me put a case.

"Chesterfield in my archdeaconry has a population of ten thousand. There is a good (too good) house; the income is only £100 a year, and sometimes £30 more for surplice fees.

"Now such a place as this would be entitled to immediate consideration without any challenge. I could mention a dozen more places which have a population of from three to four, five, and six thousand in my archdeaconry, and not £150 a year.

"I wish I had time to give you more details. I hope all this and more will come out on the Commission, which is calculated to do great good if fairly dealt by.

"Believe me, dear Dr. Burton, truly yours,

"S. BUTLER."

To Dr. Burton

Shrewsbury, October 21st, 1832.

"DEAR DR. BURTON, I am afraid of Lord Henley. He is a tool of Evangelicals, who are craftier than himself. Taking for granted that he is sincere, he is short-sighted, and is not to be trusted merely because he means well—so does many a simpleton who is made the tool to do mischief. No one more than the worthy reviewer you speak of.

"I grieve for the supineness of our Bishops and the timidity of the Archbishop. They are suffering their enemies to take the arms out of their hands. Nothing can be more to be deprecated than laymen legislating for the Church. They know nothing of its rights, its constitution, or its claim to protection.

"Many join in the popular yell to gain the applause of the most depraved and worthless of mankind, many because they hate tithes, many because they hate virtue, some because they personally hate the parson, some because they love dissent, some because they hope for plunder, and some because they are sure of comparative impunity when they attack a clergyman.

"I do not think a reformed House of Commons will be so hostile as the present. It will have more men of sense in it.

"I am anxious to see the returns to the Commission. Much will depend on that, and on the immediate use which the Bishops make of it in the House of Lords. They are surely mad if they suffer the inquiry to originate in the House of Commons.

"I want to see

    Translations abolished,
    Sinecures abolished,
    Pluralities greatly restrained,
    Residence greatly promoted,
    Small livings increased,
    Tithes commuted,
    Scandalous clergy easily removed.

"There must and ought to be a great disparity in the value of livings, or else no men of education and good manners would enter the Church. I would even allow of translations to the two Archbishoprics and to the three Bishoprics of Durham, London, and Winchester, but no more. Like you, I care little about the details by which these things are to be accomplished if only they are brought about.

"Another great point is to have the powers of ecclesiastical officers defined and made effectual. Neither those of Bishops nor Archdeacons are so now—and we are blamed continually for not doing that which we have no power to do.

"Believe me with great regard, dear Dr. Burton,
"Yours faithfully,
"S. BUTLER."

CHAPTER TWENTY-FOUR: A ROYAL VISIT

Visit of their Royal Highnesses the Duchess of Kent and the Princess Victoria to Shrewsbury School, Correspondence 2nd November 1832 – 13th March 1833, Pamphlet on Church Dignities, Correspondence 30th March 1833 – 29th April 1833

From Lord Liverpool

Pitchford Hall, October 28th, 1832.

"DEAR SIR, I LOST NO TIME AFTER HER Royal Highness the Duchess of Kent's arrival to take her pleasure respecting her visit to the schools at Shrewsbury, and I have now Her Royal Highness's commands to say that if quite agreeable to yourself she would visit you on Thursday morning. We shall leave this about eleven, and consequently be with you about twelve.

" As her Royal Highness's luncheon usually takes place at one, Her Royal Highness will thank you to allow her to have this at your house, and that there should be some roast mutton for the Princess Victoria."

From Thomas Brancker, Esq.

Liverpool, October 31st, 1832.

" MY DEAR SIR, I write a few lines to you in haste this morning to apprise you of the unfortunate delay which had occurred in the forwarding of your letter, and of my endeavours to execute your commission. After many fruitless inquiries I found that the only chance of furnishing you with a Royal Standard was to obtain the loan of ours at the Town Hall, in which I have succeeded, upon my undertaking to be responsible for its safe custody and return. You will therefore receive it herewith, and I hope in sufficient time, as I have given strict injunctions to have it delivered to you by daylight to-morrow morning. I feel much pleasure in having succeeded in furnishing you with a flag (although at the eleventh hour) which will do credit to your ancient tower, and enable you to receive your Royal Visitors in proper form. I wish I could have done anything as to flowers, but that was impossible for want of time; if I could have had a day longer, I am pretty certain that I could have obtained a bouquet which it would have been equally gratifying to the Princess to receive and to your granddaughters to present.

"When your gala is over, be so good as to cause the Standard to be carefully packed up and directed to John Foster, Esq., Town Hall, Liverpool, which will take it at once to its destination without any further interference on my part."

*

The following instructions to the boys were issued by Dr. Butler:

"*Royal Visit,* 1832

"A roll of green cloth along the school. A carpet and two chairs. The flag hoisted on arrival. The boys to stand on each side of the green cloth and bow as their Royal Highnesses advance.

"The lowest boys next the door. The boys then to keep their places orderly and quietly, while the address is spoken, and while their Royal Highnesses retire, and bow as they go down the room.

"The boys may cheer just on the appearance of their Royal Highnesses at the stair head, but must be quite silent as soon as they enter the school, and must be very attentive to stop cheering the instant they see my cap raised.

"They must not resume cheering till the Royal party have left the school, and must not attempt to follow them downstairs or obtrude upon them till they are down.

"They may go downstairs when their Royal Highnesses are seeing the Chapel, and range themselves round the school garden, so as not to be too near, and may there cheer them in their presence.

"If Dr. Butler raises his cap it will be a signal that the cheers are too loud, and they must cease.

"Strict silence and order to be observed while the Royal party is in the school. No boy to leave his place in order to get nearer, but to preserve the utmost decorum.

"In cheering some little boys who make a hideous squeal are desired to be careful not to do so."

A Royal Visit

From the " Salopian Journal and Courier of Wales " for 7th November 1832

"On Thursday last Her Royal Highness the Duchess of Kent, accompanied by the Princess Victoria and suite, the Earl of Liverpool, and the Ladies Jenkinson, were pleased to honour Archdeacon Butler with a visit at the Royal Free Grammar School of this town.

"Their Royal Highnesses were received soon after twelve at the archway of the schools by Archdeacon and Mrs. Butler. Immediately on their arrival the Royal Standard, a truly magnificent flag, was hoisted on the school tower, saluted by twenty-one guns from the river and by the ringing of the bells of St. Mary's Church. Her Royal Highness was conducted by the Archdeacon and the Princess Victoria by Mrs. Butler, on a platform covered with green cloth under an awning, from the archway to the entrance tower, and thence upstairs to the principal schoolroom, which was tastefully decorated with laurel, having at the upper end a crown formed of splendid dahlias, and at the lower the letters K. V. in the same beautiful flowers. The *coup d'œil* of this fine room, ninety feet long, in which the young gentlemen were arranged in triple ranks on each side, forming a lane through which the Royal party advanced to their chairs, was exceedingly fine. On the first appearance of their Royal Highnesses they were welcomed with the cheers of the young gentlemen, who bowed as they proceeded to the upper end of the room. Their Royal Highnesses then being seated received the following address, which was admirably delivered by Mr. Humphry, the Senior Scholar:

"'MADAM, As the Senior Scholar of this Ancient and Royal Foundation, I have the enviable gratification of being appointed, on behalf of the Masters and Scholars belonging to it, to express our deep sense of your condescension in honouring us with your presence this day.

"'Indebted as we are for our foundation to that good and pious Monarch in whose reign the Protestant Religion was first generally established in this kingdom, and for a very important augmentation of that foundation to his sister Queen Elizabeth of great and glorious memory, we cannot but rejoice to welcome your Royal Highness and your Illustrious Daughter the Princess Victoria within these walls which owe so much of their support and prosperity to the munificence of a female Sovereign.

"'We would apologise to your Royal Highness for their present appearance, owing to those recent and yet unfinished repairs which the lapse of near three hundred years has rendered necessary. We wish they had been better fitted for the reception of their present Illustrious Visitors, and of another Member of your Royal House, who within the last two months honoured us with a similar mark of condescension to that which your Royal Highness is now graciously pleased to confer on us. But unfinished as they must at present appear, never since their foundation have they ceased to be devoted to the cause of sound learning and religious education.

"'Even in the reign of their second Foundress they sent forth one of the most brilliant ornaments of her Court, the gallant and accomplished Sidney; and we humbly beg to add that whatever may be the fortunes in after-life of those now instructed within them, their loyal prayers are here daily offered for the health, happiness, and prosperity of our Most Gracious Sovereign and all His Royal House.'

"On the conclusion of this address their Royal Highnesses rose, and the Duchess of Kent, turning to Archdeacon Butler, was pleased to return the following gracious reply:

"'November 1st, 1832.

"'SIR, It is very agreeable to us that, on this occasion, we should receive through the Senior Scholar of this Ancient and Royal Foundation, on your behalf, that of the other Masters and Scholars belonging to it, the sentiments we have just heard. Our being in this neighbourhood permits me to bring the Princess to see this distinguished school, the reputation of which your learning and assiduity has again revived, to have explained to her how the youth of this great and free country are educated, to see the habits of sound learning and religious education gradually forming those, who now stand around us, to be loyal subjects and valuable members of society.

"'Some are destined, if we are to judge by the past, to carry from the Universities the reward of your and their labours here.

"'The Princess is taught to estimate and value an educated community, so as to be first in aiding by every means in her power, if it be her lot to fill a higher station, the intellectual and religious improvement of all classes.'

"Her Royal Highness having concluded this reply, the Masters, the members of Archdeacon Butler's family, and the Senior Scholar had the honour of being presented to their Royal Highnesses; after which they proceeded to view the library in its yet unfinished state, the noble proportions of which they much admired, and the chapel and head-master's schoolroom. In the latter, in which are placed the boards recording the long list of first-rate academical honours obtained by the scholars who are sent forth from it, their Royal Highnesses found the following inscription, with which they appeared much pleased:

"1832.

"'This Ancient and Royal Foundation was visited by three Members of the Royal Family within two months—by His Royal Highness the Duke of Sussex, September 5th, and by their Royal Highnesses the Duchess of Kent and the Princess Victoria, November 1st.'

"Their Royal Highnesses then walked from the school to Archdeacon Butler's house, conducted by Archdeacon and Mrs. Butler, amidst the loud and repeated cheers of the young gentlemen and the spectators assembled. Here they partook of *déjeuner*, and the Princess Victoria was presented (by the Archdeacon's granddaughter) with a bouquet of very elegant china flowers manufactured at Coalport; these were greatly admired, and a stronger proof of their beauty and perfection cannot be given than when we say that the Princess immediately smelt to them, supposing them to be natural.

"About a quarter before two the Royal Party left the school, on their return to Pitchford Hall. Immediately on her return

Her Royal Highness sent a donation of a hundred pounds to the Shrewsbury Infirmary."

From Lord Liverpool

Pitchford Hall, November 2nd, 1832.

"DEAR SIR, I return you many thanks for your very polite and attentive note. Everything that occurred during Her Royal Highness's visit yesterday at Shrewsbury School gave her, I am sure, satisfaction.

"It is very pleasing and gratifying to me to hear that, in making Her Royal Highness acquainted with whatever persons I consider distinguished for talents, respectability, and property hereabouts, I have given some satisfaction, and I trust little offence."

A few weeks later Dr. Butler received proof prints of H.R.H. the Duchess of Kent and the Princess Victoria, sent him by command of the Duchess, together with an autograph copy of the reply which she had made to the address. These are now among the most valued possessions of my sisters.

CORRESPONDENCE, 2ND NOVEMBER 1832–13TH MARCH 1833

From H.R.H. the Duke of Sussex

(Published by permission of Her Majesty)

Kinmel Park, St. Asaph, November 2nd, 1832.

"DEAR SIR, I have to return you my best thanks for your obliging note, with the valuable extracts which it contained, and which will be a very valuable acquisition in my library. I cannot sufficiently express to you how delighted I felt with my visit at Shrewsbury, and with the sight you furnished me with of your valuable and splendid collection as well as with our conversation. The papers which you put into my hands relative to the examination of the scholars at Shrewsbury afforded me both instruction and pleasure. Would the Masters of Eton and Westminster follow the same system, instead of sticking to the old Posting System, they would send up to the Universities more distinguished young men than they do at present, and would lay a proper foundation to work upon with every probability of success. I had the pleasure of showing the questions and the papers to Dr. Story, and my friend the Rev. G. A. Thorne, who is here with me, and both were highly gratified with what I put before them, adding, 'Now we comprehend how Shrewsbury sends up such able young men.' This communication must afford you as much pleasure to receive as it gives me to communicate it to you.

"I am happy to say that my health has derived some benefit from my stay at this delightful place, which I must shortly leave, and that with deep regret, for I love Kinmel as much for its inhabitants as for the beauty and salubrity of the spot which has so materially benefited me. I enclose you Smyth's short sketch of Dr. Parr, which I think you will admire, and remain with every friendly sentiment of good-will and good wishes towards you, dear Sir,

"Yours truly obliged
"AUGUSTUS FREDERICK."

Memorandum by the Rev. A. Willis

November 2nd, 1832.

"On Wednesday afternoon, October 31st, I called on Mrs. Jeudwine respecting —, who had got leave of absence by means of a forged note. The conversation afterwards turned to the general behaviour of the boys in her hall. She said that many of them were very rude and troublesome; specified that — had charged her in hall with giving him a false character to Mr. Wakefield and had threatened to pull the hall about their ears, had received letters addressed to him at Jackey Jeudwine's, at Dame Jeudwine's, etc. She said that the management of the hall devolved entirely on her, that Mr. J. had said he would rather not have a boy in the house than have any trouble with them, that she was worried out of her life.

"In the evening I called again respecting —, and as I was

leaving the door, the boys in the hall hissed and hooted me in the coarsest manner. Mrs. Jeudwine remarked, 'It was too bad.'

"On Thursday morning I called on Mr. Jeudwine, and, finding he had taken no notice of his boys' disrespectful behaviour to me, requested that he would leave it in my hands. He made some inquiry at the time respecting the management of the hall where I am—the monitors, etc. I told him that, whenever I found the boys untractable, I called in Dr. Butler, that Mr. Young did the same, and that all irregularities were soon checked. The impression which all these things made on my mind was, that Mr. and Mrs. Jeudwine found their boys very troublesome and beyond their management.

"On Friday evening I called on Dr. Butler and spoke of the behaviour of Mr. Jeudwine's boys to me, and also told him what I heard and thought of the state and management of that hall. Dr. Butler said that, if he had known this sooner, he certainly would not have granted the amnesty he had granted to — and others who had offended him.

"He also expressed a strong desire to reprimand the boys who had insulted me, and were generally behaving so badly to Mr. and Mrs. Jeudwine, and thought that if he went into their hall in the evening and addressed all the boys there, he might correct the present irregularities, check the influence of the bad example of the upper boys, render the whole hall more manageable, and thus be of essential service to Mr. Jeudwine. And he requested that I would make a proposal to this effect to Mr. Jeudwine. I did so, fully expecting it would be thankfully received.

"Mr. J. said that he did not wish Dr. Butler's interference; that Dr. B. had nothing to do in his hall, that he had no intention of appealing to Dr. B., and that whatever he had told me respecting the character of any of his boys had been told in confidence and was not to be made the subject of a complaint to Dr. Butler. On hearing this, Dr. Butler requested that in future I would make all complaints of the misconduct of Mr. J.'s boys immediately and directly to him. "A. WILLIS."

Correspondence

From Lord Liverpool

Pitchford Hall, November 11th, 1832.

"DEAR SIR, I am very much flattered that any hint of mine should have procured the two specimens of Latin verse composition you have done me the honour to send me. Lady Catharine, who was writing to the Duchess of Kent, has enclosed the verses, and they will be translated by the Dean of Chester to Her Royal Highness and the Princess Victoria."

The first of the two pieces above referred to is in the 1850 edition of the *Sabrinae Corolla*. It is by W. G. Humphry, and is entitled *Illustrissima Principissa Victoria in venatione vulpis interest apud Piceum Vadum, quae villa est prope Salopiam honoratissimi comitis de Liverpool*. The second was probably by Dr. Butler himself, but I have found no trace of it.

To the Rev. H. Holden

Shrewsbury, December 5th, 1832.

"DEAR SIR, I congratulate you on your son's success at Balliol, which I hope is the prelude to higher honours. I have received a letter from the Master announcing the satisfaction he received from his examination, and from that of other two Shrewsbury boys.

"This leads me to a subject which was slightly touched upon when we met, but which, now your son is actually a member of the University, I feel it necessary for his credit to revert to, and desirable for my own. I allude to your saying that Shrewsbury boys were not well received at Oxford, and that there was actually a prejudice against them on account of the success of several.

"Now really it is hard that among scholars, as at Oxford, who must be judges of learning, in the bosom of those very institutions which are founded for the encouragement of learning, and which profess to be zealous in promoting it, prejudice should be taken against those who bring with them habits of industry and diligence, aided by good talents, and fostered by such care and attention as I can bestow on them.

"I am told, however, that such is the case, and I have reason to know that your information came from a gentleman of Magdalen College, whose talents I respect, but with whom I have not the honour of personal acquaintance. This gentleman told you I was in the habit of what is in cant language called 'cramming' the boys for University examinations. Now if this charge had been alleged by a disappointed candidate in the moment of his disappointment, one should pass it over as an ebullition of momentary feeling. But when it comes from a gentleman respectable for his talents and the station he fills in the University, and who can have no motive of private pique against a person who is an entire stranger to him, it assumes a different character, and requires refutation.

"As he is a stranger to this school and to its system, he can only have said what he has believed upon report, and not from actual knowledge. Let me therefore beg you to disabuse him in this respect. If by 'cramming' he means preparing boys for a particular examination by giving them the information necessary for that particular purpose, and leaving them ignorant in other points, so that in fact their success is but a sort of humbug or quackery, pray assure him that there is nothing I hold more utterly in contempt and abhorrence. Request him not to take my word for this, but to ask from any or every one of my pupils at Oxford whether I ever bestowed one quarter of an hour on them, or any other boy to their knowledge, for this purpose. I appeal to them because they are boys of honour, and are best able to bear testimony. I appeal to your own son. I appeal to every man in both Universities who knows me personally and has the best means of judging.

"When your friend has made this inquiry, and has satisfied himself of the fact, I have no doubt he will do what any gentleman would under similar circumstances—bear testimony to the truth, and if he is conscious of having done me unintentional wrong in any quarter I have no doubt he will take his opportunity of correcting it. It is not for my own sake that I feel most anxious. It is of little consequence to me, known as I am to many of the most eminent scholars of this and foreign countries, what may be said of me on this score, because the worst that can be said is that I impart knowledge, and impart it successfully; but I think it is of material consequence to my pupils, for whom I feel the deepest interest, that when they go to the University full of generous emulation a shade should not be cast over any success they may attain in their literary competition by misrepresentations.

"I have been all my life a lover of plain and manly dealing, and an utter scorner of tricks and prestige. I only ask what every man has a right to ask—a fair field and no favour; and sure I am that every one of my boys would disdain the use of unfair advantage as much as any knight in his most chivalrous combat. With honourable men this needs but to be explained to be approved. I am confident therefore that your friend will appreciate the motives which induce me to wish him disabused in this respect, so that both my boys and myself may stand upon those grounds in his opinion on which we ought to stand. In truth I should be ashamed to show my face among the masters of other public schools, on all of whom I look with respect, and towards many of whom I entertain feelings of the deepest regard and long personal friendship, if I did not send my pupils to meet theirs in the arena of literary competition with every feeling of good-will and the most perfect desire of fair dealing—
ἀγαθὴ δ᾽ ἔρις ἥδε βροτοῖcιν.

"Believe me, dear Sir, very truly yours,
"S. BUTLER."

Further correspondence on this head will be found in letters dated 26th and 29th April 1833.

From Mrs. St. Barbe

Stockton Rectory, January 7th, 1833.

"MY DEAR SIR, As I fall into the sere and yellow leaf, I feel the female malady of curiosity fast creeping over me; and well remembering the tenderness with which you used to chuckle over the little ebullitions of this weakness in our neighbour Grundy and a few other distinguished pumpers, I venture to throw myself on your mercy, and in a fit of amiable confidence declare myself to be a martyr to this many-eyed monster. Reports (for I have ears as well as peepers) have reached me of plays and farces, splendid suppers, elegant company, and an epilogue of unrivalled wit and good-humour; and yet I have only got the tail end of these grand doings, my informant having forgotten that the head and shoulders were wanting to complete the piece.

"Now I want to fidget out of you a wee bit more on this interesting subject; and if you are sitting very prettily in your easy-chair by the library fire, who knows but you may take compassion on the little lady in Wiltshire, who lives in the world through the medium of Bath vellum, and thinks Sir Francis Freeling and the post-office establishment the grand features of England! Do, good sir, tell me if your play was Latin, Greek, French, or German, and tell me also how you mean to answer to Mr. Hume and Charles Tennyson and Sir William Ingilby and Cobbett for squandering the revenues of the Church in sports and pastimes instead of bestowing your superfluous wealth on the working clergy! Oh, shame, Doctor! I will set Lord Radnor upon you, who obligingly observed at a dinner-party at Longford Castle a few days since 'that he hoped the time would soon come when no clergyman would be admitted to the first table in a gentleman's house.' Down we go, derry down, derry down!

"That strong pillar of the Church my dear husband has had a twitch back of late in the shape of quinsy and scarlatina, both very prevalent here, but I am thankful to say he now sniffs the air again, and is many shades better than this time twelvemonths; and as I belong to the family of the hopefuls, I am not without secret suspicions he may one day point his glass at your richly furnished shelves, and join me in personally thanking you for kindness warmly remembered. For myself, I am fat and sprack —an elegant Wiltshire phrase, the very sound of which will explain itself, and which is a particular favourite of mine. It will give us much pleasure to have an equally promising report of you and Mrs. Butler, and all the olive branches and twigs; for I suppose you are a grandpapa now in the male line as well as the female. Perhaps we shall see some little good-natured paragraph about you in the newspaper as soon as the elections close; for surely the pious editor of the *Record* will record your theatricals! I shall especially expect a homily on ' bustles ' and other female artifices to decoy decent young gentlemen from their black-letter studies, and hope the truth will be brought before the public in the strongest terms: a little scandal is so savoury! If I write any more, you will think I am more crazy than ever; so whether in my senses or out of my senses, I will just add my love to Mrs. Butler, Bather, and Lloyd, and with Mr. St. Barbe's regards to yourself make graceful curtsey, and so no more at present.

" I should have taken more pains with my penmanship; but as you could read poor Dr. Parr's notes, my ups and downs will be a joke to you."

From a Clergyman in the Archdeaconry of Derby

January 14th, 1833.

" MY DEAR SIR, I find myself in a difficulty with some individuals who lately composed the choir of my church.

" It has been the custom of this body to go round from house to house during the Christmas week to serenade the inhabitants of the parish, and to collect such donations from them as they may be disposed to give. Great excesses have for several years been committed by them during their progress, and I have frequently remonstrated with them upon the subject without producing any amendment in their conduct. Previous to last Christmas I gave them timely notice that I should not allow them to proceed as they had been accustomed to do, and that it was my intention to appoint two of the most sober and orderly of the choir to go round the parish, without any band of music, to collect the contributions, which were to be divided amongst the whole body in the same way as usual. The orderly part of them assented to this plan with great cheerfulness, being well convinced that it would be more profitable as well as more creditable to them to adopt it. The disorderly part, however, formed a separate band, and proceeded, in defiance of my wishes and orders, in their accustomed orgies. Upon this I dismissed the disobedient portion, and desired them never to appear in the singing-gallery again. To my surprise they have taken their places amongst the choir, which I reorganised, and have persisted in singing with them, and their demeanour is most indecorous and insolent. I have sent to desire them to desist at the termination of every service since Christmas Day, but they have paid no attention to my messages.

"I must beg leave now to ask you what course I am to pursue. The singing-gallery is not an open one, but has always been set apart for the choir, and no persons have sat there but the members of it. I am very desirous to be prepared to take such steps next Sunday as will vindicate that reasonable authority which I have in vain endeavoured to exercise for the maintenance of decency and sobriety amongst a body who profess to sing to the praise and glory of God on a Sunday, but who desecrate their respectable office, as well as the donations they receive, by the grossest intemperance during the Christmas week.

"Churchwardens are the proper persons to prevent the intrusion of the malcontents into the singing-gallery. I should be greatly obliged to you to give me a written authority addressed to them (the churchwardens), desiring them to take proper steps to obviate the inconvenience for the future. At all events I beg you to give me your advice."

The note made by Dr. Butler for his answer was as follows:
"No power. Bishop of London agrees with me. Possibly churchwardens may displace from gallery; but though the minister may appoint what shall be sung, he cannot appoint who shall sing it. Nor can he prevent them from singing the words out of tune—or to a different tune. The best way would be to prevail on the whole congregation to join in singing, according to the original intention and custom."

To — Jobson, Esq.

Schools, February 7th, 1833.

"Archdeacon Butler begs to inform Mr. Jobson that he has seen the boys who laid the information against the proprietors of the Bangor up coach, and that they have agreed to withdraw it. At the same time he feels bound to remonstrate in the strongest terms against the overloading of the coach, which he cannot consider justified by the excuse of a wish to oblige him or the boys, when attended with such imminent danger. He begs to remind the proprietors that if any accident had happened involving bodily injury they would have been responsible for damages, and if there had been loss of life the consequences might have been still more serious to the person more immediately concerned in suffering such an overload. He begs Mr. Jobson to put this in the strongest manner to the proprietors of the coach at Chester.

" He believes that the boys withheld the usual payment from the coachman on the ground that if they gave it they would appear to sanction the overload; but as the information is withdrawn they will probably collect the amount from those who did not give at the time and send it to the coachman."

From the Rev. G. Matthews

Herstmonceux, February 19th, 1833.

" REV. SIR, So many years have passed away, and so many new races must have grown up under your care since he who thus addresses you left it, that he cannot but fear you have entirely forgotten him; he, however, through all his wanderings, has never ceased to cherish a grateful recollection of the guide of his youth. Perhaps it is but natural that things should be so: it is but for the mere passing moment that the fountain retains the features of those who crowd around and kneel in quick succession to drink of its waters; not so soon, however, do they who have partaken of those waters forget the fountain. Never, indeed, can life's traveller forget the spring from which he first imbibed health and vigour to bear him onwards in his toilsome journey. And what can be more natural than that, faint and worn down by those toils in after-days, he should direct his hopes and his steps back to that same spot again?

" Be not offended then, Rev. Sir, at an old pupil's thus coming to you, though you may have long lost all recollection of him, for I am in trouble, and you can help me; you have the power, and I do think, would you but listen to my story, you would find in your heart the will to help me; for there was a time when you were kind to me, when, though little better than a half-reclaimed savage from the mountains who knew not how to value such kindness, you had me under your roof and introduced me to your friends—among them to one who laid his hands on my unworthy head, and gave me his blessing and this charge, ' Whatever may be your lot in life, never neglect your Greek and Latin, and be a Whig.' Some twenty years and more have gone by since Dr. Parr, in your study, uttered these words; yet do I seem to hear them as distinctly ringing in my ears as though they were but this moment spoken. To the former part of the charge struggles (which with me began early) with men and with the cares of life prevented my attending as I would have done; while of the latter part, it is to be feared, I have been for my professional success too foolishly observant. In truth, as the shrub clings to the rock, so have I clung to Whiggism—and have found it, as my stunted fortunes prove, about as fertile a material to thrive upon.

"Fourteen years ago last January I commenced life as a curate, and a curate—with but little prospect of change, except occasional change of place at a time of life when all such changes become painful, or a chance in these times of not being able to get a curacy at all—a curate I still remain. I am, however, very thankful to God that for the whole of the time, excepting a few intervals arising from bad health or the difficulty of getting employment, I have been actively engaged in my duties. The highest stipend I ever received, excepting last year, when it was raised to £150, has been £90 a year. I am not complaining of my lot; I only wish a continuance of it. Five years ago my father died, and with him died a great part of his income. My mother, two sisters, and also a brother were consequently left very much, and I may say for the last two years almost entirely, dependent on me.

"To meet this I employed myself as usher in a school hard by, and thus added £40 a year to my stipend, till I could bear the fatigue no longer, and was obliged to give up the school or die; providentially, however, about the same time my salary was raised, as I said, from £90 to £150. To maintain a respectable appearance as minister of a parish, to be foremost in all local charities, and to keep my mother and three others out of £130 and £150 a year is a task the difficulty of which those only who have tried can form any idea of; with the help of the Almighty, however, and strict economy, I have been thus far enabled to do it. I have even passed for rich, though verily it has been 'passing rich with forty pounds a year,' for rarely have I spent more than £40 or £50 on my own wants for several years past. It is a bitter thing to be poor; but a far bitterer thing is it to be forced—in spite of a proud spirit and a long and fondly cherished principle of independence that would rather starve than ask a favour—to be forced to proclaim one's poverty. So it is with me; for myself I would rather starve, but it is not in nature to bear the thought that ere long my old mother may have to ask me for bread when I shall have none to give her.

"Next May my new rector, Mr. Julius Hare, of Trinity, comes into residence; and I, at a time when a curacy that will maintain me is as hard to be got as a living (for I have been on the look-out for these six months past, and can hear of nothing), must leave, and must suffer. You, however, Rev. Sir, can, if you will—God give you the will—you can be of great service to me in this need. Dr. Maltby, my Bishop, is your friend, and both were friends of Dr. Parr's. Now I do hope, I am almost sure, that the Bishop of Chichester will do something, however trifling, for one whom Parr has blessed and Butler recommends to him.

"As to my character, I can produce testimonials for the whole of my clerical life. For the last eight years I have been fixed here, and can appeal to my parish from highest to the lowest. The principal landowner is a Mr. Gillon, M.P. for some of the Scottish boroughs. He is a Scot, and loud against the English Church, etc.; yet can I safely refer you to him for my character as a parochial minister. He has known me long and intimately. Mr. Curteis also, the late, and his son the present, member for this part of the county, have known me long and intimately; they live within a few hundred yards of me. I mention these persons because they live near me and know me well; and were there anything in me to disgrace your recommendation, they must know it. Let me, dear and Rev. Sir, an old pupil who turns to you in his need, persuade you to speak but one kind word of recommendation in his behalf. You will be doing a really Christian and good deed; and if the prayers and thanks of more than one grateful heart will be anything of a reward, such reward will most certainly not be wanting to you."

In regard to the writer of the foregoing letter I take the following from the Life of Bishop Blomfield [1] by his son, to which Professor Mayor's quotation of it in his account of Dr. Butler already referred to has called my attention:

" The warmth of controversy between the Aeschylean critics extended even to Butler's school at Shrewsbury, where, although of course the majority of the boys supported their master, *one* was found bold enough to take the side of Blomfield, and to support his claims in a stand-up fight with the stoutest champion of the opposite party.

" Six-and-thirty years afterwards this anecdote was communicated to Bishop Blomfield by his solitary defender, the Rev. George Matthews, who added that he still bore the marks of the contest in a scar on his lip. Mr. Matthews having asked him to help in restoring his church, the Bishop replied:

" 'Fulham, November 23rd, 1846.

" ' REV. SIR, Such an appeal as you have made to me it is impossible to resist. It has revived many recollections of an interesting period of my life. I have often wished that I had never written the review of Butler's Aeschylus, although the criticism was generally true. It caused an excellent man to regard me for several years with suspicion and dislike, besides the lesser evil of inflaming the wrath of the Press. However, I had the happiness of being cordially reconciled to Dr. Butler some time afterwards, and of becoming intimate with him. He

---

[1] *Memoir of C. J. Blomfield, D.D.*, by Alfred Blomfield, M.A., vol. i, pp. 15, 16.

was a really learned as well as an amiable man, but his forte did not lie in verbal criticism. I am much amused by your account of the πυγμαχίη; you do not say who conquered; but I hope that as *I* was fortunate enough to beat my friend Thomas Smart Hughes in various academic contests, so you triumphed over his brother at fisticuffs, and were the Epeus, not the Euryalus, of the fight, although it might be said of him:

ἐπὶ δ᾽ ὄρνυτο δῖος Ὕησος
κόπτε δὲ παπτήναντα παρήϊον.
Iliad, xxiii, 689.

"'I enclose a cheque for £10; of which I request your acceptance, not so much, however, for a μνήμη ἀντίμισθος, as an expression of my good wishes for the success of your pious endeavours to restore the house of God to a due degree of seemliness.'"

From the Rev. G. Matthews

Herstmonceux, February 25th, 1833.

"REV. AND DEAR SIR, I am thankful, truly thankful, for your prompt reply to, and kind compliance with, my request—a request which, from the moment I had emitted it to the post, I had not ceased to wish unmade and to regret as an impudent and unreasonable one. I have also to thank you for the salutary and necessary caution 'not to trust too much to the result'; for though by no means one of those spoilt children of fortune to whom blighted hope comes the bitterer from being strange, yet I do think, had I ever been tempted to doubt the saying of Hope's being but the mother of Disappointment, it would have been on reading over your letter without the cautionary clause. But I will not punish your goodness for having read over and attended to one long and begging letter by inflicting on you another equally long one of thanks; I will therefore conclude with hoping that Mrs. Butler is well, and that you will present her my best and most respectful remembrances, while to yourself, dear and Rev. Sir, I offer without flattery, but with as much warm and devoted sincerity as though I were once more a schoolboy, all that duty and reverence and gratitude which I have always believed, and now more than ever feel, to be your due."

To Robert Scott, Esq. (who had just taken the Ireland Scholarship)

Shrewsbury, March 13th, 1833.

"DEAR SCOTT, I write to you a few lines this morning just in time to catch the post, on the receipt of the despatch Brancker so kindly sent me.

"I was anxious that you should offer, considering your very hard case of disappointment from uncontrollable causes last year, but I did not like to urge you. I am glad, however, that your own good sense led you to come forward.

"It is just the case with Hildyard, who, in the first sting of disappointment in not being Senior Classic, resolved not to go in for the medal. His friends prevailed upon him to sit, and he had no sooner done so than he received a letter from me, which the post could not convey to him time enough to influence his decision, urging him most vehemently to sit *coûte que coûte*; because, as I told him, his honour was at stake. It would be cowardly to refuse. If he failed, he would be but where he was, beaten by the man who had already beaten him; but if he succeeded, his reputation would be exalted tenfold. The result is yet undecided; but whatever it may be, it is a matter of great satisfaction to me that he sat. Your success now will convince everybody that your want of it last time was the result of mere illness. Believe me, dear Scott,

"Very sincerely yours,
"S. BUTLER."

Hildyard was successful in obtaining the Chancellor's Junior Medal for 1833.

I cannot ascertain the exact date of a pamphlet *On Church Dignities*, but it is dated 1833, and I find it referred to in letters from friends as early as 28th March, so I presume it must have been published at the beginning of the year. Its tenor will appear sufficiently from the following extract:

"Were these offices either wholly abolished or very materially reduced, I conceive one inevitable evil would be the introduction of a grade of persons lower in point of birth, habits, and education into the Church. For what man of high attainments and cultivated mind will enter into a profession which holds out no honourable distinctions as a reward for merit and a stimulus to exertion? I may—indeed I have been told by some of our own brethren that it is enough for the clergy to be humble-minded, and to seek a higher and nobler reward than that which any temporal distinction can bestow, and that in fact a lower grade of clergy would be an advantage to the interests of religion. But I must maintain that there is a fallacy in the way in which the two former of these propositions are put, and I must give a decided negative to the third. For it is thus assumed that a clergyman cannot be humble-minded in a station of dignity, and that he who seeks a temporal reward cannot seek the honour of God also. To be sure he cannot at once serve God and Mammon; but I know some of my brethren who profess, and I doubt not sincerely, to be humble-minded, and to seek nothing but the honour of God, and to look for no reward but that of His heavenly kingdom, who yet are not indifferent to the station they hold in His Church. I believe in this world men generally act from mixed motives, and even the best of us has so unavoidably the 'law of sin in his members,' that he cannot divest even his most spiritual feelings of a certain mixture of human infirmity. If this be so, few will be found to refuse temporal distinctions, when proposed as an honourable testimony to their labours in the cause of religion. Thousands, I trust, are to be found who would not make them the sole, or even the principal, motive of their religious acts, or who would cheerfully and even triumphantly sacrifice them, rather than swerve from their religious duty, or who would disdain them as the price of their acquiescence in sin; but whenever a large body of men is to be governed, there must be governors, and be certain grades of office, from the highest governing power to the second, and so on to the very last. As long then as this is the case, so long must there be distinctions; and why good men should not be willing, and even desirous, to accept of these, or should be desirous that these should be left in what they may consider less judicious hands than their own, is to me quite incomprehensible.

"As long therefore as there are honourable distinctions in the Church, so long will men of liberal and honourable minds be found to aspire to them, and to use their best exertions to attain them; and even if they were not the reward of peculiar merit or high attainments, but disposed of, as they now often are, to men who have no peculiar claims beyond those of fair character and good education, backed by good connections, there would still be strong reasons for their being preserved. For a man does not serve the altar without intending to live by the altar; and though it is to be hoped that the desire of promoting the glory of God, and the advancement of His kingdom on earth, be the highest and most prevailing inducement to all sincere and rightly thinking men for entering more actively into His service in the capacity of Christian ministers, yet in an age when we have no right to expect miraculous interference for our daily support—no ravens to be sent to us with bread and flesh in the morning, and bread and flesh in the evening—no barrel of meal to waste not, no cruse of oil that shall never fail—some regard must necessarily be had to our temporal provision and support. And though by far the majority of those who enter the Church do really and truly enter it without any certain expectation, and with nothing but a trust in the mercies of Providence to raise them up friends in the profession which they have chosen, yet there are few who do not look with the eye of hope to a participation in the temporal advantages of the Church, and few of more generous minds who do not hope to win their way to honours and distinction in it; and the more surely any one thinks he may attain these, the more ready is he to labour cheerfully in his vocation.

"So that these appointments afford a considerable inducement to men of a superior grade for entering on the profession, and it is owing to such men that the clergy in general are considered admissible into the highest circles. That when so admitted they give a tone to the morals of society, and exercise a beneficial influence over its levities and freer conversation, as well as impose a check upon its excesses of every kind, is what no reasonable person can deny. Now much, if not nearly all, of this would be lost, were the chief places of honour and distinction abolished in the Church. I would therefore still leave these accessible to the higher ranks, but I would make some additional qualifications of learning and personal merit necessary for the holding of them. In short, in selecting proper individuals to fill such stations, much the same rule might be observed as in the elections at all the best colleges in our Universities, where the fellowships are open to all, but given to the most worthy, who might there find that *otium cum dignitate* which their labours and services may justly claim. Nor can I see any reason why such men, who have worn out their best years in the service of the public and the duties of their profession, should not be allowed this dignified, even if easy, retirement. Whatever may be the popular cry against the wealth of the clergy, I assert, without fear of contradiction when the matter is brought to proof, that the clerical profession is the most underpaid of any.

" The whole revenue of the Bishops, if equalised, would not give more than about £5,000 a year; those of cathedral dignitaries not more, probably less, than £800; and those of the parochial clergy not more than £200 to each beneficed individual. Is this too much for men who have spent probably on the average not less than £1000 on their education—who have no means of embarking in any other pursuits, and increasing their fortunes by commercial or agricultural speculations, or of holding lucrative civil offices in addition to their own profession? Let us but consider the fortunes made in the law, and its snug appointments; and the governorships, colonelcies, and commands attainable in the army (a profession which is certainly not overpaid for its outlay and risks); the emoluments of a successful medical practitioner, which nobody grudges him; or the enormous accumulation of wealth obtained by mercantile or manufacturing pursuits; and we shall soon find that the incomes of the clergy are as nothing in comparison. The lawyer retires into some less laborious but well-paid appointment, with a good private fortune, the result of his talents and industry. The general has his regiment, his garrison, or his pension, the well-earned reward of his gallant services. The physician is not often remunerated by public appointments, but even these sometimes fall to his lot; yet if he has not these, he has secured an ample fortune by the public favour. The man of commercial enterprise reaps the reward of it in a golden harvest, and retires to enjoy it. The clergyman alone is rarely able to lay up a comfortable provision for his family from the income of his profession, unless he is appointed before the decline of life to some of the higher stations; and then, if there be a few unhappy instances to the contrary, he, generally speaking, finds abundant use for the means put into his hands—not in the indulgence of pomp and luxury, but in the exercise of benevolence and hospitality; and in the employment of his leisure, not in the indulgence of sloth and idleness, but in the pursuit of his literary occupations, and the instruction and improvement of mankind."

CORRESPONDENCE, 30TH MARCH 1833—29TH APRIL 1833

To the Rev. T. S. Hughes

(Original in possession of Mr. Hughes's representatives)

March 30th, 1833.

"This day fifty years I went to school for the first time, and was put in the lower remove of the third form at Rugby.

"MY DEAR HUGHES, I send you a few Greek translations (you will find the English written opposite one of them) and three Latin essays, which I shall be much obliged to you to look over carefully as soon as you can, and send me word which you think the two best of each. You will find the Greeks much better than last year. But the Latin essays really surprise me, from the quantity of reading and the acuteness of observation, in one especially.

"Underline with pencil, in each of the two you approve,

what appears to you to require alteration. You need not do this till you have decided which two you prefer. As soon as you have done this in each case, if you will write me a line containing the mottoes, I shall be able to see if we coincide by comparing with my selection.

"If we agree, you will have nothing to do but to send back the whole to me; if we differ, you will have to forward them to H. Drury.

"I have sent him the verses, and *mutatis mutandis* the same course will take place with them.

"I have been ill ever since December, very ill in London and at Watkinson's, with so severe a cough that I thought my lungs were seriously injured—long ill with that on my return, and subsequently with long-continued membranous inflammation, principally about the head and on the trachea; for the last three weeks I have had erysipelatous attacks in my eyes or ears, at present on my left ear and scalp, very burning and painful. The season has been most ungenial. I long to get into my cutter at Beaumaris. I shall leave the scientific to their own pursuits at Cambridge, and shall confine myself to exercises in quest of soles, mackerel, gurnet, and *id genus omne*.

"Believe me, dear Hughes, truly yours,
"S. BUTLER.

"Be so good as to return the parcel directed to me at the Old Hummums on April 15th. I am coming up for the Levee and Drawing Room."

To the Same

(Original in possession of Mr. Hughes's representatives)

Shrewsbury, April 9th, 1833.

"MY DEAR HUGHES, I consider 'Secure lateo' as decidedly the best—having the best Latin and the best argument, and abounding in good taste. 'Produnt auctorem vires' is solid, but heavy in its style and matter. It is the result perhaps of more reading and less tact. The third, if it were not slight and sketchy, might rank before it. There is more elegance of style, and more discrimination and cleverness of observation, but it is of the ' levis armatura ' kind.

"I am not sure that I quite agree about the Greek Iambics. But I have been, like yourself, very unwell, and my quickness of perception has been impaired thereby. Still, as far as I recollect, I found reason to give ' Πέτομαι δ' ἐλπίcιν ' at least the second place. I have no hesitation about ' Hic delectatur Iambis ' being second if it is not first, or being first if ' Πέτομαι δ' ἐλπίcιν ' is not first. I have much dubitation about these two, but I should place ' When Greek meets Greek ' the last of the three.

"Have the goodness to state the faults in each when you return them to me—some blemish may strike you which I have overlooked, and which may turn the balance; it is very nearly even: it was not till the third or fourth reading that I began to give ' Πέτομαι δ' ἐλπίcιν ' the preference. I am not sure that I should do so now. I need not say that one sees things differently at different times, according as health or illness prevail.

"I am better, but still have erysipelas about the head, eyes, and throat. I mean to go to the Levee next week, and I hope something from the change of air and the exercise of it.

"If you have any friend on whose judgement you can rely, I wish you would show the three Greeks—' Hic delectatur,' ' When Greek meets Greek,' and ' Πέτομαι δ' ἐλπίcιν '—to him, and ask his opinion.

"Be good enough to send the parcel directed to me at the Old Hummums on Monday, April 15th, or Tuesday, April 16th."

*

To the Rev. T. S. Hughes

(Original in possession of Mr. Hughes's representatives)

April 18th, 1833.

*

" Eighty-seven thousand persons were ill with ' la grippe ' in London yesterday. Theatres closed—Law Courts partly so—Banks hardly able to keep open—Levee pretty full, but Drawing

Room very thin. I like the Bishop of Peterborough's[1] conduct about the Bell exceedingly."

From the Rev. G. Booth

" 3, Halkin Street, Belgrave Square, London,
April 26th, 1833.

" REVEREND SIR, I cannot but regret, for your satisfaction and my own credit, that Mr. Holden, owing to a strange (though I fully believe involuntary) misapprehension and misstatement of my remarks (made in a private conversation to himself), should have added the further error of delaying so long to transmit to me either the original or the substance of your letter of December 5th, 1832, only this day received, with his own account of the circumstances; under which I do not wonder that you should write so warm and indignant a protest! I hope it will suffice to say, that I had understood, from a man of known probity and simplicity of character, long versed in college tuition and in examination for degrees and scholarships, that the Ireland Scholarship had of late been almost exclusively obtained by your pupils, in consequence of a sort of routine questions into which the examiners had fallen, as being hackneyed in academic system and the habitual lecture-room questions; all or most of which were within the compass of boys well taught at the superior schools, especially your own, where they were so thoroughly initiated in verbal criticism and technical philology. That, to obviate this unfair monopoly, and give a due opportunity to the matured talent, knowledge, and taste of the more adult academic candidate, subjects for essays, etc., and other additional questions, ought, and would, be henceforth set; which would elicit the powers and acquirements of more advanced age and progress.

" He neither undervalued that branch of literature, in itself, to which he thought the examination had too much leaned, to the great advantage of your pupils; nor for a moment insinuated that you prepared or made them up designedly for such examinations, nor did he entertain or mention as current any

[1] Dr. Marsh.

'prejudice' to the obstruction of their success in Oxford, or to your disparagement. He is quite incapable, I am sure, from his well-known character, of any invidious, illiberal sentiment or representation. I cannot expect you to take my word that I am equally superior to disingenuous and ungenerous reflections on the plan or detail of tuition adopted by so publicly and widely distinguished a scholar as Archdeacon Butler, and recommended to the world by fruits so manifest."

To the Rev. G. Booth

Shrewsbury, April 29th, 1833.

"DEAR SIR, I was favoured with your letter of the 26th on Saturday, but was then, and have been till this morning, so deeply engaged in preparing some important ecclesiastical papers for the Bishop of the diocese on parliamentary affairs that I could not attend to any private business. This, I trust, will be an apology for my not having written to you before this morning's post.

"I now snatch a moment to thank you for your disavowal of any such opinion as that I am accustomed to 'make up' boys for any particular examination, or using any such detestable quackery. I have ever sought to impress my boys with the highest principles of honour, and I am fully convinced that there is not one of them who would not spurn the idea of using any unfair advantage as indignantly as myself.

"But while I thank you for disavowing this imputation, I cannot but express some surprise that you should still refer to an 'unfair monopoly,' which required to be obviated by proposing other questions than those usually proposed in college lecture-rooms as being within the compass of boys well brought up at superior schools. For in such case there can be no unfair monopoly. If the questions proposed by the examiners (which rest with themselves, and must be unknown to me) are within the compass of well-taught boys, they must be within the compass of all the candidates, for it is not to be supposed that those who have not been well taught would be competent to offer themselves. If the questions are those generally asked in college lecture-rooms, they are clearly within the reach of all the candidates. I cannot therefore understand how the Shrewsbury boys could have any unfair monopoly in those questions more than in the light and air, which are equally open to all; and with regard to boys just admitted, questions usually proposed in college lecture-rooms rather tend to throw the monopoly into the hands of their opponents, who have been longer at college, than into their own.

"Again. If the alteration in the examination has a tendency to give an advantage to the more matured talent, knowledge, and taste of the more adult academic, does not this tend to throw 'an unfair monopoly' into the hands of candidates of superior standing. If the questions which are proposed tend to give an advantage to any class, I cannot think them fair questions; and if the more matured academic could not answer such as were proposed, and yet such as were usually asked in college lecture-rooms, he can have no reason to complain of unfairness in being asked what he ought to have known; whereas the junior may have reason to complain in being asked questions expressly calculated to give an advantage to his more adult opponent.

"You must pardon me, therefore, if I cannot agree with you either as to the alleged unfair monopoly, or as to the fairness of the mode proposed for obviating it. This last, however, is a matter for the consideration of the examiners, and I beg to be understood not as complaining, but merely as arguing on the subject. I have urgent grounds for wishing that you should see the original letter which I wrote to Mr. Holden, and not merely the substance of it, and I do not clearly collect from your mention of it whether you have seen it. If not, I should be much obliged to you if you would apply to Mr. Holden for a perusal of it. If he has destroyed it, a copy of it was taken by my amanuensis, which shall be communicated to you, but it would of course be more satisfactory to me that you should see the original. It was written more for my boys' sake than for my own, and I can only repeat what I said then, that they have never been taught by me to wish for anything more than a fair field and no favour; and while they can obtain that, to that I

willingly leave them. I have the honour to be, Sir, your very obedient and humble servant,
"S. BUTLER."

The reader who turns to the Honour Boards of Shrewsbury School given at the end of this work will see that Dr. Butler's pupils had taken the Ireland in 1827, 1828, 1829, 1830, 1831, and 1833.

CHAPTER TWENTY-FIVE: CORRESPONDENCE, 29TH APRIL 1833— (?) DECEMBER 1833

From the Rev. G. Matthews

Herstmonceux, April 29th, 1833.

"REVEREND AND DEAR SIR, AS YOU WERE good enough to express a wish to know the result of my application to Mr. Dallaway respecting the curacy of Slinfold, I proceed, though with a heavy heart, to communicate it. Owing to a too frequent neglect in the post of this village (it is a cross penny post) your letter did not reach me till more than a week after its date. I wrote, however, immediately, as you advised, and have had an answer, a very kind one, but lamenting at the same time that he ' had already entered into an engagement with a neighbouring clergyman.' I need not tell you how much disappointment and downheartedness I felt at learning this. If hope deferred maketh the heart sick, hope blighted may well go near to kill it outright.

" It is so great a thing for the Bishop to have so promptly exerted himself once in my behalf, that to expect him to bear me a second time in mind would, I doubt, be too much; and yet he may, for I am sure he is a kind-hearted man. At a confirmation last autumn he was almost cordially kind to me; and when I told him I had been a pupil of Dr. Butler's, he even desired me to come over to Chichester to see him. To Chichester, however, I never ventured, owing to a sort of nervousness and want of confidence in myself which has accompanied, and I may say has stood between, me and the sun all my life long. And how indeed could it be otherwise? The confidence I want is to be acquired only by early association with the better classes of society, or springs from a consciousness of one's possessing great and commanding talents: these God has not thought proper to give me. And as for society, all my boyhood, except when at school, and the better part of my early manhood, was, from peculiar circumstances, spent in a state little better than savagery, if there is such a word, shunning the haunts and dreading the face of man as much as the wild beast does. I am convinced that the only feeling I should be alive to on entering the Palace and standing before the Bishop would be that I had a label on my forehead:

> "'I know that I am nothing, and that I have done nothing to deserve your notice; yet am I come to play the courtier, to crouch and sue for favour and patronage and whatever I can get.'

"I was never bred a courtier; and if we are anything more than the creatures of after-circumstances, I don't think I was ever born to be one, the reverse seeming to be interwoven every other with every thread of my constitution both in body and mind. Nevertheless, if you think it would be right, I will go over even now, label and all on my forehead, nervousness in my limbs, and embarrassment in my brains, and pay my devoirs to his lordship, and again remind him, of what I fear no word or deed of mine would otherwise ever lead him to suspect, that I have been a pupil of yours—and seem like the weed to bring a sort of virtue along with me from having merely having grown near some herb of grace, trembling, however, all the time, lest, when handled, the native rankness of the weed should be more perceptible than any superficial fragrance it may have caught from the influences of its more fragrant neighbour. But I must leave off, lest by talking so long and so familiarly I give offence. I hope such has not been the case, but that the goodness which has extended a hand to me will forgive the rude freedom with which it is grasped. Do not yet, dear and Reverend Sir, do not yet let me go, but hold me up a little longer, and I trust that ere long, through your help and goodness of Providence, my feet will be set upon the rock and my goings ordered."

From the Bishop of Chichester (Dr. Maltby)

Preacher's Chambers, Lincoln's Inn, May 4th, 1833.

"MY DEAR DR. BUTLER, When you wrote to me in favour of your old pupil, George Matthews, I enclosed your letter to the Chancellor, who, I was sure, would be pleased to have an opportunity of serving any one who had attracted the notice of Dr. Parr and deserved the good opinion of Dr. Butler. I think

I need not tell you that if a favourable opportunity had presented itself, Lord Brougham would have been glad to have placed a small piece of preferment in the hands of your quondam pupil. It has so fortunately fallen out that what the Chancellor with his numerous claims and applications has hitherto been unable to effect, it may possibly be my lot to accomplish. The vicarage of Rudgwick, in my diocese and near Horsham, is now vacant, and is in my gift. I am afraid it does not at present clear more than £140 per annum; but as it contains near a thousand inhabitants, if funds can be found for improving small livings this must sooner or later come within their application.

" The house is delightfully situated, as I am told the whole neighbourhood is beautifully wooded; but I am sorry to add the vicarage house is itself a bad one, and in bad condition; and as the last vicar, to whom I gave it one and a half years ago, has not been able to get anything from the executors of his predecessor, and has improved the house in some degree, it would hardly be fair for his successor to expect more from him than he received himself.

" If after this description of the drawbacks upon this vicarage Mr. Matthews thinks it worth his acceptance for the purpose of residing, I authorise you to make him the offer of it; wishing you to consider it as a mark of good-will to yourself jointly from the Lord Chancellor and me; for I have conferred with him upon the subject, and he expressed himself as highly pleased with the disposition both as regards Mr. Matthews and yourself."

Mr. Matthews appears in the Clergy List for 1865 as still incumbent of Rudgwick, but disappears in the list for 1866.

To the Lord Chancellor (Lord Brougham)

Shrewsbury, May 5th, 1833.

" MY LORD, Understanding from the Bishop of Chichester that you have been so good as to express your satisfaction at his disposal of a living in his gift to a friendless, but I believe deserving and grateful, pupil of mine, Mr. G. Matthews, whom

I recommended to his protection, I feel bound to offer your lordship my most sincere and respectful thanks for the interest you have taken in the fulfilment of my wishes.

"The poor man's curacy, on which he maintained his mother, sisters, and an infirm brother, was his sole resource, and he was in despair at losing it on the death of the incumbent. He had no friend but me, and I feel the kindness which has been shown him as much as if it had been done to myself."

From the Rev. T. Rowley, Head Master of Bridgnorth School (afterwards D.D.)

Bridgnorth, May 8th, 1833.

"MY DEAR SIR, Allow me to introduce to you the Rev. W. Boulton, a friend for whom I feel great and well-merited interest. He is a candidate for the head-mastership of Stourbridge School. I have given him a testimonial which will have some weight, as I am well known to many of the respectable inhabitants of that town and neighbourhood. I am, however, anxious to do as much for my friend as possible, and I know that your name would almost ensure his success. I cannot ask you to give Mr. Boulton a testimonial, but I shall venture, from the great kindness I have always experienced from you, to ask you to back my testimonial by writing a few lines to the governors of Stourbridge School, expressing your opinion, if it be really your opinion, that I would recommend no one to their choice who was not fully qualified to discharge the duties of the school. I can speak of Mr. Boulton in the highest terms; he was the first pupil I sent to college, and had circumstances been favourable would have distinguished himself highly as a scholar at the University; since he left college he has been an assistant master here.

"I am aware that I am putting my request in a very roundabout manner; it is always difficult to ask favours, though I feel assured that in the present instance I am addressing one who will oblige me if he can do so with propriety.

"I beg my kind remembrances to Mrs. Butler, and remain, dear Sir, yours very truly, "THOMAS ROWLEY."

Copy of Dr. Butler's answer:

"Although it must be perfectly unnecessary for me to bear testimony to the value of Mr. Rowley's recommendation in a neighbourhood where he is so well known and so deservedly esteemed, yet from my knowledge of his character after twenty-three years' acquaintance with him, either as a pupil or a man, I venture to add that there is no one on whose judgement I would place more reliance, or on whose recommendation I would set a higher value, than on his."

From the Rev. G. Matthews

Herstmonceux, May 15th, 1833.

"DEAR AND REVEREND SIR, Situated as I am, and for a long time have been, I have found it impossible to keep any such sum of money by me as twenty pounds. I know not therefore how I can meet the exigencies of the time except I avail myself of your generous offer. God's blessing upon you through a long and honoured life for this and all else you have said and done for me!

"All you require shall be done; all you advise shall be attended to; for all your advice is good and wise and proper. I lament only that I can make you no return but words, of which I fear you have already had too many."

To the Rev. Charles Seager

Shrewsbury, May 24th, 1833.

"SIR, I had the honour to receive about a month ago your very beautifully edited and useful compendium of Simon's Lexicon and your analysis of the Greek cases. With regard to the first, I would observe that we do not read Hebrew here, but that I think you would afford a valuable assistance to those who are beginning to study the language if you would give a compendious grammar of the same size, or add a sheet to the lexicon containing a verbal praxis on the Psalms or Genesis, as far as a sheet would go.

*

"With regard to the *Graecorum casuum* analysis, the subject is very interesting, and as connected with the origin of language in general belongs to a subject which has occasionally occupied my thoughts, and at one time most of my correspondence with one of the most inquiring and learned Continental scholars, as well as the oldest friend I had, the Baron Merian, whose death I have to lament within the last few years. Of your book I have as yet been able to read no more than twenty-five pages, and such are my occupations that it is impossible for me to say when I may finish it, short as it is. I owe these twenty pages to an attack of *la grippe*, which obliged me to keep my bed, and you owe the trouble of this letter to my being sufficiently recovered to sit up, but not to resume my usual occupations, though I can employ my pen without the labour of talking. I therefore do so because it may be long enough before I have such another good opportunity. What I have read is sufficient to show me that the work is one of much ingenuity and research. How far I may be prepared to go with it in the sequel of course I cannot foresee, but I should think a good way, if not wholly, in the broad principle, if I should differ in detail.

"I may observe, however, that for the last twenty-five years, when lecturing my upper boys upon the Greek grammar, I have been accustomed to inform them that verbs are only substantives in action or acted upon, and that their inflections are not arbitrary, but originally meaning sounds, being fragments of words expressive of the agents or patients. I hold that original words were very generally imitative, or at least meant to be expressive, and I have illustrated this by the Greek word τυπ,[1] and its Saxon derivative, or rather congener, *thump*. Thus τυπ-(εγ)ω or τυπ-ω (by euphony τύπτω) is 'thump I'; τυπ-cυ or τυπ-τυ (by euphony τυπ(ε)c(υ) and τυπειc or τύπτειc) 'thump thou'; τυπ-έ, τυπ-ει, τυπτει, 'thump he,' etc. And a similar account is to be given of the cases.

---

[1] I have taken the sample of Dr. Butler's writing given opposite from an earlier draft of this same letter, also in Dr. Butler's handwriting; hence the variants. It is a fair example of Dr. Butler's more hurried and cursive script.—ED.

I have for the last 25 years, when lecturing on the grammar to my upper boys, been accustomed to inform them that verbs were simply substantives in action or acted on, & that their inflections were not arbitrary but on' ginally meaning sounds, expressive of the persons who were the agents or acted on, & exemplifying it by run

DR. BUTLER'S HANDWRITING IN 1833

"In the infancy of language verbs could have had no persons, and nouns no cases, and no doubt much was done by action, as is still the case among all savage nations. By degrees, as it became necessary to distinguish persons by some better means than pointing δεικτικῶc, the personal pronouns became combined with the verb, and thus the verb got its inflection of persons; and in like manner, as it became necessary to distinguish things or persons in point of possession, direction, object, locality, instrumentality, etc., inflections of case were given to nouns. I quite agree with you therefore that it is absurd for any philosophical analyst of language to suppose the nominative case the source from whence all the inflections of a word are to be derived, for it is certain that these no more depend on the nominative case than they do on any other, and in fact we might make out a strong plea for the accusative.

"From what I have read of your book already I presume we are agreed:

"1. That the primordial language in its earliest stage consisted of nouns only, expressive either of things or qualities. This is a question which I had to maintain for years against the learned and valued friend I have mentioned.

"2. That these were simple, often imitative sounds, without either number or case, which were added as necessity led to improvements.

"3. That verbs were formed from these nouns brought into relation with other objects in an active or passive sense.

"4. That verbs had no persons or numbers originally till necessity led to improvement, and that in each case fragments of significant words led to the forms of inflection, varied by the polish of language into their present form.

"Still we are not up to the mark. Language even thus considered is arbitrary and conventional: *e.g.* there must have been as much agreement necessary to make τυπ into τυπ-ω, τυπ-cυ, or τυπ-έ, as to make τυπτω, τυπτειc, τυπτει, original and arbitrary formations.

"What then have we gained by this investigation? Why this: that in the former case we see a reason for the thing, in the latter we see none. But does this show us how a whole nation could be led to adopt even a rational form? For there must have been some conventional pact to do so. No. How then could it have been effected? Perhaps thus:

"On the Origin of Language

"We do not know how long the first man was without the use of his tongue. Supposing, then, the first sounds imitative, or at least expressive, a small list of primitive nouns must soon have been formed, and observation of one thing acting upon another, or being acted upon by it, would soon lead to a small stock of verbs: thus a very narrow primordial language may have been formed, which call A.

"On the first peopling of the earth this would suffice the first congregated families. When these became sufficiently numerous they would separate, and at the moment of separation would take with them their primitive language. Let a party thus separate, which call B.

"But differences of localities, employments, wants, and associations would require additional words to be added to their primitive language A, which would be in the new settlement B, but not in the old settlement A, supposing no intercourse, which probably was the case in the earliest times. Thus we may designate the language of the colony as A B.

"In the meantime, as new events and new combinations are constantly arising, the primordial language A would be increased by a new stock of words expressive of such combinations, but unknown at B. Call this a.

"The like would happen at B. Call this b. So that the primordial language becomes A a, while the language of the colony becomes A B b; so that the language of B will now be only like that of A in respect of one-third.

"The language of both A and B is increasing by a and B b respectively, while the primordial stock A remains the same and never increases.

"The new stock continually increases, and in both languages

at once. The number of radicals therefore *common to both* languages is stationary, while the number of those not common to both is continually on the increase.

"The languages therefore become continually more and more dissimilar as to words.

"Furthermore, man is a progressive being. As the multitude of objects within the sphere of his knowledge increases, he finds it necessary to be more minute in his discrimination.

"The ways by which he marks the distinctions of time and space—distance and proximity—possession and alienation—object—intention—direction—aim—instrument, etc., etc., become more and more minute as his occasions multiply. Hence the inflections of his nouns and their relations to each other vary; and this is true in mental as well as in material objects—in matters of fact and contingency—of past, present, and future—of relation and correlation—of volition and power, etc., etc. The combinations become more varied as his faculties become enlarged and his observation more discriminative. Hence his verbs acquire not only new inflections, but new moods and tenses, as we call them.

"Thus, then, the *Grammar* of B begins to differ from that of A. And thus I think we may see how we may get two languages with some traits of resemblance, but more of discrepance.

"Now send off a third family C from A, at a more advanced period than that at which B migrated. These will have all the new combinations of A, but none of those of B. Their language will therefore at first be represented by A a, will soon become A a C, and ultimately A a C c, while that of B is A B b. The language of C therefore will have but one-fourth in common with B.

"Let B now send forth its colony D. The language of D will be at first A B b, then A B b D, and ultimately A B b D d. The language of D therefore will have but one-fifth in common with C.

"And if C sends off a colony E, its language will be represented by A a C c E e.

"And if D sends off a colony F, its language will be represented by A B b D d F f or the language of F will have only one-seventh in common with E.

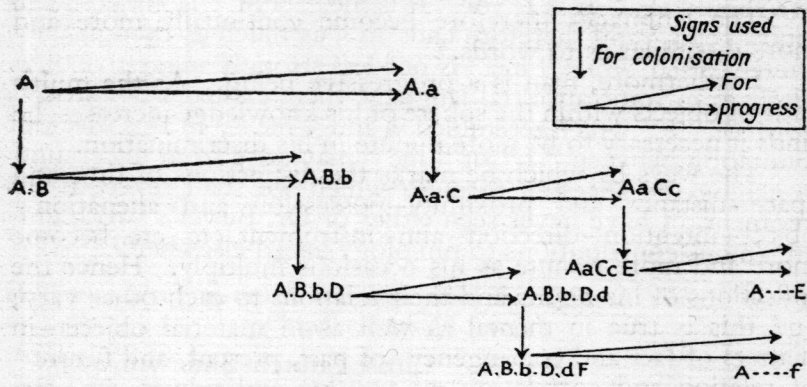

"This on the supposition that the languages of each nation vary in an equal ratio, which it is impossible can be the case, and therefore the discrepancies will be far greater and proceed far more rapidly; for though the letters A, B, C, etc., may be considered as fixed quantities, the letters a, b, c, etc., which are far more important, are variable.

"But if all these six tribes, instead of migrating to great distances, where they find great changes in natural objects and the physical effects of climate, go but to moderate distances, where they may have occasional but not very frequent intercourse, and are in other respects on the whole similarly situated, they will form not separate languages, but dialects, or at least branches of the primordial language A.

"And this is the sum of my thoughts upon the matter, which any one who has time may easily expand into a good octavo. I shall probably compress them into an essay in some periodical.

"I have the honour to be, Sir, your very obedient servant,
"S. BUTLER."

Dr. Butler never found time to develop the speculations contained in the foregoing letter, which should be compared with one to Baron Merian given vol. i, pp. 318-320. It is interesting to note that Dr. Butler's theory makes the two endings of Greek verbs ω and ΜΙ reflect the hesitation we still feel as to whether we should say " It is I " or " It is me." For " I " of course is only " ego," and therefore ends in o as much as though the o were written, while " me " is not less strongly suggestive of ΜΙ. Perhaps in some ancestral language there existed a nominative form of " I " which resembled ΜΙ and " me "; in this case our hesitation between " I " or " me " may arise from uncertainty touching the ancestral form to which we shall revert at the moment. I have never seen either of Dr. Butler's two highly ingenious contributions to philology urged elsewhere.

From Robert Scott, Esq. (who had just taken a First-class " in Litteris Humanioribus ")

Christ Church, June 7th, 1833.

" MY DEAR DR. BUTLER, Give me leave to thank you most warmly for your kind congratulations, which will, I am sure, be as gratifying to my father's feelings as they are to my own. I must in return congratulate you upon the preponderance of Shrewsbury men in the first class, and to assure you how glad I was to form one of a number which, I believe, no other school equalled. Henney, besides being either the first or among the very first in Classics, is quite sure of his Mathematics. It may perhaps not be very unpardonable vanity in me to add, in writing to you at least, that I too have reason to believe that I was among the first.

" The examination was a very curious one upon the whole, but I am not now disposed to examine it too critically. We were not allowed to bring away the questions; but if they are published, I shall take an opportunity to send them to you, if it would at all interest you; and perhaps you would like to see the papers for the Ireland Examination too, which I shall be happy to send you at the same time."

From the Rev. S. Tillbrook

Earl's Colne, July 11th, 1833.

" Thank you *mille volte*, my dear Archdeacon, for your congratulations on the birth of my second son. How many more 'latitats' there may be in my quiver God only knows and I need not seek. Time will show. I am glad to say that mamma and the baby are going on well, and such being the case I left them to the care of Providence, the doctor, and the nurse, and came hither to-day, just to jollify, etc., with Watty and Andrew Irvine till duty and the church bells summon me home again. We all of us cordially wished that you could have been of our party, and have added your superior wit to ours, and have joined in the mirth and good cheer that enlivened our host's festive board.

"Irvine has brought his wife and three children with him, and is going to stay some days at Colne. We think and talk of you and your family yacht. Neptune and sea-nymphs protect you 'when the stormy winds do blow.' For my own part I never could endure the *sickening* restlessness of the sea, and had far sooner take a trip with you by land. Nevertheless I thank you for your invitation to Beaumaris, and would gladly accept it but for the domestic duties that summon me back to Freckenham.

"We expected to have heard some tidings of you at the commencement, but I really think you proved your good sense by staying away. Only think of old Dalton, the rusty old Quaker we fell in with at the Nag's Head when on our fishing expedition to Leathes Water—only think of his being lauded and collauded and scratched and buttered by Sedgwick and Buckland, and praised up to the skies as the great Father of the Aurora Borealis race!!

"Think moreover of the rest of the Sophs, who were admitted without a degree or name to all the rights and privileges of regular men of science and philosophy. But enough of all this; you will read it in the *Cambridge News* of last week.

"Pray have you heard any more of the *Museum Piscatorium*? I believe it will end in smoke, as young Lowe, the intended editor, has left London, and has accepted some official situation under the Town Clerk of Liverpool.

"All friends here unite in kind regards to you and your household. May you sail in safety *inter alta navium* till you return to old Salop to resume the command of your classic vessels there! And now good-night. 'All's well.'

"P.S. You must come and see us next Christmas. Your godson will then be able to add his greetings to ours. He is a rare little fellow. This last is a prettier child, but does not give promise of being so stout a controversialist as Master Limborch. Has your son Tom made you a grandpapa yet?"

From the Rev. J. Wood Warter (then residing with Southey)

Greta Hall, Keswick, September 17th, 1833.

"MY DEAR SIR, You were kind enough when we parted in your study at Shrewsbury to beg that I would write soon after my arrival here. I have delayed doing so from day to day because I had no news to impart, nor indeed have I now, but I am unwilling that any semblance of forgetfulness should appear in me towards one to whom for everything I am so deeply indebted. I need not say I am very happy here. In all probability I shall remain under this good man's roof till something turns up, as I reap daily a rich harvest from his conversation and library. His cheerfulness and merry heart remind me, my ever-valued friend, of yours, with all the labours of your school thick upon you. I used to wonder at it, but it convinced me that the merry heart was a continual feast.

"My time is devoted to study and mountaineering alternately. I read a good deal of Spanish and Italian, and have a mine of curious authors to work at. I take advantage of these Southern tongues, as all the house are proficients, particularly one who was flattered that you recollected her, and who begs with her father that I will not omit their best wishes to you and yours. I have long made the old divines the object of my reading, and here too I am enabled to follow it up. At present I am engaged with a cut-and-come-again worthy in three folios, and could wish they were six—that 'reverend and learned divine Thomas Jackson,' sometime President of Corpus Christi College, Oxon, whose works it is a blot on the Syndics of the Clarendon not yet to have reprinted. After Hooker, J. Taylor, Barrow, and South, I read him with infinite instruction and delight, and that is saying much.

"But enough of myself. Southey is busy as usual. The preparation of the late Dr. Bell's Remains for the Press and the second volume of the Naval History occupies his attention at present in the main. How he finds time to do the thousand and one other things he does, besides regularly attending to an immense correspondence, I cannot make out. Of this I am sure, that he finds time to write what few can find time to read. I regret much that he is obliged to write, as he says, from hand to mouth, and that our country, as others are wont, does not set a value on time which would produce works to be had in lasting remembrance. His heart has long been set (and for the works he has the collections of thirty years) on writing the histories of the monastic orders and of Portugal, and of taking up the account of English literature where Warton left off. With all the three at once he could flood the Press. But such is not the food for the times; there is too much of hard truth in it, and without blasphemy and without reproach.

"I hope ere long to be enabled to tell you I have found some employment in the vocation I [word illegible]. Southey has had several letters assuring him that those who have it in their power will not forget me when anything drops out. The last intimations were from the Archbishop of Canterbury and from the Bishop of Bath and Wells, through the veteran Bowles. I am naturally anxious to be settled; and there is no one I shall have more pleasure in communicating any turn o' the tide to than yourself.

"P.S. I must not forget to tell you that I saw some beautiful char the other day at Coniston. We eat of them half an hour after they were caught, and certainly it was to be ἐν πᾶσι λαγῷοις. As soon as they begin to pot them I shall take care to forward some to you."

To the Rev. George Buckeridge

Shrewsbury, about October 16th, 1833.

" DEAR SIR, I should willingly sign the paper you have sent me were the third paragraph away, and consequently the second somewhat modified.

"God forbid that we should see the time when the great

truths of Christianity shall cease to be taught at the Universities! I would sooner exclude all Dissenters than risk this, but I dislike exclusive systems altogether, and I do not see why Unitarians should be excluded more than any other class.

"I come to the facts. I have educated at this school many Unitarians, and some of them sons of eminent Unitarian ministers; one such, a son of the Rev. Joseph Hunter, whose celebrity as an etymologist and antiquarian must be well known to you, is with me now, and will go to Cambridge next year. The son of another respectable Unitarian minister is also here, and is high in the school.

"Some of these have been first-class classics at Cambridge, but have been hindered from their degrees after they had passed so creditable an examination by the present absurd law of subscription.

"Now never while these boys were at school was there the slightest inconvenience from their religious principles. They attended prayers in our chapel daily. On Sundays I gave them leave to attend their own minister in his chapel (on a promise from that gentleman that he would report them to me if absent), and allowed them to miss my sixth-form lecture on the Greek Testament, which, however, they have generally chosen to attend. No disputes or sneers have ever happened between them and the other boys, and I am sure no inconvenience has arisen from their tenets when they have left me for their respective colleges.

"Why, then, should we exclude Socinians from a privilege which they appreciate, and which, be it said without disrespect to other Dissenters, they are by their general learning at least as well qualified as any others to aspire to? I believe indeed they yearn for it. And if they are left free to attend chapel and divinity lectures or not as they choose, I am confident they will be on terms of peace, and may be led even to union with their Trinitarian brethren.

"But I cannot in the compass of a letter say all I wish on this head—and indeed am still too ill to write more than I can help. I honour the liberality of feeling which dictated your first and second clauses, and I believe I understand the difficulties of your position as a member of Oxford which led to the exclusion in the third.

"I have known a Turk, and more than one Greek, and a Roman Catholic undergraduate at . . ."

(Rest of draft not found by me.—ED.)

To the Bishop of Chichester

Shrewsbury, October 30th, 1833.

"MY DEAR LORD, About a fortnight ago I was applied to by Mr. George Buckeridge, of Worcester College, Oxford, to know if I would head an association in my archdeaconry to resist any alteration in the Liturgy, doctrines, or discipline of the Church of England. He stated that many distinguished persons were desirous of becoming members of such a society, and among them mentioned the names of two persons whom I highly esteem, Hugh Rose and Walter Hook of Coventry. I replied that I must beg to be excused; that I thought any such association not only unlikely to answer the proposed end, but to be productive of serious mischief; that as to the clergy of my archdeaconry, they must judge for themselves—I should not attempt to influence their religious opinion, except so far as that I would not be instrumental in leading them into any such association by my recommendation or example.

"There the matter ended. To-day, however, he has sent me the prospectus of the society, in which I see much reason for congratulating myself at having declined to join it. I hope I have as sincere a regard for the welfare of the Church and as much attachment to her doctrines as any member of the association can have, but I will not fetter myself in the trammels of an association whose primary and avowed object is to reject all change. I freely avow that there are some parts of the Liturgy which I think capable of improvement and should like to see improved. Besides some verbal alterations, I should like to see the Athanasian Creed either wholly expunged or at least left to be read on the festivals where it is now enjoined by the Rubric at the discretion of the minister, with the same sort of ' Or this ' as we have to the prayers for the King in the Communion

Service. I should like to see a great alteration in the Marriage Service, and some in some of the other occasional services. Especially I should like to see a solemn prayer substituted for the *Veni Creator* in the Ordination Service. From supporting all this the association would tie up my hands, and even from minor points such as shortening the service and altering the proper lessons. I therefore disapprove of this and all such associations for the reasons I have assigned, and for many others which I might assign were they not sufficiently obvious to any sensible and thinking man. I have written fully to Dr. Burton on the subject."

From the Rev. W. F. Hook

Coventry, November 2nd, 1833.

"MY DEAR MR. ARCHDEACON, On my return home last night I found your letter, and am much flattered by your regarding me as a person worthy to receive from you an explanation of your reasons for not joining the proposed association. In most of what you say in that letter [1] I cordially agree, although I must protest against your classing that best of Churchmen and of Christians John Keble with the Wilberforces and that set. If you wish to learn that man's doctrines and feelings look at his poem 'Let us Depart Hence' in the *British Magazine* for last March. He is a poet, and not a man of the world, and may sometimes fail in worldly wisdom, but in all true wisdom he shines among the highest lights.

"As to the association, my opinions very nearly coincide with yours. At the end of September I received a visit from my friend Mr. Palmer, author of the *Origines Liturgicae*, and he told me that not the Wilberforces, but such men as Keble, Froude, Newman, and himself had been devising some such scheme, to which Rose gave his approval. I agreed to join with them so far as to consult on what ought to be done. Palmer returned

---

[1] I found no draft of the letter here referred to, nor yet of several other letters that were evidently written by Dr. Butler to Mr. (as he then was) Hook and others on the Oxford Movement. Everything that I found will be given under its due date.—ED.

to Oxford, and just before I started for London (the evening of Sunday, October 30th) I received the suggestions. I sent off a few copies to some friends in the neighbourhood, according to orders received. But I clearly perceived the next morning that the thing would not do. Who would commit himself to an association of the very fundamental principles of which he is ignorant? Finding my friend Archdeacon Bayley in town, I sent for Palmer, and we persuaded him to give up this plan of an association (which, however, has so far done good that it has opened a correspondence between many good men in different parts of the country), and to join us in framing an address to the Archbishop of Canterbury.

"Nothing could have been more admirable than the conduct of the Oxford men, who, in finding that several other practical men agreed with us, immediately relinquished their schemes. Accordingly Joshua Watson, Archdeacon Bayley, and myself (for Palmer returned to Oxford) have been at work to draw up an address to the Archbishop, stating to him our great respect for his personal character as well as his office, our determination to maintain the doctrine and polity of the Church as at present established, but at the same time our readiness to co-operate in any measure of reform which, rendered necessary by lapse of time, should meet with his approbation and sanction. Something to this effect is requisite to induce the Government to consult his Grace, which they have not hitherto done in any case, and to strengthen his hands. The address is so worded that I think it must meet with the approbation of almost every one. I have stated that this is private and confidential, because of course we sent up this address to the Oxford men with whom the measure originated, and we must not talk of it till we hear again from them. In the meantime I am sure that you will not fear anything that emanates from such men as Joshua Watson and Archdeacon Bayley, who is quite a man after your own heart.

"As to Buckeridge's applying to you to be a member of any such association, it was highly injudicious. You are so circumstanced that he but ill-befriends the Church who could wish you to commit yourself in any way.

"You ought to be asked to sign nothing but what we could expect a bishop to sign—among which order I hope soon to see you.

"Archdeacon Bayley introduced me to three friends of yours —Tate (a delightful fellow, if he were not a Whig!!), Dr. Burney, and Dr. Sleath."

From Dr. Burton

Oxford, November 3rd, 1833.

"DEAR DR. BUTLER, If you do not actually think that I am telling a white lie, you will at least be amused when I tell you that I had not even heard of the association which you mention till I read your letter. Whether it is owing to my long absence from Oxford, or whether the framers of the association did not think me likely to attend to them, from some cause or other the measure seems to have reached you at Shrewsbury before it was communicated to me, though I am now living, as it appears, in the place of its birth. I infer from your letter that the association is virtually, though not perhaps professedly, opposed to all reform in matters relating to the Church, and I now remember that about a week ago a friend of mine, who is a reformer in the same good sense with you and me, told me something of a society being instituted, or about to be instituted, by some members of Oriel College, which was to protest against all reform; but I had ceased to think about it till your letter brought it to my recollection. There is probably some connection between the two associations; but I think I can undertake to say that no countenance has been or will be given to such a measure by the senior members of this University, nor by any persons of much weight and influence."

*

To the Lord Chancellor (Lord Brougham)

Shrewsbury, November 3rd, 1833.

*

"I wish, however, to avail myself of this opportunity to mention two subjects, one of which I submitted to the Duke of Sussex when I had the honour to see him here two years ago—namely, whether it might not be practicable to exempt from subscription to the Articles of our Church at the two Universities all persons matriculating and taking A.B. degrees, and all laymen taking higher degrees, at least till they should be appointed to some office or place of emolument in the Universities or their respective colleges.

"One of my pupils, the son of the Rev. Thomas Broadhurst, a very respectable Unitarian minister at Bath, after passing an excellent examination and being seventh in the Classical Tripos two years ago, was prevented from proceeding to his degree on this ground. And another now with me, the son of that very distinguished antiquary the Rev. Joseph Hunter, will be under the same disadvantage.

[" The other point respects a very recent and yet inchoate measure, calculated, I think, to do great injury to the Church, by preventing all such reform as may be necessary to keep pace with the spirit of the times. I allude to an association now forming among the clergy and laity to resist *all change* in the doctrines, *ritual*, or *discipline* of the Church of England. This I was lately invited to head in the Archdeaconry of Derby, and refused, and have written my opinion on the whole subject in detail to the Bishop of Chichester.] . . ."

This last paragraph was erased by Dr. Butler.

From the Rev. W. F. Hook

Coventry, November 5th, 1833.

"MY DEAR MR. ARCHDEACON, I have just received your letter, and hasten to reply to it, for the same post has brought me a letter from my friend Mr. Palmer, in which he states that the society is still to be formed, and that vast numbers of the clergy have sent in their adhesion.

"I had understood otherwise. But you would not have honoured me with your friendship if you were not prepared to believe me when I say that I had no intention to deceive you, and that when I wrote to you last I fully thought the business of the society had, for the present, been entirely laid aside.

Occupied as you are, you will be annoyed at having to write over again your letter to a certain person (I can guess who he is), and I beg to apologize for having caused you this trouble. At the same time you will see that it could not have been my wish to prevent your adopting such a course; because, as far as my opinion goes, while you will, on the one hand, be only doing as, from your station, your influence, and your mode of thinking, you ought to do, we shall, on the other, be gaining one of our objects, which is, to let our rulers see that, however they may interfere with our temporalities, there is a spirit abroad prepared to resist unto death any undue tamperings with our spiritualities. Let them do what they will with the first; but as to the *jus divinum*, if they encroach upon *that*, I confess that I am fully prepared to relinquish my preferment and to quit the Establishment. We can obtain the *jus divinum* from America, if the English Establishment renounces it. I agree with you, as I said in my last, in what you say of the suggestions. Nothing can be more injudicious than to ask men to pledge themselves to anything so indefinite; but Mr. Palmer's letter, in answer to my objection on that head, informs me that something definite is now to be done.

"I think your friend Evans and my friend Keble might run together in a curricle, except that your friend (read his sermon on obedience) is a little wee bit inclined to Calvinism. As to Keble's sermon at Oxford, if you mean that which was published and entitled *National Apostasy* I would only request you to read it, and I think you will agree with me in admiring it. Your story of Newman and Froude is amusing. You have let off your bomb in defence of Lord Nugent. But we may, I think, agree with men in principle, though we think them unwise in some details of practice. For my part, the longer I live the more determined I am to pray to God that I may ever strive to do what I think right myself without regard to others. And whenever I differ from anybody, my rule has always been to believe that his motives are good until I clearly ascertain them to be wrong.

"I don't think, my dear Mr. Archdeacon, that you and I shall in the long-run very materially differ. At all events, when we do differ, we can agree to differ; for I am very grateful for all the kindness I have received from you, and shall always entertain for your opinions the greatest respect.

"P.S. I am sorry to say that, in these days when all men's minds have been shaken, I observe an opinion gaining ground among High Churchmen against an establishment. A man said to me the other day: 'that is the point we must drive at—a separation between Church and State.'

"Twelve or fourteen years ago my own opinions coincided with these; but I have grown, as I hope, wiser. The Church in America is no doubt, as a Church, far better off than the Church in England, where we are sadly shackled by our alliance with the State. This is one side of the question: on the other I look at the state of religious feeling throughout the respective countries, and then I see the advantages of an establishment in creating as it were a religious atmosphere, so that rather than have none I would uphold an establishment to which, as in Scotland, I could not conscientiously conform."

From the Bishop of Chichester (Dr. Maltby)

November 7th, 1833.

"MY DEAR DR. BUTLER, I thank you for your communication, and agree in all you say respecting it. The only end of such an association would be to invite attack, when it is both our duty and interest to be as quiet as possible. I am glad, however, to find from your second letter that it is given up. The Church and country are much indebted to you for the judicious and manly course you have pursued respecting it."

*

To the Rev. W. F. Hook

Shrewsbury, November 21st, 1833.

"MY DEAR FRIEND, Your letter is not of ordinary interest, and it occupies my most serious attention, as coming from one whose integrity of heart and purpose is unimpeachable, whose theological learning is most extensive, whose piety is unaffected, and whose moral courage is undeniable. With what face can I oppose all these, or with what arms can I combat them, except with the simple garniture of heart and purpose?

"Your address, you say, is somewhat altered. I do not, however, see much ground for saying that it is somewhat improved. It is a little more verbose; but my rule for writing addresses (an evil which has fallen to my lot oftener than I could wish) is to make them as short as possible, and retrench every word but that of titles and dignities, which I am ready to pour out as Alexander did his frankincense—ὅλῳ τῷ θυλάκῳ. All that, however, is a matter of taste, and I do not mean to do more than make a courteous salute so far.

"You say that the object of the address is to let our civil rulers know that the clergy of England are determined to stand by their spiritual head, whom they (our civil rulers) have slighted, if not insulted, and that they (our civil rulers) must consult with him before they venture to propose any changes in spiritual matters.

"If you mean to show this to our civil rulers, I think the address had better be directed to them than to our spiritual head. But, my dear friend, I am quite confounded with this assertion from you, an ultra-Tory, a High Churchman to the backbone, and, as you are pleased to describe yourself, 'a most illiberal dog' (which you are not, for your better feelings prevent you from the imputation, Ἡ γλῶσσ᾽ ὀμώμοκ᾽ ἡ δὲ φρὴν ἀνώμοτος). Your spiritual head *de jure divino* is the King; and if you make your spiritual head the Archbishop of Canterbury, you incur the penalties of a *praemunire*, and I may yet hope to see your own spiritual head adorning a spike upon Temple Bar. Besides which, admitting for the moment that your spiritual head is the Archbishop, allow me to ask whether you know that he feels himself insulted, and wants *auxilium et defensores istos*?

"With regard to your wish for the revival of ancient discipline, you tell me it is wished for in the Commination Service —a service which in all its damnatory parts I heartily wish to see cut out of the Prayer Book (I know all that is said in its favour), and in which it is distinctly implied, if not expressly acknowledged, that even in the times when it was compiled there was no prospect of restoring it, and which it is therefore idle to think of restoring now.

"You say that the association has assumed a more definite character, but you do not give a definition of its character, and it is this which I am most anxious to know. You admit that you belong to the association 'because it is exclusive,' and you state your fears that they who wish to render the Church as little exclusive as possible will destroy its catholicism. This is a contradiction in terms which I cannot understand, and which I must leave to wiser heads than mine to reconcile. I am a stupid fellow; and though your University has done me the honour of admitting me to an *ad eundem* D.D. degree, she did not at the same time pour into my brain a sufficient portion of Aristotelian logic. By your 'catholicism' I cannot understand anything but 'the principles of the association,' which may be a part of the Catholic Church, and I am sure is so while it has men like you in it, but which is not the whole of it. Do not break my head with the Fathers, and tell me that Catholic and Orthodox are the same. I shall question your orthodoxy if you do.

"When you say in the first place, 'Pity us,' I do a great deal more: I love and esteem you and all who are like you, but I do pity you and grieve for you when I see you surrendering your high honour and your powerful judgement to the shibboleth of a set of men who are not fit to brush your shoes, and whose fears are excited by any possible alteration in a Liturgy which has been already altered fifteen times.

"When you say 'Beware of us,' then I grieve indeed. Surely your own high spirit must tell you that such language is of all others the most likely to lead to a fatal collision. I seek and wish and pray for the peace of the Church. I am among those who think that the best way to secure it is for the clergy to keep quiet—at least till called upon by their spiritual rulers. I do not think the Bishops will sacrifice the doctrines in which they have been bred, which they teach, and which they have sworn to preserve and maintain in any essentials, though I think some changes in the Liturgy of the Established Church are necessary, and others desirable.

"No man of common information can be ignorant that they

who framed the Articles of that Church endeavoured so to frame them as to comprehend as many as possible within its pale. I see no reason why the same principle should not be adopted in the nineteenth century which was acted upon and admitted in the sixteenth. Do you think that all–I had almost said that any–of those clergy who are unwilling to adopt the exclusive sentiments of the association are such latitudinarians in principle as to be indifferent to any creed, or so obsequious as to be ready to surrender a single point which they think essential to the opinions of any man or body of men whatever? If you do, believe me that you have formed a wrong estimate of one at least of them, who is, in spite of your prejudices, your ultra-Toryism, your Church and State, your inquisitorial dogmatism, and your hundred thousand political offences, your very affectionate friend,
" S. BUTLER.

"P.S. After knowing what your address means, I won't sign it. There's the pith in the P.S. But you, who argue for the exclusiveness of the Church, told me that you wished the address to include as many as possible."

From the Rev. W. F. Hook

Coventry, November 23rd, 1833.

"MY DEAR MR. ARCHDEACON, For your amusing and learned letter accept my thanks. I will follow your advice, and keep quiet. Indeed it is seldom that I busy myself out of my parish except to write an article for the *British Magazine*. With respect to the address, I do not much transgress the boundaries; I have merely undertaken to make the thing known in Warwickshire. All the clergy in this neighbourhood and the members of our Clerical Society have signed. The saints of Birmingham, headed by their pompous Archdeacon, refuse. You will remember that I did not open the business to you in the first instance, but you very kindly wrote to me, and of that letter I shall always feel, as I ought to do, proud. Having entered upon the subject–a subject which I should never have touched upon unless you had written first–I am sure you would not desire me not to speak out boldly and manfully for what I hold to be God's truth.

"I repeat what I said in my last letter—that if alterations are to be made, it is only fair that the prejudices of those who think that our reformers went too far should be considered, as well as the prejudices of others who think that they went not far enough. I am not, nor ever have been, one of those who look upon the Church of England as the best and purest Church in existence; I much prefer the Church of[1] America. And I admit that our Liturgy has been altered many more times than you mention since its first introduction into England by the great apostle of the Church of England, Augustine. I should be sorry to see alterations made now, chiefly because I fear that they would not be such as I approve. I should be in the minority, I fear, although I really find every year new acquaintances who hold the same principles as have actuated me for fourteen years. I belong to the Church of England, not because it is the purest Church or best Church, or anything of that sort, but because I believe it to be in England the only Church—that is, the only Catholic Church. In Scotland I conform not to the Establishment, because I believe the Scottish Establishment not to be a Catholic Church. What I mean by a Catholic Church (between *a* Catholic Church and *the* Catholic Church Archbishop Wake points out the distinction) you may see in a sermon preached at Bishop Luscombe's consecration[2] which I once sent to you, or the accompanying tract will show. It is not published. It is printed that the opinions of different persons may be obtained. Some of the English Bishops, all the Scotch Bishops, have seen it and approved highly, though several alterations as to details have been suggested. It is to be sent to the American Bishops. You will believe me that I honour the Scotch and American Churches more than our own when I say that I believe there is scarcely an exception to the

---

[1] "Of" is probably a mere slip of the pen for "in," for Dr. Hook was very particular on this point—but the word is "of" in the original letter.—ED.

[2] This sermon is published in *The Church and her Ordinances*. Sermons, etc., edited by the Rev. W. Hook. Bentley, 1876, 8vo. Vol. i, p. 14.—ED.

soundness of their Bishops, and when I believe we can scarcely predicate even orthodoxy of some of our own. Is not, for instance, Archbishop Whately a Sabellian heretic? Look to his definition of Persona in his *Logic*. However, I will hope and believe that he can explain this away. I only remark that he is generally supposed to be a Sabellian heretic. And I can tell you besides that he has sent, with his compliments, to several of the clergy Cox's suggestions with respect to alterations in the Liturgy, implying of course that the suggestions on the whole meet with his approval—and suggestions they are which, if acted upon, must have the effect of causing a secession from the Establishment. We know that his Grace is much looked up to by the King's Ministers.

"As to what you say about the King being the spiritual head of the Church in this country, I can only say that if I thought he was I should instantly leave the Establishment, because it would cease to be a Catholic Church. Our Church (as it is the fashion to speak, thereby making it appear that we are a sect instead of *the* Church) exists in America, purer in spite of all our boasting than here in England. Will the republican Bishop of New York admit his Majesty's headship? How can he be our spiritual head who is not a spiritual man? Have not the Articles drawn up when our Church was (not founded, for it was founded by Christ and His Apostles, but) reformed expressly provided against our making this mistake? Our temporal head indeed he is.

"I am nothing of a politician, but I hold no divine right in kings. Divine right in bishops I do hold, because the Bible and all antiquity teach me that they are the successors and in the place of the Apostles, and are thus commissioned by the Lord Jesus Himself; and I hold no ministrations (except where it is impossible to obtain episcopal orders) valid except those performed by bishops and the other orders instituted by the first Apostles and acting under the sanction of bishops. But as to any divine right of kings, I utterly reject the idea. If circumstances indeed shall drive me from my country I shall settle in a republic—namely, New York, under good Bishop Onderdonk, because in America I find a pure reformed branch of the

Catholic Church; all the Catholic Churches in Europe, excepting those of Sweden and Norway, being more or less corrupted, some by their connection with Rome, others by the barbarisms of Russia.

"With you, my dear and most respected Mr. Archdeacon, I wish and seek and pray for the peace of the Church, but peace itself must be sacrificed, nay even life and all that is dearer than life, to preserve it in its integrity and purity. For this it was that those good men contended by whom the Church in this country was (not founded, but) reformed. Peaceful she was before, but peace they sacrificed to render her pure, to wash her venerable though somewhat dirty face. For her face had become dirty by her flirtations with the Pope of Rome. If the face of our dear old mother is dirty again, let it be washed; we who sanction the work of the Bishops who washed her before cannot complain. What I fear is that her vitals will be attacked. There are men on the Bench—and you know it—who, to save their temporalities, would sacrifice anything. I am among those who say, Perish the temporalities! if it be necessary—but let us die in defence of the Faith once delivered to the Saints. Place us in the same position as the American Church, and we shall be able to fight with the sectaries and maintain our cause. I shall regret the loss of the temporalities, but let them be taken before any Uzzah with unhallowed hands venture to support our Ark by unhallowed means.

"And here ends the sermon of one who is to the backbone a Catholic, although no Papist. I do not think that the Episcopal Bench will in these days be a bed of roses, but I hope when the mitre is offered that you will accept it, if not from reverence to the divine right, yet at least from regard to classical authority, for I presume that you are aware that Hector assumed the lawn sleeves before he departed this life.

πρὶν γὰρ πόλις ἥδε κατ' ἄκρης
πέρσεται· ἦ γὰρ ὄλωλας ἐπίσκοπος ὅς τέ μιν αὐτὴν
ῥύσκευ.[1]

"And when you are on the Bench I trust you will plead the

[1] Iliad, xxiv, 728-730.—ED.

cause of those High (sound?) Churchmen, who are certainly of ancient date, since St. Cyprian has admirably described our principles: 'Unde scire debes Episcopum in ecclesia esse, et ecclesiam in episcopo, et si qui cum episcopo non sint, in ecclesia non esse.'

" P.S. With respect to what you said in a former letter touching the Calvinists, you know that I am not a Calvinist. Indeed, as neither Calvin nor Arminius come within the Church, I trouble myself little with the opinions of those mistaken individuals. But as the Catholic Church has never in any General Council condemned the Augustinian doctrines, I should never refuse to act with a man on account of his holding them. Herein on the part of any national synod I should condemn anything like exclusiveness. Bishop Bull and Bishop Beveridge, as well as Archbishop Chrysostom and Bishop Augustine, may find ample room to walk in the Church, yea and to dispute too; but the Catholic Church has in her General Councils condemned Arians and Sabellians, and *a fortiori* Socinians—therefore a national Church must watch closely to prevent their coming into the fold. The Church in this country has, I think, guarded as much as possible against this. How such a man as Dr. Whately can belong to it I know not: that is his look-out. Do what we will, we may miss a case now and then, but we do not do it willingly.

" It is remarkable that the American Bishops and Clergy, in remodelling the Liturgy, rejected the Liturgy (properly so called, or Communion Service) adopted by the Elizabethan Bishops, and received that which was first revised in the reign of Edward VI—thus retaining the material oblation and the invocation for the illapse of the Spirit on the Elements. They went back, not forward, in their work of reformation. If you can secure for us that Communion Service instead of our own, I will be a reformer. The American Bishops are high authority because they have no temporalities like ours to blind them to the truth; not that temporalities always do this, but they that do, too often, induce worldly men to seek the mitre for the pomp and wealth of the Peerage. In America it can seldom be that any but a sound Churchman can desire an office which brings no emolument.

"You say that if it were impossible in the times of Archbishop Parker to revive primitive discipline it is equally so now. I think not. Our first reformers saw not how the Church could be separated from the State. We see that this is possible; and if our alliance interfere with our discipline, there are some who say, Give us the discipline and dissolve the alliance."

To the Rev. W. F. Hook

Shrewsbury, November 26th, 1833.

"MY DEAR FRIEND, I have received, have read with very great pleasure, and have lent to Archdeacon Bather your sermon, and I have also lent him the anonymous Catechism. And I most sincerely thank you for your long letter. I wish I could write like you, but for my life I cannot conquer a propensity to jest on important cases when most men are serious. I always feel disposed to this when in great affliction or in great earnestness. It is very foolish, but I cannot help it. This will account for what you have taken for serious in my letter.

*

"Seriously then, my dear friend, valuing and honouring you as I do, admiring, deeply admiring, your high moral courage, your inflexible firmness in defence of the truth, and your very extensive theological as well as profane learning, I sigh over parts of your letter. I sigh to think that your high principles should probably make you a martyr (I mean in fortune and temporal prosperity) without a cause to a Quixotic admiration of Churches which you hold to be purer than our own at this moment, and which you will hold to be the only pure ones, if certain changes should take place in our present Established Church. But are you sure that these will take place? Who is Mr. Cox? I never heard of him; and being wholly unacquainted with Archbishop Whately, I do not expect to receive a pamphlet with his Grace's compliments. I do not suppose that Archbishop Whately or Mr. Cox can make any alterations in the Liturgy *de suo*: whatever is done in that way must, I suppose, either be done by a special commission directed to certain Bishops and Clergy, to prepare and report, or by a convocation summoned for that purpose. I do think that we need not anticipate troubles. Of Archbishop Whately's religious opinions I have no means of judging, having never read any of his works. I suppose from your term of Sabellian that he makes some distinction between Person and Essence; but I am content to believe in the divinity of Christ because I find it in Scripture, and I hold those who attempt to explain the doctrine to be anything but wise. I am content to say, not ' Credo quia impossibile est,' but ' Credo quia revelatum est,' and, without attempting to understand the divine mystery, to pursue the duties resulting from it. As to the mitre, my dear friend, of which you mention, if such a thing should ever fall upon my head, it would be impossible for my worst enemy to say I had accepted it ' for the lucre of gain,' or for the love of idleness, as I should give up a better income and an easier life for one of far greater care and occupation and much less worldly gain. But this I can say, were it to rain mitres, I would not put my head out at window to have one fall on it on condition that I should renounce any doctrine which I hold to be essential. Still I am not averse to concession as far as it can be granted, and am anxious as far as possible to admit rather than to exclude.

"Do pause and consider what you are about. Think well what claim your wife and children have on you before you go to live under good Bishop Onderdonk at New York. How is it that the Birmingham clergy refused to sign what some of the Oxford fanatics have proposed? Do they think it a child of many fathers, and refuse to baptise the bantling till its various parents have undergone the discipline of the Church in that ancient form which is not entirely abolished in the Kirk of Scotland, and which ' it is greatly to be desired ' might be restored among us? I shall rejoice to see you on the cuttie stool. Why do you speak so contemptuously of the Arminians? Which of their five articles do you reject? And why? I ask really for information. I know that they were most unjustly treated at Dort for political reasons, and that their enemies have accused them in subsequent times of Socinianism, but nothing whatever of this is to be found in their five articles. You know also that that High Churchman Archbishop Laud was accused of being an Arminian, and the Puritans could not have given a worse name to him, for it made every Calvinist at once his foe, and they have more than once given the same name to the clergy of the Church of England. And I expect that many honest uneducated people have been frightened at it, who have confounded Arminian and Arianism, and have always heard the latter to be a very bad thing."

From the Rev. W. F. Hook

Coventry, St. Andrew's Day, 1833.
(November 30th.—ED.)

"MY DEAR MR. ARCHDEACON AND MY MOST RESPECTED FRIEND, I am quite penetrated by the kindness, the friendship, and the warmth of your letters. And what a goose was I to make *ex musca elephantem*! But, you know, every man is a little crazy on some points, and your observations in your last letters have pointed that way in which my madness lies.

"But surely, my good Mr. Archdeacon, I may have recourse to the retort courteous, with respect to the very friendly but very earnest exhortations you have addressed to me touching my proposed migration to Brother (or rather Father) Jonathan. I may have somewhat of a *cerebrum fanaticum*, but I am not so far gone as to think of leaving, except upon compulsion, my own dear country, my beloved parish, and my most happy home. Indeed so contented am I that I have but two wishes at present: viz. first for an increase of income to the amount of about two hundred pounds a year, so as to have a little pocket ease; and, secondly, for the improvement of the Coventry trade.

"When a man is thus happy and contented, and has such very few wishes, he is not likely to desire to change his home. All I said or meant to say was, that if a revolution takes place and I am driven from my home, while others betake them to Italy or France, I shall depart for America, and see if I cannot get professional employment under the good Bishops there. This surely is not Quixotic.

"With respect to Calvinism I believe we perfectly agree in opinion. I am opposed to it as strongly as you can be, and I always have been so since the day of my ordination. I deem the meeting at Dort to have been what the Greeks called the second Ephesian Council, cýnoδon λhctpikhn.

"I do not like the name, or rather nickname, of Arminian. I indeed disclaim it, because Arminius not being of the same Church as I am, he is no more authority to me than Calvin is or Luther. I thank them with Bishop Bull for what good they have done with respect to papists; but as they all despised the authority of the ancient Catholic Church, I hold with none of them. I daresay Arminius was right as to the five points, but I have never read his works, and probably never shall. To him our reformers could not have had respect, since he was an infant muling and puking in his mother's arms when the Church in this country drew up the Thirty-Nine Articles. I *know* that they rejected the proffered assistance of the blood-stained murderer of Servetus. A man cannot be really a Calvinist if he remains in the Church. But he may be in error as regards some of the five points, being an Augustinian (though commonly called a Calvinist, and yet remain with us. I will oppose, I will fight with him, I will endeavour to prove him to be wrong, but I refuse not communion with him as I do with an Arian, because our Church in the Council of Nice has pronounced Arianism to be a heresy—it has never pronounced Augustinianism (for instance the doctrine of Predestination) to be so. *I* think a Predestinarian to be wrong, but the *Church* is silent—the *Church* has pronounced an Arian to be a heretic. To the decision of the Universal Church I bow; as for my own opinion I may be in error. With respect to the Church of England we cannot say that she has decided the question, because this is a matter of dispute. I think she ought not in this particular matter to be exclusive, though, believe me, I hate the Calvinists. So you see all this is only logomachy, occasioned, it may be, by a little theological pedantry upon my part."

*

To —— (?)

December 1833 (?).

"MY DEAR SIR, I would most willingly communicate at your request all information in my power to M. Renouard, whose admirable work on the Aldine Annals is a model for bibliographers, and to which I feel under great and daily obligations—but I really do not know how he would receive it. He has never mentioned my name, though he has made a sort of supercilious allusion to a book in my possession in his *Annales des Alde*, vol. ii, p. 301, without noting my communications either on that subject or on some others, especially on the *Astronomi veteres* [?], on which I sent him some detailed information long before the publication of his last edition. You may also remember that when you introduced me to him in your house at London, he received my information respecting a doubtful edition with a smile of sardonic incredulity.

"You know what I could communicate respecting his own publication [amounting almost to a supplemental volume], and how much I could add in respect to the illustrative works if M. Renouard should intend to go into them—and you know that my Aldine library, as Dr. Dibdin, who was here last week, can confirm to you, [very considerably] exceeds Lord Spencer's, and has even more rare books, though it has not so many vellums and large-paper copies. I must therefore know from Renouard himself that he both wishes for such information as I can give him, and is disposed to receive it in the friendly way in which I should offer it, before I send him any further communications. I have not the least wish that he should pledge himself to adopt my opinions, for I think the caution he uses is what stamps the great value on his work. I only expect such occasional acknowledgement in his work as may become any liberal editor to give when he makes use of the friendly and disinterested communications of a correspondent."

It does not appear to whom the foregoing letter was addressed. The words enclosed in brackets were erased in Dr. Butler's draft. In a note prefixed to Messrs. Christie & Manson's

1833]   *Correspondence*

Catalogue of Dr. Butler's Aldine Collection, it is stated that many of the additions, alterations, and corrections in the 1834 edition of Renouard's *Annales des Alde* were made from information contributed by Dr. Butler.

CHAPTER TWENTY-SIX: CORRESPONDENCE, 6TH APRIL 1834—(?) DECEMBER 1834

To the Rev. T. S. Hughes

(Original in possession of Mr. Hughes's representatives)

Shrewsbury, April 6th, 1834.

"MY DEAR HUGHES, I THOUGHT YOU HYPERcritical last year when you found fault with the Latinity of a prize essay which has been universally admired and of which I send you a printed copy, though you have had one already: there are not a dozen words altered since you saw it in MS. One short sentence, I believe, is omitted.

"I now send you what I shall not think you hypercritical in abusing—a translation from the *Spectator*. I send you only two copies, as I know your time is much engaged. It is a new prize instituted here, and as you may see by these specimens much wanted, but neither boys at school nor young men at college will take to write prose Latin. I do not say tell me which is the best, but which you think the least bad. I have made some little alterations, as I could not keep my pencil quiet while I was reading.

"I am still nearly as ill as when you saw me; my eyes are better, but I have a severe cough still and great deafness. Dugard says there is continual membranous inflammation which no medicine will relieve till the weather becomes mild, but that the vitals are yet safe. It keeps in all the upper membranes. If my eyes get better my ears get worse, and *vice versa*; or if both get better, then my cough increases and gets tighter. I have had one outbreak of erysipelas since I saw you, and that complaint I think is still lurking about me.

"Do not let anybody see the translations: they ought to be kept to ourselves this year.

"I have some very good verses and very good Greeks. I have sent them to different friends to decide."

Correspondence

From the Rev. T. F. Dibdin, D.D.

April 17th, 1834.

"MY DEAR DR. BUTLER, I have unfeigned pleasure in announcing to you your election this day to the fraternity of Roxburghers. I have not time for another word, except that the dinner installation takes place on the second or third Thursday of next month.

"You were elected in the room of Sir Walter Scott."

To Professor Sedgwick

(Original in possession of J. Willis Clark, Esq.)

April 30th, 1834.

"MY DEAR PROFESSOR, I grieve to see from the papers that you are laid up by an accident. I have been very ill ever since January, and I hope both you and I may yet meet in health again.

"I have had a letter containing a counter-declaration to the Oxford one, from Dr. Arnold. I do not like the third clause at all, and do not much like the wording of the second. The first (there are but three) is very well.

"I have sent it by this day's post with a copy of my answer to the Bishop of Chichester, with a request that he will forward it to you; and when you have read it, I shall thank you to enclose it to me.

"I think we ought to circulate among the non-resident members of the Senate a copy of your petition, which was signed by the resident members and presented by Lord Grey, that all may have an opportunity of recording their sentiments.

"It is necessary as a counter-declaration to that circulated by the other party. I will do them the justice to say that they did not send me a copy, which I think was gentlemanly on their part, and I should be glad that we exercised a similar forbearance towards those whom we know to be decidedly opposed to us, *e.g.* to those who have signed the counter-petition to ours.

"I write to an invalid, and am one myself; therefore no more. I have said enough to make myself intelligible, and you will have the correspondence I allude to in a day or two. In the meantime think of it. *Valeamus*, in every sense that is good."

The counter-declaration proposed by Dr. Arnold and circulated by him for signature is given in Dean Stanley's *Life of Dr. Arnold*, vol. i, pp. 341, 342 (London: 1844), and is as follows:

" The undersigned members of the Universities of Oxford and Cambridge, many of them being engaged in education, entertaining a strong sense of the peculiar benefits to be derived from studying at the Universities, cannot but consider it as a national evil that these benefits should be inaccessible to a large proportion of their countrymen.

" While they feel most strongly that the foundation of all education must be laid in the great truths of Christianity, and would on no account consent to omit these, or to teach them imperfectly, yet they cannot but acknowledge that these truths are believed and valued by the great majority of Dissenters no less than by the Church of England, and that every essential point of Christian instruction may be communicated without touching on those particular questions on which the Church and the mass of Dissenters are at issue.

" And while they are not prepared to admit such Dissenters as differ from the Church of England on the most essential points of Christian truth, such as the modern Unitarians of Great Britain, they are of opinion that all other Dissenters may be admitted into the Universities, and allowed to take degrees there, with great benefit to the country, and to the probable advancement of Christian truth and Christian charity among members of all persuasions."

I must refer the reader for a fuller account of this whole matter to Clark and Hughes's *Life and Letters of Adam Sedgwick*, vol. i, p. 418, etc. No petition, in the same sense as that presented by the sixty-two resident M.A.'s, was eventually presented from non-residents; I gather that it was dropped in consequence of the singularly outspoken manifestations of hostility to the Church referred to in Dr. Butler's letter of 21st May 1834 to J. Herford, Esq. It is needless to add that the good cause has long since triumphed.

From the Rev. S. Tillbrook

Ludlow, 1834 (?).

"DEAR ARCHDEACON, I had as much delight in killing the pike which accompanies this as the old hawk-eyed scout had in bringing down Magna the Huron. My credit as an angler was at stake, and I persevered till I killed the tyrant in the most correct style of the art. Once he baffled me, but I changed my bait, and he took a poor frog just as kindly as you or I should have swallowed a bit of green turtle. I daresay the rascal had swallowed thousands of trout and graylings. He lay surrounded by them when I caught him, and the poor lad whom I sent to hunt for a frog said, 'I'se sure he likes graylings; there's such a-many all about him.' Yes—just as there are swallows about an owl, or small birds about a hawk. The grayling when in full season are so highly scented that the pike do not like them. I saw pike chasing the grayling without taking them, and this induced me to try the frog.

"I hope the pike, which weighed ten pounds, will prove good: cook him *à la* Barker if possible, and drink old Piscator's health."

Here, to my great regret, I take leave of this delightful writer, no more letters from whom were found among Dr. Butler's papers. I shall be grateful to any one who will lend me any other letters, no matter about what, which they may possess from Mr. Tillbrook's hand.

From the Bishop of Chichester (Dr. Maltby)

Lincoln's Inn, May 2nd, 1834.

*

"In regard to the correspondence it appears to me very desirable that some such document should be brought forward, in order that the short-sighted, narrow views of the rusty old residents at the University may not be mistaken for the views of all. I entirely agree with what you say of the Unitarians, who are among the most respectable and intelligent of Dissenters, yet always the object of attack and abuse. For my part I cannot make a very nice scale of error. Why should a Unitarian be an object of more dread and suspicion than a Catholic or High Calvinist? I differ from all in opinion; I think them wrong, but, if I could choose to be wrong myself, I would quite as even be a Unitarian with all his defects of all [kinds?], as either of the others with all their superfluities. After all, of what little consequence is it in the ordinary intercourse and business of life what speculative opinions are held? If the Universities only did away with subscription, I have little doubt but Dissenters of all denominations who could afford it would flock to them, and trouble themselves little enough about chapel and theological lectures—at least at Cambridge.

"I am now going to tell you a secret as far as it is known to myself. The question between the Dissenters and the Church appears to me of so much consequence that I propose to make it the subject of my primary charge, which I intend to deliver at Lewes the 16th inst. and at Hastings the 21st. My object is, if possible, to bring both parties to a better understanding; and while I make some concession to the Dissenters, I protest with all my might against anything like separation, or injury to the Establishment. This of course will be a difficult and delicate task. I have mentioned it to no one but the Chancellor, who much approves the sketch I have shown him; and if I persist in my intention—and now I know not what should prevent me— we may mutually aid each other in promoting a work of charity and peace.

"But you will be so good as *not to open your lips to a soul* upon this subject till the charge is delivered. I wish you were here, that I might have the benefit of your sound judgement and experience. What does the good Archdeacon think on this subject? My notion is that with some difference of arrangement, such as I think of pointing out, the admission of Dissenters would be beneficial to the Universities and the Church.

I am just going to the House, where I shall put your letter into the Chancellor's hands, and desire him to forward it to Sedgwick. I should be sorry to see the declaration adopted with the third paragraph intact.

"The present crisis is, I am sure, formidable. The best way of stemming the torrent is by prudent and well-judged concession—by charitable and conciliatory language—by expressing respect for the persons while you firmly contest their opinions. But this, alas! is a course few of my brethren seem disposed to adopt. I hope you admire the Bishop of Exeter's views of subscription.

"I was sorry to hear from Mr. Whateley how unwell you had been, but trust you will take care of yourself, and not run up to Levées to the injury of your health. If you have been at a Drawing Room, you might have come up on the Birthday, the 28th. I leave town for my eastern visitation on the 14th. If you are here, and could breakfast on that day or preferably on the 13th, I need not say I shall be happy to see you."

To Professor Sedgwick

(Original in possession of J. Willis Clark, Esq.)

Shrewsbury, May 3rd, 1834.

"MY DEAR PROFESSOR, Probably ere this letter reaches you the Lord Chancellor will have forwarded to you my letter in reply to Dr. Arnold. The Bishop of Chichester agrees with me in thinking that we ought to come forward, and I cannot see what can be done better than to signify our assent to the petition of the sixty-two or sixty-three, whichever the number may be.

"In the *Oxford Journal* of this week the whole convocation seem to have signed the declaration of intolerance. It will be a great thing for us to put out a counter-declaration respectably signed. I shall be in town at 14, Suffolk Street, and always to be heard of at the U.U.C. from May 12th to May 16th, but I hope to hear from you before that time.

"I see some observations in the *Cambridge Chronicle* of yesterday on the petition of the sixty-two, from a correspondence of the *Times*, which I think remarkably well put. But I think our declaration should be as short and comprehensive and unprovoking as possible, and on that ground I should prefer a declaration of adhesion to the petition from the non-resident members. Still such a thing can only be got up and arranged by a committee in Cambridge or London, or both, and should, I think, be set about forthwith.

"Would it not be enough to print the petition and to add such a paragraph as this:

"'We the undersigned non-resident members of the Senate hereby declare our concurrence in the prayer of the above petition.'

"Of course the whole should be introduced by a short letter from the committee, or some member of each college, acting for them. An active and intelligent friend in each college would soon manage the business. A small fund only would be requisite to pay for printing and postage, to which I would very readily subscribe.

"I do not approve of Dr. Arnold's plan of a joint declaration from Oxford and Cambridge. The Oxonians can give us but very few names, and our opponents would say that we were forced to eke out our numbers by an unfair addition. We can make a good list of our own at Cambridge, and I think we should do so, to set it against the list of our opponents. Let the Oxford men take their own course; were they to join us, being very few in numbers as I fear they are, their opponents there would say that they were forced to join us to shield themselves from contempt. If they are enough in numbers to form a respectable list, though much less than ours, they should do so. In short, I want it to appear that neither University is unanimous in the exclusion; and this will be best done, and with the best results, if each University acts apart on this occasion."

From Dr. Arnold

Rugby, May 7th, 1834.

"DEAR SIR, I thank you very much for your Letter. My Feeling about Unitarians is this, that they could not be included *at present* in the religious Instruction of the Colleges without such Omissions in that Instruction as no good Church of England Man would think it right to make. On the other Hand, if you allow them not to attend your religious Instruction or religious Worship, you seem to me to countenance what I certainly shrink from, the separation of Education from Christianity; you stand to a Person *in Loco Parentis*, and yet waive a Parent's highest Duty and Privilege, the instructing his Child for Eternity. This, I think, affects all such Places of Education as Colleges and Schools, where the Tutors and Masters have not only the Charge of their Pupils intellectually but morally.

"But I should agree with you in admitting Unitarians to the University, if the true University System were restored, and it was not necessary in order to belong to the University to belong to some now existing College or Hall. The University being a National Institution, I would have it open to all Christians—that is, to all to whom I would open Parliament—for the Bill I am strongly opposed to on every Ground. I would then allow Unitarians to be at a Hall or Halls of their own, under their own Instructors, or of course allow them to enter at our Colleges if they liked to attend our religious Service and Instruction; and I would so far alter the Examination Statute as to make the Divinity Examination refer only to the Evidences of Christianity generally, and the Substance of the Old and New Testaments, dismissing all Examination in the Thirty-Nine Articles. I believe with you that if thus brought into friendly Juxtaposition with enlightened Members of our Church, Unitarianism could not stand—at any Rate it is clear that every Unitarian who had Scholarship enough to take a Degree would be ashamed of the Blunders of their 'Improved Version' of the New Testament, and would either give up Unitarianism or avow himself an Unbeliever altogether.

"I have long thought on wholly independent Grounds that the Restoration of the University, by allowing every Master of Arts to open a Hall with the Chancellor's Licence, and to receive Students amenable to all the public Discipline of the University, besides his own domestic Discipline within Doors, and by restoring the Government to the proper University Officers, *i.e.* the Professors or the Doctors in the three Faculties, or a

Body chosen by them without any Reference whatever to the Colleges, would be a most important Improvement, and nothing, I think, would so readily obviate the Difficulties of the Dissenters Question.

"In the Matter you and I and others in our Situation are quite as much concerned as the College Tutors, and I very much wish that our Sentiments should be expressed publicly. I think that you quite agree with me in the main Points; indeed our only Difference seems to me to arise out of the College System, not at all with Reference to the University. I have had Unitarians here, but they attended our Chapel and Divinity Instructions like other Boys. In one Case where the Boy was likely to be in the Sixth Form I wrote to his Father, telling him that when he came under my immediate Instruction he must hear much against Unitarianism, and that I thought it fair to give him Warning, that he might remove him if he liked. I only said that I would never go out of my Way to attack his Tenets, nor make any Difference in the ordinary Christian as opposed to controversial Instruction which I gave my boys. The Father wished him earnestly to attend my Lectures, and so he would have done had he stayed at the School long enough to have come into the Sixth Form.

"I was very sorry to find that you had been and still were unwell. Your Letter has increased my Wish to become personally acquainted with you, but our Occupations sadly interfere."

All the substantives in the MS. of the foregoing letter are written with initial capital letters. This was very usual in the letters of the time, though Dr. Arnold has been more consistent in his adherence to the then custom than any other of Dr. Butler's correspondents. I have received more than one letter from old pupils of Dr. Butler's still living in which I have noted survivals of this now obsolete practice. Dr. Butler himself never observes it. To avoid giving an appearance of singularity to the writers, I have generally substituted small initial letters for the capitals which they actually wrote.

Correspondence

From the Rev. T. S. Hughes
Cambridge, May 8th (?), 1834.

*

"You have no conception to what a flame the *odium theologicum* is blown in this our Alma Mater; we are held up as Apollyons, and infidel or heretic is a name too good for us. I was told by the most moderate of their party that the only excuse he could make for us was that we had lost our senses, *i.e.* were fit for a madhouse, and all this for the simple wish of reducing the University to the rule of Elizabeth. The most outrageous in their cries are those who were in heart at first with us, and dare not join us – Whewell and Smyth. I have brought my mind to such a pitch of resolution that I laugh at all they say or do – but I have a sharp fire to withstand at home, I assure you."

From Professor Sedgwick
Trinity College, May 9th, 1834.

"MY DEAR SIR, I this morning sent a note directed to you at 14, Pall Mall, East. After I received your second letter, Professor Wingrove at my request wrote to some of our active friends in town, explaining your views and wishes. He has received a reply, from which it appears that they have met and done nothing, considering that the smallness of their numbers might tell more against than for the prayer of the petition. This morning I sent a note to this effect, but it has struck me that if you and Dr. Arnold and a few more good men concerned in education and well known to the world could join in supporting the prayer of the petition to the House of Lords (and of Commons if there be time) the effect might be excellent. I write to suggest this in the hopes of reaching you before you start for London. I am scrawling with the left hand in a great hurry to save the post, as it only wants a few minutes of the half-past ten when the post starts."

To Professor Sedgwick

(Original in possession of J. Willis Clark, Esq.)

Shrewsbury, May 11th, 1834.

" MY DEAR PROFESSOR, *Rebus sic stantibus*, I think we must rest on our arms. My opinions are well known to Lord Brougham, the Bishop of Chichester, and many other friends in the House of Lords, and to several members of the House of Commons. I would have readily signed an address or declaration from the University such as the petition of the sixty-three, but it would be difficult to frame one of any other description in which we could agree. Dr. A[rnold] and I certainly take different views — I have heard from him again,[1] and am satisfied about that. He is a very honourable and respectable man, but he does not appear to see things as I do, and he is exclusive, which I am not.

" Yours is the true view of the matter — not to petition or say anything about Dissenters *eo nomine*, which, besides alarming and giving weight to the objections of our antagonists and supplying them with an argument that may excite popular clamour against us, would tend to confirm the Dissenters in their dissent. They would then perhaps make it a point of honour to continue Dissenters; but if we quietly withdraw the obstacle to their taking degrees, and allow them to come not as Dissenters, but as not refusing to conform to our established regulations and discipline as to chapel and lectures, many, I know, would come over to the Church, and we should have at least all the *élite* of their body on more friendly terms with us.

" I speak from experience in my own parish. The principal dissenting family in it, Socinian, having the curiosity sometimes to come to church when I am there, and not finding themselves preached against, had also the curiosity to see if my curate preached against them, and finding he did not they came oftener; now all the females of the family have joined us, and regularly stay the Sacrament, while the men are friendly, and some stay the Sacrament also. There cannot be more firm Trinitarians than my son and myself. My son has married the daughter of a Socinian, who with all her family have conformed

---

[1] I did not find any letter from Dr. Arnold except that of 7th May. — ED.

to the Church, except a brother whom I have often seen there, and who I am sure bears us no ill-will.

"Can there be a stronger ground to argue that we might expect similar instances of good-will (if we would remove barriers) in the general body of Dissenters? They are now, it is true, united against us, and, I think, urge unreasonable demands, and injure themselves thereby—but is there nothing unreasonable in the way in which we unite against them to repel them? On Tuesday morning I shall breakfast with the Bishop of Chichester, and if anything occurs worth mentioning between us you shall hear."

To J. Herford, Esq.

Shrewsbury, May 21st, 1834.

"DEAR SIR, I very sincerely thank you for your little pamphlet and your obliging letter. Nothing can be more seasonable than such a publication at a time when I fear that worst of evil spirits the *odium theologicum* possesses so many on both sides.

"I confess I am no less surprised than concerned at the turn things have taken among the generality of Dissenters, who, speaking in the name of the whole body, virtually declare that their great aim is the subversion of the Established Church; for such must be its separation from the State.

"Among many of the most enlightened Churchmen I know that there was a very conciliatory spirit. Will you pardon me for saying that I do not think it has been met on the side of your friends with the cordiality it deserved?

"I have long been an advocate for the abolition of subscription for lay degrees at the Universities. I mentioned it, years ago, to the Duke of Sussex, when H.R.H. honoured me with a visit at this house. I have mentioned it more than once to Lord Brougham. I was actually in correspondence with Professor Sedgwick and my Cambridge friends on the subject, when the declarations of the London Deputation and the Glasgow Petitioners burst upon me.

"What can I say now? I cannot come forward with any zeal or confidence to advocate a measure which avowedly would be made use of for the destruction of that Church which I am bound both by oath and principle to defend. I cannot act a treacherous or suicidal part, or advise a measure which I once thought would be conciliatory and highly beneficial, but which I now find would neither be accepted with cordiality nor used with forbearance. I therefore rest inactive. I am unwilling to join the violent on either side, or yet to go further than self-defence requires.

"I have but one consolation, which is that the sentiments publicly avowed on the part of the Dissenters in general in the declaration I have alluded to are not, I trust, approved by all the individuals of their body. By yourself they clearly are not. It has been my lot to know and enjoy the friendship of many excellent men, among whom I may reckon the Rev. Joseph Hunter, Thomas Broadhurst, John Currie, J. H. Bransby, as dissenting ministers, and several more of their brethren, and among the laity the excellent family of the Cottons at Kenilworth, that of my daughter-in-law at Bristol, and many more. And I cannot believe that there is any hostile or acrimonious feeling among these to the Church in general—to me individually I am sure there is none.

"I only wait therefore for a period which I fear recent events have rendered more remote than I could wish, when the voice of moderation shall once more be heard. But it will be no easy matter for many minds to become calm after so much excitement, or after the late avowals to devise such securities as may satisfy the members of the Established Church that, if Dissenters are admitted to the academic privileges it still enjoys, no mischief shall result from such participation."

To Professor Sedgwick
(Original in possession of J. Willis Clark, Esq.)
Shrewsbury, May 28th, 1834.

*

"I now rejoice that no declaration of approval of the petition was put forth by the non-resident members of the Senate. After the avowal made by the Dissenters of their being content with nothing less than a severance between Church and State—in other words, the destruction of the Church—I cannot sign a petition on their behalf. They have cut their own throats in their eagerness to cut ours. Still, my dear Professor, I am not inclined to be unjust because they are unreasonable, and I do hope there are many among them who would not go the lengths of these decided enemies. The most violent are not always the most numerous though always the most prominent. Let us hope that this extreme excitement will in time subside."

From the Rev. E. C. Hawtrey

(Then just appointed to the Head-Mastership of Eton)

Eton College, August 16th, 1834.

*

" If you can spare time to answer inquiries which I must allow are purely selfish, perhaps you would have the kindness to tell me some particulars of your system with the highest class at Shrewsbury. 1. Are all, or part, or none of that class admitted for merit solely, without reference to their place in the school? 2. Are their lessons part of a regular routine, or are whole authors, or long portions of authors, read by them from time to time, according to your choice? 3. Do your examinations go entirely through the whole school, and is the classification in consequence honorary, or does it change the place of each boy in the school?

" I am here in great embarrassment. A large body of malcontents who have no responsibility abuse our whole system, and advise all sort of absurd changes. On the other hand I am checked by an attachment to the old course of things in the ruling power of Eton, which it is very difficult indeed to make any impression upon. I am desirous therefore to get all the authority I can for improvements which seem to me absolutely necessary to meet the demands of the Universities upon us. No one can dispute the transparent results of your method, and I wish as much as I can to engraft it upon the one change which

I am allowed to make by the Provost. The Newcastle Scholarship and 'sending up for good' are at present the only public stimulants to emulation for the fifth and sixth forms. I am afraid this is making a very unconscionable demand on your time and good-nature.

"I should be unfit to enter upon an office of such responsibility if I were not anxious to gain from every quarter, and *a fortiori* from the best, whatever may be conducive to good in the administration of the school.

"I heard a few days since from my young friend George Selwyn that you were expected at Lord Clive's. I have therefore ventured to put this letter under cover to him."

From H.R.H. the Duke of Sussex

(Published by permission of Her Majesty)

August, 1834 (?).

"MY DEAR SIR, My friend Mr. Alexander, who is going down to Shrewsbury to place one of his sons under your tuition, affords me an opportunity of recalling myself to your memory, and at the same time of recommending the young lad to your particular attention, whom I understand to be a clever boy, and consequently I am sure you will make something of him. Should I prove a true prophet, I shall be delighted. Mr. Alexander is to restore me to light when the time comes, and gratitude as well as personal regard for his own private merits make me feel a great interest in the son's welfare.

"We have closed our work for the season in a gloomy way. I do not like to dwell upon the mischief which I fear to anticipate; but the rejection of the fair claims of the Dissenters, particularly to University degrees, is, I think, both unwise and injudicious, and unkind even to the Universities. I should like to have conversed with you upon the subject; for although I have not seen your charge, I have perused extracts with which I was much pleased. Perhaps you will send me one. As to the Irish Bills, the Lords who have thrown them out have taken a great responsibility upon themselves.

"More I will not say; and therefore, apologising for the

scrawl of a blind man, I conclude with signing myself very sincerely yours,
"AUGUSTUS FREDERICK."

From the Rev. E. C. Hawtrey, Head-Master of Eton

Hastings, September 2nd, 1834.

"MY DEAR SIR, I am infinitely obliged to you for your prompt and kind answer to my inquiries, though it leaves more strongly impressed on my mind than I ever felt it before the enormous disadvantage under which the Head-Master of Eton must always labour, as compared with those of any other school. He is blamed for every defect in a system which he cannot alter, because he is under the check of a superior power.

"If I understand you right about numbers, I conclude that, where twenty is the maximum, one is worth as much as five would be in actual merit where one hundred is the maximum. But this is just one of those cases in which I should have understood the plan better could I have had the liberty I had hoped for in these holidays. There is another question which I meant to have asked. Are the sixth-form lessons prepared before school with any assistance from the tutors? or is the tutor's attention confined solely to correcting the exercises and to the private lessons?

"I should like very much to get rid of the sixth form at Eton being previously construed by the tutors, for I am persuaded it has done much more harm than good—has oftener been an encouragement to idleness than a help to diligence.

"I have gained one great point from the Provost. He has permitted me to make a subdivision which will reduce my class to thirty. Still I want your half-yearly examinations, without which there will be no general emulation to keep up with the great demands of the Oxford and Cambridge scholarships and degrees.

"I think the whole system, as you describe it to me, excellent, and admirably calculated to produce the results which every one knows it does produce. Much of it, however, would be impracticable with us, from the nature of the materials which we have to work upon—sons of people who do not care about Latin and

Greek, and would much rather hear that a boy was captain of the boats than that he had gained the Newcastle Scholarship—and again, from the difficulties we have with the Collegers, who cannot be moved from their place without material injury to their prospects in life.

"Still I do hope that I shall be able, by degrees, to engraft something of your system on ours. I had already determined on having a half-yearly report from the different masters of their respective divisions, that being one of the few things which I can do without reference to the Provost.

"I take it for granted that during your examination week no other business is done. This, however, I have found the great difficulty with our Provost, who will not admit of this improvement if a single school lesson is to be given up for its introduction.

"I think Drury's histories, both Greek and Latin, are excellent, and I wish to introduce them, if the Provost will allow it.

"The not reading by routine in the sixth form must be an excellent part of your system.

"I will remember to ask no more unreasonable questions, and must only remark as to that for which you reprove me, that I would not have repeated it except to clear myself of ignorance.

"Can you give me but two lines in answer to my inquiry (1) about tutors construing; (2) about omitting the lessons of the week during examination? For these will be important points with me in my next discussion with the Provost.

"I regret more than I can express that I was unable to reach Shrewsbury. I need not say that I am not now thinking merely of the opportunity I should have had of making selfish inquiries.

"Believe me, my dear Sir, very truly yours,
"E. HAWTREY."

From the " Analyst," a Worcester Paper (reprinted in the " Cambridge Chronicle," 1st October 1834)

Shrewsbury, September 22nd, 1834.

"SIR, Permit me, as a well-wisher to the success of your spirited undertaking, to correct an error which appears in the

Biographical Memoir of the late S. T. Coleridge in your second number.

"It is there stated that when he was at Jesus College, Cambridge, 'it does not appear that he obtained, or even struggled for, academic honours.'

"As I was his contemporary at the University, and enjoyed his youthful friendship (the kindly remembrance of which continued between us till his death, though we had few opportunities of personal intercourse), I beg to state that his biographer has under-valued both his struggles and his success.

"In the summer of 1792 he gained the 'Browne Medal' for his Greek Ode on the slave trade, which contains some highly spirited and poetical passages, tinged with melancholy and moral pathos. In the months of December and January following he was a competitor for the University Scholarship then vacant by the election of the illustrious Richard Porson to the Greek Professorship, Porson himself being the principal examiner. Although he was not successful, he was so far distinguished as to be one of the four who at a certain period of the examination were selected from the general body of candidates, and formed into a separate class for a second more severe and decisive trial.

"I believe no other opportunity occurred for his exertion during his stay at College; he may therefore be fairly said to have distinguished himself on every occasion of competition for first-rate honours while at the University, and I feel happy in this opportunity of testifying my regard and doing justice to the memory of a man whom we cannot but admire for his talents and high attainments, pity for his severe and protracted sufferings, and reverence for the patience and Christian resignation with which he endured them.
"S. BUTLER."

From the Bishop of Chichester

(Private and confidential.)

Palace, Chichester, October 6th, 1834.

"MY DEAR ARCHDEACON, It is always painful to be a messenger of bad tidings, especially to a friend whose interest I have at heart. Nevertheless, although I am not authorised to say that another appointment is actually made, yet I have no doubt that the first offer of the vacant See will be made to Dr. Allen.

"The Lord Chancellor came hither with his daughter on Saturday evening, on his way to the Isle of Wight, and left me yesterday. As soon as he came he took me into the garden, and told me he was excessively mortified, and so were other members of the Cabinet, to learn that Lord Althorp had obtained a promise from Lord Grey which Lord Melbourne thought himself bound to act upon. I am, however, allowed to say that many, if not all the Cabinet, looked forward to your being placed on the Bench with great anxiety; and I am satisfied that you cannot be kept from being there longer than the next Cambridge turn, even if there should be no departure from the usual routine on your account.

"It is possible, you understand, that Dr. Allen may not accept the See of Bristol, for he would not be allowed to retain more than the Stall of Westminster, if that—and the two together would be considerably under £3,000 per annum. Now you could afford to take a moderate or rather a very poor bishopric till something better fell in your way. And of this the Chancellor is fully aware.

"I am persuaded that no one takes a warmer interest in your promotion than the Chancellor; and if he had had any good to communicate, you would have heard from him. For the present you must receive through me the expression of his apprehensions."

To the Bishop of Chichester

October 9th, 1834.

"MY DEAR LORD, I wrote a few lines to you yesterday to thank you for your truly kind wishes and active friendship, and to request that you would say to the Chancellor all that I do and ought to feel for his kind exertions. With the exception of Mr. Canning, whom I never saw, and whose intention of placing me on the Bench I never knew till after his death, Lord Brougham is the only high official person from whom I have ever received more than ordinary encouragement, and I perhaps feel my obligations to him the more keenly from his being the first living person to whom I have owed any.

"Perhaps when I asked you to express these to him the matter might there end—but you will permit me, I am sure, to have the comfort of giving vent to my feelings to one on whose tried friendship I can rely.

"Look at the Bench—with the rare exception of yourself, can you find a man on it who owes his preferment to his actual merit? Can you name one other, not even excepting the Bishop of London, superlative as his merits are, who does not owe it to private tuition or family connection? Look at one, the utmost amount of whose private tuition consisted in teaching writing— but then that was all he could teach—to a late Premier, and who has not undergone even the common course of academic education; yet this man is a bishop at least, though not a peer of Parliament.[1]

"I speak not this to disparage Dr. Allen, whom I believe to be a man of real learning and great respectability, but merely to prove a general proposition.

"I will not pretend to say that I am not disappointed, but I should have been less so had the disappointment been softened by giving me something else *ad interim*. I confess to you what it would be very injurious to me to confess to the public, that I feel worn out by thirty-six years very laborious occupation, and I see Mrs. Butler's health and activity impaired by it. I see Carey[2] with his bishopric, Keate with his canonry of Windsor, Russell with his great living and his stall at Canterbury, Tate with his canonry (God bless him with it dear, honest fellow!); I see Goodenough with his deanery, and my namesake of Harrow with his living; but I see myself without any of these good things. I do not grudge others their success, but I know that I have laboured as much as any, more than most, and longer than all; with what success I have laboured let more than one hundred University scholarships, medals, and suchlike first-rate honours tell for me. But the labour is becoming too

[1] I have not been able to discover the bishop here referred to.—ED.
[2] William Carey, Head Master of Westminster, 1803-1814, Bishop of Exeter, 1820-1830, and of St. Asaph to his death, 13th Sept. 1846.

much for my wife and myself; and, what is worse (for I must not conceal the painful fact from you), I fear my school is declining, and I would wish to quit it before the fact is too evident. The cause I am sure is not from any want of exertion on my part, for I would die in harness before that should happen, but partly from the general opinion that something would be done for me, which has prevented many parents from sending their boys to me for the last three years, and partly from the traffic in joint stock company schools, which is ruining, and will ultimately ruin, the old foundations.

*

" I am quite of Yorick's opinion, that if it were to rain mitres none would fall on my head. I need not remind you of the old proverb, ' Senis mortem expectare longum est.' Besides I am not a young man myself, and must take five things for granted: the King's life, which God grant—the continuance of Ministers in office—the occurrence of two vacancies on the Bench—and my own survival. Well—there—my spleen is at an end, and now I feel much better, and I think you will be none the worse for a laugh at it, which when you are indulging you may say to me in your (lawn) sleeve, ' Solventur tabulae risu, *tu missus abibis.*' Farewell, and believe me with great truth, my dear Lord,
"Your much obliged and affectionate
" S. BUTLER."

From the Bishop of Chichester

(Private.)
Palace, Chichester, October 15th, 1834.

" MY DEAR ARCHDEACON, I cannot tell you one-hundredth part of what has passed between the Chancellor and me respecting you, but depend upon it good will come out of evil. I may quote one passage from a long letter received this morning entirely about you:

" ' You may assure the excellent Archdeacon that Melbourne as much as myself feels this severe disappointment. He volunteered his expression of it.'

"He adds:

"'Unfortunately the Durham stall is not Crown patronage, and the Windsor is the King's *peculium*, who immediately named to it.'

"I could not help giving you this drop of comfort. Depend upon it you have a most anxious friend at headquarters watching for your good."

To the Rev. H. B. Greenlaw, Blackheath

Early November, 1834.

"DEAR SIR, Last January I was obliged to employ an amanuensis to write to you. My complaint continued till the end of April, and within the last month it has returned severely. Your book has never been off my table, but my arrear of business accumulated as much during the time I was prevented from using my eyes that I could not proceed with it, and have made no further progress. It was necessary to say this in order to explain my seeming inattention to one of the ablest philological tracts I have ever met with, and I hail with delight your announced exercise-book, which I shall not fail to introduce to my boys, as I have your treatise.

"Your observations about boys being taught to analyse propositions, so as to see the subject and predicate, I admit as far as in the simpler cases of direct propositions; but in cases where other independent clauses are introduced, or where the subject is qualified by a subsequent clause, or where the subject is latent in some clause, or where the clauses are hypothetical or dependent or oblique, I find great difficulty in making them analyse properly. They will do so in a Latin sentence (reasoning upon it because they find a subjunctive mood to be accounted for, which leads them to a right conclusion) more frequently than they will do it in an English sentence which is to be turned into Latin. For this reason I would venture to suggest the propriety of your being full on this head in your introduction by giving a considerable number of examples both of Latin sentences and of English sentences analysed, in order to familiarise boys to the practice before they begin the exercise

—in short, to clear the way for the exercises, much as you have in your treatise by the preliminary chapter before you come to chapter v.

"With regard to your observations on *ob* and *propter*, in both which cases I have mentioned the reason or cause of a thing, would not the word *reason* in its common acceptation apply both to *ob* and *propter*? But is the other distinction which you take, that *propter* always expresses the efficient or moving cause, and *ob* the reason, *i.e.* object or purpose, invariably true? May not both be rendered ' on account of '? When we say ' propter vitam vivendi perdere causas,' and ' clarus ob id factum,' may we not translate ' *on account of* ' in both cases? But you will say *propter vitam* is *for the sake of life*, and so expresses the moving cause, and that *ob id factum* is *by reason of that action*. I grant you the first but not the second of these interpretations; for though you may say that the *reason* you cannot say that the *object* or the purpose of his renown is expressed by *ob*, for the man went on neither of these accounts, but, as Horace expressly says, simply from despair. But then I say that this action was the efficient cause of his renown, for he would not have been renowned but for it. The reason therefore and the efficient cause are one and the same thing in this case, and therefore either *ob* or *propter* might be used, just as when the same author says ' propter onus segnes ' the efficient cause of their being slow and the reason why they were slow are both expressed by *propter*; but *ob* in this case would not have expressed object or purpose, though it would express the reason, *i.e.* the cause. When Cicero says, *Ob eam enim ipsam causam Erectheus Athenis filiaque ejus in numero deorum sunt*, is not the efficient cause as well as the reason of his being worshipped expressed?

"For what was the cause which moved the Athenians to esteem Erectheus a god except *augendae virtutis gratia*—which is mentioned by Cicero in the preceding sentence? You will find it in the last paragraph of *De Natura Deorum*, iii, 19, Olivet—. Again, when we say in our own language, ' What is the reason why the sun appears to rise in the East and set in the West? ' the answer is, ' Because (by cause—the efficient cause, or the cause which produces this effect) the earth revolves on its axis from W. to E.'

"Perhaps, however, you will say that a distinction exists between cause and reason which I have not noticed. I am aware that in the material world the cause of anything is that which makes a thing to be, and the reason of an effect produced is the explanation why it is so. But after all what is this explanation but an assignment of the efficient cause? And in the moral world the cause of any act is the motive in the mind which leads the man to do it, and the reason of the act is the explanation of the motives which lead him to it. What, however, is this but an assignment of the moving causes?

"So Hor., *Sat.* I, iii, 91, *ob hanc rem*, ' on this account.' But does it not also express the efficient cause why his friend should be less dear? What is the cause of their coolness but this? You can hardly say that the object or purpose is expressed. The reason is; but that is also the moving cause. If therefore I have used the words *cause* or *reason* in too lax a sense, as perhaps I may have done, I shall be gladly set right; it is because I wish to be set right that I have entered upon this discussion, and without any view of maintaining an erroneous proposition.

"Pray think the matter over. With your clear and logical head, you will, I am sure, come to some definition more perfect than the present appears, which seems to me hardly to stand the test of strict examination. Pray use my book, refute me, and set me right without scruple, and remember that no man can less wish to be pertinacious or captious than I do. I never wish to prolong an argument from the shame of acknowledging an error; the shame would be in prolonging the argument, not in the having sense enough to correct a mistake: therefore consider me as not only open to conviction, but anxious to be convinced, and as merely stating what I state for your consideration before you go to press.

"*Propter* expressing the efficient, *ob* the final cause: perhaps in the former case I ought strictly speaking to have avoided adding ' or cause,' and in the latter to have omitted ' or reason,' but I was not, and to say the truth am not satisfied, even by the help of the distinction which you take, of the invariable application of the rule proposed. After all it is perhaps a dispute about words, but I will try to explain myself.

"When we speak of the cause of a thing, we mean that which

makes an explanation why a thing is, and produces or effects anything. And by the reason for anything, we mean an explanation of the way in which a thing is effected or produced. What is this after all but an explanation of an efficient cause. So that the reason of a thing is but a kind of periphrasis for the cause of a thing.

*

"I am not sure therefore that your proposition, though generally true, is universally so, but I speak with diffidence."

(No more of this draft was found.—ED.)

From H.R.H. the Duke of Sussex
(Published by permission of Her Majesty)

Kensington Palace, December 8th, 1834.

"DEAR SIR, Many thanks for the kind interest which our friend G. A. Thorne informed me you had taken to promote my interests in case I had offered myself for the Chancellorship of the University of Cambridge. Under existing circumstances it would neither do good nor be advantageous to myself. The unfortunate intolerant line which the University adopted last year quite sickened me as to any hope of amendment in that quarter, and what must inevitably be the consequences if such a system be persisted in is too painful to me to predict, but certainly I should feel still more distressed were I by accident at the head of that Institution.

"The *Edinburgh Review* has, I think, placed the matter of the Dissenters very fairly before the public. Professor Hamilton, who, I believe, is the author of that article, is a man of profound knowledge and great industry. How unfortunate that the masters of the colleges are such unreasonable beings! *Mais ainsi va le monde*.

"I do not think heads of colleges the fittest persons to draw up rules for colleges; they have too little knowledge of the world, as it is progressively changing and improving, while their personal inclinations lead them to arbitrary measures.

"Excuse this scrawl, for I can hardly see, and believe me, with great sincerity, your obliged and devoted, etc.,
"AUGUSTUS FREDERICK."

From the Bishop of Chichester

Palace, Chichester, December 15th, 1834.

"MY DEAR ARCHDEACON, I met Sydney Smith since this deplorable change.[1] He said, 'You and I must have a good cry together.' Now I confess I am much more inclined to cry for my friends than for myself, and I really believe that nothing was such a vexation to Lord Brougham on going out of office as that you had not been put on the Bench. He expressed this strongly to me the day before he left town and concluded by saying, 'But surely Butler is such a man that any Administration must make him a Bishop!'

"I do not see myself what chance a Tory Government has of staying in a month after Parliament meets, but I dread their being succeeded by men who would go much farther than our friends."

To the Bishop of Chichester

December, 1834 (?).

"I think the plurality a good measure when a man has a large living, say £500 or upwards, but not for a smaller sum. Even with £500 a year much convenience and benefit to a parish may arise by allowing him to hold a contiguous living not exceeding £100. 'Six hundred pounds a year' is not an enormous income for a clergyman.

"What Lord Brougham can mean by allowing an archdeacon whose archdeaconry does not exceed £20 a year to hold one living, if within the limits of his archdeaconry, I cannot conceive. He can hardly think £20 a year a sufficient income for an archdeacon. He cannot be ignorant that there are not six archdeaconries in England which produce £100 a year, and not above three or four which are so much as £200, and that their estimate in the King's books is not like that of livings,

[1] Lord Melbourne's first administration had just resigned.—ED.

greatly below their actual value, but very nearly approaching to it. The returns of the different archdeacons will show him this.

"Then as to residence—archdeacons are not required to reside; they have no houses, as bishops, deans, and canons have, and their residence is not at all essential to the discharge of their duties—nay, even as to the residence of bishops in their dioceses and within their episcopal houses, the requisition of this latter condition defeats all the value of the former. For a bishop's diocese is in fact his parish; the value of his residence in it is not to be estimated by his regular episcopal visitations, but by his communications with his clergy in different parts of it. I have known bishops take a house in their diocese fifty, nay almost a hundred miles from their episcopal residence, and by residing in it two months do more good in regulating disorders among a distant part of their clergy than any visitation or any residence in their episcopal house could have done; so far from requiring residence in the episcopal house, the contrary should, as much as may be within the diocese, be encouraged.

"Two months is too short a leave of absence for the clergy in the year, but when reduced to thirty days at any one time it is absolutely intolerable. It is actual imprisonment, with rules somewhat wider perhaps than those of the King's Bench, as it confines a man to a parish, which may be more extensive. Suppose I had a living here, and wanted to see a friend in Essex or Northumberland (perhaps a sister or a parent, and to take my wife and children with me), I am hardly able to get there, after an expensive journey, before I must take it back. But this thirty days' liberty will assuredly have one bad effect. If a man had three months' liberty, to use when he pleased, he would perhaps once or twice in his life avail himself of it, and but generally would not take half or one-third of the time. Give him his thirty days, and twice a year, most assuredly every clergyman who can afford it will be absent from his living. He will naturally take it as a vacation—*Exiguo gratoque fruetur tempore raptim.*"

Terms at Shrewsbury School [1834]

The following statement of Dr. Butler's terms is the only one that I found among his papers. It being dated 1834, I have thought it better to place it here.

1834.

SHREWSBURY SCHOOL

Rev. Archdeacon Butler, D.D., F.R.S., F.S.A., etc., etc., Head-Master

Terms:

Board	Forty Guineas	⎫
Tuition	Eight „	⎬ Per annum.
Washing	Four „	⎭
Entrance to the House	Three „	
„ „ School	Two „	
Single Bed (if required)	Four „	Per annum.

No boy can be admitted unless qualified to begin the Latin Accidence immediately on entering the School, being also not less than six nor more than sixteen years of age at the time of admission. And three months' notice, or a quarter's board, is required before removal. Each boy is requested to bring six towels. Woollen stockings are worn from Michaelmas to Lady Day.

There are two vacations in the year, of six weeks each — the one beginning on the Monday before Midsummer Day, and the other on the Monday before St. Thomas. No other holidays are granted.

Masters of Accomplishments attend on the following terms per quarter:

	£	s.	d.
Dancing	1	1	0
Drawing	1	11	6
Fencing	1	1	0
French	1	1	0
Writing	0	16	0

Private tuition — per quarter; Classics, £2 2s. ⎫ or both together,
„   „   „   Mathematics, £2 2s. ⎭ £3 3s.

CHAPTER TWENTY-SEVEN: CORRESPONDENCE, 17TH FEBRUARY 1835–28TH NOVEMBER 1835

From the Rev. W. F. Hook

Coventry, February 17th, 1835.

"MY DEAR MR. ARCHDEACON, THE MAJORity of the clergy in this archdeaconry have refused to support the Diocesan Church Building Society unless there be a rule to prevent the Society from acting in any parish without the consent of the incumbent. For in more instances than one the Bishop, in conjunction with Mr. Archdeacon Hodson, has united with a party of the parishioners against the Rector, and actually in one case prevented, by personal interference in London, the Rector from enlarging the church, in order to compel him to sanction the erection of a chapel which would be in fanatical hands. This was before the passing of the present Act; and what therefore may we not expect under existing circumstances? In another case, since the present Act, an archdeacon was discovered endeavouring to collect money and form a party, in the most underhand manner, in order that a party chapel might be erected in opposition to an incumbent who did not, in his opinion, preach the gospel.

"At the same time we feel that the Society is a good one, and we wish to unite with it; and I am therefore commissioned by three or four gentlemen who think that their example would influence the rest to inquire of you whether you think the interests of the incumbent are sufficiently protected. It is clear to us, from what you said at the meeting at Birmingham, that your proposition had in view the same object as ours, and if you are contented there can be no reason why we should not be so too. You are the only prelate in this diocese to whom we can apply for advice, and I hope therefore you will not refuse to give it. If you write a private letter to me, I can show it to the few persons who have requested me to write, in confidence; and as to the others it will suffice to say that Archdeacon Butler, who fought our battle at Birmingham, is satisfied, provided that such is the case. You may rely on my discretion not to mix up your name improperly in the affair.

"To put the whole case in one sentence before you, our wish, our earnest desire, is to join the Society: all we wish to know is, Can we do so consistently, and without sacrifice of principle? our principle being to secure the rights of incumbents and to prevent schism in our parishes.

"I hope I have written intelligibly. I am far from well. Indeed I should have delayed writing till to-morrow, in the hopes of being better, were it not that a few of us mean to meet together on Friday, and I should like to be armed with your opinion."

To the Rev. W. F. Hook

Shrewsbury, February 19th, 1835.

"MY DEAR FRIEND, Your letter has grieved and would have surprised me, had I not had too much experience of the Jesuitical proceedings to which some of the so-called Evangelical party will have recourse in order to carry a favourite point. After the startling instances which you mention, and which are new to me, I grieve to think that I cannot confidently say the interests of the incumbent are securely protected; at least I must own that there is at present no rule which provides expressly for his protection. The only existing protection is to be found in the provision which enacts that no case shall be brought before the general committee for consideration which is not recommended by the district committee. I should think the general as well as the district committee would pause before they recommended or sanctioned a grant which they were given to understand, by letter from the incumbent, was directly at variance with his wishes. But, on the other hand, in the prevalence of what I must take the liberty of calling pseudo-evangelical sentiments, there is no saying what either committee might do where the majority consisted of persons so disposed.

"I said very little in the public meeting at Birmingham, not knowing in fact that I should be called upon to say a single word. I was in an agony of pain with a gathering in my face, and the meeting was above half over before a motion was put into my hand, with a notice that I was to say something.

"But I had said a great deal in the committee previous to the meeting, both on the Monday and the Tuesday, and previously at Eccleshall, and believe what I said had some effect in stopping the grant of any sum towards endowment, where I suspected mischief was lurking; and I said much upon granting aid, not only to large places, but to smaller churches, where £30 or £50 would enlarge galleries for schools and make free sittings for poor, instead of granting large sums for building new churches; and this is a point on which I always mean to take my stand.

"I have been lately in correspondence with some members of the House of Peers and of the Church Reform Committee, whom I feel I can rely on, respecting the matter. I do not alter one tittle of what I have already said about Church dignitaries. I confirm all; but I wish to go a little farther, and open the eyes of some staunch old Church of England men to the game that is going on. Who are to be benefited? The Evangelicals principally, who have bought up, by what I think an unconstitutional, if not illegal confederacy, all the advowsons they can lay hold of in populous places to an immense extent, which are generally of small value, and to increase which what some people are pleased to call the superfluous wealth of the Church will go. Besides there are some good names in the commission, and some which frighten me."

From the Rev. George Peacock

Trinity College, Cambridge, March 4th, 1835.

"MY DEAR DR. BUTLER, Humphry[1] was this morning elected Pitt Scholar—an event upon which I most sincerely congratulate you. I believe that all the Pitt Scholars have been your pupils—a circumstance which must give additional value to the almost endless distinctions of Shrewsbury School. Humphry is a most excellent person, who is respected and beloved both by old and young. You would be glad to hear that Harris passed a most admirable examination, and ran close upon Howes. He was very considerably above the fourth man."

[1] The late Rev. W. G. Humphry, Rector of St. Martin's, Trafalgar Square.

Correspondence

To the Rev. A. Irvine

(Original in possession of the Rev. J. Irvine of Colchester)

Shrewsbury, March 5th, 1835.

" MY DEAR IRVINE, ... I am glad to say that Mrs. Butler, who has been severely ill, and if she had not had a copious and instant bleeding would have been dangerously ill, is now nearly well. Of myself I cannot say much. I am nothing to brag of. February and March are my bad months, and I suppose will some time or other make an end of me. I am never well in them, but have been worse this year than usual. I thought it was disease of the heart, but Dr. Dugard, who examined my chest, found a thickening of the liver; and now I think the complaint is not in the heart, but I think we have only scotched the snake, not killed it.

" When the weather gets warmer they are to have another turn at me.

*

" I am, ever was, and ever will be a decided anti-radical. I certainly will support Sir Robert Peel against that party, as I believe many of the old-fashioned Whigs will—though I am vexed at the divisions on the meeting of Parliament on the Speakership and the Address, for I should think it contamination to make fellowship with O'Connell and his tail, and with Messrs. Duncombe, Wakley, and their gang."

*

From Lord Berwick

March 11th, 1835.

" I would not have thanked you so soon but for your P.S.

" Are you sure the stalls are to augment small livings? I have not heard a word of this, but only that a fat parish may be thrust upon them. Perhaps this is your meaning.

" Have you read the article taken from a magazine in the *Morning Post* of yesterday? (Tuesday). I protest from the first sentences I could have sworn it was your appendix, but some other passages are not precisely your opinions.

"You are quite right about my difficulty of a proper parson for Sutton; but when I mentioned 'higher views' in my last, you might guess I had thought of some small means of stipend, and indeed had written to Salt about it.

"Of Lord Powis's twelve Apostles the division of last night will show that many at least are not *His*. To save the revenue the Opposition joined the Government, and at the same time placed the latter for the moment in the same mire with themselves regarding agriculture, and left a very comfortable finance system for themselves in case they come in again. There seems to be a growing opinion, in spite of the farmers, that repeal of malt would not be a very great relief, while it would utterly ruin finance, and something else is to be done.

"There are speculations about an administration of which Peel is to be still the prominent feature, but many others vacating the Cabinet. This would be no mortification, as the others were chiefly placed because Stanley refused.

"Yours ever,
"B."

The article above referred to is given in the *Morning Post* for Tuesday, 10th January 1835, and I have thus been able to give the year in which Lord Berwick's letter was written, he having omitted this. The "article" is headed as "from a correspondent to the *British Magazine*," and I have little doubt that it is by Dr. Butler; it is upon Church property and preferment generally, and is written with both point and moderation.

To a Parent

Shrewsbury, May 7th, 1835.

"SIR, Mr. Henney has just put into my hands your letter dated May 3rd, which requires an explicit and prompt reply.

"Your son had been flogged twice, and twice only, when you saw him, and each time with neither more nor less than the usual degree of punishment, which consists of six cuts with a few twigs of loose birch held in the hand. With regard to the punishment itself, it is one which I hold to be the best for little boys and the worst for big ones, and which I administer accordingly. As to its frequency, I may observe that out of two hundred and sixty boys not three are punished on the average in the course of a week. There may sometimes be more, or there may be less. From the day your son was punished, on March 25th, to April 27th, there was not one case.

"With regard to allowance being made for your son's backwardness, I have only to state that ample allowance has always been made for the backwardness of him and of every backward boy; but to great backwardness he joins great idleness, and it is necessary for any master who means to do his duty faithfully to a boy or his parents, to correct this when he sees fit—of which he certainly is the most competent judge.

"I beg leave to state that your son is allowed to say his lessons separately from the other boys for the most part, than which a greater allowance cannot be made, and that of those he says with them he has a very reduced portion to learn.

"He copies English to improve his spelling. Two or three easiest sentences of Ellis instead of a page. Sets his own lesson. He does six lines—fixes his own quantity; they do twenty. He does no verses; they do. He has only three rules of grammar; they have six. He fails principally in writing and English; has never been punished for dulness, but for refusing to do what he was ordered and what he acknowledged he could do.

"Permit me, sir, to add that thirty-seven years' successful experience, independent of all other considerations, is some guarantee to parents that their sons are not likely to be ill-taught or ill-treated under my care and that I anxiously and earnestly request you, if you cannot consign your son to me with the fullest confidence in this respect, that you will remove him at Midsummer, for I must candidly say that unless you can place him in my hands with a full reliance on my kindness and discretion, as well as my zeal for his improvement, I should be very sorry to have him here. And I am bound to add that, if he is here, I shall punish him as often as I see cause, just as I should any other boy. I have the honour to be, etc."

Life and Letters of Dr. Butler

From Robert Scott, Esq.

May 12th, 1835.

"It would give me the highest pleasure to avail myself of your kind invitation to the Speeches, if the College term permitted it. But as we unfortunately are thrown back this year by the lateness of Easter, I shall be tied down here with my pupils till the beginning of July, which I am sure must be far too late for your festival. But I hope to be able to witness them some other year, when our vacation begins more seasonably. Your account of the prizes is indeed most satisfactory to every one who has the interest of Shrewsbury at heart, and I shall look forward with no ordinary interest to seeing them.

"I must certainly plead guilty to all that you say about the Latin rhymes, but in fact they were written very much off-hand for the amusement of a party at Stackpole Court, and I afterwards gave them to the man who manages the Magazine without further correction. I confess that *tribus* and *ibis* are a simple rhyme, *erant* and *deciderunt* a bad rhyme, and *terret* and *cucurrit* no rhyme at all. But as to the ictus, it seems to me that, in repeating them as English verses, an emphasis does fall on the first syllable of *iterum*; for they are throughout on the plan of *freménsque équus íterum*, so that it is very difficult to pronounce the last word otherwise than as *it-terum*.

"But do not suppose that I give my time to such things, for it was merely the accidental employment of a few hours; and no one can more dislike than myself the frittered scholarship, the Boudoir Classics, which you refer to. Still I do not think that once a year or thereabouts is much too often to try that species of amusement.

"I have not heard anything about the Ireland Examination, nor have I seen the papers; but the selection of examiners struck me as a very poor one. Gordon, however, our successful candidate, is a very particular *protégé* of Gaisford, who gave him a studentship at Christmas, so that I suppose he is a good man, but he was not known or thought of much beforehand.

"I think I mentioned to you how narrowly I had escaped being virtually dismissed from Christ Church, for my audacity in presuming to answer Lord Cawdor's application before I had asked Gaisford's leave.

"Pray remember me particularly to Mrs. Butler and my other kind friends at Shrewsbury, and believe me

"Ever most truly yours,

"ROBERT SCOTT."

The foregoing letter refers to Mr. Scott's well-known translation of "John Gilpin" into Latin Iambics—of which a copy in Mr. Scott's handwriting is among Dr. Butler's papers in the British Museum. Dr. Butler was rendered, no doubt, fastidiously hypercritical by his desire to discourage Scott from attempting such translations at all.

To Robert Scott, Esq.

Shrewsbury, May 16th, 1835.

"DEAR SCOTT, I am just returned from London, and should not trouble you with an answer to your last but for its conclusion—which moves my righteous bile.

"What say I, or what can I say, at such a possible indignity offered to yourself or even thought of? What can I say but what Prometheus said before me:

ΝΈΟΝ ΝΈΟΙ ΚΡΑΤΕΊΤΕ ΚΑΊ ΔΟΚΕΊΤΕ ΔΉ
ΝΑΊΕΙΝ ἀΠΕΝΘΉ ΠΈΡΓΑΜ᾽· ΟΎ᾽Κ ᾽ΕΚ ΤΩΝΔ ΕΓΩ
ΔΙΣΣΟΥΣ ΤΥΡΑΝΝΟΥΣ ᾽ΕΚΠΕΣΟΝΤΑΣ ᾽ΗιΣΘΟΜΗΝ;
ΚΑΙ ΤΟΝΔΕ ΤΟΝ ΝΥΝ ΚΟΙΡΑΝΟΝΤ᾽ ΕΠΟΨΟΜΑΙ
ΑΙ᾽ΣΧΙΣΤΑ ΚΑΙ ΤΑΧΙΣΤΑ.

So I hope at least. By the way, I have been quoting from memory, and suspect I have introduced a false reading in the last line but one; with regard to the τρίτος τύραννος, however, for many, many reasons πνέω τοι μένος ἄπαντά τε κότον —and so do hundreds more who have reason to stand in awe of him.

"We have awarded the prizes to-day. The magnificent ode turns out to have been written by Robert Dukes,[1] whom the Dean rejected from Christ Church, and who has also gained the

[1] Robert Middleton Dukes took a First Class Litt. Hum. in 1838.

twenty-guinea trustees' prize for the Latin essay. Of course you shall have some copies when printed.

"As to the Latin rhymes, I am sure I have no right to cast a stone at any one—I, who have been guilty of the same nonsense so often myself. I by no means object to such occasional *délassements*; it is only to the too frequent publication of them, as in Wrangham's case, that I put in my *caveat*. My objection to *iterum* was not perhaps very clearly stated. The extreme thinness of the *i* makes it an unfit word for an ictus to sustain. Such a word as *odium* or *opera* would be less thin, and might be tolerated *sed de his satis*.

"Believe me, dear Scott, truly yours,
"S. BUTLER."

From a Lady

(Original destroyed by me.—ED.)

About May 20th, 1835.

*

"This young man is an undergraduate, of whom in fact we know nothing. His father was Mr. P—'s curate for a little while some twenty years ago, having been curate to the late vicar; but Mr. P— did not like him. He was a shabby man in his ways—rather busy, and not too sincere. In fact they are all shabby. This young man's aunt sold all her father's old sermons for wastepaper at three halfpence a pound, to wrap butter and bacon in, at a shop in this town; and many of the inhabitants, out of respect for their old vicar, actually paid twopence for a whole sermon. However, to do this young man justice, he had no hand in that, not having been born at the time. We look with some suspicion therefore on intelligence from that quarter."

*

From the Rev. George Matthews

Rudgwick, May 25th, 1835.

"MY DEAR AND REVEREND BENEFACTOR, Herewith you will receive the halves of two notes, a £10 and a £20. As soon as I am advised of the safe arrival of these, the remainder shall immediately follow. I have been dilatory, for the date of this ought to have been May 17th, and perhaps somewhat wilfully, though not dishonestly so, in making this remittance. I feel sad in parting with the money, and yet, believe me, it is no covetous sadness I feel, and fear that the connection between us is about to be broken, that I must now part convoy with the good ship that bore so promptly down to my aid at the sound of the first signal gun of distress, supplied me with stores, with chart and compass, and has up to the present moment allowed my shattered bark to sail under the protection of her lofty lee. She is now distancing and leaving me, as I must expect, to hold on her own proper course. God send I may soon hear of her arrival, captain and crew all safe and well, at Durham or some such other desirable and deserved harbour of rest. But I fear, my dear sir, ere you have got as far as this you will think that with all my nautical phrases I have been quite far enough ' at sea,' and would be glad were I to leave you at Durham seated quietly on the Cathedral Chair. God send, without a metaphor, you were there!

"I am as busy as an attack of low typhoid fever will allow me to be in preparing to mend up my house under Gilbert's Act, and hope ere winter closes in to bring my poor old mother, should it be God's will that I survive her, to end her days and sorrows and wanderings—and few in romance even have ever met with more—under the roof which you have been the means of procuring for me. It will be an arduous undertaking, but I feel that I shall die myself the easier for doing it. But I will not take up more of your precious time, and will therefore hasten to write what must ever be the cordial subscription of every letter of mine to you, viz. that I am yours by every tie of gratitude and affectionate respect, "GEORGE MATTHEWS."

From the Rev. Thomas Hill

Vicarage, Chesterfield, July 8th, 1835.

"REV. AND DEAR SIR, I feel that I have need of your utmost indulgence in the liberty I take in troubling you with this letter. My best apology will be found in the motive which dictates it, in the grateful respect which I owe to you, and in the desire I feel to preclude even the appearance of disunion in the members of our Zion.

"I have discovered that several of the clergy, who are by no means agreed in their general views of religious truth, are of one mind in regretting some of the statements contained in the charge delivered at your late visitation. I allude to the passages in which you affirmed that the members of the Church of England had dissented from the Church of Rome, even as the Nonconformists had dissented from her, and that the Church of Rome, notwithstanding all her errors, is an ancient and venerable part of the Christian Church. To the latter of these statements not a few demurred; in the former scarcely any, I believe, were able to concur.

*

"I have thus, Rev. Sir, used the freedom to lay before you the objections which are strongly and extensively felt to the statements in question. It would ill become me to take the further liberty of offering any suggestion to you on points which you have no doubt well considered. But as I am persuaded that these passages will, on publication, become the subject of attack or protest, I feel that I would rather incur the charge of presumption or officiousness, painful as it would be, than withhold from you such information as may (notwithstanding the insignificance of the quarter from which it emanates) lead to the abatement, if not removal, of this ground of offence."

To the Rev. Thomas Hill

Beaumaris, July 13th, 1835.

*

"You, I am sure, my dear sir, will be pleased to know that I had anticipated in great measure the contents of your letter by sending my charge the day before yesterday to London to be printed, accompanied with a few notes, two of which were explanations of the very points your letter alludes to.

"It only remains for me to consider whether I shall let those notes stand, or whether I shall expunge them and qualify the expression in the text so as to be less obnoxious to the scruples of those who certainly put a meaning on them which I never intended, and which I do not think, when taken with the context, they can fairly bear. I have previously spoken of the Protestant Church (if I recollect, for the charge is with the printers, and I must speak from memory) and of the Protestant Dissenters; I have also, if I forget not, said something about the Reformation. Now though the Protestant Dissenters dissent from us of the Church of England, yet *a fortiori* they dissent even more from the Church of Rome; for they originally dissented from us (the Calvinists and Anabaptists formed the great mass of Dissenters) because we kept Episcopacy, and in our restoration of the Church discipline as well as doctrine retained several ceremonies which they, the Dissenters, considered as idolatrous or superstitious, and even retained in a set form of Liturgy many of those beautiful prayers which we and the Church of Rome found in one common storehouse—in the forms of primitive worship. I need not go further in their dogmatic theology.

"So far then it is strictly true, I presume, that the Protestant Dissenters, according to their first principles, dissent from the Church of Rome as much as or more than we do, and as much or even more than they dissent from us.

"I suppose my reverend brethren will admit that they do not themselves agree with the Church of Rome. Now they must either assent, or if they do not assent they must dissent. If therefore they dissent, they must be Dissenters from the Church of Rome; but I suppose they think I ought to have used a stronger or more grandiloquent term. The objection is something like what might be expected from a man brought up in the prejudices of the ultra High Church school of Oxford, and I answer that it did not suit my argument to use the stronger term. I was speaking of the contradiction of the Protestant Dissenters to their own original principles in now inconsistently taking part with the Church of Rome against us of the Established Church; it suited me therefore to use the minor term instead of the stronger. That is all. I must alter my note on Dissenters in consequence of your letter. My note upon the word ' venerable ' I need not alter. My only doubt is whether I may not expunge both by slightly altering the text; but I have my doubts how far I may be justified in altering the text even by a mere explanation of my meaning. That I should unsay what I said, you are, I am sure, far too honourable and too sensible a friend to propose yourself, or to recommend any one to propose to me.

*

" I cannot close this letter without assuring you how very sincerely I thank you for communicating to me the scruples of some of the clergy of the Archdeaconry, because it is my sincere desire to respect even those which I do not understand or feel the force of, and certainly to promote, as far as in me lies, the union of all our brethren in times so critical as these. Believe me to be with the most sincere regards and respect, dear Sir, very truly and affectionately yours,   " S. BUTLER."

In Dr. Butler's note on the word " Dissenters " he says:
" I am told it has been said by some zealous members of the Established Church that I have placed its claims too low; that a Christian Church existed in this country long before the Romish Church usurped dominion over her; that the Reformed Church is not a dissenting but a protesting Church, and reformed on the same principles as those of the pure early Church in this kingdom in the sixth century; and that the term 'dissent' ill applies to the re-establishment of that portion of the pure and Apostolical Church in this land which existed before the usurpation of the Church of Rome. I agree in the main to these remarks, and have not the slightest intention of abandoning this higher ground because the course of my argument makes it more convenient to place myself on the lower. . . ."

There was no note on the word " venerable." The passage stands:
" I must be understood therefore not as intending to upbraid

the Dissenters or to revile the Church of Rome, which still is a Church venerable from its antiquity, however fallen from its purity, and with all its errors is, in common with ourselves, a part of the Holy Catholic Church on earth; but it is impossible that we should again assent to its domination. . . ."

To the Trustees of Shrewsbury School
Probably Autumn, 1835.

" GENTLEMEN,

*

" While I am on this subject, I hope I shall not be thought as stepping out of my province if I call your attention also to another part of your Act of Parliament. I mean that unfortunate clause towards the end, which takes away the patronage of the livings formerly in the gift of the Mayor and Head-Master, and vests them in the Corporation.

" Whether livings so vested can be sold by the new Town Council is a point for professional men to advise you. Whether, if the livings are so sold, you can be compelled to pay the same stipends which you now pay to their respective ministers is another point requiring much consideration. And whether, in case you are thus compellable, you would at once withdraw those augmentations for fear of having them made a permanent charge on the School property (reserving to yourselves the power of giving an annual gratuity to the incumbents to the amount of their present salaries), or whether in any case you would obtain an Act of Parliament enabling you to purchase these livings from the new Town Council (they can be of very little value if you have the power to reduce the stipends at present paid), are points which I respectfully submit to your consideration, and hope that I may be excused for having done so, although not directly concerned in the decision, because they are of great importance to the interests of this institution, and may indeed hereafter affect the Head and Second Masters, who have a kind of claim to the preferment, according to the Act. I have the honour to be, Gentlemen,

" Your obliged and faithful servant,

" S. BUTLER."

To — (?)

Shrewsbury, October 12th, 1835.

"DEAR SIR, Your brother stated to me that he did not choose to stay at Shrewsbury to be kicked about and bullied by everybody, and that the boys would not let him learn his lessons. On my asking him if he had ever complained to me or any master of this, he said, No; he knew what a public school was too well to do that. On my endeavouring to obtain any particulars, I could obtain no other answer than the one above mentioned, and I confess I doubted the fact.

"The head boys, I find, unknown to me, have been making inquiries carefully on the subject, and I can find no ground for believing it to be true. I have also made inquiries from boys in the house with him, under circumstances which I think would ensure me true answers, and find that none of the boys whom I have examined ever saw or knew of his being bullied or prevented from learning his lessons. But on being asked by some of them before he left what boys had bullied him, he said, None; it was I that had bullied him and flogged him unjustly.

"I merely state these facts that he may not circulate a calumny (if it be one) on his schoolfellows. And I could wish therefore that you would examine him, and make him come to particulars of time, place, and person. I need not say to you that a casual annoyance is a distinct thing from a systematic course of bullying for oppression. To the former every boy at a public school is occasionally subject; to the latter no boy ought to be; and if any such system prevails, or has prevailed, I cannot too soon put a stop to it. If none such prevails, I cannot too soon put a stop to so injurious a statement."

To Professor Sedgwick

(Original in possession of J. Willis Clark, Esq.)

Shrewsbury, November 3rd, 1835.

"MY DEAR PROFESSOR, I am President of the Shropshire and North Wales Natural History Society. We want some *magna nomina* to support such humble ones as mine.

"We have got permission from Murchison and Whewell to propose them as honorary members at our general meeting to be held on the 12th instant, when I am to deliver an oration, and we greatly wish and earnestly beg that you will give me leave to propose your name with theirs. These will be a triumvirate! A few more good names, but at an immeasurable distance from these, will be proposed at the same time. There will be no cost to you, and a great deal of honour and glory to us; therefore I hope, studious as you have been of the geology of Shropshire, we shall have your consent, which I am desired by the council to ask, and which I prefer doing by autograph letter rather than ask our amiable and modest secretary, Dr. Henry Johnson. Therefore, Sir my brother, surrender at discretion.

"Your affectionate brother,
"S.B.

"We muster one hundred and seventy subscribers, and have got a reasonable good quantity of alligators, lizards, serpents, butterflies, numerous idols, coins, ores, stones, fossils, shells, fish, and monstrosities, considering that we have only been four months in existence, and have as yet purchased hardly anything. Colonel Wingfield and Dr. Dugard are among our members. When shall I ever see you again?"

From Professor Sedgwick

Trinity College, November 7th, 1835.

"MY DEAR SIR, I have been away three days, and consequently only received your kind letter at a late hour last night. I am rejoiced to hear that you have established a Natural History Society at Shrewsbury, and I shall be highly flattered in being enrolled as honorary member of your body. In some parts of North Wales I have worked very hard, and may perhaps have it in my power to be of some use to you—at all events you have my congratulations on your good beginning, and my hearty good-wishes for your success in your great voyage of discovery. But what a list of fine things you have sent me! If you go on in this way for many years, the world will be turned inside out and Shrewsbury will hardly hold your museum. I don't know when I can promise myself the pleasure of visiting Shrewsbury, but I can never want motives for so doing. Have the kindness to give my best remembrances to Colonel Wingfield, Dr. Dugard, or any other friend who may attend your general meeting on the 12th, and believe me, my dear Sir,

"Most truly yours,
"A. SEDGWICK.

"P.S. I suppose my friend Dr. Darwin is a member. His son is doing admirable work in South America, and has already sent home a collection above all price. It was the best thing in the world for him that he went out on the voyage of discovery. There was some risk of his turning out an idle man, but his character will be now fixed, and if God spares his life he will have a great name among the naturalists of Europe. Before I close the sheet let me thank you again for your kind remembrances of me in sending me copies of your charges, all of which I have read with very great pleasure."

From Mr. Serjeant Talfourd

Temple, November 9th, 1835.

"MY DEAR ARCHDEACON, Our friend Whateley has communicated to me great pleasure in the form of a message from you, by which I learn that you have honoured my drama by sanctioning the translation of some of its passages into Greek Iambics, and that they have been found not uncongenial by the young composers to whose graceful scholarship they were submitted. Having just received from the press some copies of a new edition, which is, I hope, rendered rather less unworthy of your indulgence by considerable alterations, I take this opportunity of sending you a copy, and I presume further to trouble you with six copies, and with the request that, if you have no objection, you will present them from me to the gentlemen who have made my verses classical by employing their own skill upon them, or any other of your scholars to whom you think the work adapted. If you see nothing in the play which may render it unfit for such a destiny—as your kind message encourages me to believe—your compliance with this desire will cause me peculiar gratification, in the consciousness that the images and thoughts which the admiration of the noble production of antiquity has awakened in the mind of so poor a scholar as I am, are presented to the imagination of those whose enviable lot it is to receive that introduction to classical learning which, according to the splendid experiences of Shrewsbury, will ensure them its rarest delights and happiest rewards. Do not allow your regard for me to induce you thus to dispose of the books contrary to your own judgement or inconsistently with the usages of the school, but in such case give them any distinction you think fit, or keep them till I can relieve you of them at the Assizes. If, on the other hand, you do not object to honour me by placing them in the hands of your embryo poets and statesmen, and think they would be acceptable to more than I have ventured to assume, I shall be most happy to forward you a further supply. Believe me, my dear Archdeacon, ever faithfully yours,

"T. N. TALFOURD."

From the Rev. J. D. Hustler

Euston, Thetford, November 28th, 1835.

"MY DEAR SIR, After a long interruption of our friendly communications, I am at last driven to trouble you upon a melancholy subject, which I doubt not has pained your heart as severely as it has mine—the untimely and unexpected removal of poor dear Tillbrook.

*

"I was heartily sorry, when you approached me once as near as Freckenham, that I could not tempt you to come nearer. To Freckenham probably neither you nor I may ever go again, if we can help it. The loss we have both sustained there would make us both prefer to go round another way rather than pass through it. I shall be truly happy if at any future time you will give me an opportunity of being poor dear Till's representative in hospitality.

"Mrs. Tillbrook has taken a house at Bury, where I hope she is comfortably situated. . . . I feel that the whole world cannot supply the loss I have had in the friend of so many years, of such rare and delightful talents, and of good-will which continued warm and unvaried between us up to the last moment."

CHAPTER TWENTY-EIGHT: INTENDED RESIGNATION

Intended Resignation, and Appointment of the Rev. B. H. Kennedy to the Head-Mastership—Correspondence, 1st December 1835— 9th April 1836

IN SPITE OF EVIDENTLY FAILING HEALTH, DR. Butler might perhaps have held on for another year or two to the school which he had made so glorious, if Mrs. Butler's health had not also broken down. In the autumn, however, of 1835 she had a severe paralytic seizure, and the anxiety which the care of so many boys inevitably caused her determined Dr. Butler to resign. He had set his heart on being succeeded by Kennedy, and the following letters will show how essential he considered this for the future prosperity of the school. Probably Kennedy would have been appointed even though his claims had not been so strongly backed, but Dr. Butler's eager advocacy of his cause is a point which all who are interested in Shrewsbury School will note with satisfaction. It should be remembered, however, that Dr. Butler's cordial advocacy of Kennedy's claims implies no disparagement to other favourite pupils, as, for example, R. W. Evans and Robert Scott; for not being Johnians, none of them stood the remotest chance of being elected.

At this time the second mastership was vacant; for Mr. Jeudwine, as I have said in an early chapter, died 22nd October 1835. But Dr. Butler does not seem to have interested himself in favour of any candidate for this post, which indeed was filled up immediately before he had well time to move, and without his being consulted in the matter. He was well pleased with the choice made by the College, and appears to have held that if he could secure the appointment of Kennedy to the Head-Mastership all would be well. There was, however, another uncertainty over and above that attendant upon the decision of the Master and Senior Fellows of St. John's. Kennedy (not yet D.D.) had been for some five years an assistant master at Harrow; and though there was as yet no indication that Dr. Longley was anxious to resign, it was thought not improbable that he would ere long be promoted to the Bench, and some of the trustees were as anxious to see Kennedy at Harrow as

Dr. Butler was that he should be at Shrewsbury. In fact there can be no question that if Kennedy had chosen he might have had Harrow whenever Dr. Longley should resign, and it was a difficult question both with himself and Dr. Butler which school it would be most advantageous for him to take.

It is to be feared that for himself it would have been better if he had stayed at Harrow, in spite of the many difficulties which he would unquestionably have had to face as headmaster at that school; but it is easy to be wise after the event, and the combination of adverse circumstances that for so many years told against the numerical prosperity of Shrewsbury could not in 1835 have been reasonably foreseen. Foremost among these, so far as I am able to form an opinion, was the growing renown of Dr. Arnold, which made Rugby resume the place as leading Midland school, of which for a time the prestige of Shrewsbury had deprived her. When Dr. Arnold took Rugby the numbers were one hundred and sixty. These increased till June 1832, when they stood at three hundred and nineteen. From this point they declined slowly but steadily, till at Christmas 1836 they were only two hundred and seventy-three. This was probably due to the growth of many good Midland schools, which led to a corresponding and contemporaneous decline in Dr. Butler's own numbers. They began to rise again with 1837, and continued to do so as long as Dr. Arnold lived.

Dr. Butler, always in touch with his own old school, was well informed of all that was doing at Rugby, and the decline in his own numbers made him naturally watch to see whether those of his great neighbour declined correspondingly. It was not, however, to be foreseen in 1835 that Rugby would be on the London and North-Western Railway, while Shrewsbury was for many years to be without any railway at all, nor yet how great a development was to take place in the views of parents with regard to the material comforts which they expected for their boys.

CORRESPONDENCE, 1ST DECEMBER 1835–9TH APRIL 1836

To Robert Scott, Esq.

(Mr. Scott was ordained Deacon 20th December 1835)

Shrewsbury, December 1st, 1835.

"MY DEAR SCOTT, I am truly glad that you have so honourably left Christ Church for Balliol, and that the little warrior with the ineffable name, *quod versu dicere non est,* bore you no grudge on that score. Indeed no man could, who had common sense and common humanity.

"I am also glad to hear your account of Lonsdale. He is a clever idle fellow (*inter nos*), and has done quite as well as I expected.

"Within the next fortnight I shall have occasion to write to you on very different matters.[1] In the meantime
"Yours affectionately,
"S. BUTLER.

"Do remember me most kindly to Pain. [Slip of the pen for Payne.—ED.]"

To the Rev. B. H. Kennedy

(Confidential.)

December 6th (?), 1835.

"MY DEAR KENNEDY, After a sleepless night, in which my thoughts have been entirely employed on considerations respecting you, I have determined to give you the result of them.

"If the College will elect or promise to elect you to Shrewsbury, I advise you at once to decide on it; and I advise this most unquestionably.

"If they will make no promise, and Harrow should be offered to you, I dare not advise you to forego the offer—but I am

---

[1] This must refer to Dr. Butler's intended resignation. Is it possible that he may at the moment have contemplated trying to secure Scott as his successor? If so, he must have come to the conclusion that it would be hopeless to get the Master and Fellows of St. John's to elect any but a Johnian, and abandoned the idea.—ED.

sensible that it will be attended even then with great hazard, and this it is my duty to lay before you as fairly as I can. I think that if the College are unjust enough both to you and to me to give no pledge nor hold out any promise, the hazard of your remaining at Harrow as head-master is not greater than that of the College not electing you at the time of the vacancy. For I have now written a most urgent letter to the Master, authorising him to announce my resignation if that will induce him to influence the College at once to elect you—not otherwise; and I have also written very strongly to Tatham. Now if that does not produce either an absolute election or a promise, I must say that we have no good ground to trust them when the actual vacancy occurs. My letters will reach Cambridge to-morrow (Tuesday), and I might have an answer by Thursday, but I cannot well hope for one before Friday—and I am afraid, as their fellowship election day is this day fortnight, that, with their usual procrastination, they may not come to any decision or hold any meeting till then. I have urged despatch. Now to-morrow fortnight you break up at Harrow; in the meantime you will be sounded.

"I wish you could avoid giving any answer till Friday next, if you are sounded in that interim. You might ask till Friday for consideration without assigning a reason. You might then fairly avow that you have sent in your name as a candidate for Shrewsbury, and have given the people connected with that school reasons to expect you would offer yourself for it; that you therefore wish permission to write to the College, desiring to know their determination in the course of—say five days, as your other prospects would be materially affected by it; and that if you do not hear by that time you will not oppose the wishes of the Harrow Trustees.

"This is on the supposition that, weighing all the *pros* and *cons*, you choose to run the risk at Harrow. The *pros*, as you state, are honour and glory, and the prospect of a good income if you succeed. The *cons* are a sure and desperate rebellion, the possibility of failure after it, and the possibility of having all your assistants dissatisfied. You are in the hands of a man who professes to wish you well and who may be your friend, but he is a known meddler and *intriguant*, and he is a man who I believe would flatter and betray any one to serve his own views. They are plain to me. His apparent object is specious and laudable. His real one, as I firmly believe, is to make it a school for his own evangelical clique, and still more to bring about a purpose which I might tell you in conversation, but which I dare not trust on paper. See the mischief that man is now doing in an old and long established society. He is the real mover of the levers which in the hands of his agents will make the P. C. K. Society split into parties and factions, and ultimately break up to the great advantage of the Bible Society. I dread him for my friends, and I despise him for myself, as our poor dear friend at Hatton did.

" I don't know what you mean by Arnold's reform of Rugby. You are probably better informed than I am, and allude to something with which I am unacquainted, but I can only say that I never heard of such an act. I know he increased the numbers very much, and I hear that they are now considerably on the decline again, but I do not know anything more.

" All this letter is confidential, and must be read and burnt immediately. What I have said of one person you may think arises from prejudice. I avow that I dislike him, but that would not influence me. Is not the very act of sounding you a proof of his meddling and intriguing spirit? Do you think the proposal to do so came from the two lords without his previous suggestion and application to them? And what name will you give to that? Ask for three days.

" Write as often as anything important occurs – especially if you hear from St. John's."

It must be remembered that any proposals made at this time to Kennedy must have been informal and provisional, for Dr. Longley had not yet announced, nor even, so far as I can learn, contemplated, his resignation.

To the Master of St. John's College, Cambridge

December 9th, 1835.
(Redrafted and sent 11th Dec. (?): *cf.* letter of 4th Feb. 1836.)

" DEAR MASTER OF ST. JOHN'S, I send you enclosed a letter which speaks for itself. It is one of great importance to the

College; for the appointment, if in the hands of an able and efficient man, is far beyond any other preferment which the College has to bestow. In those of an inactive or inefficient person it is merely equal to a college living. I write to you in great confidence, founded on my deep respect for you, and the high value I have set upon your friendship during more than forty years. I have therefore no reserves with you, and I tell you without the slightest concealment what I should be very sorry to commit to the discretion of a less tried friend. If in what I say I am obliged to make some allusion to my own exertions and expenditure here, you will, I doubt not, place it wholly to the account of unreserved confidences, and not to any motives of paltry vanity—for though of course I place the substance of this letter at your discretion, I depend upon that sound judgement which you have always exercised in the use you will make of it, and am confident that a letter like this, which is for your private information and to guide your judgement by putting you in possession of facts, will not itself pass into any hands but your own.

"When I came here the salary of the Head-Master was £120 a year, from the foundation, and continued so for many years. The house was inconvenient, and would accommodate about thirty-six boys, and the school was desolate. There was a public carriage road, in fact a street, by the house, and most of the adjoining houses were occupied as almost pauper cottages—in some cases tenanted by disreputable people. The only two decent houses were perfectly unconnected with the school.

"I came also a stranger. In my attempt to establish the almost unheard-of principle of discipline, I had all the mammas in Shrewsbury against me, and for nearly twenty years I struggled on almost without a friend. More than once I was strongly urged to resign, and was inclining to it from ill-usage and neglect, but had a degree of pride that prevented me. At last my boys having gained high University honours, and my perseverance itself having gained me some credit for consistency, I found, at the very moment I had determined to resign if there was no improvement, that we were beginning to increase. We proceeded progressively, and by degrees I was enabled to buy all, and to pull down and rebuild all the objectionable houses in the school lane, and, what was of still greater importance, to stop up the thoroughfare. All this, however, was done at a great sacrifice of money. I have spent above £14,000 on the improvement of this house and the adjacent premises. On this house alone I have expended £4,000, £1,000 of which was granted to me by two separate grants from the Trustees. I also by my exertions and remonstrances contrived to get an end put to a ruinous law-suit, which had lasted (with some interruptions, when the belligerents became exhausted) for above two hundred years, from the reign of James I to that of George IV— and the termination was also in our favour. The school, therefore, which when I came to it had an income of £900 a year with a heavy debt, has now an income of about £2,600 a year, and is not only out of debt, but is annually putting by money, though it has considerably more than doubled all the salaries of the masters and incumbents, has more than trebled the exhibitions, and has founded, and is still preparing to found, new ones. The numerous bye-exhibitions, several of which are principally in the management of the Head-Master, are also trebled in value. The school, which had two boarders when I came, has now one hundred and sixty; and had there been a second master with the least capacity for managing boys, would have had, as it had a few years ago, two hundred—but he lost all his boys for want of knowing how to govern them. Besides these there are about eighty more boys day scholars—about one-fourth not on the foundation.

"Such is the appointment to which, if a properly qualified man comes, he may succeed me with every reasonable hope of keeping it up, but which must fall instantly with one who is not first-rate. I shall retire, it is true, with only a moderate income, but this is no criterion of what an active and able successor might do, for I have had it all to make, while he will come to it ready-made.

"I can tell you in confidence that, in spite of the heavy demands I have had upon me, to the extent of £14,000 and upwards (of which a very considerable sum must be sacrificed), and notwithstanding the settlement of my three children in marriage and other heavy drawbacks made to secure a large landed property to my eldest grandson,[1] in which I have been obliged to make great investments at a very low rate of interest, and have consequently much reduced my income, on the average of the last ten years I have been enabled, though keeping a carriage and living in good style, to put by full £4,000 a year. No one else can do this. I will explain in conversation.

"Now suppose my successor at first experiences some diminution in the school, which may be reasonably expected, even admitting that for the first two or three years he is able to put by but a quarter of what I was able to do myself, you see what a great appointment he may make it. He never can make what I have, for reasons which I will explain hereafter.

"No doubt a large sum will be required for his outfit, or what I think you call income in college; for although I shall be ready not only to treat liberally with him, but to give him every accommodation in point of payment, still so great a concern as this will require a large outlay. But yet in a few years he may clear this; and I am ready to enter into any arrangement that any two friends, appointed one by him and one by myself, may suggest. In short, if a high man comes, he will find no difficulties; if an inferior one, it will be ruin to him.

"He should be not only a first-rate scholar, but a man of good tact, of some knowledge of the world, and of gentlemanly manners—one who can always command his temper, and never show himself to the boys under the influence of passion. Boys are not what they were fifty years ago. They are brought to manhood early (too early in my opinion, but I cannot help that—I can only go with the manners of the age); and unless they find that they have to do with a scholar and a gentleman, they will leave him, or will do nothing.

"Again, whoever succeeds me (I may say it to you without arrogance) must have attained high classical honours at the University, or else the boys will compare his name in the Cambridge Calendar with mine, to his disadvantage; and he must not only be a good scholar as far as construing goes, but an elegant and tasteful composer also, in Greek and Latin, in prose

[1] Not the present writer.—ED.

and verse. For if he cannot qualify boys to compete on all occasions for the highest classical honours, they will look to the boards of my school—on which above one hundred such prizemen are recorded, and among them thirteen University Scholars in succession in the two Universities, besides others when the succession was interrupted—and they will find something wanting.

"All this I say not for my own sake, but for that of the man who is to come after me; and though you cannot actually elect him till you have my formal resignation at midsummer, it is of the very greatest importance that you should previously fix on the man whom you determine to elect, that he may avail himself of the offer in my enclosed letter, and come and live with me for the last quarter. This will be a great inducement to parents to continue their sons here, [and will be nothing new or strange to the boys. Dr. Longley, on being appointed Head-Master of Harrow, came into school here with Mr. Henry Drury to hear me teach. Several other distinguished scholars have done the same—among them I may mention that first-rate scholar Mr. Lonsdale] and will bring him acquainted with the boys and the mode of teaching, and be of essential advantage to him in all respects.

"Having now put you confidentially in possession of all the details, it only remains for me to say that I shall be at Cambridge during the first six days in January for the express purpose of answering any further inquiries which you may wish to make. Meantime believe me, dear Master, yours most faithfully,

"S. BUTLER."

The part of the foregoing letter which I have enclosed in brackets was cancelled by Dr. Butler, and does not appear in the second draft of this letter. From part of what seems to have been a third draft I take the following:

"I have had advantages here of which perhaps no successor of mine can avail himself; for though my expenses have been enormous, I have been able, through Mrs. Butler's activity, to keep three houses, each containing fifty boys, in my own hands. Now I think no man who comes after me will be likely to do this. The best thing he can do will be to leave two of the houses for the accommodation of boarders in the hands of assistant masters, and thus to content himself with the tuition money only from the boys in those houses, leaving the profit from the boarders in them out of the question.

"No doubt this will make a most important alteration in his income. But supposing this to be the case, and supposing the school to fall off at first (the degree in which it will fall off will greatly depend upon the tact as well as the literary character of my successor), still I cannot think, on the most reasonable calculation, that his actual profits will be less than £1,000 a year on his first coming; and when he is well established they will hardly be less, I should conceive, than £2,000, and may be considerably more. My data are very easily understood, and I shall be ready to show them to you when we meet. It is so much more easily explained in conversation than on paper that I prefer this. I have taken a low calculation in order to be safe."

The letter referred to in the first draft of the letter to the Master of St. John's contains nothing but a formal announcement of Dr. Butler's intention to resign at the following midsummer, and an offer that whoever the College might appoint should come to reside with Dr. Butler during the last three months of his own tenure.

From the Bishop of Gloucester (Dr. Monk)

Palace, Gloucester, December 12th, 1835.

"MY DEAR ARCHDEACON, I am seriously obliged to you for your letter, and for your kindly making me acquainted with the interesting, I had almost said the affecting, fact of your intended relinquishment of the post which you have held with such unparalleled honour and efficiency for so long a time.

"Were not the health of Mrs. Butler one of the causes, I should cordially congratulate you while I condoled with the public on the event. There is nothing in scholastic history which can be fairly compared with your career, except that of Busby—and he did not, like you, find a school with only a single scholar. I am sorry that it has never happened to me to have an opportunity of expressing publicly how much in my opinion the cause of good education owes to you.

"My charge ought to have reached you two months ago.

"Having passed six months continuously in town in attendance on the Church Commission, I had hoped for a little repose at home—but last month I had again to go to its sittings, which are to be revived in the middle of January. Our report will, I expect, appear before the ensuing Session.

"If I am able it will give me sincere pleasure to go to Shrewsbury in the autumn next year.[1]

"Mrs. Monk joins in best regards to Mrs. Butler. Believe me always, my dear Sir, your faithful servant,

"J. H. GLOUCESTER."

From the Rev. R. Wilson Evans, afterwards Archdeacon of Westmoreland

December 22nd, 1835.

"DEAR DR. BUTLER, I have just been assured beyond all doubt that you intend to resign your office at next midsummer, and hope to be not among the last of your old pupils who will write to you on an occasion in which they feel so much concern. Regretting as I do the deep loss which not only the school itself but the education of the whole country will suffer, yet I cannot but warmly congratulate you on your release from so protracted and arduous exertion, and on your entrance upon a well-earned retirement. God grant you long and happy enjoyment of it! This, I am confident, is the hearty prayer of all your old pupils. Henceforward we may be proud of a more peculiar privilege and distinction in having partaken of an instruction which is so soon to cease, although we may hope to receive it still, in common with the world, under another shape. For myself, who went through your school from the bottom to the top, and am therefore, I am proud to say, every inch a Butlerian, I delight in ascribing my purest enjoyments, with whatever success I may have had, or good service which I may have been

[1] It was at that time intended that Dr. Butler should take up his residence at the Whitehall, Shrewsbury.—ED.

called upon to perform, to this beginning. Even after so long a period as eight and twenty years, and after having advanced into pursuits removed by some steps from those of my younger days, I am perpetually reminded amid my progress by traces not to be mistaken of your most valuable instruction. Nor have your friendly offices ever been wanting since those times, whenever I needed them. Trusting that I shall never forego the sense of such benefits as I have enjoyed at your hands,

"I remain with sincere affection and regard, dear Dr. Butler,
"Yours faithfully and gratefully,
"R. W. EVANS."

From the Rev. H. Drury

Cockwood, December 29th, 1835.

"MY DEAR BUTLER, In common with all who have the slightest love for or pretence to literature, your secession from Shrewsbury is the cause of my regret. The advance of learning among the young has decidedly at all English schools of any note generally taken its impulse from you; and where it has not, as at Westminster, the decadence has been doleful.

"Whatever Eton and Harrow may be, I can safely say they would not have reached even any moderate excellence if you had not been 'the Agitator.' I admire much the manly, conciliatory, and kind tone of your circular in what refers to a successor, when, I think, you had no reason to be well satisfied with the Johnians—who, as far as in them lay, ought in sheer gratitude to have made you the 'Grand Elector' in both instances. Whoever goes to Shrewsbury must follow in your steps, or his reputation will perish. He must aim at a proximity where he cannot attain a parity—one might say to him,

'Nec tu divinam Aeneida tenta,
Sed longe sequere et vestigia semper adora.'

"Enough. No man after such service can be happier than you among your books and amusements."

*

Correspondence

To the Rev. Philip Gell

December 31st, 1835.

"DEAR SIR, I know not whether you have yet had any meetings or collections in Derbyshire on behalf of the clergy of the Church of Ireland, but I feel, in common with, I presume, every brother of our profession, a deep sense both of their merits and of their extreme ill-usage. I therefore agree in thinking that though the Protestant laity of England, from their numbers, their fortunes, and their attachment to the Protestant Church, should take the lead in contributing, still the clergy of England may, and ought to, unite cordially with them in this good work, and to stir up the benevolent liberality of their respective flocks.

"May I therefore hope that you will confer with some of your clerical brethren in the town and neighbourhood of Derby; and if you should not think it expedient to call a general county meeting (which can hardly be done if subscriptions have already been entered into, and which if called at all should undoubtedly be headed by influential laymen), yet still should adopt such methods as may seem to you most expedient by committees or otherwise, composed of lay and clerical members in different districts, to collect contributions, which may be paid into the hands of one or more treasurers, and remitted by them to the Bishop of the Diocese?

"In the *Staffordshire Advertiser* for December 19th, 1835, which if you have not seen you probably will find at some newsroom in Derby, is an account of the proceedings at Stafford, which you will find on the second page. In the first page of it is an advertisement containing the resolutions of the meeting and a list of subscribers, and in the second page is an advertisement containing the proceedings and resolutions at Burslem, which seem to me well calculated to form the basis of any proceedings short of a county meeting.

"Considering Derbyshire to be so divided as almost to form two districts, North and South, I have sent a copy of this letter to Mr. Hill at Chesterfield, requesting him to communicate with you, and either to act separately or in conjunction, as may appear to yourselves expedient.

"My address till the 27th inst. will be at Kenilworth, Coventry. I shall be at Dr. John Johnstone's, Birmingham, on the 28th and 29th; and if I do not hear from you sooner, shall hope to do so by some of our Derby friends deputed to the Diocesan Meeting on the 29th. I shall then be at the Rev. T. S. Hughes's, Regent Street, Cambridge, where I am obliged to go on very important business connected with my approaching resignation of this school. Of course I shall subscribe to the fund at Derby, but wish first to hear from you—and am, dear Sir, faithfully yours,

"S. BUTLER."

From the President of Magdalen, Oxford

Magdalen College, Oxford, February 2nd, 1836.

"DEAR MR. ARCHDEACON, Having seen in the account given in *Thorpe's Collection of Autographs*, p. 129, of a letter of Henry Stephens to Bonaventura Vulcanus, the following passage, 'Nevertheless books have appeared from the other offices, but edited, it must be confessed, in such a manner as not to be worthy of me; take, for example, the Plato recently published. I hope soon to give a second edition, etc., etc.,' and being informed by Mr. Thorpe that you have purchased the article, I should be much obliged by your sending me an extract of the original of this passage, and so much more of what follows as relates to that edition of Plato. This notice of it is extremely curious, but does not surprise me. I am, with great respect and regard,

"Yours very sincerely, "M. J. ROUTH."

From the Rev. B. H. Kennedy

Undated: postmark, February 2nd, 1836.

"MY DEAR SIR, Butterton's answer leaves me at liberty. Tatham says nothing to the purpose. I asked him whether the College desired the application of any candidate, but he does not reply to this part of my letter. He tells me Isaacson has withdrawn his name, but that if he does another Fellow is expected to come forward. That Fellow I believe to be Merivale (C.); and I have little doubt, if Isaacson gets the Oratorship, that Merivale will be the man of their choice for Shrewsbury.

"However, I have obeyed you; and what would I not do to show my sense of your great–too great–kindness, and my reverence for your authority? I have sent the enclosed letter to the Master, and my cause is now in their hands and yours. Whatever you think right I shall now be satisfied with. You see that I have said nothing of a testimonial from you, because I wish to leave you quite free to act as you may deem best. If you think proper to write to St. John's, you may consider this letter as an application for your testimony. I await the result with calmness. If defeated, I shall find solid consolation in the reflection that

'Victrix causa Deis placuit, sed victa Catoni.'

If successful, I shall gird myself for the task encouraged by your good opinion, though painfully feeling how much you overrate my powers. Believe me I shall be more than satisfied to be the Pallas to your Jove.

*

"Believe me ever your truly grateful and affectionate
"BENJAMIN H. KENNEDY."

To the Master and Fellows of St. John's College, Cambridge

About February 4th, 1836.

"GENTLEMEN, The Rev. Benjamin Hall Kennedy, formerly a Fellow of your College, has informed me of his having offered himself as a candidate to succeed me in this school. I hold it absolutely unnecessary to give him a testimonial–indeed he asks for none–considering the distinctions he has obtained in your own College, as the most brilliant scholar I ever sent out from this school, but I cannot forbear saying that in becoming a candidate he has most highly gratified me, and if he should be judged at the time of election the best qualified to succeed me I shall see the fulfilment of the dearest wish of my heart. Whoever you may elect, you will find me ready to redeem my promise, but in his case I shall do so with the warmth of almost paternal affection.

"He was educated here, was the most distinguished of all my pupils, and has a name which itself will be sufficient to maintain the reputation of this school. In fact he will be a tower of strength to it, and will more than continue it in its present credit. He was also an assistant master here till he went to Harrow, where he has now, I think, had about five years' experience not only in teaching but in managing boys as boarders—a thing which requires no small tact, and in which if a master fails he cannot maintain the credit of his school.

"Let me not be understood as writing with any mercenary views for Mr. Kennedy. He is well off where he is; and well as I wish him, I need not in that respect wish him better. I write from a deep and anxious feeling for the prosperity of an important and now flourishing foundation, which I have made what it is, and to which I have devoted the best thirty-eight years of my life. I am anxious, too, for the honour and welfare of my College, that it may receive a succession of boys qualified to keep up the reputation of the school from which they came, and to adorn the prize-lists of the University as Johnians; and though I would by no means be thought to say that no other scholar can be found to succeed me but Mr. Kennedy, I feel bound to say that in my most sincere and firm belief no one can be found so fit to succeed me, so acceptable to the boys and their parents, and so completely realizing public expectation as he.

"I therefore most respectfully, but most zealously and affectionately, beg to recommend him to your notice. I have stated the grounds on which I do so. I ask not for interest or favour, for I remember that you are to elect on oath. I ask only this—that, considering the deep interest I feel in the prosperity of this school, you will forgive me for stating my opinion as to the suitableness of this candidate, and will take it at a proper time into your serious consideration. I remain, etc., etc.

"If by my immediate resignation I can facilitate his election,

I am ready to resign immediately, but only on the understanding that he should be elected my successor, as I must stay here till midsummer, and could easily arrange that with him and the Trustees. Still I must add, that should the College elect any other candidate, I am ready to do all I have undertaken in my letter of December 11th. I will never fail in duty or promise, whatever may be my disappointment. I only hope that my successor may reap greater advantages than I dare to expect for any man who comes here as superseding Kennedy."

From the Rev. B. H. Kennedy

February 6th, 1836.

"MY DEAR SIR, For your generous testimonial accept my warmest thanks, and be assured that to have been recommended by you, and so recommended, will enhance beyond measure the value of success, while it will fully compensate defeat.

"You will have learned Isaacson's failure for the Oratorship. I was there and voted for him; but the small colleges by no means supported him as might have been hoped. They appear not to care about having none but Trinity men examiners for the scholarships and medals. A Trinity man was elected Plumian Professor the day before, so that ere long all offices of honour and emolument in Cambridge will be absorbed by one college.

"I got no information about Shrewsbury. Indeed I only stayed to take a hasty dinner at my brother's rooms, and returned immediately. Isaacson will probably, though I should say not certainly, be still a candidate. Nobody knows when they are likely to come to a decision, but I have desired George to give me any information of importance.

"I have thought it useful to have a testimonial from the Bishop of London as the parent of one of my pupils, and he has written very handsomely to the Master of St. John's in my favour. Dr. Longley says for me all that is kind. If the boys at Shrewsbury really wish to have me I cannot fail to rejoice, though I trust they may be reconciled to the event whatever it may be. Isaacson is not only a good scholar, but an honourable and well-intentioned man, but he has for many years been living monastically in a monastic college, and this, I fear, will be against him at Shrewsbury.

"Your men, I hear, have been fortunate in having for the University Scholarship 'Columbus' for Latin verse, and a passage from *Comus* for Greek Iambics which had been done at Shrewsbury. It is said to lie between Thompson (your man), Vaughan (a Rugbeian),[1] and my brother William. I will write whenever I hear anything worth your hearing, and meanwhile believe me

"Ever yours with the greatest gratitude and affection,
"BENJAMIN H. KENNEDY.

"P.S. They cannot be mistaken about the fact of my being a candidate. I told one or two of the Fellows, who are sure to mention it, that I had now no motive for keeping it quiet."

From the Rev. B. H. Kennedy
Harrow, February 8th, 1836.

*

"Not only would I not be a candidate for Harrow, but I would not take it if offered me. I would rather have Shrewsbury, if, after twenty years, I could retire with £1,000 a year, than Harrow with a prospect of a quintuple income. I am not fit for it, nor it for me. Lucre cannot make me happy unless I feel myself to be doing good and see the good I do. I will take no school where fagging is a legalised system. Learning cannot flourish in it.

*

"As to Harrow boys, I have not found them in any respect superior to those at Shrewsbury. No doubt they can be very well mannered, and there are many of gentlemanly habits and feelings; but as a body they are more reckless than at Shrewsbury, more idle and careless of self-improvement. The upper

[1] Vaughan, now Dean of Llandaff, took the Porson 1836 and 1837. – ED.

boys exercise little or no control over the mischievously inclined, and the games of cricket and football are so zealously pursued, and with such organisation of the whole school, that it is vain to expect anything like extensive reading and sound scholarship."

*

The letter from which I have taken the foregoing extracts is the only one of those I submitted to him about three weeks before his death which Professor Kennedy did not wish me to publish. I can see no reason for his wish, but I should not even have ventured on printing as much as I have if Dr. Vaughan had not assured me that it gave so true a picture of Harrow as it was when he took the head-mastership in 1845 that he should wish it published. Believing that if he could have known this Professor Kennedy's objection would have been removed, I have allowed myself, with some hesitation, to give so much as is above found. As regards the accuracy of the comparison drawn between the then states of Harrow and Shrewsbury, it must be remembered that not only had Professor Kennedy been a pupil at Shrewsbury, but he had been a master there during parts of the years 1827 and 1828. The tone of the school therefore was well known to him.

From the Same
(Original given by me to Professor Kennedy shortly before his death.—ED.)

Harrow, February 9th, 1836.

"MY DEAR SIR, I need hardly say how much my heart is gladdened by the enthusiasm of the boys in my favour. It increases tenfold, if anything could increase, my desire to be with them, yet I am sorry they depreciate Butterton. There is more in him than perhaps they think. If I had got to Shrewsbury, I would have given anything in the world to have had him second master. His attainments, his temper, his manageableness, and his affection to me would have been worth £5,000. But it is too late to talk of this, and perhaps he would not have come down from the throne at Wakefield, even for an increase of emolument.

*

"No more news about the Oxford chair, saving that rumour couples Hampden's name with Longley's as a probable candidate."

*

To the Rev. T. S. Hughes

(Original in possession of Mr. Hughes's representatives)

February 18th, 1836.

"DEAR HUGHES, Your question is hard to answer, but I can do it pretty well for round numbers, so as that there shall be no mistake of importance.

"You will be surprised at the smallness of the numbers, but recollect that boys who complete their education stay on the average seven years, and that we have not been above fifteen years in full bearing.

"The whole number of boys admitted by
me from 1798 to this day is   1,626
Of these known to be dead are   154
Left after one or two years' stay, about   300
Army, India, Law, Merchants, about   150
Burgesses of Shrewsbury in lower grades   100
Unknown, or dismissed, say   50
Boys now at school   243
                                    997
                                    629

Leaving 629 for the two Universities here and also for Dublin, to which you may assign the twenty-nine at least, for I have had many there.

"I cannot reckon therefore more than 600 at the outside for the two Universities, and as during the last twenty years the numbers have been pretty equal at each, I may say perhaps 340 for Cambridge and 260 for Oxford. There cannot be more. I have perhaps rather underdone Oxford."

Correspondence

From the Master of St. John's, Cambridge

St. John's, March 7th, 1836.

"MY DEAR MR. ARCHDEACON, We met this morning to take into consideration the propriety of fixing upon your successor in the mastership of Shrewsbury School, as far at least as we are justified in expressing an opinion upon the future conduct of the Master and Seniors in an election which cannot be completed until the actual vacancy occurs; and it gives me a singular pleasure to say that the unanimous opinion of the assembled seniors was that the Rev. B. H. Kennedy is the proper person to receive the appointment.

"Whilst we all regret that from particular circumstances you are induced to retire from so laborious an employment, it is a great gratification to the society that we have so eminent a scholar, and one in every point so highly qualified for the situation, to succeed to the mastership of the school, as it will be I trust to all who feel for the prosperity of the institution. As to myself, I cannot but look forward to the great advantage which the College will derive from such a choice. Whilst we have so eminent a master of the school, and such excellent college tutors to follow up the instructions received there, we cannot fail to send into the world men who will stand foremost in the ranks of Literature and Science.

"As there can be no doubt of Mr. Kennedy's appointment, it will, in my opinion, be unnecessary for you to take measures for premature resignation; you may on this point consult your own convenience.

"I cannot conclude without expressing in the strongest manner, and which I have omitted no opportunity of doing, the sense I have felt of the value of your labours to the kingdom at large, to the two Universities, and more especially to that society at the head of which I have had the good fortune to be placed.

"That you may yet receive that reward which is due to your extraordinary exertions is the sincere wish of, my dear Mr. Archdeacon,
    "Your faithful and obedient, humble servant,
            "J. WOOD.

"Mr. Tatham desires me to acknowledge the receipt of your letter, to which, as it relates to the above subject, he feels it unnecessary to trouble you with an answer."

To the Rev. A. Irvine

(Original in possession of the Rev. J. Irvine)
(Confidential.)

March 10th, 1836.

"'*Ridentem dicere verum*' is not only good Latin, but sometimes sound policy, and therefore, my dear Andrew, though you do ask some questions '*Ut qui jocularia*,' I am aware of their serious import and will answer you faithfully and unreservedly.

"Mr. Willis, bating his original sin of being a High Tory, is a man of very high principle. I have no master whom I value so much for his steady undeviating attention to the boys, both in and out of school. He is a disciplinarian—if he were not he would not do his duty by them and by me; he is a kind-hearted man; but as regards tact—which you inquire about—I am afraid he has not all that I could wish, and his manner sometimes does not appear quite so gracious as his meaning.

"I am afraid he is nervous—not with nervous cowardice, for he is fearless enough, but I am afraid he has some degree of nervous irritability arising from not over strong health. As to his beauty, he is not near so handsome as I am, perhaps not even more than you are; his voice is not that of the Thunderer, for it has a little shake in it; and his form is, alas! about five feet three or four. His body is small also, even in proportion to his height, for he is thin. Valuable as he is, here, in a subordinate situation, anxious as he would be to fulfil his duties in a superior one, and capable as he is of doing so, as far as instruction goes, I confess to you, but I think I may depend upon your most confidential secrecy when I say so, that though I think him sure to succeed as a second master, I am not so sure that he would have all the trappings of dignity about him and all that tact that might be expected in a first. He is an excellent preacher. Now I have told you the truth, the whole truth, and nothing but the truth. The boys who are under him are divided in opinion: the idle ones do not like him; the industrious like him well, for he encourages and instructs them. His pupils among the upper boys one and all like him; and I believe all the masters admit that he is a good master and does his duty.

"Now upon this you must act, and your first action must be to burn this letter, that you may neither lose it nor be tempted to show it to anybody. I have a scheme—I do not know whether I can effect it—of sending him to Leicester for a day with an introduction to you."

*

Mr. Willis afterwards became Head Master of Ludlow Grammar School, and held the head mastership for many years, greatly liked and respected.

From the Rev. Thomas Hill

Chesterfield, March 10th, 1836.

"REVEREND AND DEAR SIR, At the monthly meeting of some of the clergy of this neighbourhood, on Tuesday last, the address to the King from the clergy of the Deanery of Bath in reference to the recent ecclesiastical appointment was read, and a strong feeling was expressed in favour of a similar petition from this district. It was, however, the unanimous desire of the meeting that I should in the first place write to you, and request the favour of you to inform me whether it was likely you would promote any measure of this nature. With any such expectation, they would, of course, desire that it should originate with yourself.

"I trust, reverend sir, you will pardon this intrusion, and whatever may be your sentiments on the subject that has occasioned it, that you will be assured of the sincere respect of the clergy in whose name I write, as well as of,

"Reverend and dear Sir,

"Your obliged and faithful servant,

"THOMAS HILL."

Life and Letters of Dr. Butler [XXVIII

To the Rev. Thomas Hill

Shrewsbury, March 12th, 1836.

"MY DEAR SIR, I take it for granted that by 'the recent ecclesiastical appointment' you mean that of Dr. Hampden, for I presume there can have been no address on that of my very dear and old friend Dr. Maltby to the see of Durham. But I have seen none from the Deanery of Bath, and I have always congratulated myself that on the appointment of Dr. Hampden at Oxford, being myself a Cambridge man, I did not consider myself called upon even to offer an opinion. For this reason I have not read, and do not mean to read, either Dr. Hampden's lectures or the strictures on them.

"Will you therefore be so good as to offer my kind and respectful compliments to the clergy who have done me the honour to consult me through you on this occasion, and to say that I consider it my duty—and I trust they have always found my conduct to be in conformity therewith—on all occasions to abstain as much as possible from controversy, and to promote peace and goodwill amongst ourselves?

"I adopt the precept of the Greek moralist—πῦρ σιδήρῳ μὴ σκαλεύειν. I therefore must beg to decline any participation in the matter you propose, and must leave yourself and your brethren to the exercise of your private judgement. I remain, dear Sir, faithfully yours,   "S. BUTLER.

"In the present state of the Bishop's health also, I think the archdeacons should be particularly careful not to originate any measure of a public nature."

From the Rev. H. Drury

Harrow, March 14th, 1836.

"MY DEAR BUTLER, I was just stepping into the carriage to pay a visit to Keate and Goodall at Eton when yours arrived. I desired my wife to answer it for me in the rough.

"There are, I understand, innumerable candidates[1] in the

[1] *I.e.*, for the Head Mastership of Harrow.—ED.

field, and it is supposed the boarding-house will be separated from the Mastership—which it ought to be—but then whence will there be sufficient emoluments to the Master?

"I am perfectly indifferent as to who comes here, provided he is a Gentleman, Scholar, and Public School man and can do verses. Eton, Harrow, Winchester, Shrewsbury, Rugby, perhaps Westminster, and from no other place whatever.

"The sixth form as well as the fifth is on my hands, so I write in school slovenly. I know none of the gentlemen who have presented themselves, but have written to Hughes to press him to be a candidate. I suppose he is now too much of a historiographer to grammaticise.

"I failed in an application I made to Eton for a good man and true.

"I am glad that Kennedy has succeeded, as it was his wish; and should have quaked if Charles Merivale had been the successful candidate. I cannot understand, however, how the former could be discontented with the goods the gods provided for him there. At all events, may Shrewsbury flourish though docked of its most brilliant beam—which is a nice mixture of metaphors. Let me know who your man is, and if Hughes (which I deem he will) declines, I shall be happy to assist him both now and hereafter.

"Give my best regards to good Mrs. Butler, and believe me
"Your faithful and fagged friend,
"H. DRURY."

From Dr. Longley, afterwards Archbishop of Canterbury

Harrow, March 14th, 1836.

"MY DEAR ARCHDEACON, Your congratulations [1] were not, I assure you, a whit the less welcome though not conveyed under the privileged cover; and as I believe I must wait for the new Act of Parliament before I can avail myself of the advantage which my future office will give me, I will not any longer delay my thanks for your kindness in greeting me on the prospect that awaits me.

[1] On the writer's being appointed Bishop of Ripon.—ED.

"We may mutually felicitate each other on our approaching relief from our arduous duties; but I will not presume to compare my own feelings on the occasion with those of one whose long and most honourable career has been distinguished by a degree of splendour and success unrivalled in the history of Public Schools."

From the Rev. P. B. Symons, Warden of Wadham College, Oxford

Uxbridge, April 9th, 1836.

"DEAR SIR, Your letter was placed in my hands on my way to the coach which was to take me from Oxford. I remember however the state of my engagements sufficiently well to say that I will readily receive a pupil of Dr. Butler's at Easter, 1838, for admission, and will make every effort, and I trust successfully, to receive him into residence in the following October. Be good enough to send me his age, and the name, condition, and abode of his father. I shall be in Oxford on Friday week.

"I began a letter to you on the announcement of your resignation, but what I meant for a sort of congratulation turned out of so doleful a cast that I abandoned and burnt it. I have met with good scholars from other schools, but none at all to my taste like those from Shrewsbury. How could I write therefore without forebodings?"

CHAPTER TWENTY-NINE: OFFER OF A BISHOPRIC AND FAREWELL SPEECH-DAY

Offer of a Bishopric, Correspondence, 6th April 1836 – 6th June 1836, Dr. Butler's Farewell Speech-day, and Resignation of the Head Mastership

IF DR. BUTLER HAD KNOWN HOW SERIOUSLY HIS health was impaired, he would hardly have resigned one arduous task to undertake another not less wearing; but, however this may be, his sanguine temperament and the assurances of his physicians forbade him to decline the bishopric that was now very shortly offered him. His only hesitation appears to have arisen from uncertainty whether or no he was expected to support the policy of the Government in regard to the Irish Church; on learning that his liberty was unfettered in this respect he accepted Lord Melbourne's offer.

No other close of such a career would have been adequate. Those, therefore, by whom Dr. Butler's memory is still cherished must feel that, though his life may have been shortened, as it possibly, though very uncertainly, was by his elevation to the Bench, nothing less than this would have rounded it in a way that would have satisfied them. They will also reflect with pleasure that, short as his episcopal career proved to be – hardly three and a half years from the day of his consecration – it was long enough to show that he was not less able and laborious in the administration of his diocese than he had long proved himself in a sphere of less ample scope.

I have often heard people regret that he was not made Bishop some ten years earlier. As one jealous for his fame I rejoice that he did not leave Shrewsbury a day before he did. The last ten years of his head mastership were the most lustrous of them all; had he left in 1826 he would have been nothing as compared with what he was ten years later. Granted that he had made his mark by 1826, still another ten years or so were wanted before he could so impregnate the abiding spirit of the place as to haunt it benignly and go in and out for good among pupils whom he had never seen. Moreover it was during these last ten years alone that his private means became sufficient to enable him to accept a position which entailed expenses far exceeding not only its emoluments but his own income as well. On every ground, therefore, it was well that his elevation to the Bench was delayed as long as it was.

The affectionate tribute paid to his memory shortly after his death by his examining chaplain and former pupil R. W. Evans will show what was thought of his administration of the see by one who had the fullest knowledge of it. In the preface to his *Bishopric of Souls*—a book which he inscribed to the memory of Dr. Butler—Mr. Evans wrote:

" Such a work may not be without its use to others also; I have, therefore, digested it into regular form, and published it, with the additional view of offering some public tribute, such as I was able, to the memory of the lamented prelate whom it was my privilege to serve. It will declare my will, if not my power, to be found in some way ἐκτίνων καλὰς τροφὰς to the instructor of my youth, and the kind friend of all my life. I am even bold to think, that it may, as every monument should, reflect here and there the likeness of his mind. In anything which will be worthy of the dedication of the work it assuredly will. For who of those who are enjoying the fruits of his instruction are not continually reminded of the seed which he sowed in their minds, by means of information conveyed through his deep learning in large store, made interesting by the form in which his exquisite taste presented it, and obvious by the accommodating powers of his clear and vigorous conception? Who of us who have drawn from his pure fountain are not conscious of its fertilising stream in every field of mind, upon the proper cultivation of which we can at all congratulate ourselves? And who of us can forget those admirable endowments, any more than we can that high tone of feeling, that kind parental regard, that openness and candour of mind, which marked all his communication with us?

" When he entered upon his high and sacred office in the Church of God, all who knew him not were surprised to see how he rose at once up to the standard of its rare requirements; while all who knew him were delighted to see proper room and scope afforded to the vigour and largeness of his mind. A bodily affliction, with which the Lord was pleased to visit him soon after his consecration, only made his spiritual vigour more remarkable. . . . Not only was the business of his diocese regularly transacted within doors, and his palace open with hospitable reception to his clergy until within a few days of his death, but long after a common regard for the ease of his suffering body would have counselled him to remain at home, he appeared at his post in public. He presided at meetings where every person present had been in almost daily expectation of hearing of his death. He traversed the wild moors of Derbyshire when every one who saw him wondered that he should have quitted a sick chamber. Truly he approved himself a good soldier of Jesus Christ."

The reader will judge from letters that will appear in due course how far the sketch given above is likely to have been too highly coloured by the personal affection of the writer. I should not, however, have decided in favour of laying these letters before the public if my only object had been to show that Dr. Butler administered his diocese with energy and discretion. My object rather is to give a bird's-eye view of the state of the Church and of the working of a diocese some sixty or seventy years ago. Both the see and its administrator were, I take it, very typical. Bishops are more like one another than schoolmasters are; they are chosen as being of a certain type at an age when all sensible men begin to assimilate more to one another. They are known, to use Baron Merian's word, as bishopable men, and to be bishopable is to be safe as well as energetic. Bishops and clergymen are probably familiar with the kind of questions that in any diocese make demands on the sagacity and forbearance of its Diocesan, but laymen know very little about them; and even clerics may be glad to see, on the one hand, how much quiet unobtrusive good work was being done by the clergy even at a time that we are apt to stigmatize as still lethargic, and, on the other, how impossible scandals have now become which as recently as 1836-1840, if not common, were still existent.

My selection, therefore, from the letters which the authorities at the British Museum have thought fit to render accessible to the public will be guided by the considerations above briefly indicated. " Do they," I shall ask myself, " illustrate the times? Do they throw the same kind of light upon the working of a diocese in the earlier half of this century as those already given throw upon the state of public education? " If I think they do, I shall venture at this distance of time to make them more accessible to the general reader than they now are in the MS. department of the British Museum. If they do not appear to justify their publication on these grounds I shall leave the curious to search for them.

Nearly three months elapsed after Lord Melbourne had named Dr. Butler to his Majesty before it was decided which see he was to fill. He therefore remained at Shrewsbury till the end of the half-year, which would have been impossible had he been nominated at once to the then see of Lichfield and Coventry.

CORRESPONDENCE, 6TH APRIL 1836–6TH JUNE 1836

From Lord Melbourne

Panshanger, April 6th, 1836.

" SIR, I have great satisfaction in being able to reply at once to your letter of the 3rd instant that it is my intention to name you to his Majesty as a proper person to fill the vacancy which has just taken place upon the Episcopal Bench. Although I have not the pleasure of your personal acquaintance, your general character both as a clergyman and a scholar is such as not only to justify, but in some measure to demand the promotion, and the most useful but most laborious occupation in which you have passed the greater part of your life gives, if any human exertions can give, a paramount claim to encouragement and reward. I can assure you it has given me great concern that circumstances which I could not control have prevented me from doing you justice at an earlier period.

" I do not designate any particular see because, so many vacancies happening contemporaneously with a general plan of ecclesiastical reformation, it is necessary to consider very maturely the particular arrangements, with a view of carrying the recommendations of the Commissioners into the most speedy and the most complete execution. I remain, Sir, with great respect, your faithful and obedient servant,

" MELBOURNE."

To the Rev. T. Butler

(Original in possession of Mrs. G. L. Bridges and Miss Butler)
(Private.)

April 7th, 1836.

" MY DEAR TOM, The Bishop of — sends his blessing to his dear son and daughter-in-law and grandchildren.

*

" I have had no intelligence from Lord Melbourne, and therefore you must not talk of it till my next, as it would be contrary to all etiquette to do so before the Premier's announcement. My intelligence is from the congratulations of the Bishop of London, whose letter by the mail has either outstripped the King's Messenger bearing me official intelligence, or else it is not the etiquette to make an official announcement before the funeral of the late possessor of the see. The Bishop of London does not mention the see to which I am appointed. I presume therefore it is Lichfield. God bless you all."

I did not find the letter from the Bishop of London above referred to.

From the Rev. W. F. Hook

Coventry, Easter Tuesday, 1836.

" MY DEAR MR. ARCHDEACON, I have just received a letter from London informing me that you are to be our new Bishop, and in the joy of my heart I cannot for the life of me help writing to offer you my real, genuine, heartfelt congratulations. Thinking as I do of the episcopal office and of its awful responsibilities, it is not to every friend receiving such an appointment that I should thus write. But to a man of active mind who has been all his best days a working man, retirement is generally only another name for disease and discomfort; as one, therefore, who has been honoured with your friendship, I do rejoice that you are now to die with harness on your back. On public grounds I have a twofold ground of rejoicing: first, that we have not had a *bad* man appointed over us, as we feared; secondly, that we have had appointed over us a man *pre-eminently* good, which was more than we could expect. I am prepared to show that you are pre-eminently fit for the situation from high authority. There is a passage which strikes me as very curious in St. Chrysostom, in which he makes nearly the same complaints as to the episcopal appointments as we do now, showing that under the primitive system, as well as under our own, it was impossible to prevent abuses. He complains that one person is appointed 'ὅτι γένους ἐστὶ λαμπροῦ,' another 'ὅτι πλοῦτον περιβέβληται πολύν,' etc., etc.; but he (St. Chrysostom), so far from admitting the justice of these pleas, would not prefer a man even for his *distinguished piety* εἰ μὴ μετὰ τῆς εὐσεβείας πολλὴν καὶ τὴν σύνεσιν ἔχων τύχοι. His description a little lower down of what a Bishop ought to be is very much in the antithetical style which Dr. Parr seems to have admired: καὶ γὰρ καὶ σεμνὸν καὶ ἄτυφον, καὶ φοβερὸν καὶ προσηνῆ, καὶ ἀρχικὸν καὶ κοινωνικόν, καὶ ἀδέκαστον καὶ θεραπευτικόν, καὶ ταπεινὸν καὶ ἀδουλωτικόν, καὶ σφοδρὸν καὶ ἥμερον εἶναι δεῖ. I will not turn this into a compliment lest I should be involved in the censure he passes on those who flatter their Bishops, but I suppose Dr. Parr would have rendered the passage, 'Grave without haughtiness,' etc.

"As in my next letter I shall have to sign myself, and I shall do so with great pleasure, as your dutiful *son*, I hope you will pardon the freedom with which I write for the last time, in all probability, to a brother-presbyter. Although I may be dull in understanding a playful allusion to a subject which lies very near my heart, you will always find me very serious when I subscribe myself yours, my dear Mr. Archdeacon, most sincerely and respectfully,
"W. F. HOOK."

Offer of a Bishopric

From Sir F. L. Holyoake-Goodricke, Bart. (a Former Pupil)

Arlington Street, (April 9th, 1836.—ED.)

"DEAR DR. BUTLER, It gives me great pleasure to communicate to you that the meeting at which I had the honour of presiding yesterday could but feebly express all they felt of kindness and friendship towards you. Believe me that the satisfaction of assisting at such a meeting is more than ever I could have expected, and is one of those opportunities of manifesting long and deeply felt esteem that may warrant some feelings of pride.

"I hope that the announcement that Mr. Kennedy made of your new honours may permit me to congratulate you upon the occasion, and may you have many, many years to enjoy the well-merited promotion. I have the honour to remain, yours most faithfully,
"F. L. H. GOODRICKE."

Committees consisting of Dr. Butler's old pupils had been formed both at Oxford and Cambridge as soon as his intended resignation had become generally known, for the purpose of presenting him with a testimonial. It was resolved that the two Universities should combine, and that a meeting should be held in London at the Thatched House to which all old Shrewsbury men should be invited. The day was fixed for 8th April, and between that date and 1st June, when the subscription list was closed, between £700 and £800 was collected, with which a massive service of plate was purchased. This was presented 6th October 1836, as will appear in due course.

From Lord Melbourne

Panshanger, April 10th, 1836.

"SIR, I have this morning received your letter of the 8th instant, and have to inform you in reply that I have received his Majesty's approbation of your elevation to the Episcopal Bench.

"Having read your last charge to the clergy of your archdeaconry which you were good enough to send me, I was of course aware of your opinion with respect to property which had been set apart for ecclesiastical purposes, and with this knowledge I made you the offer contained in my former letter.

"Dr. Longley, when I made him a similar offer, stated to me in reply an opinion similar to yours upon the Appropriation Clause in the Bill for the settlement of the tithe in Ireland, and he added that, if I considered agreement upon this point indispensable, he was willing in perfect good-humour and without feeling any offence to relinquish the preferment proffered to him. I replied that what I looked for was a general agreement in political opinion, and a general disposition to support the measures of the present Government, and that if that existed I did not wish to bind him down to support upon every question, and that I had hopes of being able to bring forward a measure upon the Irish Church which would meet with a more general concurrence than the Bill of last year. I have not the correspondence before me, but as far as my recollection goes I believe I have correctly stated the substance of it, and I hope that what I said to him will also be satisfactory to you. I remain, Sir, your faithful and obedient servant, "MELBOURNE."

From the Rev. R. Watkinson

Earl's Colne, Sunday, April 10th, 1836.

"MY DEAREST FRIEND, A thousand thanks to you for your kind consideration of the suspense we have been in for the last week, in so early sending us the joyful news. During the whole course of my life I do not recollect any intelligence which gave me so much pleasure, and Mrs. Watkinson said the same. After reading your letter I ran with it to my wife, and we sang, capered, laughed and cried by turns, and prayed heartily to God that He would grant you many years of health and strength to enjoy the elevation which has so long been due to you."

*

The writer of the foregoing letter was one of Dr. Butler's most valued and intimate friends, and had rendered him inestimable assistance in the matter of the school lawsuit. Much of the negotiation between the contending parties was carried on through him, and on his death a very large number of Dr. Butler's letters were found among his papers. These were destroyed a few years since, it being not foreseen that any one would ever wish to see them; it is not likely, however, that they would have told me more than I have been able already to put before the reader as derived from other sources. Mr. Watkinson died in 1869, aged ninety-three. His wife died in 1884, aged over ninety.

To Lord Melbourne

Undated: probably 10-12th April or perhaps May (?), 1836.

"MY LORD, I hope I am not venturing too far when I beg to represent to your Lordship that having been sixteen years an archdeacon in the diocese of Lichfield, and well knowing the circumstances respecting one hundred and seventy of its churches and above two hundred of its clergy, I should feel extremely gratified if I might be permitted still to preside over them by being appointed to the see of Lichfield.

"Another circumstance which would enhance my satisfaction is that the Bishop is Visitor of this school, and that everything related to it is submitted to his consideration, and must receive his sanction. Should it therefore be consistent with Ministerial arrangements, it would be a great satisfaction to me to be placed in a situation where I may probably be more efficient from my previous knowledge of the diocese than I could be elsewhere—besides having my family and connections settled within forty miles or less."

No more of this letter was drafted.

From J. Bather, Esq., Recorder of Shrewsbury

April 15th, 1836.

"MY DEAR SIR, I will not apologise to you for addressing you by letter on a point which I feel of some importance to the schools, since perhaps I shall thus occupy less of your already over-occupied time than by a personal conference. You mentioned that you proposed as suiting your convenience and Mr. Kennedy's, and as a natural expression of Jubilee to the boys on your promotion, to add a week to their holidays—*præfigere*, as Lord Brougham says. This natural indulgence I apprehend neither parent nor trustee can object to, but it brings more forcibly to my attention both as parent and trustee the subject of the holidays generally. They are stated in your half-yearly accounts as being six weeks, and the day of their termination, *e.g.*, is fixed for Monday the 1st of August; then follows a notice that 'a week is allowed for assembling,' the effect of which is that no boys, except perhaps a few recent ones by mistake, come till the Saturday night, or, what is still worse, the Sunday night, say the 7th. The masters and yourself are at their posts, but if any boys do come they are (with the exception of those who are to be examined and placed) idling and guttling about the town (a reason which has always led me not to send mine till Saturday night), and, as I said before, many travelling on the Sunday, which I think a scandal.

"Now I assure you I have heard this very generally remarked upon and objected to, and nothing but a desire not to stir any question that could in any sort convey a shadow of censure upon one to whom the school is so deeply indebted prevented my mentioning it to you sooner, and obtaining your opinion as to remedying it. Now seems the natural time for the Trustees to do so. They clearly have a right so to do, and I should propose (unless you can convince me that I am wrong, and indeed I am open to conviction) to make a regulation that the holidays should actually finish when they profess to do, and as in the case of the Universities, all boys should be in Chapel on the Sunday morning before the Monday of the school exercises commencing, still allowing them the one, two, or three days they now have before the first Monday of the holidays, so that they need not travel home on a Sunday. I understand that this is the case in most great schools, Rugby for instance (not that I am a worshipper of Dr. A.), where if a boy is absent he must get up all the lessons of the absent time, the Military and Naval Schools, and various others. I think you will feel that if in course of thirty-eight years this is the only relaxation of discipline that the Trustees have to complain of, or rather the only practice which they think capable of amendment, that they and still less I am doing nothing disrespectful to you in taking the opportunity of improving the practice. I should therefore propose if you take the week at the beginning of the present holidays that the boys should return to the day, and that for the future the rule should be imperative. The preliminary week in the present instance would mitigate the rule to the boys, and I think the alteration would be no additional severity on the masters, who are most to be considered. The loss to the boys who are not fortunate enough to have parents who can and will guide their studies during the holidays, both in actual attainments and regular habits of exertion, is very serious. I have spoken to my brother on the subject, who concurs with me."

The writer of the foregoing letter, brother to Dr. Butler's son-in-law Archdeacon Bather, was a man for whom Dr. Butler felt the warmest affection and respect. There cannot be a doubt that all he said was accurate. Neither can there be a doubt that Dr. Butler knew what went on to the full as well as his correspondent. He was so astute, so well informed, and so watchful over the individual characters of his boys that any licence he permitted was certainly deliberate. Perhaps he thought that snatches of greater liberty, even though pretty sure to be abused, were useful as teaching boys how to make better use of greater liberty when they attained it. He may have deemed it well to give them a chance of making mistakes on a small scale when little harm was likely to follow, and when he was sure one way or another to know where they had been and what they had been doing. I cannot say what his motives were, but there is not a shadow of doubt in my mind that, whatever they were, they were the result of mature reflection. Unfortunately I found no draft of Dr. Butler's answer, which was very likely verbal.

From the Rev. Robert Scott

April 18th, 1836.

"MY DEAR DR. BUTLER, I have been waiting very impatiently until I might be quite sure of having really to congratulate you, and as I now understand that there is no doubt whatever of your elevation, I hasten to express to you how glad, and how proud, I am that your retirement from Shrewsbury is not to involve the public loss of your services, but that a new and wider sphere of utility is opened to you, which will reward your past exertions without releasing you from the claim which the public has upon you for their continuance.

"It is indeed a proud thing to all of *us*, that, while we were endeavouring to show some token of regard to our master, our proceedings should be so ratified, and the claims which we advanced so satisfactorily acknowledged. But there can be very few, I will be bold to assert, that can feel it so much as myself, because few—very few indeed—have owed so much to you. And without speaking of the success which has attended me in the University, which, whatever it has been, is wholly and entirely yours, the parental kindness which both in sickness and in health I always met with from Mrs. Butler and yourself, and the continuance of your regard, which I trust I may boast of even to the present time, give me a peculiar claim to rejoice in your exaltation.

"And your satisfaction will be the more unmixed from the consideration that you are leaving your school in the hands of the one person who above all others is likely to enable it to retain its present character.

"I have not heard positively where you are to be placed; and at any rate it would still be too early to direct to you as anything but 'Dr. Butler'; but I am not sorry to have an opportunity of taking a farewell of him, when I can do it under these circumstances."

From Lord Melbourne

(Original in possession of Mrs. G. L. Bridges and Miss Butler)

South Street, April 19th, 1836.

"SIR, So many sees having fallen vacant at once, and such vacancies being contemporaneous with a general plan of reformation of the Church, considerable difficulty has naturally arisen, which has prevented anything as yet from being definitely settled except the translation of the Bishop of Chichester to Durham. I have no doubt that much inconvenience will be occasioned by the delay, which I will try to render as short as possible. The evil which your letter points out as arising in the see of Lichfield and Coventry is not inconsiderable, and shall, if possible, be remedied. I am much concerned to hear that you have been indisposed, and I remain, Sir,

"Your faithful and obedient servant,
"MELBOURNE."

From Lord Berwick

April 28th, 1836.

"You have, I fear, too deep a knowledge of Materia Medica ever to feel quite well, but certainly this weather and the suspense in which you are kept is enough to shake any man's constitution.

*

"You will recollect I said Grey would try for Ely as it is on the North Road, besides the Dover Street House, but you said it must be given to a Cambridge man, and if Lord M. is consistent about alternate nominations, he certainly should not make an Oxford man visitor of Cambridge colleges, not to mention the patronage; but they want Whiggery at Ely, and dare scarcely refuse anything to Lord Grey at this moment, after their open defence and recognition of O'Connell, which gives Lord Grey such a favourable opportunity of withdrawing his support. I forgot to mention Wooler in my last, and you may depend upon it some dreadful job is contemplated either for Grey or otherwise. If he goes to Ely, Cambridge will be up in arms, like Oxford; and what is the King to do with two Universities offended at the same time?

"The papers report the delay to be owing solely to the See of Durham Bill not having passed into law. This cannot be entirely true, as all the jobbing will give the Tories a triumph which Lord M. can ill afford, even at the exposure, though countenance, of Lord Grey.

"Ever yours, "B."

Life and Letters of Dr. Butler

To the Rev. A. Irvine
(Original in possession of the Rev. J. Irvine)
June 6th, 1836.
*

"On Saturday, if I am well enough, I set out for London, accompanied by my friend Dr. John Johnstone of Birmingham. I hope to reach it, resting on Sunday at Birmingham, on the 13th or 14th. A journey down to Leicester and back in my present state is out of the question, and it is important that I should now be in town as early as I can.

"Still they say I have no organic disease, but a tedious affection of a great nerve connected with the heart and stomach, and they try to prove this by various arguments; they assure me that at some time or other, but they are too wise prophets to fix the time, I shall be *qualis eram*.

"I doubt, but what can I do?
*

"Dr. John Johnstone is to see Sir H. Halford with me."

I take the following account of Dr. Butler's last Speech-day – the day which ended his Head Mastership – from a small pamphlet now in the British Museum, evidently a reprint from one of the Shrewsbury papers.

Shrewsbury School Speeches and Distribution of Prizes, 7th June 1836

"Dr. Butler, in delivering the prizes to the successful scholars, was evidently imbued with feelings of the deepest emotion, and the chords of sympathy were struck in no slight degree in every breast among his numerous auditory.

"The number of persons assembled on this interesting occasion was, for reasons readily appreciated, very great, and comprised all the leading families resident in this vicinity, and the speeches were delivered by the young gentlemen respectively with so much taste and feeling as to render individual distinction invidious, where all excelled.

Dr. Butler's Last Speech-day

"After the recitation of the speeches had concluded, Archdeacon Butler requested the company present to partake of his accustomed hospitality in the library, upon which the whole body of Trustees present rose, and John Bather, Esq. (in the absence and at the request of the Hon. Thomas Kenyon, who was prevented by accident from attending), in their name, presented to the Archdeacon the unanimous vote of thanks of that body for his long and eminent services. The resolutions were as follows, which Mr. Bather read verbatim:

"'At a special meeting of the Governors and Trustees of the Royal Free Grammar School of King Edward the Sixth, in Shrewsbury, held the 23rd day of May, 1836;

"'Resolved unanimously, that the thanks of the Governors and Trustees be given to the Venerable Archdeacon Butler, for the unremitting assiduity and eminent ability with which he has performed the duties of Head-Master of this School for a period of thirty-eight years; restoring and augmenting, by his energy and learning, the utility and celebrity of this ancient foundation, imparting to the sons of the free burgesses of Shrewsbury the full advantages of that liberal education which was provided for them by the munificence of their Royal Benefactors, and pointing out to them, and to the youth of this and the surrounding counties, that road to academical honours and distinctions which so many of his pupils have successfully pursued.

"'That the Governors and Trustees further desire to congratulate Archdeacon Butler on the prospect of his immediate advancement to that eminent station in the Church to which he has been designated by the well-deserved grace and favour of the King; and to communicate to him that, in order more fully to testify their own sense of his services, and to perpetuate the memory of them, they have determined to found an additional Exhibition of £100 per annum, to be called for ever "Dr. Butler's Exhibition," and to be tenable according to the provisions and limitations of the Act of the 38th of George the Third, by the sons of burgesses entering at either University.

"'In witness whereof, they have hereunto ordered their common seal to be affixed, the day and year above written.'

"[The preceding resolutions were exquisitely written on vellum, and the common seal attached was enclosed in a beautiful silver box, the manufacture of Messrs. Rundell & Bridge.]

"'And now, Sir' (said Mr. Bather), 'I might well conclude, and neither dilate nor dilute the simple language of these resolutions by addition of my own; but, Sir, satisfactory as it has been to the Trustees to do as they have done, yet they do feel regret that they have not been able to extend their plan farther; and this I wish to state publicly, and in the presence of the gentlemen who hear me: By the provisions of the Act under which we are incorporated, the beneficial interest on exhibitions is strictly limited to the sons of burgesses: we wish it were otherwise, and that we could throw open to the emulation of these young gentlemen those rewards of their diligence which we feel they amply deserve. For, Sir, I must assert that the sons of the inhabitants of Shrewsbury are deeply indebted to the scholars who have joined them from every part of the kingdom for the high and gentlemanly spirit which they have contributed to nourish in the school, and for the kindness with which they have treated them as friends and companions. Having, Sir, thus broken my original intention, and, I suppose, from habit, whether good or bad, ventured to trouble this meeting with my own sentiments, I cannot resist the temptation of addressing a few words to your scholars, whom I for many reasons have always viewed with the sincerest regard and affection. Gentlemen [turning to the boys], you may extract a most useful moral from the gratifying proceedings of this day. We have recorded before us active services of thirty-eight years' duration. How large a portion even of a long life! how much larger of a life of sixty-two years! and you witness its reward. But the wonder is not that the gratitude of the country and of the King should select a meritorious man for promotion after such a length of service, not that a great scholar should be made a Bishop at sixty-two. But look at the beginning of his career. The marvel is that he should have been at the head of such a foundation as this at twenty-four. And how did this happen? Not by sloth, not by delay, not by procrastination, not by losing the first term or two at the University in idleness and dissipation, but by a strenuous and determined application from the hour he entered school to the day he was selected (from his known merit) for this appointment. Go, then, and do ye likewise. Many of you are leaving the school this half-year, and entering at the Universities. Few, perhaps, may reasonably hope to rise to the height of your revered master's learning or celebrity; but you may all try to do this; and in one point, if you will try, you may equal him – in his industry. Do this, and you have gained much, whatever else you fail to attain. Possibly in time your industry may be equally rewarded. *Otium cum dignitate*, in some form or other, and at some time or other, is the aspiration of us all; but they are but Epicurean translators who would construe it into dosing in a stall or fattening on a sinecure. The repose of great minds is a variation of labour, adapted to their age and circumstances; their dignity consists in the power and the consciousness of being useful. Long may you, Sir, enjoy this repose – long may you flourish in these dignities! And when at length your eye shall grow dim and your strength fail you, may there arise from amongst these, many, very many, to fill your place, to edify and defend the Church, and to do good and faithful service to the State, guided by your precepts and stimulated by your example! And now, Sir, let me place this document in your hands. We have indulged a harmless fancy – a sort of efflorescence from the taste of the learned – in adorning our plain language with beautiful and ornamental writing. May we hope, Sir, that you will not disdain to place it among your literary treasures; and that your family – and long may they flourish! – will preserve it and hold it not the least valuable of their title-deeds?'

"Archdeacon Butler said:

"'Mr. Recorder, I receive with the greatest respect and gratitude this most honourable and truly valuable testimonial. Having devoted the best part of my life to the duties of my station, it is a matter of no small delight to me to find at my retirement that I have so conducted myself as to obtain the approbation of those to whose guardianship this important foundation is entrusted, and I hope also with the satisfaction of the public.

"'Encouraged, therefore, as I am, to believe that my efforts have not been in vain, may I be allowed to say that they never were exerted with greater anxiety, nor, I am sure, with more probable advantage to this foundation, than in securing for it the services of my distinguished successor. Let me add, Sir, from my long knowledge of him, and from the experience of the last six months which I have had of the gentleman who has been appointed Second Master, that the College have nobly fulfilled their part, and that I could not desire to leave the school in better hands, nor, as I must in justice also say, with a set of better disposed, more studious, or more promising boys in it.

"'Sir, I ought to say more, but I trust, under all circumstances, you will excuse me. I will therefore detain you no longer than while I offer to yourself and the rest of the Trustees my most grateful thanks, accompanied with every good wish for the prosperity of this ancient and royal foundation. It is owing, Sir, to the cordial co-operation of yourself and your colleagues with my own humble exertions, during the long period of thirty-eight years, that I am able to take leave of it in the words of the great Roman Emperor, and to say, *lateritiam inveni, marmoream relinquo.*'

"Mr. Marsh (the senior scholar present) then stepped forward, and, respectfully addressing Dr. Butler, said:

"'Mr. Archdeacon, Before the present party adjourn to partake of your accustomed hospitality, will you permit me to acquit myself of a duty imposed on me by my schoolfellows, in presenting to you this sincere, though inadequate, testimonial of their gratitude and affection, a testimonial purchased (I may say) by the united contributions of every pupil now a member of this school, and one which we hope you will consider as worthy of your acceptance as we know you to be deserving of it? To yourself, Sir, and to scholars, the comprehensive brevity of the Latin inscription would sufficiently indicate by what feelings we are actuated in offering it to your acceptance; but, Sir, however incompetent to the task, I feel myself called upon on this occasion, and before this assembly, to advert somewhat more fully to the circumstances which seem peculiarly to establish your claim on our gratitude. You are quitting us, Sir, after an almost unexampled length of laborious service of thirty-eight years. In that period you have raised this royal foundation from a state of comparative insignificance and obscurity to that of high rank and reputation which it may at present claim among the public institutions of the country. You have covered the very walls of your school with the records of the successful exertions of your former pupils in both Universities, and we presume to hope that the spirit which you have infused will not be extinguished by your retirement, but that there may still be found among ourselves some to emulate the acquirements of our predecessors, and repay your cares and those of your successor by the attainment of equal honour. We believe, Sir, that we could express no sentiment more gratifying to yourself than the assurance of our cordial and respectful acceptance of that successor. He has long lived in the annals of the school as one of its most eminent and successful scholars, and we congratulate you, Sir, on your handing over the institution which you have renovated to one so competent to pursue your plans and uphold it in the reputation which you have established. Although, therefore, we cannot but feel that in your departure, and that of the excellent partner of your cares, we are deprived of an affectionate superintendence, only less than paternal, we should do ill to indulge in any selfish regrets; rather we would rejoice in the knowledge that your prolonged labours are about to be rewarded by an appointment to an eminent station in the Church, alike honourable to those in whom the appointment rested and to yourself, and perhaps still more in the gratifying expectation that, though in a different sphere, you may still be enabled, as Visitor, to watch over the interest of those whose welfare, as a master, you have always so cordially promoted. Should this, however, not be the case, should the episcopal arrangements remove you to a more distant diocese, we may still hope that your position in the immediate vicinity of the Cambridge University will, in some degree, tend to preserve your connection with this foundation. But, Sir, I have too long trespassed upon you; accept this memorial from your pupils at my hands, and pardon—as I trust they will pardon—my inadequate expression of their feeling.'

"Mr. Marsh then delivered to Dr. Butler a massive silver candelabrum, value three hundred guineas, the manufacture of Messrs. Rundell & Bridge—the subject a Vine Branch with Genii pressing the Fruit.

"The Venerable Archdeacon Butler said:

"'My dear Pupils, I am at a loss for words to thank you as I ought for this splendid mark of your affection, a gift of great intrinsic value, but which is enhanced beyond expression by the kindness with which it is conveyed to me; and I regret that neither my health nor my feelings on this occasion permit me to thank you as I could wish. Of this, however, be assured, that in whatever station I may be placed, nothing will ever be more gratifying to me than to reflect on the affectionate kindness you have shown me on this occasion, on the good discipline which I leave behind me, and on the generous ambition and love of learning which I am sure many of you possess.

"'My endeavour has been to educate you, and all who have gone before you, in the principles of true religion and sound learning. In regard to the former, I have the comfort of reflecting that I have supplied the Church with many valuable ministers, and that few of my contemporaries have sent more tutors to colleges or masters to preside over schools.

"'With regard to learning, you have the walls of that school in which you are accustomed to see me, covered, as you may observe, with a splendid list of names of those who have gone before you, distinguished by the highest academic honours in both Universities, and I doubt not you will endeavour to tread in their steps. I trust, indeed, there never will be wanting within these walls a succession of ingenuous youths, fired with noble emulation, to imitate those who have gone before them; and that such of you, my dear pupils, as are about to go to College, and those of your schoolfellows who are now pursuing their education there, will take good care to fill up the vacancies that still remain on the last blank board, and thus oblige my successor to undertake the pleasing task of beginning his career with tables in another apartment. Let me, however, observe to you, that of near one hundred and twenty first-rate honours recorded on those boards, your future Head-Master and his

Dr. Butler's Last Speech-day

brothers claim more than one-sixth, and himself more than one-twelfth for his own individual share. Under him and his able coadjutor, and my long-tried and much-valued friends the Assistant Masters, may you pursue your career with the same success as those who have gone before you; and to my most affectionate wishes for your welfare and happiness, let me add, as my last official words, " Floreat Salopia! " ' "

The Speeches and Speakers were as follows:

1. COPE — The Grove of the Druids.—Lucan, iii, 399.
2. J. BATHER — Buckingham going to Execution.—Shakespeare.
3. MORSE — Providence avenging Guilt.—Cicero, *Milo*.
4. BARSTOW — Galgacus to the Britons.—Tacitus, *Agricola*.
5. E. BATHER — Agricola to the Romans.—Tacitus, *Agricola*.
6. ROTHERY — Cassius on Caesar's Greatness.—Shakespeare, *Julius Caesar*.
7. FOULKES — Descent of Orpheus.—Virgil, *Georg. IV*.
8. MUNRO — Sheridan against Hastings.—Sheridan.
9. THRING — Catiline to the Conspirators.—Sallust, *B. C.*
10. MACNAB — Pitt's Reply to Walpole.—Earl of Chatham.
11. E. LEVIEN — Sir Balaam.—Pope.
12. CARR — Ellen and Fitz-James.—*Lady of the Lake*.
13. CASE — The Revellers.—Mrs. Hemans.
14. BLAND — Brutus to the Romans.—Shakespeare, *Julius Caesar*.
15. LONSDALE — Antony on the Death of Caesar.—Shakespeare, *Julius Caesar*.
16. MARSH — Greek Funeral Lament.—Mrs. Hemans.
17. FRASER — Apollo Belvedere.—Milman.
18. SALE — Marino Faliero's Dying Speech.—Byron.

Rank in the School

MARSH.	COPE.	BLAND.	SALE.
MUNRO.	MACNAB.		BARSTOW.
FRASER.	ROTHERY.	MORSE.	E. LEVIEN.
CASE.	J. BATHER.	FOULKES.	CARR.
THRING.	LONSDALE.	E. BATHER.	

Distribution of the Prizes

Pelham Prizes

Latin Verse	20 Guineas	GEORGE GILPIN.
Greek Iambics	10 Guineas	FRANCIS FRANCE.

Trustees' Prize

Latin Essay	20 Guineas	FRANCIS FRANCE.

Assistant Masters' Prize

Latin Translation	10 Guineas	J. G. LONSDALE.

Head-Master's Prizes

Latin Essay (extra prize). Aristophanes, 5 vols., 8vo.
                J. MYNORS BRIGHT.
Greek Iambics (extra prize). Tacitus, 5 vols., 8vo.
                H. AUG. MARSH.
First in Examination. Ernesti's Cicero, 8 vols., 8vo.
                FRANCIS FRANCE.
Second in Examination. Livy, 5 vols., 8vo. H. AUG. MARSH.

Dr. Butler in his reply to the Recorder's speech said that he could not desire to leave the school in better hands, nor, he continued, "as I must in justice say, with a set of better disposed, more studious, or more promising boys in it." Let me take the boys whose names appear on the foregoing page as at the head of the school, and trace their careers as far as I have been able to ascertain them.

The list does not profess to be a complete one. It gives the rank of the several speakers in the school, but omits the names of three boys who did not speak. These were Francis France (then head boy), who was suffering from a painful disfigurement which had broken out on his lips and made him keep much out of sight; Mesac Thomas, who came next after Foulkes, but whose strong Welsh accent may perhaps have been the reason why no speech was set down for him; and E. Montagu, who stood between Thomas and E. Bather.

Dr. Butler's Last Speech-day

1. FRANCE, F., had been long under Dr. Butler. Left Shrewsbury and went into residence at St. John's, Cambridge, October 1836. Senior Classic 1840. Many years Full Tutor, President of the College, and Archdeacon of Ely.
2. MARSH, H. A., went to Shrewsbury in 1831, and left Midsummer 1836. He was prevented by illness from going in for the Classical Tripos, but was elected to a Fellowship at Trinity in the same year. He was for many years Vicar of Tuxford, Notts. Still living.
3. MUNRO, H. A. J., went to Shrewsbury in 1833, left October 1838. Second Classic and Senior Chancellor's Medallist 1842. Afterwards Professor of Latin at the University of Cambridge.
4. FRASER, J., went to Shrewsbury from under Dr. Rowley at Bridgnorth in 1834, left October 1836. Ireland University Scholar 1839. Fellow of Oriel, and afterwards Bishop of Manchester.
5. CASE, W. A., went to the Schools from his father's school in Shrewsbury 1830, left in 1836, but did not go either to Oxford or Cambridge. M.A. Lond. 1842. Elected Fellow of University College (Lond.) 1845. An excellent Scholar, and highly successful Schoolmaster. Some time Vice-Master of University College School (Lond.).
6. THRING, H., went to Shrewsbury in 1831, left, I believe, October 1837. Third in the First Class of the Classical Tripos 1841. Afterwards raised to the Peerage. Still living.
7. COPE, E. M., was at Shrewsbury in 1833, and left October 1837. Senior Classic 1841.
8. MACNAB did not graduate at either Oxford or Cambridge. He adopted his father's profession and practised as a medical man, but I have been unable to trace him.
9. ROTHERY, H. C. I do not know in what year he went to Shrewsbury, but he was a year and a half in the sixth before Dr. Butler left, and left when he did. He was 10th Wrangler in 1840, and afterwards Commissioner of Wrecks.

10. BATHER, J., was many years at Shrewsbury under Dr. Butler, and left October 1837. He was second in the First Class of Classical Tripos 1841. A much respected landowner and Magistrate near Shrewsbury.
11. LONSDALE, J. G., was an excellent scholar, but for some reason or other took no degree at the right time for taking honours. Now living as Canon and Chancellor of Lichfield Cathedral.
12. BLAND, G. D. I have not been able to trace him, beyond the fact that he went to Trinity, Cambridge, and graduated in 1841.

The foregoing were the twelve praepostors. Of the remaining boys who I learn from my cousin Archdeacon Lloyd were in the sixth form,

13. MORSE, F., left in 1837. He was seventh in the First Class of the Classical Tripos 1842. Afterwards Vicar of St. Mary's, Nottingham, Prebendary of Lincoln, and Chaplain to the Bishop of Lincoln. One of the most impressive preachers of his time.
14. FOULKES, E. S. I do not know when he entered. He left presumably in 1837, took a Second Class Lit. Hum. in 1841, wrote many learned and valuable theological works, seceded to Rome, returned to the Church of England, and died Vicar of St. Mary's, Oxford.
15. THOMAS, MESAC, left October 1836. Graduated in 1840, and was appointed Bishop of Goulburn 1863.
16. MONTAGU, E. W., was a Senior Optime, and in the Second Class of the Classical Tripos 1842. Still living as Rector of Kettlestone, near Fakenham.
17. BATHER, E., was many years at Shrewsbury. Left in 1836. Took a First Class Lit. Hum. in 1840. Afterwards Rector of Meole Brace, near Shrewsbury. Died early.
18. SALE, C. J. A most popular boy and admirable actor, both tragic and comic. Third Class Lit. Hum. 1840. Now living as Rector of Holt in Worcestershire.

Dr. Butler's Last Speech-day [1836]

19. BARSTOW, T. I., was many years at Shrewsbury under Dr. Butler. He was fourth in the Second Class of the Classical Tripos 1842. For many years a most respected and popular London Magistrate.
20. LEVIEN, E. I know nothing of him but that he was long an assistant in the MS. department of the British Museum. Levien edited a good many school books in " Weale's Series " (*Athenaeum*, 24th October 1896). See also *Bibl. Cornub.* of Boase and Courtney.
21. CARR I have been unable to trace. I doubt his having been actually in the Sixth Form.

Gilpin and Mynors Bright, whose names appear as prizemen, had just left the school. Gilpin went to Oxford, where I am told he was seized with a religious mania and burned his books, but I cannot vouch for the truth of this story. Mynors Bright headed the Second Class of the Classical Tripos in 1840. He was a most useful Fellow of Magdalene, Cambridge, where he continued to reside for many years, and is well known as the editor of Pepys's Diary.

To one of the twenty-three boys above-named, but I do not know to which, I was told by Dr. Welldon that on bidding him good-bye Dr. Butler said he had every confidence that he would do well in after-life—" but," he added, " you must avoid the particle ἄν."

I should no doubt be able to date the entry and departure of all these boys but for the loss of the last of the four volumes in which Dr. Butler entered all the salient facts concerning the progress while under his charge, and the subsequent careers, of all his boys from the commencement of his Head Mastership. Three of these volumes exist in the possession of Archdeacon Lloyd, to whom I am indebted for much of the foregoing information. It is believed that the fourth volume was left at Shrewsbury for the guidance of Dr. Kennedy, but this has never been positively ascertained. Dr. Butler also chronicled all the principal events that took place in the school. I found a paper dated 21st October 1828, relating to some boyish absurd conduct of three of his most brilliant pupils. The first page of this paper is numbered 273, and is now in the British Museum; but I found none of the preceding 272 pages. I mention this as showing the minuteness with which Dr. Butler noted everything that threw light on the individual character of his boys.

Returning to the careers of those whom he left as his head boys, I would ask, Is it likely that any other school of the time can show a greater, if indeed an equal measure of success? Granted that the education of these boys was completed by Dr. Kennedy; but could Dr. Kennedy have done what he did if he had been at any other school than one in which the spirit infused by Dr. Butler was still living? I mean no word of disparagement to Dr. Kennedy; I was six years at Shrewsbury under him, and from the bottom of my heart can say that he treated me with great forbearance—far more than I deserved. He lost nothing of what he found at Shrewsbury save only numbers; and this loss, as I have already said, was due to causes in no way connected with himself. Nevertheless I cannot think that he could have done at Harrow what he so brilliantly achieved at Shrewsbury. He was several years at Harrow, but I have never heard that he sent thence even one pupil who was at all eminent in scholarship. I do him no injustice when I say that it was because he found Shrewsbury in so sound a state that he was able, to his lasting credit, to keep it so—and that with for many years hardly a third of the number of boys that Dr. Butler left him. I sometimes hear it said at Shrewsbury Dinners and School Speeches that the school was rough. I do not doubt it. It was rough in my time; our beds and our board were identical with what they were under Dr. Butler, but I can truly say that I remember no complaints. If it was rough, it does not seem to have been rough enough to do anybody any harm; at all events it was robust, and free from either priggishness or blackguardism. I have never felt that I should have done better anywhere else. If I were not a Shrewsbury man, I would be one. Dr. Butler had left exactly twelve years before I went to Shrewsbury; if there had been any marked change of system or discipline I am confident I should have known of it. There was none, and it is precisely because Dr. Kennedy had the wisdom to make none that he was able to surpass his predecessor in the proportion of his academic successes.

One word more before I close my account of Dr. Butler's career at Shrewsbury. His spirit has never left it. If I were asked what I flattered myself upon as being the pre-eminent virtues of Shrewsbury, I should say sincerity, downrightness, hatred of sham, love of work, and a strong sense of duty. What little of these noble qualities I dare pretend to, I owe hardly more to my parents than to the school at which they placed me, nor do I believe that Shrewsbury would have possessed them in the measure in which they certainly existed among my own schoolfellows but for the deep impress of Dr. Butler's masculine and sagacious character. That the impress has not been dimmed by those who have succeeded him is my firm and comfortable belief. That it never may be dimmer than it now is, is my fervent hope; and so let me repeat the last words of Dr. Butler as Head Master—*Floreat Salopia*!

CHAPTER THIRTY: APPOINTMENT TO LICHFIELD AND COVENTRY

Correspondence, 6th June 1836–24th August 1836, An Episcopal Judgement, Correspondence, 31st August 1836–4th October 1836, Presentation of a Service of Plate by Dr. Butler's Former Pupils

HENCEFORWARD TO THE END OF DR. Butler's life my work will consist of little else than Dr. Butler's episcopal correspondence. His tenure of the see was without history save for the severance of his diocese in 1837, to which attention will be called in due course. I have already stated the principle by which I shall be guided in my selection of the letters to be published, but would add that many of the most at once typical and fatherly have been omitted as being of a nature that might cause pain to surviving relatives.

To a Clergyman

June 6th, 1836.

"SIR, I cannot at present say whether I shall be placed at Lichfield or elsewhere, but as I apprehend if I should be at Lichfield you intend to bring some charge before me, I trust I need hardly observe to you that any private correspondence on the subject previously to my hearing it is contrary to those principles which I doubt not you as well as myself respect in dealing out even-handed justice. I have had now two letters from you, and not the slightest communication from Mr. Meredith or Mr. Sandford. As to any right I may have of hearing the case, even should I be placed at Lichfield, I am at present quite ignorant. I do not know the constitution of the school, or the powers of the Bishop over it. What the late diocesan stated to you is perfectly correct respecting the limitation of the powers of Bishops. But such is the law of the land, to which they are bound to submit, they can only administer it as they find it, and to whatever see I may be appointed I trust my administration of it as a Bishop will be found as impartial as a desire to do right can make it.

"In these observations you will have the goodness to consider me as giving no opinion, but merely stating the line of conduct which I think we ought mutually to pursue, that your

appeal, if it should turn out that I have a right to hear it, and my decision upon hearing it, may be free from any possible imputation on either of us. I remain, Sir, your very obedient servant,
"S. BUTLER."

On 13th June 1836 Lord Melbourne wrote appointing Dr. Butler to the See of Lichfield and Coventry.

From John Herford, Esq.

Manchester, June 20th, 1836.

"MY LORD BISHOP, Although I am sensible of the small value which can attach to any expression of the feelings of so unimportant a person as myself, I cannot resist the desire of assuring you the high gratification I experienced at the confirmation Saturday's *Gazette* afforded of an appointment which does far more honour to those from whom it has proceeded than to the distinguished individual upon whom it has been conferred.

"Although a Dissenter, I earnestly desire to see the Church of England placed upon a basis which shall secure it from all danger and render it truly a national Church. I sincerely rejoice therefore at every circumstance which tends to its prosperity and to its increased usefulness and popularity, and nothing appears to me better calculated to effect this object than the appointment of those to its highest offices who are alike distinguished for harmony, liberality, and a constitutional regard for the rights and liberties of the people. Let a fair proportion of the dignitaries of the Church be found amongst the supporters of a popular Government, friendly to the advancement of knowledge, and promoters of every scheme having for its object the real welfare and happiness of the people, and there will soon be an end of the absurd desire for their removal from the House of Lords. Living as I do amongst the Dissenters, and well acquainted with their views and feelings, I have no hesitation in saying that the Church has far less to apprehend from their hostility than from the mistaken zeal of its professed friends.

"The day is gone by when religious establishments might depend alone upon their antiquity and splendour. All institutions are now tested by their utility, and can only be maintained by their conformity with the spirit of the age, and the wants and feelings of the people.

"Your Lordship will I trust excuse these remarks, offered in a spirit of profound respect for yourself and of sincere anxiety for the permanence and increasing usefulness of that Church of which you are so distinguished an ornament. In the hope that you may live many years to strengthen and adorn it, and that your high reputation may advance as your sphere of honour and usefulness becomes more extended, I remain, my Lord Bishop, very respectfully yours,
"JOHN HERFORD."

From Mrs. Butler

June 23rd, 1836.

"MY DEAR BISHOP, I am endeavouring to collect my scattered senses to enable me to send you my affectionate congratulations upon your new honours. I went over Eccleshall yesterday, with less fatigue than I could have supposed. I have been over to the schools, and found everything as backward as possible. I think if Kennedy does not come down to see after the workmen himself, he will never be ready for the boys against they return. Though it is his concern, not mine, I cannot help being worried about it. I have sent to Trail this morning, to beg he will write to Mr. Kennedy. I have had a very pleasant visit to Langar.

"You cannot think what a lovely grandchild[1] you have; he is only waiting for you to christen him after yourself."

From the Bishop of Durham (Dr. Maltby)
(Original in possession of A. R. Malden, Esq.)

28, Curzon Street, June 29th, 1836.

"Who could look into the Book of Fate, and conjecture that, when you and I were dining with Lord Berwick forty-four years ago, we should go to Court on the same day, you for the See of

---
[1] The present Editor.

Lichfield, I for that of Durham? I am sure you are thankful, as I am, to a gracious Providence who has thus been pleased to notice (beyond *my* deserts) our honesty and independence.

"Now to business. Do you go to Court alone? If you do, will you take my son, who is not going to the Levee, but wishes to see the humours of it, as my Chaplain attending me when I do homage?

"My reason for asking is, that Lord John Russell has offered to call for me in his carriage; therefore I shall have mine to come for me, but not to carry me. Lord John is to call for me quarter before two; therefore if you set off at two you will be in good time.

"If you prefer that my carriage shall take you and him, we can squeeze home together, as my son's spareness will not make him a great addition to the weight and robes of two Bishops.

"Pray send me a frank of yours to Mrs. A. Urquhart, St. Colme Street, Edinburgh; and if you want one of mine to Mrs. Butler or any of your family to-day or to-morrow you shall have it.

"Wishing you an increase of health to enjoy your well-merited honours, I am, my dear Bishop, yours most sincerely,
" E. DUNELM.

"I think you should put on your two cards:

BISHOP OF LICHFIELD *elect*,
on his appointment.
Presented by Lord Melbourne (I suppose).

Remember, that is *extra metrum*."

Dr. Butler was consecrated 3rd July 1836 at Lambeth, by the Archbishop of Canterbury, assisted by the Bishops of Durham, Lincoln, and Bristol.

To a Clergyman

Pulteney Hotel, Albemarle Street, July 9th, 1836.

"DEAR SIR, I have only been two days in possession of my full episcopal functions; you will therefore, I hope, not consider my delay in answering your letter as attributable to any neglect.

"Previous to that time your petition has been the subject of my serious consideration, and that of older and more experienced Bishops than myself, whom I have consulted—it being an object of the greatest importance with me, although very desirous of complying with your wishes, not to make a false step in so important a matter as granting licences of non-residence to a pluralist in two livings.

"One thing appears certain, that it will be impossible for me to grant the licences without an augmentation of the salaries of each of the curates. I am aware that you were instituted to each of these livings before 1813, but I must have a strong justifying ground before I can grant the licences required, and I can find no stronger than that. Will you therefore let me know, with the least possible delay, when you are disposed to grant this? Marston has a population of about a thousand, and the stipend is even below the lowest sum allowed by the Act of 1813.

"Longford is a widely scattered parish, with a population not short of thirteen hundred. The surplice fees at either parish must be very small.

"I would also beg the favour of your stating in what the inconvenience of the houses to receive your family consists; for instance, what may be the number of rooms in the houses, and the number requisite by your own family.

"Had you been instituted after 1813, I believe that the full amount of stipend which I might have required for each of your curates would have been £150. I propose, however, that you should add £20 to each, making Marston £90 and Longford £100 per annum. Under such circumstances, and a more specific account of the inconveniences of the houses for your residence, which I consider as necessary for my justification, I shall be happy to grant you the licences required, in the hope that your residence so near as Sudbury will enable you occasionally to perform some of the . . ."

(No more drafted.—ED.)

Correspondence

From Lord Melbourne

South Street, July 13th, 1836.

"MY DEAR LORD, I am much concerned to hear of your illness. Do not make yourself uneasy about the House of Lords. There has been nothing here to make your presence necessary. Take care of yourself and attend to Sir Henry. He called upon me the other morning and repeated some of his Latin verses, which appeared to me good, but an Etonian ear does not like *Videbo Deum* for the end of a pentameter. We always avoided using these final *o*'s as short syllables, and, according to my recollection, it is very unusual in Virgil, Ovid, and the *Odes* of Horace.

"Yours faithfully,
                                        "MELBOURNE."

Sir Henry Halford had been turning "I know that my Redeemer liveth" into Latin elegiacs.

To a Clergyman

Pulteney Hotel, Albemarle Street, July 15th, 1836.

"REV. SIR, Though you are personally unknown to me, I have always heard you spoken of in such high terms that I address you on rather a painful subject in the fullest confidence.

"Mr. — called on me yesterday to inquire when I should hold my next ordination, telling me that he had from you the promise of the curacy of Montford, and signifying his intention of offering himself for Deacon's Orders. He seemed much surprised at hearing that there had been an ordination at Lichfield on the 3rd of this month, when the Bishop of Bangor ordained at the request of the Archbishop; but as I got further into conversation with him he appeared to me to have formed a very low estimate of the requisites for ordination and the deep importance, not only of due preparation in point of learning, but in the examination of his own heart as to his fitness for the sacred office for which he is a candidate, and the devotedness of his life to fulfil its duties.

"He was once my pupil at Shrewsbury—not remarkable there

for assiduity. On my telling him, among other papers that would be requisite, that it would be necessary for him to have a college testimonial, he told me that this would be of no use, as his tutor had left and the dean was dead, and nobody could tell anything about him. This appeared to me strange language for a candidate to use to his Bishop, and I replied that all Bishops require a college testimonial as a *sine qua non*, and that he had better write and procure it. As he was going out he met my secretary, Mr. Burder, with whom he returned, Burder having told him precisely what I had said on the subject. On his coming to me a second time he said he must confess to me that he could not obtain a college testimonial, that Mr. Hughes, the tutor, had shown him great unkindness (I rather think he called it spite), and that unfortunately Mr. Jones, the dean, having rooms adjoining his, every little noise in his rooms was noted far more severely than it ought to be by Mr. Jones. He then showed me a part of Mr. Hughes's letter, which satisfied me that he had been extremely irregular in college, and that it was quite impossible for Mr. Hughes to advise the college to pass his testimonials. Mr. Hughes and Mr. Jones were both very well known to me, and I am confident that neither of these gentlemen would do an unkind thing. Mr. — pressed me to say at once whether I would admit him to orders without a testimonial or not, that he might know whether it would be 'worth his while' to read for orders or not, and said he had been reading very hard for them. I was not a little shocked at the levity of this remark, but was consequently induced to ask him how long he had been reading hard; whereon he replied, Two months.

"I told him I had a letter lying before me at the moment from a man of high family who appeared of a very different spirit, and who had been reading with an excellent clergyman for two years.

"I must say that there was much in Mr. —'s manner and replies which gave me pain and made me entertain strong doubts of his fitness to be admitted into our sacred profession. The complaints in Mr. Hughes's letter were more than once of intoxication, and I am so well persuaded that you would not knowingly recommend a candidate for orders who was not likely to do credit to your recommendation that I write to inquire whether you promised him the title from the representations of a common friend, or whether from your own knowledge you can vouch for his having laid aside all those habits which appear to have induced the college to refuse him a testimonial. I both make the inquiry and await your answer in strict confidence.

"If you can speak favourably of him from your own knowledge I shall send for him again and have some further conversation with him, that I may judge how far it may be expedient to admit him as a candidate at my next examination (for which even the four months and a half which will elapse from the time when he began his studies some two months ago will be but a very short preparation) or to allow him to offer himself at a future period. It would be painful to reject an old pupil at an examination for orders, but in so serious a duty there is no room for ill-placed indulgence. I remain, Rev. Sir, your faithful servant,

"S. LICH. & COV."

To the Rev. Jeremiah Walker, Long Itchington, Southam

Draft undated: August 1st, 1836.
See Mr. Walker's answer.

"REV. SIR, It is with great regret that I must inform you of a letter I have received from the Rev. James Monkhouse Knott, the Vicar of Wormleighton, enclosing a handbill with his signature and some other documents which contain a heavy charge against you—namely, that of purchasing poles, of having had them cut up into bludgeons, and of distributing these among your parishioners to take to the late election for South Warwickshire.

"It is my duty before I proceed further in this matter to acquaint you with this accusation, and to express my readiness to receive your answer, and my hope that it may be satisfactory. Your reply will find me as above. I remain, Rev. Sir, your obedient servant,

"S. LICH. & COV."

The handbill above referred to was as follows:

Wormleighton Vicarage, Monday, June 27th, 1836.

"*To the Clergy of the Southam District of the Southern Division of the County of Warwick, and the friends of the Rev. Jeremiah Walker, Curate of Long Itchington.*

"GENTLEMEN, As a zealous supporter of that party which has no other object in view than the Correction of Abuses in our various Institutions, and the general prosperity and Welfare of the *United* Kingdom, I cannot pass by a case of such enormous Wickedness as that in which the REV. CURATE of LONG ITCHINGTON stands charged as the PRIME MOVER; I mean the Purchasing of Poles, having them converted into BLUDGEONS, and attempting to hire Ruffians to use them against their Fellow Creatures; if not with intent to Murder, certainly to intimidate.

"Now I frankly assure you, that unless the REV. GENTLEMAN shows his contrition, by a Public expression of Regret for so doing, I pledge myself (in the absence of a Bishop) to bring his conduct before the Arch-Bishop. I am, Gentlemen, your most obedient humble servant,

"JAMES MONKHOUSE KNOTT,
"*Vicar of Wormleighton.*"

On the receipt of the foregoing letter and handbill Dr. Butler made inquiries from the Rev. T. B. Bromfield, a neighbouring magistrate, and received a letter detailing the facts as they will appear presently, and at the same time expressing great respect for both parties to the dispute, each of whom he knew well as hardworking clergymen, very much liked in their own parishes and in the neighbourhood. Mr. Walker he signalizes more especially as a man of "peaceable and benevolent disposition."

Dr. Butler then wrote to the High Sheriff, and, after stating the contentions of the two parties, concluded by saying:

"Under such contradictory statements I feel it my duty to request a sight of the bludgeons, poles, or wood, seized by the Under Sheriff, which I presume remain in his custody, and as I shall be at Kenilworth in the course of Saturday, August 27th, I shall esteem it a favour if you will order him to exhibit them to me when I call, which will probably be about twelve o'clock, or earlier. In the meantime, if you would take the trouble to give me a short account of the facts of the case, I should feel much obliged to you. I conclude of course that Mr. Knott and Mr. Walker are on opposite sides, and should be glad to learn the facts from less interested and less prejudiced authority. I trust no bludgeons were actually used, at least I infer so both from Mr. Knott and Mr. Walker's letter. I have the honour to be, Mr. High Sheriff, your obedient and faithful servant,

"S. LICH. & COV.

" An answer will find me at Eccleshall Castle."

To this the Sheriff replied in due course, promising to send the report of the Under Sheriff at the earliest possible moment, and to procure that the bludgeons should be brought for Dr. Butler's inspection. The Under Sheriff's report was as follows:

Sheriff's Office, Warwick, August 24th, 1836.

" An information in writing having been lodged in my office by two very respectable gentlemen complaining that the Rev. Mr. Walker of Long Itchington had employed his clerk, named Isaacs, to make bludgeons for the purpose of the Election, and that he had engaged several men at 7s. 6d. per day to go to Southam, one of the polling places, with them, and the gentlemen having at the same time stated that they had personally inquired into the matters complained of and that they were true, I considered it my duty (acting as the representative of the highest civil authority in the county, on whom the responsibility would rest if any riot or disturbance took place at Southam) to proceed at once to Mr. Walker. This was on the Friday preceding the Election. I found him at home, and told him the purpose of my visit, and requested him to accompany me to Isaacs to ascertain whether my information was correct, and in that case to use his influence to induce Isaacs to deliver them up to me. I added that, in the event of Isaacs doing so, it was not my purpose to inquire by whom or by whose order they were made, and that having them once in my possession my interference would cease. He at once refused to go with me, and stated it to be his firm conviction that it was altogether a fabrication and without the slightest foundation, and he wondered how and where such a 'scandalous report' could have originated. This he repeated many times in reply to my earnest requests that he would go with me, and he stated many times that he did not believe I should find anything of the sort at Isaacs'. My pressing him so much made him at last say that I appeared to doubt his word. I then proceeded to Isaacs and asked him if he had been making any bludgeons or staves; he said he had. I blamed him for doing so, and he replied, 'I was against it at first, but I was ordered to make them.' I inquired by whom, and he said Mr. Walker. I requested to have them, and he consented, saying he should be glad to get rid of them. I asked him where they were, and he said he had hid them by Mr. Walker's orders the evening before. He took me to an outbuilding, and took part from a loft and part from under a quantity of straw. He carried them out himself and placed them in the car. Just as I was leaving his door Mr. Walker came up, and I at once reminded him that he had stated his disbelief in the information, and he replied, 'Dear me, sir, you don't suppose those things' (pointing to the staves) 'could have been made for the Election; they might be used for hurdles.' I said it was of no consequence what they might be used for, as I had the clerk's assurance that they were made for the Election and by his order. He said Isaacs must be mistaken. I called Isaacs and in the presence of Mr. Walker asked him who ordered them, and he said again Mr. Walker; and that they were made for the Election, and that Mr. Shirley was to pay for them, as Mr. Walker had told him. Mr. Walker remonstrated with me then for removing them, saying they were Isaacs' property. I said I was determined to remove them, whereon he asked me not to take them, as it would make a great noise in the neighbourhood, and do injury to him and Isaacs. I then reminded him that all exposure would have been avoided if he had complied with my original request; but having found such things, and it being my duty to suppress everything tending to create disorder and riot at the Election, I was bound to remove them to a place of safety, and so prevent their being used.

An Episcopal Judgement

"The other part of the charge, relating to the hiring of men at 7s. 6d. per day, I did not inquire into, considering that having secured the weapons themselves no danger was to be apprehended, but I informed Isaacs that if any of the men I had heard of were seen at Southam I should have them taken into custody.

"THOMAS HEATH, UNDER SHERIFF."

Judgement
August 29th, 1836.

"At the Coventry Visitation, the Bishop having summoned Mr. Knott and Mr. Walker, in the presence of the Chancellor of the Diocese, the Archdeacon of Coventry, Mr. Bromfield, a magistrate, Mr. Biddulph, and Mr. —, friends of Mr. Walker and Mr. Knott, addressed them as follows:

"'I have received and carefully investigated the charges brought by Mr. Knott against Mr. Walker, together with the answer of Mr. Walker thereto, and I am highly dissatisfied with both. Under the very peculiar circumstances in which I am placed, at the very eve of relinquishing this part of my diocese, I feel that although I ought not to shrink from a duty which has been imposed upon me by Mr. Knott's appeal to the Archbishop, and by his Grace's reference to me, yet that I ought not to follow up the consequences as if I were to continue in the uninterrupted possession of my episcopal powers. With regard to Mr. Knott's charges against Mr. Walker, and the mode in which he has chosen to give them publicity, I can never sufficiently lament the want of consideration he has shown for the true interests of his profession, the honour of which a clergyman does not vindicate by bringing a charge against a brother-clergyman (even supposing it to be ever so well founded) in so intemperate a shape.

"'With regard to Mr. Walker, with great grief I say it, I am far from satisfied with his defence.

"'I observe that thirty-three rods, or wands, or whatever he may please to call them, were provided. I observe that there were in all fifty-eight persons who voted in the parish of Long Itchington. I observe further that of the fifty-eight only twenty-two voted on the side he espoused. He could therefore want at the most but twenty-two wands, supposing each voter was to be conducted by a separate assistant; but when I deduct the voters on his side who came from London, from Northampton, and other distant parts, I can find the voters actually in the parish of Long Itchington on his side to amount in all only to thirteen.

"'For these, wood for thirty-three staves or wands to be borne by assistants was provided. On comparing the rods or wands or staves to be borne by these assistants with those usually borne by Sheriffs or Under Sheriffs, benefit societies, and the like, which Mr. Walker states them to resemble, I find this material difference—that the wands borne by Sheriffs and Under Sheriffs, etc., are almost constantly made of deal, and so, I believe, are those borne by the conductors of benefit societies. I have examined and carefully measured these various staves or wands. I find that borne by the Under Sheriff, which I believe to be similar to that borne by the High Sheriff and other officers, to be a thin wand of deal, a mere badge of office, of about an inch and a half in circumference at the thickest end, tapering to an ending, and totally incapable of being used as a weapon of offence or defence. There are about twelve smaller and twenty-one larger wands or staves, not of deal, but ash, provided by Mr. Walker. Of these a few are peeled, and measure in that state on the average three and a half inches in circumference; the remainder of these, not so prepared, measure about four and a half inches. But the larger poles, all of which appear to be unprepared, being twenty-one in number, measure from six to six and a half inches in circumference; and all these, especially the twenty-one larger, are capable of being used as offensive or defensive weapons. But, on the other hand, I must observe that of each description of these none are cut in half, which would make them much more dangerous weapons than in their present state, and that none are either in the shape of bludgeons, or were actually used, and it is also stated to me that Mr. Walker had disavowed his intention of using any. These circumstances operate to a certain degree in his favour, and though I cannot acquit him of great indiscretion, in having thought of such a mode of taking voters from his parish to the poll, I cannot go the length of imputing to him those evil intentions which are insinuated in the handbill published by Mr. Knott.

"'I therefore content myself with censuring Mr. Walker for his want of discretion, and admonishing him to be more circumspect on any future occasion. At the same time I must express my deep regret that Mr. Knott should have thought it necessary or becoming to bring a charge against him in so public and unusual a way, and cannot but express my disapprobation of the course which he has adopted, as little likely to vindicate " the cloth," as he expresses it, " from so shameful a stain," or to promote the reputation of the clergy or the interests of the Church.

"'In conclusion, as both these gentlemen appear to me to have mistaken their respective duties, I would earnestly press upon them the best reparation they can make to the interests of the Church and to each other, by mutually forgetting all past grievances, and real or imaginary causes of offence, and studying to live in peace and harmony with their neighbours and with each other. They are both, as I am told, attentive and diligent parochial ministers. In that legitimate sphere of duty they will find abundant opportunities of redeeming their past error by active and useful exertion.'"

CORRESPONDENCE, 31ST AUGUST 1836—4TH OCTOBER 1836

From a Clergyman

August 31st, 1836.

" MY LORD, About six years ago two paupers (a male and female), inmates of the Atcham House of Industry, who had obtained leave of absence for the day, upon their return at night presented to the Governor a certificate of their having been married on that very day, by banns at Wombridge, by Mr. —. Meeting with Mr. — shortly afterwards, I took the liberty of telling him that he had acted contrary to law in marrying the above-named parties, and that I humbly thought it would be better for him if in future he would make stricter inquiries as to the residence of parties who presented banns for publication.

"Upon my return from London this year at the end of June last, information was given me that a mere boy, an infant in law, a *bona-fide* resident in my parish of Atcham, was about to be married by *banns* at Wombridge, and that on the ensuing Sunday the banns would be published for the third time. I immediately wrote to Mr. — to acquaint him with the above circumstances, and, mentioning the boy by name, said I could take it upon myself to say that he was a *bona-fide* resident in this parish, where his banns ought to have been published, that I was positive he never had resided in Wombridge at all, and moreover that I had every reason to believe that the woman to whom he was about to be married was similarly situated, and that after this information I trusted he would not proceed to marry them.

"A short time after I met Mr. —, junior, who I believe officiates at Wombridge; he informed me that my letter had been duly received, that he had consulted with his father upon the subject of it, who had desired him to marry the parties, and therefore he was obliged to do so. Having some reason to fear that this marriage would turn out anything but well, which has unfortunately proved to be the case, I was rather annoyed to find that he had proceeded to solemnise it after the receipt of the information which I had forwarded to him, and told him that as it was the second time that the thing had been done within my limited experience, and the second time that my parishioners had been affected by it, I should certainly complain of it to the Archdeacon. This I have done, and our worthy Archdeacon said that it was a gross case, and a great deal too bad, after the receipt of my letter, and that he advised me to state the case to your Lordship prior to the commencement of your visitations. I trust, therefore, that you will accept this as my apology for troubling you thus at length.

"Mentioning the above circumstances to the clergyman of a parish adjoining to Wombridge, he told me that he considered he was annually deprived of some pounds in the way of fees by residents of his parish going to get married at Wombridge without any inquiry being made as to their residence.

"If your Lordship would be good enough to say something to Mr. — on this subject (should it be within your jurisdiction), so as to prevent Wombridge from being considered, as it now is, a sort of little Gretna Green, I do humbly venture to think that it would be of advantage to the community in checking these clandestine, foolish, and improvident marriages which but too often have been known to have taken place at Wombridge, or at any rate would put a stop to a practice which, to say the least of it, is very irregular."

Appended to this was a note in Dr. Butler's handwriting: "Spoke to Mr. —, who seems sensible of his error."

To a Clergyman

Langar, Bingham, September 11th, 1836.

"REV. SIR, In a population like Atherstone there must be two services. The canonical hour is three, but if a better attendance can be obtained, and the expense of lighting the church can be defrayed by the congregation voluntarily, I do not object to the change to six. If you give a third service it will be a gratuitous act.

"The Moravians, as far as I know, are not like the Vaudois, a poor persecuted sect, but a community flourishing under regulations calculated to preserve them in competence and prosperity.

"Why therefore should you go out of the way to advocate their cause, when there are so many objects within the pale of our own Church on which you may have to solicit the liberality of your congregation? Contributions of this sort bring the Church too near the Conventicle.

"With regard to your licence of non-residence, I am inclined to think that, as you have no cure of souls, a licence is not necessary. Your curacy was decidedly without cure of souls till augmented by Queen Anne's Bounty—was augmented by lot without any contribution from the incumbent, and therefore, I conceive, remains exactly *in statu quo*. I am, Rev. Sir, your faithful servant,

"S. LICH. & COV."

To the Archbishop of Canterbury

Langar, Bingham, September 12th, 1836.

"MY LORD, I wish to communicate with your Grace on some important particulars, which it is necessary should be known to the Ecclesiastical Commissioners, previously to their completing the scheme for severing that part of the Diocese of Lichfield and Coventry which is in Warwickshire from that See, and annexing it to the See of Worcester.

"In the Archdeaconry of Coventry, which comprehends, I believe, the whole district to be transferred, there are several charities or foundation endowments, which belong to the Clergy of the See, in its present extent, generally, or to children born within the present Diocese, of which it seems to me neither the one nor the other should be despoiled.

"There is a very valuable foundation for the widows of the Clergy of the whole Diocese, called Newton's College, in the City of Lichfield, and as this bequest was left without any alteration in the extent of the Diocese being then contemplated, it seems hard that the benefits should not be continued to the objects whom the founder designed.

"At Brazen Nose College, Oxford, there are certain fellowships to which natives of the Diocese of Lichfield and Coventry have a superior claim, of which I presume the Commissioners would think it unjust to deprive them.

"There are also innumerable trusts devolving on me, and Acts of Parliament in which I am concerned as Bishop of Lichfield and Coventry: may not these become disputable, unless care is taken in the transfer that in that part of the Diocese which is to remain with me, the same rights and powers shall be granted to the Bishop of Lichfield as were exercised by the Bishop of Lichfield and Coventry?

"There are also livings in my gift as Bishop of Lichfield and Coventry, both in and out of the severed part of the Diocese, and many charities for the poor and aged similarly circumstanced.

"The Proctors also of the Court of Lichfield, who received a great part of their emolument from Birmingham and Coventry and the severed district, are likely to suffer great loss by the separation, unless they are allowed to continue to practise in the Court of Worcester for that part of the Diocese which is to be severed from the See of Lichfield.

"I have felt it my duty to lay these circumstances before your Grace, for the information of the Ecclesiastical Commissioners, humbly and confidently looking to them for such provisions as the justice of the case may appear to require.

"With regard to the See of Lichfield itself, I am sorry to say it is likely to fall lamentably short of the income returned by the late Bishop to the Church Commissioners. The defalcation will arise from three causes:

"1st. The diminution of fines on renewals arising from the diminished value of tithes. I have already had one refusal to renew on this ground.

"2nd. The extent of endowments granted or promised by the late Bishop from the revenues of the See for the augmentation of small livings.

"3rd. The great depreciation that will take place in the value of the woods, which has already begun in part, and will most fatally increase after next year. The timber used to average near or quite £1,000 each fall. This year it will not produce £500, next year less, and I am informed by the very experienced manager of the woods, who has been employed for the last six years or so by the late Bishop, but most extensively by other great proprietors of wood land, that for the nine years ensuing they will produce scarcely anything, owing to the necessity of bringing the new system which he recommended for their management into effect. After that period, which with my present state of health I can never hope to see, they will become more valuable than ever.

"As I do not think the See will produce me more than £2,500 or at most £2,800, I hope that the Commissioners, considering I have no means of holding any preferment *in commendam*, will take this case into consideration when they increase the smaller Sees.[1]

[1] My cousin Archdeacon Lloyd, who possesses Dr. Butler's account books, has assured me that his annual expenditure as Bishop was never less than £9,500 per annum.—ED.

"With the greatest respect, I remain, my Lord, your Grace's most obedient and faithful servant,

"S. LICH. & COV.

"I am now on a visitation tour, but shall be at home on September 23rd, and at Sir H. Halford's, Wiston Hall, Leicester, from the 15th to the 18th instant inclusive.

"P.S. I have reserved for a postscript a different business. A clergyman in my diocese informs me that a Roman Catholic (of whom there are many) dying in his parish, the friends of the deceased applied to him for leave to bury the corpse in the churchyard, without any ceremonies of their own, but with the omission also of the funeral service of our Church; that he was inclined to allow this; but that subsequently they came to him and requested him to read the service as usual, which he did. As the case is likely to occur often, he asks me what he should do.

"I have told him to say, if it happens before he has any decisive answer, that whatever he may grant in such an instance must not be considered to his prejudice, should he refuse hereafter on having consulted his Bishop.

"I observe the Rubric specifies cases in which the service is *not* to be used, which exceptions are not applicable in this instance, but does it necessarily follow that it must be used in all others, though the parties interested are willing to dispense with it, substituting no formula of their own in the churchyard, as they always perform the service in the house of the deceased?

"May I beg your Grace's advice on this subject?"

From the Archbishop of Canterbury (Dr. Howley)

Addington, September 15th, 1836.

"MY DEAR LORD, I will lay your letter before the Church Commissioners at their next meeting; the particulars stated in it are important, and will, I am certain, be taken into consideration by the Board, as soon as the business which presses immediately, and which, as it involves many preliminaries, may perhaps take some time—the erection of the See of Ripon—is completed.

"In respect to your postscript, the Rubric specifies three descriptions of persons over whom the office for the burial of the dead is not to be read—unbaptised, excommunicate, and those who have laid violent hands upon themselves. In all other cases the clergyman is required to read it. The clergyman, therefore, who has applied to your Lordship was right in refusing leave to bury a corpse in the churchyard without the performance of the service, and also in reading the service over a Roman Catholic, and should continue to act in the same manner. This is in substance the advice which I received from an eminent ecclesiastical lawyer in a similar case. I remain, my dear Lord, your Lordship's faithful servant,

"W. CANTUAR."

To a Clergyman

Eccleshall Castle, September 29th, 1836.

"REV. SIR, I hardly know how to answer so singularly unprepared an appeal as that which you have sent me relative to the new pewing of Newport Church.

"There are no reports from a committee—no estimates—no grounds for the very vague calculations expressed in print, one of which is in fact founded on an illegal assumption.

"Moreover I find myself publicly advertised as a contributor without the form even of asking my consent, and I beg to say that it is very improbable, considering the numerous and more important claims on my income, that I shall be able to spare any sum whatever towards the object for which you have announced my expected donation.

"I should be very well pleased to see the church of Newport better pewed and with more accommodation in the way of pew sittings, but it is quite impossible that, with an exceedingly diminished income from the See, I can support my station in society and at the same time subscribe to every object which persons in this extensive diocese may think fit to pledge me to even without asking my consent.

"The way in which I could be of service to you would be

by supporting your cause before the Diocesan Committee, when you are enabled to send a well-digested plan for your improvements, accompanied by estimates, which, I apprehend, if properly made, will be found much below the present mere guess. Besides, it will remain to be considered even then whether Newport Church is a building which would justify the laying out so considerable an expenditure upon it. I remain, Rev. Sir, your obedient servant,

"S. LICH. & COV."

To a Clergyman

Eccleshall Castle, October 3rd, 1836.

" REV. SIR, It is my painful duty to inform you that a serious complaint was brought against you this day by the trustees of — School, who from the kind and feeling way in which they expressed themselves towards you appear to be actuated by no motive but a desire to fulfil their duty to the public, though at the expense of their private feelings.

" They allege against you frequent intoxication, neglect of duty in your own school and in your superintendence of the subordinate departments, neglect of weekly registration of the boys' conduct and improvement, neglect of your ecclesiastical duties, especially by the omission of sermons; all which charges they say they are ready to prove, but with much good feeling towards you have contented themselves merely with stating in conversation what they have to bring forward against you, should your future conduct compel them to do so.

" Now I entreat you to consider what must be the consequence, should these charges be proved against you. The trustees by their Act of Parliament have in such cases a power of dismissing you, subject to my concurrence.

" I must call them and you before me, and hear their charges and your reply, and if it should appear to me that they have made good their allegations, it will be impossible for me to refuse my consent to a measure which my public duty as well as theirs will force upon me. I cannot, I ought not, and I will not in such a case protect you.

"And let me beg you to consider the consequences. You will lose an appointment worth £250 a year to you, together with a good house rent free. Who or what is to supply this? How are you, how is your family, to be provided for and taken care of? What have you to expect but absolute poverty and ruin, with a lost character and a troubled conscience?

"Be warned therefore by my admonition while there is yet time; it is given with much kindness but with earnest seriousness, and if you slight it remember that I cannot repeat it. There is no trifling with men whom I see resolved to discharge their duty faithfully, however painfully to themselves; depend upon it, if their charges are proved to my satisfaction of your culpability, I shall feel it my duty to concur in their sentence of dismissal. They have most kindly, at my suggestion, and I believe agreeably to their own wishes, allowed me to write to you, and to grant you from now till Christmas for an opportunity of amendment. Avail yourself of it, I entreat you. Lay aside the odious and brutal habit of intemperance, disgraceful to any man, but most especially to a minister of the Gospel and a teacher of youth. A teacher! Gracious Heaven! do his precepts square with his example?

"But remember that a short amendment will be productive of no real benefit. The trustees are willing to overlook the past only on condition of permanent amendment for the future. They grant you the present opportunity only as an earnest of future and increasing diligence and sobriety. For the sake of your temporal, for the sake of your eternal welfare, avail yourself of it and be warned by the admonition of your sincere well-wisher,
"S. LICH. & COV.

"I shall send the trustees a copy of this letter."

From the Rev. W. F. Hook

Coventry, October 4th, 1836.

"MY LORD, I have again to request your Lordship's permission to administer the Sacrament of Baptism to an adult, James Smith, aged fifty-nine, of Far Gosford Street in this parish. The case is one of great interest. He has led a very wicked life, but has lately married the woman with whom he lived; he has attended church, and is most anxious to amend his ways. It is quite painful to witness the agony of his remorse. He applies for Baptism as the means of obtaining grace for the future, and especially as the means of applying to his soul a full absolution for the past. Having prayed with him to-day, I desired him to remain on his knees in secret prayer; he continued on his knees, but prayed out loud, and his prayers were beautiful and touching. He concluded with the Lord's Prayer. I thought it not necessary to interrupt him at the time, but I have prohibited him from using that prayer until he has been baptised, and he immediately perceived the propriety of not addressing God as his Father until he had been received as His adopted son in Jesus Christ. I mention these circumstances, as when I had the pleasure of seeing your Lordship you seemed to feel a particular interest in these applications for Baptism. In the course of a little time he will, I hope, be prepared for the other sacrament, which he is also anxious to receive, if your Lordship will either appoint him a time and place to wait on you for Confirmation or signify to him your willingness to dispense with his observance of that sacramental. I state this in order to save your Lordship the trouble of another letter.

"During my absence, my curate baptised a young woman of the name of Freeman, aged fifteen. Perhaps your Lordship will kindly inform me what age we are to consider a person as an adult, so far as this sacrament is concerned."

I found no draft of the answer to the foregoing letter.

I take the following from a newspaper cutting which I found among Dr. Butler's papers. The name of the paper is not indicated.

Presentation of Plate to the Lord Bishop of Lichfield

"On Thursday, the 6th of October, a Deputation of Members of the Committee for the management of the Testimonial to be presented by his late Pupils waited upon the Bishop of Lichfield and Coventry at his Lordship's residence, Eccleshall

Presentation of Plate

Castle, to present a Service of Plate which had been purchased for that purpose. The following gentlemen composed the deputation:

> Rev. B. H. Kennedy, D.D.
> E. Massie, Esq.
> P. H. S. Payne, Esq.
> Dr. Johnstone.
> Rev. E. H. Grove.
> T. Brancker, Esq.

"The Service of Plate was laid out in the dining-room, and his Lordship was then invited to wait upon the deputation, when the presentation was made by Dr. Kennedy in the following speech:

"'My Lord, We are deputed by a large body of gentlemen, formerly your Lordship's pupils at Shrewsbury School, to present you with a Service of Silver Plate, which they design to be a sincere though very inadequate testimonial of their veneration, gratitude, and love.

"'My Lord, your pupils regard you with just veneration. They behold in you the most accomplished and successful instructor of modern days. They revert to the vast difficulties you overcame, and they admire your dauntless perseverance. They can estimate the large outlay you made in improving the facilities of education at Shrewsbury School, and they laud your enterprising spirit. They take a proud delight in the fame of that school, earned by its unequalled victories in each University, and in your Lordship they recognise the founder of that fame. You found Shrewsbury School at its lowest ebb, without credit, without discipline, almost without scholars; its funds from year to year consumed by a long-pending lawsuit. You raised it to the rank of one of the largest and most flourishing schools, and (if University distinction be received as a fair test of success) the most successful school in the country. And this you did in the face of many and formidable obstacles, independent of rank and influence, unaided by the prestige of fashion. You did it by the force of learning, skill, industry, courage, and enterprise, in dependence on the Divine blessing.

You established a wise and wholesome system, all the parts of which work together in perfect harmony,—a system which creates and maintains emulation, the main-spring of youthful improvement; where advancement depends on merit alone; where industry can calculate on its sure reward, and idleness cannot avoid discouragement and disgrace. This, my Lord, and much more than this, you did for Shrewsbury School. No vain boast is it to say you found it of brick, but you left it of marble. Surely then we, who love the fostering abode of our boyhood, may express unblamed our veneration for you, its benefactor and second founder.

"'You possess equal claims to our personal affection and gratitude. From your lips we received the precious lessons of early wisdom and learning-lessons, to which most of us owe the foundation of our worldly success, and more, far more, the establishment of our best habits. Why should I speak of your unremitting solicitude for our improvement? why of the indulgent care which the inmates of your family received from yourself and from your excellent and beloved lady? why of the kind interest with which you continued to watch our opening career, of the friendly readiness with which your counsel and support were extended to all who sought or seemed to need them?

"'Inspired by such feelings, my Lord, was it wonderful that your pupils should desire to give common and public expression to them at the moment when you retired from a situation which you had filled for so many years in so remarkable a manner and with such brilliant results? Many indeed there were who regarded the ordinary sort of testimonial as being inadequate to this extraordinary occasion. The sentiments of these gentlemen were natural and just. Yet, viewing the time which must have elapsed, and the difficulties which might have interposed, to delay the fulfilment of their wishes, they wisely yielded to the voice of the majority, and concurred in the completion of our common object. At this moment, when we were united to express our sense of your exalted merits—merits which all the world recognised, but to which we were especially indebted—what was our delight to learn that the voice of Royalty had confirmed the universal verdict, by calling you to that dignified office which you fill with so much benefit to the Church, reflecting back upon the mitre more lustre than you receive from it.

"'My Lord, in the name of your pupils at large we respectfully beg you to accept our testimonial, and to believe that it is presented with feelings which far outweigh its intrinsic value. We pray, most anxiously do we pray, that confirmed health and strength being added to your numerous blessings, this plate may long continue to grace your hospitable board. We desire that, passing as an heirloom to your children and your children's children, it may often recall the memory of their revered ancestor, and incite them to emulate his signal virtues.'

"His Lordship then replied as follows:

"'My dear Friends, and former Pupils, When I say that I want words to thank you as I ought and wish, I convert a commonplace expression into a simple truth. So magnificent a gift, the intrinsic value of which is so exceedingly enhanced by the kindness with which it is bestowed and by the relationship in which the givers once stood to me, cannot but excite feelings in my mind which go beyond all description. For it proves to me that I have not laboured in vain, but that my exertions have been appreciated and affectionately remembered by those who are best capable of estimating them. And when I reflect on the numbers of my pupils who are now useful and honourable members of society, and see myself here surrounded by some of those distinguished men who have done so much honour to my instructions, and are so fast rising to fame and eminence, I cannot but feel a conscious satisfaction that my efforts for their improvement while under my care have more than met their reward, and a proud gratification in the honours reflected on myself from those which you, my dear friends, have attained.

"'To my successor in particular I would say that, when a similar course of literary triumphs achieved by his pupils, which I am sure none who hear me will think I am presumptuous in anticipating, shall have crowned his exertions on their behalf, I trust he will retire with the same feelings of mutually affectionate attachment between himself and them that it has been my happy lot to experience. He cannot reap a richer or a nobler reward.

"'Gentlemen of the Committee, let my earnestly, though imperfectly, attempt to express to you, and through you to the rest of my former pupils who have contributed to this splendid mark of their goodwill, my assurance that I shall recommend the preservation of it as a sacred deposit to those who come after me; and let me add my most sincere and grateful thanks to you all, and my earnest prayers for your welfare and happiness.'

"The service was executed by Messrs. Storr & Mortimer, of Bond Street, London.

"His Lordship afterwards entertained the deputation at dinner, when the service was used for the first time."

CHAPTER THIRTY-ONE: CORRESPONDENCE, 7TH OCTOBER 1836–28TH DECEMBER 1836

To a Clergyman

Eccleshall Castle, October 8th, 1836.

"REV. SIR, IN THE SINGULAR CASE IN WHICH you have been good enough to consult me, I should imagine that it will be necessary for you to have some witness present who has been used to the signs of the woman, and can interpret them, so that if she makes her usual sign of affirmation, whether by nod or other gesture, her consent may be taken for granted.

"If to this you add a certificate from the mother, which you may draw up and get the mother to sign by her name, or mark, in the presence of one or two witnesses, that she verily believes her daughter knows for what purpose she is brought to church and is a consenting party to the marriage, and subjoin to it after the marriage a further certificate that her mother was present at it and saw her daughter give the usual sign of consent, I think in such case you may fairly be at ease as to the legality of the marriage. I remain, Rev. Sir, your very faithful servant,

"S. LICH. & COV."

The woman above referred to knew no deaf and dumb language of any kind, and could not write. There were specially urgent reasons for the completion of the marriage without delay.

From the Bishop of Durham (Dr. Maltby)

Auckland Castle, Rushyford, October 9th, 1836.

"MY DEAR BISHOP, I wanted to know how you were. I wanted to reply to a letter I got from you soon after my arrival, and I have intended to write continually, but the ponderous letter-bag every morning, fraught with more trouble, if not more mischief, than any bag in the keeping of Æolus, with the routine of ceremonials, visits, etc., have engrossed me since I came here, more completely than I have ever been as Bishop. Last week I began a course of Confirmations which hitherto has been uncommonly prosperous. Whether the weather will favour me from the 17th to the end of the month is very uncertain, but I ventured to fix that time (partly indeed by compulsion) from an understanding that October was usually very fine.

"I was very sorry to hear that you intended a visitation this year, and think you were very rash going to Lichfield, as you did. I trust, however, that you will be warned by experience, and take more care of yourself in future, as the only means of enabling you to be useful at all.

"I am sure you will be glad to hear that my reception here throughout has been very gratifying, and that all matters have gone on in every respect as well as possible. If I were to judge from my present experience, I should say there is a higher tone of religious feeling and greater reverence for the Hierarchy in the North than in the South. I laid the first stone of a new church in Darlington (a town abounding with Dissenters), in a procession which was accompanied by high and low, and so thronged as completely to fill the town, after which a most handsome collation was given to me and the Clergy. At Newcastle a similar feeling was manifested when I went to preach, and the Confirmations in which I have been hitherto engaged have been conducted with unexampled order and very strong appearance of the right feeling among the young people.

"Of course I am not speaking of the pitmen, nor others of the lowest class, for I have at present not had much intercourse with them, though I daresay some of them were mingled with the crowds at Newcastle that attended me."

*

To a Clergyman

October 11th, 1836.

"REV. SIR, I saw Archdeacon Hodson yesterday, whom I requested, during a very severe attack of my illness, to write to you respecting the church at Lowton.

"He tells me you have had one or two applications for the curacy, and are about to appoint a curate when Mr. — goes.

"I shall be very glad when you have arranged the affair satisfactorily, and shall readily receive any person of your appointment whom you may think duly qualified, but it may save you some inconvenience if I state to you what I think essential and indispensable qualifications—namely, that he be of an active and zealous mind, likely to make himself acquainted with his flock and interested in their welfare—also that he is to be a native of England educated in this country.

"What I stated to you when you did me the favour to call in London, as well as your own experience, will, I hope, satisfy you of the disappointment which almost invariably results from application to clerical agents. It is a mode of supplying curates that scarcely ever ends well, and I shall be most particular in my inquiries before I license any such. You will, I trust, avoid this, and take care to ascertain that whoever you may appoint may be a man of unexceptionable character, and possessed of the qualifications I have stated as absolutely essential to his obtaining a licence. I am, dear Sir, your faithful servant,
"S. LICH. & COV."

From a Clergyman

September 19th, 1836.

"MY LORD, According to the directions of the Rubrick, I have to inform you that I yesterday repelled Thomas Hood of this parish from participating in the Sacrament of the Lord's Supper. The circumstances under which I so acted were as follows. The curate, Mr. Swainson, and myself were in the midst of the service, administering the sacred elements, when, on Thomas Hood presenting himself at the rails, Mr. Swainson begged me not to administer to him, and on my demanding the reason, he said the man was a notorious blasphemer. I then asked whether he, Mr. Swainson, was prepared to prove the charge; and on his answering 'Yes,' I desired the man to retire to the vestry till the service was concluded. This he did, and on my stating the grounds upon which I had refused to administer to him, he denied the charge, and expressed a willingness to meet it. Having thus laid the facts before your Lordship, I await your directions how to proceed. I remain, my Lord, with much respect, your faithful servant."

From the Same Clergyman

October 7th, 1836.

"MY LORD, I have had the honour to receive a communication from Mr. Hawarth purporting to be a reply to my letter to your Lordship of the 19th ult. I hope I may be pardoned for again addressing you upon the same subject, for truly, my Lord, I feel myself placed in a great dilemma, not with respect to the particular case mentioned in my letter of the 19th ult., but generally as to what course I ought to take when the Rubrick speaks plainly and clearly. Making use of the case in point as a ground for argument, the Rubrick is very definite, but Mr. Hawarth says, ' I am of opinion that his Lordship is not called upon to express any opinion on the grounds for, or the propriety in, repelling Thomas Hood from participating in the Sacrament of the Lord's Supper on Sunday last, nor do I think that his Lordship has sufficient or even any jurisdiction in the matter to give any directions as to your future proceedings connected with that act'; and then Mr. Hawarth adds, ' I quite agree in the opinion expressed to me by the Bishop, that no responsibility can devolve upon him either for opinion or advice on the subject-matter of your communication.' This, my Lord, is so diametrically opposed to the opinion and judgement of the Church Universal, as to episcopal jurisdiction, as also I believe I may say to common usage, that I cannot refrain from again troubling your Lordship. According to Mr. Hawarth's letter, I am given to understand that the Rubrick, in some instances at least, is a dead letter; that spiritual jurisdiction and power has ceased; and, more than all perhaps, that a Bishop can at any time be freed from giving advice to the ministers of his diocese when they apply for it, as they are directed to do in all doubtful cases. If such be the case, if there exist legal trammels which interfere with the exercise of that spiritual power which has devolved upon the Bishops of Christ's Holy Church by an authority superior to any which is human, we may indeed tremble for the well-being of that Church in this country.

"As to the case of Thomas Hood, I must, my Lord, beg

leave, with all due respect, to refuse to accept a lawyer's letter as a proper answer to my application for advice, according to the rules of the Church, to my Spiritual Father and Superior, and I again ask for directions, aid, and counsel, to which I am entitled, from my Bishop himself. I remain, my Lord, with all respect, your Lordship's dutiful son and servant."

Answer to the Foregoing

Eccleshall Castle, October 10th, 1836.

" REV. SIR, I received on Saturday, but too late to answer by that day's post, your letter, in which I confess I find several observations which might have been better spared. Passing these over, however, without further remark, I now hasten to reply to those parts of it which appear to require notice on less personal grounds.

" It is a very serious, and I believe, a rare thing to repel any one openly from the Sacrament of the Lord's Supper. It involves consequences of much importance both to the person repelled, whose character is thereby seriously injured, and to the repelling minister, who becomes liable to an action at common law for damages on that account. I beg you to remember, Rev. Sir, that I am not advocating the cause of common law against ecclesiastical, or condemning or setting light by the Rubrick, but am stating a mere fact.

" In all cases of penal enactment I believe it is necessary to construe the law literally, and not loosely; and I have never understood that it was to be interpreted less strictly in ecclesiastical matters than in civil.

" Now I examined the case you stated in your former letter very carefully and anxiously with the Rubrick, and I could not find that it fell very strictly under it, or that you had complied with the directions there given. Nay, from your own statement it was evident you had not, for you appeared to know nothing about the man Thomas Hood, till at the instigation of your curate, and he only a deacon, you repelled him during the administration from the Holy Table.

" But you seem to have used no previous admonition, as the

Rubrick requires, for you had no previous knowledge, and so far was the man from being a notorious evil liver that you did not previously seem to know what ground there was for repelling him, or how far the charge might be proved.

"Perhaps the 26th and 109th Canons may have been considered by you as justificatory of your proceeding, by which such notorious offenders as are to be sent out from the Communion as bringing scandal on it are described. But here the statute laws, which supersede the Canons, interfere.

"By 1 Ed. VI it is enacted that the minister shall not without a lawful cause deny the sacrament to any person that devoutly and fervently desires it.

"Again, you will find in Bishop Andrewes' notes on the Common Prayer, that the law of England will not suffer any man to be considered a notorious offender who is not so convicted by some legal sentence.

"Nay, persons who are declared by the canon law to be *ipso facto* excommunicated for certain offences, cannot by the statute law be legally excluded from the Holy Communion till sentence of excommunication has been regularly passed and pronounced against them in the Ecclesiastical Court. Nor can schismatics, according to the statute law, be denied this sacrament, when not lying under any direct and specific ecclesiastical censure pronounced against them.

"I might multiply instances, were it necessary, to the same effect. But still I admit it is a great hardship and difficulty for a conscientious minister to know how to act when the ecclesiastical and civil laws of his country are at variance with each other. It is a case in which every man must be the keeper of his own conscience, according to the circumstances which may occur.

"For instance, suppose a communicant were to present himself at the Lord's Table who was not hindered by any bodily infirmity (as the loss of both legs), and yet should refuse to kneel, I should say that the officiating minister ought not in such a case to administer to him the sacrament.

"But to return to the case of Thomas Hood. The way in which it ought to have been treated, I apprehend, was this. If

Mr. Swainson was aware of the man's habits of profaneness, and that notwithstanding these he was likely to present himself as a communicant, he ought previously to have informed you.

"You ought to have called on him, and told him that the very fact of his intending to present himself as a communicant was a proof that all sense of religion was not extinguished in him, but that you had heard he had adopted profane habits, which were a scandal to the neighbourhood, and which disqualified him from admission, without repentance and due preparation, to the Holy Communion. You then ought to have shown him the Rubrick and Canons, and talked mildly and persuasively with him. Such a course would probably have been effectual, and on his testifying his concern, and his desire to amend, you should have prayed with him that God would give him grace to feel the wickedness he had committed, to strengthen his good resolutions, and to grant that his repentance might be both lasting and sincere.

"Had he presented himself at the sacrament after this, persevering still in his profane courses, you would at least have had the satisfaction of having done your duty; and if you had thought it necessary in such case to repel him, and he had brought a civil action against you, and succeeded therein, you would have had the consolation of suffering for conscience' sake.

"But in the present case both your curate and yourself appear to me to have acted injudiciously and hastily. I do not think that, under all circumstances as at present before me, you were justified in repelling him (I hope he will not take proceedings which will make you too sensibly feeling of this), and I think that if you had admitted him, had called upon him the next day, and had pursued the course with him which I have above recommended, essential benefit might have resulted.

"And now, Rev. Sir, I must add a brief defence of myself, by assuring you that it was from no want of courtesy, far less from any desire to save myself trouble, that I requested Mr. Hawarth to write to you instead of writing myself.

"Mr. Hawarth is a man of excellent sense, a Proctor in Doctors' Commons, and a very good ecclesiastical lawyer. He is the chief agent for my secretary, Mr. Mott, when that gentleman is absent from home or confined, as he too often is, by severe illness. Both these events took place when he wrote to you at my request, for Mr. Mott was both ill and absent. I knew it was a rare, a difficult, and a hazardous case to repel a man publicly from the Holy Communion, though I think a minister may and ought to exercise a conscientious discrimination in his private administration of that Holy Ordnance. I therefore thought I was doing the most kind and friendly act possible towards you, by desiring him to write to you who could give you a better legal opinion that I could give myself. What he wrote I never saw, for I was obliged to go to a Diocesan Meeting, but I cannot imagine that he would write anything but what became him as a man of business and a gentleman; and I certainly adhere to my opinion that no responsibility attaches to me, for an act undertaken by you without my privity or concurrence.

"Your concluding sentence, in which you say that you 'beg leave, with all due respect, to refuse to accept a lawyer's letter as a proper answer to your application [to me] for advice,' etc., etc., may perhaps appear to you worthy of reconsideration. But I leave that to your own discretion. I remain, Rev. Sir, your faithful humble servant,

"S. LICH. & COV."

To this there was evidently a reply, which I did not find among Dr. Butler's papers.

To the same Clergyman

Eccleshall Castle, October 20th, 1836.

"REV. SIR, I must confess that expressions occurred in more than one part of your letter of the 7th instant which I think few people could read without supposing they were intended to imply something very short of respect. As you disavow any such intention, I beg to express my satisfaction at such a declaration and to thank you for it.

"With regard to the case of Thomas Hood, and what should be done in it, I have little to remark which, I apprehend, may not already be inferred from the answer I have already given.

"I think that you should call upon him, should talk mildly with him, show him the Rubrick, and stating that on being called on by your curate to refuse the administration of the sacrament to him, you felt bound to suspend his admission to that rite. You may show him the 26th, and especially the 109th Canon, and endeavour to make him sensible that a clergyman has no more power to alter the ecclesiastical law than a magistrate the civil; and as a magistrate is often compelled in the discharge of his duty to pronounce decisions which are very painful to his private feelings, so must a clergyman in the discharge of his duty be liable to the same.

"My object is that, as far as you can do it without unbecoming concessions, you should endeavour to conciliate the man. For it strikes me that a man cannot be utterly destitute of religious feeling, or absolutely hostile to the Church, who comes voluntarily to the Lord's Table.

"I should advise you, therefore, to proceed in the manner I have already laid down in my former letter of the 10th instant.

"If this does not answer, your future conduct becomes a matter of conscience, the responsibility for which, as I have already said, rests with yourself and not with me, and in which I cannot direct you further than to advise you well to consider before you act, and to lay aside all prejudice and party feeling, if any such exist.

"You should take into account in such a deliberation whether the course you propose to adopt is likely to promote the spiritual improvement of your flock in general, and of the offending individual, or to harden the one and alienate the others from attendance at the Holy Table, through fear of being publicly repelled.

"You should also consider whether your proceedings are likely to prove beneficial or injurious to the Established Church.

"Having thus pointed out what I conceive to be the principal points for your deliberations, I can do no more than add my hearty prayers that you may be led by the Divine guidance to a just conclusion. I remain, Rev. Sir, your faithful humble servant, "S. LICH. & COV."

Answer to the Foregoing

October 24th, 1836.

"MY LORD, Permit me to thank you for your last letter, and whilst I do so to reassure your Lordship that nothing has been further from my mind than disrespect. I humbly therefore crave excuse for any expressions I may have used, which has caused your Lordship to interpret them to my disadvantage.

"Your Lordship's advice as to Thomas Hood shall be attended to, and I have every reason to believe that the act of suspension to which he has so justly subjected himself, instead of being prejudicial, will be most beneficial to the interests of the Church. It has been—I speak it with all deference—the assertion of proper spiritual authority, and it has occurred, I am happy to think, in a parish in which it will be duly and properly appreciated. We are not, my Lord, living here without the exercise of some ecclesiastical discipline, and I state with conscious satisfaction that no new-comer to the Sacramental Table has for a great length of time presented himself without first subjecting himself to examination and approval by me.

"Again thanking your Lordship for your letter, I remain, with respect, your Lordship's dutiful son and servant."

From H.R.H. the Duke of Sussex

(Published by permission of Her Majesty)

Kinmel Park, St. Asaph, October 26th, 1836.

"MY DEAR LORD, Many thanks for your kind letter of the 20th instant, which I received two days ago; I wish, however, that it had contained a better account of your own health. Having suffered for upwards of thirty-five years from asthma, I can easily conceive your sufferings, and therefore have a fellow feeling for you. Thank God, since the year 1817 I have lost it entirely, and never did mortal render more devoutly prayers of thanks and gratitude to the Almighty than I do at this moment, and have ever done since my recovery.

"The tribute of gratitude paid to you by your school at your retirement, as likewise by your former pupils, must have been most consolatory to you at a very painful moment, and I may add most gratifying to your friends and well-wishers, amongst which number I reckon myself. My noble host, who requests of me to offer you his kindest regards, is certainly much improved in health and spirits, although there remains still a good deal to be done. We lead a very quiet life, and this agrees with him as well as it does with me.

"My eyesight continues improving, but the left has the advantage over the right. Of this I do not complain, and being able to read and write with moderation I am perfectly satisfied, and most grateful for being restored to a blessing, the immense value of which was unknown to me until I was nearly deprived of it. My stay here will be prolonged towards the end of the ensuing month, when I must go up to town for the election of the Presidentship of the Royal Society. For nearly two years I have been absent from my duties, but I hope now to make amends for a temporary absence which was not occasioned by my own fault or with my own free-will.

"Praying that your Lordship may soon be restored to health, believe me, with great sincerity, your Lordship's obliged, etc., etc.,
"AUGUSTUS FREDERICK."

To Messrs. Webb & Hiern, Solicitors, Stafford

Eccleshall Castle, November 1st, 1836.

"GENTLEMEN, I am sorry that I was far too unwell to venture to the meeting of the trustees of Bradley School, and the more so because I hear a resolution was adopted which appears to me severe on the master, if not beyond the power vested in the trustees.

"By the decree of Chancery the master's salary is limited to a payment of £70 a year from the trustees, which I understand is a considerable curtailment of his former income, and was done for the purpose of securing a fund for repairs, the estate having been much dilapidated, as it is said, by the negligence of the present master.

"In such case I am not disposed to contend that he ought not to suffer for his neglect, and the taking away of so considerable a portion of his income may be a necessary measure for the preservation of the estates, as well as a punishment for his negligence.

"But it is a sufficiently heavy one, and I think the insisting on his paying ten guineas a year for a house in which he has resided forty years without paying any is pressing too severely on him.

"In almost all cases the master has a right to live in the schoolhouse rent free, and that is accounted no part of his salary. In many, rates, taxes, and repairs are also paid by the Trust fund, and I am confirmed in my opinion that the master has a right to reside in the house rent free, independent of his salary, by observing that by another of the rules of the decree the trustees are to do the repairs.

"Should it please God to grant the restoration of my health, I may perhaps be unable, from my Parliamentary duties, to attend the next meeting of the trustees. I shall therefore beg you to lay this matter before them, in the hope that it may induce them to reconsider their resolution. I remain, gentlemen, your obedient faithful servant,
"S. LICH. & COV."

To a Clergyman

Eccleshall Castle, November 3rd, 1836.

"REV. SIR, A charge has been presented against you for marrying a couple at Upton Magna who were actually resident in the parish of Condover. It is also stated to me that you are in the habit of committing these irregularities, and that on being remonstrated with on the subject by the parish clerks of St. Chadd's and St. Mary's at the time of my visitation at Shrewsbury, you acknowledged the fact, but pleaded in excuse the smallness of your income.

"I am sorry to say that I cannot consider this as the justification of so great an irregularity, and my duty is to insist on your discontinuance of this practice; otherwise I shall be obliged to resort to measures which will be very painful to me, and very serious to yourself. Let me beg you to take this warning from
"Your friend and well-wisher,
"S. LICH. & COV."

Correspondence

To a Clergyman

Eccleshall Castle, November 3rd, 1836.

"REV. SIR, Mr. Goddard, who has filled the office of curate of chapel, Chorlton, greatly to the satisfaction of the parishioners, has given me notice of his intention to leave, and I have it very much at heart that he should be succeeded by a person who will be equally attentive and acceptable. I cannot, therefore, but earnestly beg of you that you will be careful in your choice, unless indeed you should feel disposed to leave it to me, as I understand has been the case of late.

"Whether the appointment is made by you or by myself, I shall require two full services each Sunday, towards which some of the inhabitants so liberally contribute, and shall not license any one till upon trial he is found acceptable. I shall expect him to reside on the spot, and to take as good care of the school and of the congregation as Mr. Goddard has done. I remain, Sir, your faithful humble servant,

"S. LICH. & COV."

To a Clergyman

Eccleshall Castle, November 3rd, 1836.

"DEAR SIR, I have received, with very great concern, a deputation from — with a petition signed by many of the principal inhabitants, requesting me to endeavour to prevail on you, for the sake of peace and harmony in the chapelry, either to resign it altogether or to take some measures to effect an exchange.

"I need hardly observe that it is a very unusual request, but I could not help being much struck with the remarkable quiet and forbearance both of the document itself and of the persons who presented it. There is no harsh language or reflections on your conduct in the petition, and no *gravamina* were alleged by the persons who presented it. One of them showed me a note from a person who was to have accompanied them, merely as a document to show that he was kept away by unavoidable cause. The effect, however, produced on my mind by the reading of it was very striking, and what the person who showed it to me could never have contemplated. I mean the earnest and sincere desire expressed by the writer that the petition might be successful, without the slightest angry word or allusion to yourself.

"I told the parties that I would write to you on the subject, but that, of course, they must not expect me to come to any conclusion on the subject till I had heard from you.

"In reply to my inquiries they stated that they did not wish to enter into particulars in the way of aggravation. I collected from them that they considered you as intemperate in your language, and tenacious of superiority in trifling claims. But from one, in consequence of a question which I put to him, I elicited that you had threatened to repel Mr. — from the sacrament, when he should next present himself. I entreat you to pause before you venture on a step which may involve you in highly penal consequences, and which no man should venture on unless he has a very strong case. It was also stated to me that, having engaged your curate till Christmas, you had given him notice that you should not require his services after next Sunday, or at most the Sunday after.

"Now I do not attempt to prejudge this matter. I only say that I am very much struck with the calm and serious manner of the parties, and am thereby satisfied that they are in earnest. It is for you to consider whether you feel, as a minister of the Gospel, that you can continue there with benefit to the souls of those that hear you—whether with comfort to yourself and family—or whether (as I hear with much pleasure that you have an independent income) it may not be as much for your interest as your duty to adopt one or other of the alternatives above proposed. I remain, dear Sir, your affectionate and faithful servant,
"S. LICH. & COV.

"P.S. Since I wrote the above letter Mr. —, your curate at —, has been here with complaints which it is most distressing to me to hear. He says that you called on him within the last few days and gave him notice to quit on November 13th, because he stated to you that, owing to his wife's expected confinement in March, he could not leave the curacy then, and must consequently do so at Christmas. He further states that on asking you for £17 10s., the amount of his half-year's salary due at Michaelmas, you flew into a violent rage, accused him of being a cheat, declared that the agreement was but for £30, and terrified his wife so much, who was in a room adjoining, that he was obliged to leave the room, but did not pay him even the sum which you admitted was due, though I believe he will be able to produce a witness to his veracity as to the £35 stipend.

"He further states that you accused him of being a pot companion of the innkeeper, because he called occasionally, accompanied by his wife, on the master and mistress of the inn, who are his near neighbours and principal parishioners, without taking any refreshment in their house, but merely fulfilling his pastoral duties.

"These are heavy charges, which I hope you will be able to refute, first by paying him his whole salary due at Michaelmas, and secondly, as some acknowledgement for this effervescence of passion, by allowing him to continue quietly in the house and to perform the duty of the parish till Christmas next, and then paying him the quarter due. I expect an early answer to this.

"S. LICH. & COV."

To the same Clergyman

Eccleshall Castle, November 10th, 1836.

"DEAR SIR, I can readily give you credit for good intentions, but still I am afraid there has been something ungracious in your manner of carrying them into effect. I need hardly tell you that of two men, each having the same fit and becoming object in view, one may completely succeed by a little tact and temper in the management of it, and the other as entirely fail for the want of these.

"In the present case there may very possibly be faults on both sides, but the forbearance shown towards you by the complainants satisfies me that, however impracticable you may find them now, they might have been brought to act with cordiality towards a minister who began mildly and won them by persuasion.

"With regard to Mr. W—, I shall make the inquiries you suggest from him.

"As to the complainants, it does not appear to me expedient in the present state of things to communicate their names to you, which might only lead to exasperation of both parties.

"In the affair of the sacrament the churchwarden acted improperly in seizing the remaining wine, which the Rubrick says the officiating minister shall have for his own use. By which I understand so much as remains in a bottle which has been actually opened, but not an unopened one—and I conceive it was intended that such wine should be considered as a compensation for any of his own wine which he might expend in visiting the sick.

"But it has been stated to me, since our correspondence began, that you are in the habit of taking the whole of the sacrament collection into your own hands, and applying it to the purchase of clothing for the poor at Xmas. No charge of peculation is implied in this, but simply a violation of the Rubrick, which says that the money so collected shall be applied by the Minister and churchwardens to pious uses, wherein if they shall differ it shall be disposed of as the ordinary shall direct. You are therefore clearly in error when you assume to yourself the sole disposal of this collection.

"It is just one of those ungracious acts I have alluded to which makes men tenacious of trifling rights, and disposed to quarrel with those who unfairly assume them. They often feel and resent these petty encroachments more keenly than serious injuries.

"With regard to the appointment of the chapel warden, I have more doubts than you appear to entertain. I cannot interfere with the official parties Archdeacon Hodson and Mr. Chancellor Law, who must decide the point. I will, however, talk with the former.

"In conclusion, I must say that if you are determined to retain —, I really see no end to the discord and disunion of the parish unless you will authorise me to endeavour to be the peacemaker. In that case I should send for two or three of the complainants, including Mr. W—. I should tell them that I had advised you, without neglecting or abating from your duties as a Christian minister, to cultivate a friendly understanding with the inhabitants, totally forgetting past animosities, and that I recommend an equal degree of forbearance on their part towards their minister.

" On your part I would exhort you to be careful in abstaining from all encroachment on their rights, and from all ungracious language and demeanour; you may admonish and exhort when necessary with mildness, and more effectually than by a harsher tone, and be careful not only not to give, but not to take, offence too easily.

" By these means only, if by any, can tranquillity be restored, with my best wishes for which I remain, dear Sir, your obedient faithful servant,
"S. LICH. & COV."

From the Bishop of Durham (Dr. Maltby)

Newcastle-on-Tyne, November 15th, 1836.

" MY DEAR BISHOP, Your letter followed me hither, and found me either immersed in business, or blowing glass or melting iron; otherwise I would have answered it sooner.

" I think I should say to the candidate that I saw no reason for departing from the usual course, and therefore he should have the certificate from the Regius Professor. If he replied that his College would not let him attend him,[1] I should say I would not have a certificate from the Margaret Professor, because it appeared to be a wanton and uncalled-for insult to Dr. Hampden; but if it were a hard case I would ordain him without any.

" I shall be glad to find your charge in town, but you must allow me to say you have undertaken too much, considering the state of your health. You want repose, and must, in point of fact, lie by, if you expect to recover completely. Between myself and others of your brethren you may escape a great deal of labour, and if it were not too great a distance I would say, Send

---

[1] The appointment of Dr. Hampden to the Regius Professorship at Oxford had roused such strong feeling that Dr. Gilbert, then Vice-Chancellor, forbade the men of his College to attend the Regius Professor's lectures.

all your candidates to me for ordination. You have confidence enough in your Chaplain, as I have in mine, not to render it necessary for you to examine yourself. In short I must urge old Trebatius' injunction: *Quiescas*.

"If you take this advice, I shall soon have a better account of your health, and do not fail to rely upon me if I can do anything for you.

"I am delighted with this diocese. There is a very strong feeling of religion in the North, and one highly favourable to our Church. But then the immense increase of population calls for more chapels or churches and better endowments.

"I am now here for the third time since I came to the See, and nothing can exceed the attention paid me in every part, but most particularly here.

"Mrs. Maltby and Mr. Raymond are with us, and claim to be most kindly remembered with the sincerest wishes for improved health to yourself and Mrs. Butler.

"Let me hear from time to time how you go on, if it is but two lines. Yours most truly,
"E. DUNELM."

From the Rev. H. Drury
Harrow, November 29th, 1836.

*

"How my mouth watered at the account of the Presentation Dinner! Indeed I envy your happy feelings at the display, beyond what any two schools ever awarded to their instructor, however rich or aristocratical. But indeed it was no more than due to such an informant. Your reflected light is imparted to my son Ben at College by G. Kennedy, his tutor, who has a good opinion of him.

"I trust we shall meet with none of your youths at the competition for the Bell.

"How capitally the abuse of the Roxburghe in the papers is answered in *John Bull*! I think I trace Markland's hand. Why can it not so be managed that the Duke of Sussex, having heretofore expressed his willingness spontaneously, should be requested to become one of us?

"To Mrs. Butler all my family who have the pleasure of knowing her unite in regards. I am chary of writing to ask Kennedy aught about Shrewsbury; but I trust all is going on to your satisfaction; then it is all well."

To E. Strutt, Esq., M.P.
Eccleshall Castle, November 29th, 1836.

"DEAR SIR, The same post which brought me your letter and enclosures brought me also an introductory one from the Bishop of Chichester. Pray allow me to say, although I have not the advantage of personal acquaintance with you, that your character stands too high in my opinion, for all that is upright, liberal, and humane, to require any other introduction than its own intrinsic weight.

"Writing therefore to a gentleman whom I thus esteem, I shall venture to drop the formality of a stranger, and use the privilege of an acknowledged acquaintance; and though my present wretched state of health, and the multifarious and almost overwhelming business of the diocese, especially for the next two or three years, should I live so long, arising from the Tithes Commutations Act—although, I say, this alone would be a sufficient plea for declining the honour proposed by the Derby society to be conferred upon me, there are other considerations which weigh with me, and which I shall not scruple to avow to you.

"From the moment that I had finished my own course of education, up to Midsummer last, I have been engaged in imparting it to others, and for thirty-eight years have been Head-Master of a public school of ancient and important foundation. There I have formed my habits, and what many will call, and perhaps not altogether unjustly, my prejudices, though they have not been taken up with blindness or bigotry, but are indeed the result of reflection and observation. Therefore I should incline to claim for them the milder term of opinions, or at least not a stronger one than prepossessions.

"These are not favourable to the great changes which the advocates of normal schools and all the machinery of Continental systems are likely, I should say almost certain, to introduce. I know that they will exceedingly reduce the high standard of learning which is at present required in all who would be esteemed first-rate scholars, and they are not a few in number.

"That they might diffuse a more general stock of knowledge may or may not be true, but if it be true, it would only be of that superficial kind which tends to foster vanity, or that detestable mediocrity which is the *summum bonum* of dulness. All of the same class, being educated alike, might be educated up to a certain point, but few would go beyond it, and if any did so, the others would exclaim *Cui bono?*

"I am of opinion that there should be no more compulsion in education than what arises from the influence of the moral principle and the example of society, without any of those legislative measures of enforcement which arise from the military system of the Continent and are not congenial to the freedom of English feelings.

"No one can doubt that there is now a great demand for education, and where that exists there will always be found a supply adequate to the demand, without the necessity of associations for the purpose.

"I am willing to admit that many improvements might and ought to be made in some of our most celebrated foundations for classical instruction; that abuses may have existed in the minor ones; and that much may be done to improve those of a still humbler, though in their way not less important description, and those of a higher, at the Universities. But I have been a labourer in that vineyard very near forty years, and I know how much has been done within the last fifteen or twenty, and how much more is still doing. I may perhaps be allowed to say, without boasting, that what I have done myself at Shrewsbury School has awakened a spirit of emulation in other celebrated ancient foundations, and that the number of able men whom I have sent out to preside over schools that were fallen into decay has been a means not only of restoring those, but of shaming idle or awakening ambitious masters of others also to exertion.

I need instance, among many others, only two in my own diocese—Coventry under its able Head-Master Mr. Sheepshanks, and Derby under Mr. Fletcher, both of whom were my pupils, and recommended by me to the electors.

"Again, see what a change there has been of late years in the accomplishments possessed by Head-Masters of great schools. They were formerly classical scholars, and perhaps very little more. Look now at Eton, with Dr. Hawtrey at its head, one of the most accomplished scholars in modern as well as ancient literature whom you can find; who writes German, French, and Italian with as much elegance as a native, and who sent me not long since so exquisitely beautiful an Italian canzonet that, after vainly taxing my memory and reading, I was forced to write to him, and acknowledge with shame that I could not tell who was the author of it—who turned out to be no other than himself. Dr. Kennedy at Shrewsbury, Dr. Wordsworth at Harrow, Dr. Arnold, I believe, at Rugby, and Dr. Moberley at Winchester are all accomplished in modern literature and languages.

"Now if a classical school were a place where nothing else has to be done for eight or nine long years than to hammer the words of a language (and that a dead one) into a boy's brains, I should say it was indeed a singular contrivance for misspending the time. But it is not so at any good school. The taste is there formed, the mind is habituated to the contemplation, and the memory is exercised to the rehearsal of all that is noble in genius, lofty in eloquence, or profound in reflection. From the Poets, the Historians, the Orators, and the Philosophers of antiquity the solid materials are drawn that form the foundation of all modern superstructures; and as I cannot but foresee the certain neglect of these noble sources of intellectual usefulness and enjoyment, should the neoteric system be adopted, I cannot but deprecate any measures which may tend to its introduction.

"My advice would be to let things alone; let the improvements gradually develop themselves. I am a great advocate for boys at classical schools paying some attention also to modern languages and modern history, and of keeping pace with the advancement of mankind. But this is already set on foot. Dr. Kennedy has introduced it, for instance, at Shrewsbury

School, not only by my recommendation, but by his own wish. Dr. Arnold has introduced it at Rugby, and I believe Dr. Wordsworth at Harrow. Can we suppose that the other principal schools will sit down quiet spectators of these improvements without adopting them? But then these have been introduced cautiously and wisely by men who have understood τὸ πόϲον καὶ τὸ ποῖον καὶ τὸ πῶϲ—and no committees or associations could do this.

"I have written as much as my health now permits. Your letter found me at Shrewsbury under the care of my physician, Dr. Dugard, and too unwell to write on a subject in which I am most deeply interested, but on which I am afraid I cannot concur with you.

"Believe me, dear Sir, this lessens not the respect and esteem with which I remain your obedient faithful servant,
"S. LICH. & COV."

From the Bishop of Durham (Dr. Maltby)

Auckland Castle, December 4th, 1836.

"MY DEAR BISHOP, I am anxious to know how you are going on, I sincerely trust favourably.

"I like your pupils Peile and Whitley extremely, as indeed I do the Professors and Tutors of our University. They are able men, zealous in the discharge of duty, and in great cordiality with each other, so that everything augurs well for the institution, which must be a great benefit to the North, if they can but get sufficient funds.

"I send you the copy of what I have said upon two subjects to the Bishop of Ely. I have said nearly the same thing upon the first subject to the Bishops of Ripon and Chichester. It really does appear to me that *we* are called upon to take some steps in opposition to this persecuting edict of Dr. Gilbert."

*

(Copy above referred to.)

"Have you seen the notice from the Vice-Chancellor of

Oxford forbidding all students of his College to attend Dr. Hampden's lectures?

"It is quite clear this arbitrary act is as much political as it is religious. It is intended to throw an odium upon the King's Ministers, and upon all whom they may please to recommend for high preferment in the Church. Besides, it is dictating to the Bishops as to whose certificate they shall accept. I therefore think it incumbent upon us more especially to show our sense of such a proceeding, and to intimate to the Vice-Chancellor of Oxford that we will not accept any candidate for orders unless he be furnished with the usual certificate from the Regius Professor.

"The Pastoral Aid Society is making a vigorous effort to get into this diocese, and I am sorry to say, through the ill-timed interference of the Bishop of Chester, has got a footing in Newcastle. You may be sure that I give it no encouragement, for it appears to me founded upon the principle that a layman is equally qualified as a clergyman for the offices of religion, and therefore it will in time be contended that ordination is unnecessary."

To Edward Radford, Esq., Tansley Wood, Matlock

Eccleshall Castle, December 12th, 1836.

"SIR, I received on Saturday your very interesting letter, which demands my prompt reply and thanks.

"I shall be ready to license any suitable building which you may erect for the administration of the Church Service by a minister of the Church of England. But I feel, in common with some others of my brethren on the Bench, a very great objection to the introduction of lay teaching, which is a part of the plan adopted by the Pastoral Aid Society, and which militates against my notion of Ecclesiastical Polity. I must therefore beg to be understood as promising to grant the licence with the restriction above alluded to. I remain, Sir, your very obedient and faithful servant,
"S. LICH. & COV."

To a Candidate for Ordination

Eccleshall Castle, December 15th, 1836.

"SIR, I am afraid I shall disappoint you, but I cannot ordain you myself, much less give you letters dimissory under the circumstances you mention.

"Indeed there are far more difficulties in the way, had you even taken your degree at T. C. D., than you appear to apprehend, and I think it a very hard thing upon young men who are waiting for orders, and who have been at the expense of a regular college education and have kept three and a half years' residence there, that they should be superseded by candidates who have never resided at college, and thus had no regular academic education, but have merely gone up for a few days to answer and pass at a general examination. It will therefore require no ordinary combination of circumstances to induce me to submit such candidates at any time to examination.

"Especially now we have a third University in England at Durham, chiefly devoted to theological studies.

*

"I am glad, however, to have saved you a useless journey here, and as I know that some Bishops are more easily induced to ordain candidates circumstanced as you are than I should be, I cannot but recommend you to look out for a nomination to a curacy in such a diocese. Wolverhampton being thirty miles from Shrewsbury, you might, I should think, find such an appointment at no greater distance from your friends than you would have been with Mr. Dalton. I remain, Sir, your obedient humble servant,

"S. LICH. & COV."

From the Rev. W. F. Hook

Coventry, December 21st, 1836.

"MY LORD, After the account of your health contained in your last letter, I feel great reluctance in intruding upon your Lordship, but I am compelled to do so, hoping that a short answer to my application will be all that is necessary.

"A respectable tradesman named A—, a friend and parishioner of mine, some time ago married a Scotchwoman who was bred a member of the Established Church in that country. Since she has been here she has conformed to the Church, and is now desirous of becoming a communicant. I am now attending her to prepare for that sacrament. But of the regeneration of a person baptised in the Established Church of Scotland I have my doubts, and I am, of course, in duty bound to express them; that I have good ground for my doubts appears from this, that the same doubts are visibly expressed in Scotland, where, when the members of our Church make converts from the Establishment, they baptise them under the conditional form—the course, I believe, always sanctioned by the venerable Bishops of Scotland. And my application to your Lordship is for permission to act in the same manner towards Mrs. A—. After raising doubts in her mind, I am naturally anxious to dispel them.

"Should your Lordship not approve of this course, I presume that there could be nothing wrong in my urging her to go to the Presbyterian meeting-house instead of the church, though were she to attend at church I should not feel compelled to refuse her the Eucharist, since of the validity of her baptism I only entertain doubts. I should have done my duty in warning her of the sin of receiving the Eucharist if not baptised, and then the responsibility would rest with herself. In short I am ready to obey your Lordship in whatever you may direct. I have only to add that the parties concerned are friends, and are willing to act entirely according to my advice."

*

To the Rev. W. F. Hook
December 22nd or 23rd, 1836.

*

"With regard to the case on which you consult me, we may perhaps differ partially in our view of it, but still, I hope, not so widely as to prevent a satisfactory conclusion.

"There are two things to be considered—the form of baptism, and the person by whom it is administered.

"With regard to form, unless you can satisfactorily ascertain that it was administered in the name of the Father, the Son, and the Holy Ghost, and accompanied with immersion or sprinkling of water, or at least if you ascertain to the contrary, I hold that it is no baptism, and that the regular form for the baptism of adults should be used. If you have a doubt upon this matter, I think you should use the conditional form 'if thou art not already baptised.'

"With regard to the person, our Church does not at present recognise any authority in laymen to baptise, and some very strict and conscientious churchmen may perhaps consider Presbyterian ministers of the Kirk of Scotland, however regularly called and ordained according to the form of that Church, as having no episcopal commission, and therefore being in fact only laymen. Without entering into discussion on this point, I can only say that the Church of England, while it does not recognise the authority of laymen to baptise, does nowhere maintain that baptism so administered is invalid, and it does recognise this fact, that the validity of a sacrament is not annulled by the unworthiness of the minister.

"But then perhaps you will say that a minister of the Church of England is meant. I must then go on to observe that in the earlier periods of the Reformation, and indeed till the Hampton Court Conference, the Church of England did allow lay baptism, and that at the Lambeth Conference, held so late as 1712, at which both the Archbishops and all the Bishops who could be assembled in London attended, it was resolved unanimously, 'That lay baptism should be discouraged as much as possible, but that if the essentials had been preserved in a baptism by a lay hand, it was not to be repeated.'

"Now I have already told you what are, in my opinion, the essentials—water, and the form of sound words 'In the name of the Father, and of the Son, and of the Holy Ghost.'

"Influenced by these feelings, I should, were the case my own, admit the person to the sacrament on her acknowledging herself to be a member of the Church of England, and showing herself properly instructed in its doctrines, without rebaptising. At the same time, should any scruples exist in your mind or her own which press upon the conscience of either of you, you might, I think, use the conditional form of baptism.

"With our kindest regards to Mrs. Hook, believe me, dear Sir, faithfully yours,
"S. LICH. & COV."

From the Rev. W. F. Hook

Coventry, December 24th, 1836.

"MY LORD,

*

"My present letter will require no answer, if your Lordship approves of the plan I propose to adopt, which is to send your Lordship's letter to Mrs. A—, and to leave it to her to decide as to the course she will pursue. If she wishes for baptism I understand that I have permission to use the hypothetical form. We are going to the Monument on Monday, and I shall not return till Saturday, when, if I do not hear again, I shall conclude that your Lordship approves of this plan. The letter is one which on many accounts I should like to show, and I beg to express my thanks for your having entered so much into detail. I am not competent to form an opinion on the subject of lay baptism, and your Lordship will recollect that I only expressed my doubts in the validity of the sacrament when administered in the Scotch Established Kirk. I was, of course, aware that at a very early period lay baptisms were regarded as valid, though irregular. And such was the doctrine of the Church of England from the time of Augustine, or at least Archbishop Theodore, till the reign of James I; but during that period we all know many wrong practices crept into our Church, and whether that was or was not a proper subject for reformation I will not take upon me to decide. But this fact does not, in my opinion, meet the present case, because the baptisms, though lay, were authorised, whereas the baptisms administered in the Scotch Kirk are not only unauthorised but administered in defiance of the Canonical Bishops of the Catholic Church in that country. I do not for a moment doubt the salvability of the members of that Establishment, but I doubt whether we, as Catholics, can recognise the ministrations of a society from which, because not a branch of the Catholic Church, we in Scotland are compelled to dissent. I only mention this to show that I have grounds for doubting (notwithstanding what your Lordship so ably advances), on different principles from those that bear upon the general question of lay baptism.

"With respect to the Conference of 1712, your Lordship will find, on reference to Archdeacon Sharpe's Life of Archbishop Sharpe, that the Archbishop of York and his Suffragans refused to sign or sanction the document to which your Lordship alludes, though they did not differ from the principles expressed in it. It was merely a private paper expressive of the private opinions of certain Prelates, to whose opinions I should be slow to defer, seeing that some of these were actually schismatics and usurpers of other men's Sees, and that probably, had I lived at that time, I should not have been in communion with the Church of England. But even were it otherwise I should protest against the decision of a few Bishops of two provincial Churches, and acting without the advice of their Presbyters, being considered as authoritative and binding in any way. The decision of even a general council was only received as authoritative when it was found to be in accordance with the universal tradition of the Catholic Church. I should no more think of deferring to the opinion of Archbishop Tenison and his Suffragans than I should to that of the Bishop of Rome and his Suffragans. I apprehend that the question can only be decided by Scripture and tradition. Scripture seems to be evidently against lay baptisms, as the commission to baptise was delivered to the Apostles and their successors. At an early period certainly lay baptism was tolerated, but the very accurate Dr. Waterland tells us 'that the ancients do for above three hundred years condemn lay baptism, not so much as putting in any exception for cases of necessity.' If this is the fact, the question is decided. As I have not examined the case, I fear to express an opinion, and only doubt.

"I am afraid your Lordship will rejoice in getting rid of me out of your diocese, as I torment you with such long letters. I intrude upon past kindness, as you have for so long a period permitted me to write to you freely, an honour which I hope you will permit me to continue when your Lordship has ceased to be my Diocesan, as I naturally feel (I hope no improper) pride in holding a correspondence with one of the most, I ought perhaps to say the most distinguished scholar of the day, and have a strong desire at all times to show that we poor High Churchmen (as they nickname us) have, at least, something to say for ourselves, and that, instead of being *in extremis*, as we are misrepresented, we always wish to hold that *via media* between Romanism and Protestantism which the Church in this country has always held in theory since the Reformation, protesting equally against Protestant and Romish errors, and holding steadily to true Catholicism."

To the Rev. Edmund Carr

(Confidential.)

Eccleshall Castle, December 26th, 1836.

" REV. SIR, I have only just received (last night) your interesting and in several respects painful letter, and I shall readily give you my opinion on the matter, though I fear it can be productive of little good. I am well known to be an advocate of religious freedom, and averse to all persecution on account of sect. But that does not one jot abate my attachment to the Church of England, and it is one thing to live in peace and quietness with persons who differ from me in their religious sentiments, and another to admit such persons to be engaged in duties which properly belong to none but *bona-fide* members of the Church.

" It is true that of all sectarians I hold the Wesleyan to be the most respectable, and decidedly the least inimical to the Church. Nay, they profess to be in communion with it, and many sincerely are so, I do not doubt. But still they are sectarians, using also a separate place of worship, which they frequent more than the church, and calling themselves by a sectarian name. Now we have a right to assume, so long as we have an Established Church, that all children belonging to that Church should be brought up according to its doctrines. With regard to the children of every class of Dissenters, I do not interfere with them—I speak of our own only.

"Now let us see Mr. W. W—'s argument. 'I will not give you a member of the Established Church for your schoolmaster, because the Union is for all, not for the Church of England only.' How then does he go on?—' But I will enforce every precaution you wish taken: he shall teach the children the doctrines of the Church of England, and these only; he shall constantly attend the Church of England with them, and, in short, adhere in all things to the doctrines laid down by the National Society.' Does not the latter part of his argument refute the former? Are you not entitled to say, 'Well, sir, if the children are to be brought up in the doctrines and discipline of the Church of England, we have no need of a Wesleyan minister or any other sectarian to teach them that. We should be more secure, whatever the man's character—which we do not impeach—that it would be done heartily and effectually by a master of our own Establishment.'

"Again, what perplexities does the former part of the argument involve! 'You shall not have a master of the Established Church,' says Mr. W—, 'because the Union is meant for all, and not for the Church only.' Of what sect then are you to have a master? Will the Wesleyan Methodists approve of their children being taught by a Unitarian—the Unitarians of theirs being taught by a Calvinist—the Calvinists of theirs being taught by an Arminian, and so *ad infinitum*?

"The argument, therefore, is in my mind futile, but two difficulties still present themselves to me. The one is that you deputed two clergymen to confer with the chairman, whom he persuaded to assent to giving the man a trial.

"Now if you deputed these to act with any authority in your name, I am afraid you are bound by their assent. If you gave them none, then you are free.

"The second point is that, unless you can succeed in beating the chairman on an appeal to the directors, you will be acting indeed according to your own conscience, but you will, I am afraid, only be introducing discord and strife, and the question is whether you ought to do this, when you know that no good can result from it.

"The W—'s are a powerful family all around, possessed of large estates, probably in the very parishes that form the Union, and likely to have much influence with the board of directors.

"They are also many of them, at least, strongly attached to one portion only of the Church of England—I mean that party which is commonly called Evangelical.

"Now I advise you well to weigh this before you make any appeal to the board—to look at the character, connections, and political feelings of each individual before you act, and to judge whether you are likely to have a majority on your side.

"If you cannot ascertain this, your best way, I think, will be to forbear your appeal, but to tender your protest, and request it may be entered on the books. In such case I think I should be inclined to tell Mr. W—, were I in your place, that as you could not in conscience agree to the appointment of Garland, you felt bound to tender your protest against it, and if this was received and entered on the minutes of the directors, you would be content with having this evidence of your sentiments on record, but that if that request, which you felt but just and reasonable, was denied you, you would not be satisfied without dividing the board upon the question. In that case all the charge of rancour, disunion, party spirit, etc., would recoil upon himself, as he would have refused the proffered alternative.

"Mr. W. W— is a Member of Parliament, and I can easily imagine had his own motives for bringing in this man, and for supporting him—and he will do it, I doubt not, tooth and nail.

"I am happy to see in the account you have given me that there is no trace of your having forgotten the courtesy of a gentleman, or the meekness of a Christian minister. I remain, Rev. Sir, your obedient faithful servant, "S. LICH. & COV."

To *J. W. Whateley, Esq., Rennett's Hill, Birmingham*

Eccleshall Castle, December 26th, 1836.

"MY DEAR SIR, The Bishop of Lichfield has, I believe, some undefined powers under the last Act of Parliament respecting

Birmingham School. I have applied to the Ecclesiastical Commissioners to relieve me of these, and to transfer them to the Bishop of Worcester, who is decidedly the proper person to exercise them, together with the other episcopal functions of the severed part of the diocese.

"Their reply is that they have no power to do so.

"I have heard, however, that you are about to apply to Parliament for a new Act. To this I look for relief, and I hope you will insert a clause, to which I hereby give my full consent, transferring to the Bishop of Worcester whatever powers touching the school I may at present possess as Bishop of Lichfield.

"This will be but equitable to all parties, and will have my cordial concurrence and support.

"I remain, dear Sir, faithfully yours,

"S. LICH. & COV."

To Philip Seckerson, Esq., Stafford

Eccleshall Castle, December 28th, 1836.

"DEAR SIR, The bailiff of the Manor here, who is loud in his complaints respecting the encroachments and refusal to pay amerciaments, has already had a note from me to you, or in your absence to your partner Mr. Fowkes, to request that you will take active proceedings in the business.

"My wish is to prosecute the ringleader of the whole, the man who keeps the Post Office here, unless he has got stronger and better ground of defence than any of the rest, and in such case to prosecute the next sturdy adversary, who may have only ordinary ground of defence.

"I dislike the idea of putting any of these poor people to unnecessary expense, and therefore should be unwilling to take measures against more than one, or the smallest number that the forms of the law may require, should more than one be necessary.

"It is my particular desire, and I beg your early and careful attention to it, that if a trial at the next Stafford Assizes be necessary, Mr. Whateley and Serjeant Talfourd may be engaged for me. Two Counsel will be enough, and I suppose I must have two. If one only, let Mr. Whateley be engaged.

"Of course you will take all the necessary preliminary steps, both with the man at the Post Office here and all others, that the matter may be brought to trial as soon as possible, and that all previous demands and so forth may be duly made, by a person properly authorised on my behalf. I remain, dear Sir,
"Faithfully yours,
"S. LICH. & COV."

CHAPTER THIRTY-TWO: CORRESPONDENCE, 1ST JANUARY 1837– 30TH JUNE 1837

To the Archbishop of Dublin (Dr. Whately)
(In reply to a circular addressed by him to all the Bishops)
Eccleshall Castle, January 1st, 1837.

"MY LORD, BEFORE I PROCEED TO OFFER an opinion on the question submitted to me by your Grace I would wish to clear the way by a definition of the term on which it mainly depends. This perhaps may appear unnecessary, as the circular letter of your Grace, to which the clergy who sign the address allude in their opening sentence, probably makes the question plain enough, but as I have not seen that, I should be writing vaguely were I not to state on what grounds I conceive the argument to rest.

"The question proposed by your Grace is whether extempore prayer in a congregation is allowable, consistently with the discipline of our Church.

"Now the whole turns on the word ' congregation.' If by the ' a congregation ' is meant in its ordinary sense a body of Christian members of the United Church, assembled as usual for the purpose of Divine Service, and of hearing the Word of God preached to them according to the rules prescribed in the Liturgy and Canons of the United Church, I should say that a man must be mad to assert that extemporaneous prayer may be introduced into such an assembly. And yet that such an assembly is meant I have some ground to infer when the subscribers to the address say, in their third paragraph, ' In providing a form of prayer for general use,' etc., etc. They allude to the congregation evidently as the body of Christians assembled in the church for public worship, and attempt to defend themselves, most unfortunately, by quoting the 55th Canon, respecting what is commonly called the bidding prayer.

"Now I hold that this Canon, so far from giving any sanction to excursive extemporaneous prayer, strictly limits the preacher either to the exact words there set down, or to the substance of them, and admits no other topics. For what says it? ' Before all Sermons, Lectures, and Homilies, the Preachers and Ministers shall move the people to join with them in prayer in this form, or to this effect as briefly as conveniently they may.' Here is no choice of topics, no licence for excursion given.

"The only other instance in our Liturgy that can be referred to extemporary prayer in the congregation, is that in the Ordination Service where the congregation are desired secretly in their prayers to make their humble supplications to God for all these things, for which prayers there shall be silence kept for a space. Here the prayer may be extemporaneous or may not, according as each member of the congregation is disposed or prepared, but at all events it is to be secret, and neither the ordaining Bishop nor the priests, nor the candidates, nor any of the congregation are authorised to utter it. Can there be a stronger proof of the feeling of the Reformers with regard to extemporary prayer in a congregation?

"Let us now go to the three articles in the 39th Canon. What does every clergyman of the United Church subscribe? In the second of these articles he solemnly subscribes that he himself will use the form in the said Book [of Common Prayer] prescribed, and public prayer and administration of the Sacraments, and none other. Your Grace having already quoted the Acts of Uniformity, there is no need of my referring to them.

"I hold, therefore, that it is totally inconsistent with the intentions of the Reformers, or compilers of our Liturgy, and with the spirit of the Liturgy itself, and with the subscriptions of the clergy requisite both before ordination and appointment to any cure in the Church, to introduce extemporary prayer into the congregation, taking that word in its ordinary signification of a body of Christians assembled in their usual place of worship for Divine Service.

"In other words, I hold it is not allowable consistently with the discipline of our Church to use extemporary prayer in a congregation.

"Now if by a congregation is meant a religious meeting in a private house, called together by no public authority or sanction of the ordinary,

"In the first place I must question the lawfulness of any such meeting. I am sure, at least, that it is contrary to the spirit of the 72nd and 73rd Canons, by the latter of which in particular ministers are not allowed to hold private conventicles, for I cannot conceive anything more likely to deprave the doctrine of the Church of England than the substituting the extemporary prayers of A, B, or C for the pure and primitive form of our Liturgy. Fully agreeing with your Grace that such religious meetings 'are calculated to foster spiritual pride, love of display, contention, scepticism, etc.,' I doubt their lawfulness, and I do not doubt their inexpediency.

"I have thus freely ventured to offer my sentiments to your Grace, together with the reasons on which they are founded. I have not had the opportunity of consulting any of my brethren on the Bench, and perhaps your Grace will prefer my unbiassed opinion.

"I must, however, beg pardon for sending your Grace this occasionally interlined αὐτοσχεδίασμα, but I have been long labouring under so severe an illness that it would be painful for me to copy it, and perhaps I should not be able to do without occasion for interlineations in the transcript.

"I will therefore trespass on your time no longer than to subscribe myself very respectfully,

"My Lord, your Grace's most obedient and faithful servant,
"S. LICH. & COV."

From the Rev. W. F. Hook

January 8th, 1837.

Writing of a time some fifty years earlier, Mr. Hook said:

"The Doctrines of religion were less thought of and discussed than the Evidences. To admit the truth of Revelation was then thought a great thing, and too many persons thought they might rest there. Thanks to the Paleys and the Watsons, the present generation commence on higher ground. The truth of Revelation is a *datum*. And our religion in consequence is in theory much nearer what it ought to be: we are more busied with Doctrines than with Evidences.

*

"I confess I often think with comfort on the saying of St. Ambrose to Monica, the mother of St. Augustine—'the child of such prayers and tears must be saved'—confirmed as it is by Scripture, which teaches us that the prayers of the righteous avail much for others as well as for themselves. How this can be, or why it is, we know not: it is a mystery; and what a blessing it is that we are surrounded by mysteries! We know that faith is necessary, but we know not how much is required. We know that good works are necessary, but we know not to what extent; and though we know not to what extent, our prayers for others will not be offered in vain. We know, moreover, that the atoning blood of Christ must be applied to the soul, but there are many ways in which this may be done of which we have no knowledge. I hate the dogmatism of those who take *one* doctrine of Scripture (a most important one, I admit) and represent it as *the* doctrine, the *only* doctrine of Revelation, and then make all religion to consist in faith in that one doctrine. There are, as the primitive Church believed, many ways in which the atonement is applied to the sinner's soul, and there are many kinds of faith and degrees of faith."

*

From the Rev. W. F. Hook

Coventry, January 14th, 1837.

*

"As I came in the coach I was reading Neander's History of the Church, and I came to a passage which describes what I have often thought to be Dr. Johnstone's feeling with respect to religion—most mistaken and I think unphilosophical, but which will account for much that we may regret. Speaking of the Alexandrian Jews, more particularly the Therapeutae of Philo, he remarks: 'They said the observance of outward worship belongs to the multitudes; we, who know that all is only the symbolic garb of spiritual truth, have all and quite sufficient in the contemplation of this truth, and need not to trouble ourselves with the outward part of religion.'

"I am afraid this kind of feeling is gaining ground among

those whose thoughts are not immediately directed to religious subjects.

"I can assure your Lordship that though I am illiberal in the assertion of Principle—that is, though I hold that we ought fearlessly to promulgate the whole truth regardless whom it may condemn, though we ought to warn men of their error when they deviate from that truth—I am quite ultra in my liberality when thinking of others, of whom we are commanded, not merely not to judge harshly, but not to judge at all. I would state boldly the general rule, nor fear to say when by the general rule a man is condemned; in each individual case I hope and look for an exception to that rule, God having reserved those exceptions to Himself, and not having revealed when or how they will be made. I remain, my Lord, your Lordship's grateful and dutiful servant,

"W. F. HOOK."

From the Ven. Archdeacon Hodgson

Vicarage, Bakewell, January 24th, 1837.

"MY DEAR LORD BISHOP, It is a long while since I heard from you—not since you wrote a few lines from Shrewsbury, some time before Christmas.

"Now I am most loth to trouble you, not knowing exactly how you may be in health at present. Too ill for the wishes of all your friends I know unfortunately. But I cannot avoid sending you a line without further delay.

"'The Archdeacons of England and Wales, as the constituted guardians,' etc., etc., have two or three times written to me, and now, among other things, request my signature to a petition to Lords and Commons which has this sentence in it: 'Nothing more is required than additional enactments for better raising or making the rate, and for securing to the ratepayers every possible satisfaction as to the faithful application of the moneys raised.'

"Now really, if the ostrich hides his head in the sands and sees not his pursuers, thereby thinking himself safe, it is no reason for those 'patulis captantes naribus auras' to do the same. I am convinced that something more is required, to meet the spirit of the age, and to give it a salutary turn to the cordial reception of the Church.

"The present system of raising Church rates must obviously be altered. The question is, how? I cannot answer it, but surely it is plain that no Government, had it either Lord M. or Sir R.P. at its head, could act upon the plan of the Archdeacons, as intimated in this sentence. How then with such persuasions can I sign their petition? However, it is most painful to refuse to do so, and will expose one to the imputation of being a total abolitionist. They speak of sending down forms for parochial petitions, but I am quite sure that no such petition would be signed in this neighbourhood, except by a very insignificant number, and it would be the signal for more counter-petitions for the total abolition of the rate, one of which has already been prepared at Chesterfield.

"My own impression is that we ought to wait and see what the Government proposes, and then act accordingly.

"Pray tell me (however briefly—by yourself, or by an amanuensis) what you think of this, and as soon as convenient.

"Tell me also what you think of yourself (if you choose to do so), and, at all events, remember me ever affectionately,

"F. H."

The reader will remember that there were two Archdeacons in the diocese of Lichfield with nearly the same name, Archdeacon Hodgson of Bakewell, afterwards Provost of Eton, and Archdeacon Hodson of Colwich. The following letter, which may appear to be an answer to the foregoing, is in reality not so.

To the Ven. Archdeacon Hodson

Eccleshall, January 29th, 1837.

"MY DEAR ARCHDEACON HODSON, I trust I need not say that I have great reliance on your good sense and sound judgement at all times, but especially since Tuesday last, when my poor brains were so mystified by the enfeebling effects of a severe attack of the prevailing malady. I have been considering the truth of your observation about the very inconsequential inference in the principal article of the grand archidiaconal scheme.

"The more I reflect the more I fear that the whole proceeding will produce mischief. Some archdeacons will probably not join, for the silence of sixteen cannot be in all cases accidental. The clergy in some places and the laity in many will not join, and what I most fear is that it may lead to counter-petitions. Still the word from the London meeting of archdeacons has gone forth. You have acted in obedience to it as one of the body, and having already given your assent to them in London you must abide the consequences. I am sure you will take care as much as possible to avoid any expressions which might be laid hold of by the adversaries of Church rates.

"But the fact is the public voice will have a change. If the reasoning on which continuance in the present mode of collection is founded be ever so just in theory, it will not be borne in practice, and by trying to support what indeed is not, but what in public opinion is, an unjust tax, far more may be lost than could in any case be gained. Only see what the principle of non-concession adopted by the Duke of Wellington did in the Reform Bill. Still more mischief do I think would arise at present from an address of the archdeacons and clergy to the King. They ought at least to wait and see what measure Government bring forward before they address at all, at least to be sure that they have ground for complaint before they make any.

"Such have been my reflections, which I communicate to you in the confidence of private friendship, and not with a view to have them laid before the meeting, which, being called by the archdeacons as guardians of the funds for Church repairs, I cannot and would not in any case interfere with. But if anybody should ask you what you think my opinion is, you may say what I told you when we met, and what I tell you now—that I do not think any good will result from the measure. And if you choose to go further, you may add that I think it should have been postponed till the plans of Government had been developed."

(Here the draft in Dr. Butler's handwriting ended.)

Correspondence

From Mr. James Wood, Bailiff of the Manor

Eccleshall, February 10th, 1837.

"MY LORD, My son saw the Rev. Mr. Moore a little before he left home yesterday, who said, in the event of our hearing anything relative to the late attack upon my house, it would be proper to inform your Lordship.

"I have not been able to ascertain facts, but I very strongly suspect a dangerous party connected with amerciament-payers, so that, if an investigation in the manner named by Mr. Moore were immediately set on foot, I believe a discovery must follow. It is evident that at least three persons, probably more, made the attack. Two large paving-stones, one weighing four pounds and the other five pounds, were thrown through my bedroom window, about half-past twelve on Sunday night; the one knocked over a washstand on the opposite side of the room, and the other fell not half a yard from my wife's face. A third stone, smaller, broke a pane, but fell outside. In all there were three panes broken, and as all the three stones were thrown at once, there must have been at least three persons concerned.

"I have yet a long list of persons refusing or neglecting to pay amerciaments, and to-morrow I have to see Mr. Seckerson at Stafford by appointment, to report what I have done. But unless I am protected during the progress of this business, I dare not seem active in it, as your Lordship will admit the apprehensions of my family subjected to nightly attacks, by whom we know not, and from their number so formidable...."

From the Rev. B. H. Kennedy

Shrewsbury, February 21st, 1837.

"MY DEAR LORD, I quite admit that some of the Examination Papers were too laborious, and I shall pare them down in future. The Examination was on the whole very satisfactory, but I find that my explanations and remarks in school have been too often (though unconsciously) addressed to the best scholars, and that I have taken too much for granted with respect to the knowledge of the rest. Cope turns out an excellent scholar.

What a pity that he should throw himself away on Oxford! Trinity, Cambridge, is the place for him. He ought to have had a Balliol Scholarship, but his English Essay, forsooth, was not good enough for them. This is the complaint I have against the Oxford system. Their successful men are not (unless perhaps for University Scholarships) necessarily the best men in any one thing. The best Classic of his year may be in the Second Class for lack of Logic, or Divinity, or English Composition."

*

To a Clergyman

Eccleshall Castle, February 22nd, 1837.

" Sir, It seems to me a most surprising instance, either of ignorance or apathy, that you should not have found out from the tone of my former letter that I was highly displeased with you. I will not, however, leave you in any doubt as to that fact or the reasons for it.

" You were put down in my ordination paper as B.A. of St. John's College, Cambridge. This you will say was no fault of yours, but of the clerk who drew out the paper. Granted. My object, therefore, in asking the questions you have last received was partly to ascertain whether you were yourself in any way privy to the assumption of that degree prefixed to your name.

" It does not appear that you were, and that fact is both very important and pleads with me in mitigation of your misconduct in other points.

" The coolness with which you wrote to your diocesan, whose leave it was necessary for you to ask before you left your cure, that you had quitted it without leave, having heard of a better curacy, was absolutely astounding to me. A man who is ordained deacon is always supposed to engage himself on that cure for at least two years, if the incumbent who gives him the title lives so long, or his successor allows him to remain. After being ordained a priest he is expected to remain at least twelve months. The reason is obvious. It prevents people from stealing into the Church by a bye-way, through a nominal or false title (a thing which appears to have been done by you in the case of deacon's orders), and your conduct in leaving Mr. Kennedy's curacy before you had actually served it three months shows you had well planned in your mind the way of getting priest's orders by a similar imposition, not indeed on Mr. Kennedy's part so much as on your own.

"For these offences I could have you suspended, and if I had found that you had lent your assistance towards prefixing the title of A.B. to your name, I would have done it,—and if I find it to be the case hereafter I will do so.

"There is great disingenuousness in your answer to the fourth question. For you tell the truth, but not the whole truth. The whole truth is that you wished to get your name (as is the case with many half-educated schoolmasters) inserted on the boards of St. John's, that it might appear for once or twice in the Cambridge Calendar as a puff, without any intention of proceeding to the degree, but to assist you in obtaining orders. Now you do not appear so much as to have shown your face at the University in the capacity of a member of St. John's College. In answer to my inquiries there, I am informed that your name did appear on the boards as a ten-year man some four or five years ago, but that having continued there nearly two years it was struck out, for non-payment to your tutor of your caution money and fees. Dare such a man call himself a member of a College on which he practised what the tutors must justly consider as a downright fraud?

"Your examination, I must tell you, was so indifferent that Mr. Evans, Archdeacon Hodson, and myself were long in deliberation whether we should admit you to orders. Unhappily, being obliged to reject three other candidates, I leaned to the side of mercy in your case, who of all others appear to have been the least deserving.

"The Archbishop of York, like his predecessors in that See, is obliged to ordain men who have not had the benefit of a University education, on account of the poverty of some of the cures in that county.

"These persons are called by a name they do not always deserve—literates. But more Southern Bishops are extremely shy of this, and in very, very rare instances admit such, as you must have well known by going out of your way to get a nominal title in Yorkshire. There are many occasions on which Bishops may think it right to give £5 or £10 to a clergyman in narrow circumstances, without thereby meaning to express any particular testimony of their general approbation. I look upon the ten-year system at Cambridge, which was instituted by Queen Elizabeth at a time when it was difficult to supply churches with Protestant preachers, to be one of the greatest evils under which that University labours. It has been the means of introducing into the Church, and decorating with University degrees, persons who would have been much more usefully employed in other occupations of life, and I am happy to say that, since your case has occurred, such a regulation has taken place at St. John's as will prevent the possibility of laymen thus putting their names on the boards for a short time, for the purpose of calling themselves members of the College. The College will henceforth admit none but such as are actually in orders.

"Though I do not find cause to connect you with the assumption of the A.B. degree, and for that reason shall not pursue my complaint against you to the Archbishop, yet still I have given you abundant reason, both respecting your removal from Birmingham without so much as asking leave or giving notice, your evidently having made use of that appointment for the sole purpose of getting priest's orders (which your examination very barely entitled you to receive, and which you never would have received if your want of a degree or your intention of quitting your cure had been known to me), and your assumption of the title of member of St. John's College when your name had been struck off the boards for non-payment of fees and caution money, so that in fact you cannot justly be considered as having ever belonged to the College—I say under all these circumstances I have given you abundant reason for my displeasure, and if I were still your diocesan, I would certainly neither sign nor approve of any testimonial on your behalf.

"I am, Sir, your humble servant,
"S. LICHFIELD."

The reader will observe that Dr. Butler is now no longer S. Lich. & Cov., but S. Lichfield only. This is because the severance of the Archdeaconry of Coventry from the See of Lichfield had been completed on 24th January 1837. Dr. Butler therefore was the last Bishop of Lichfield and Coventry, and the first of the modern Bishops of Lichfield.

To F. Finch, Esq.

Eccleshall Castle, February 25th, 1837.

"DEAR SIR, Having had occasion to reply to a letter from Mr. — on the 16th inst., it occurred to me to ask from him your address, as from the warmth and friendly interest you took on his behalf I wished to have some further communication with you, which, as we have both the same object in view, I trust you will allow me to consider as confidential.

"If you have not yet seen that letter I think it would be well that you should ask Mr. — to show it you, as it will enable you to understand the objects I have in view. I need not go into the detail of it, therefore, further than to say that it is an answer to an inquiry from Mr. — whether, in case of bringing a certificate from his parishioners of their being well satisfied with him, I would countersign a testimonial in his behalf to enable him to hold a curacy in another diocese, or permit him to hold one in my own. You will see my answer, and I hope be convinced of the reasonableness of it, but the great point on which I wish to hold communication with you is as to the possibility of keeping him in a state to fulfil the conditions I have laid down to him.

"I am not to say to a gentleman of your good sense how extremely difficult it is, when habits of drinking, especially ardent spirits, have been formed, to wean a man from pursuing them.

"But I wish to set before you a strong proof of this in the unhappy case in point. When poor Miss —, for whom I was most deeply concerned, assured me that not a single drop of spirits had been brought into the house by her unhappy brother from the moment she entered, I am sure she spoke what she fully believed to be true, with as little intention to deceive as if she had been on her solemn oath in a court of justice. Yet on glancing my eye over the bill sent in for spirits, I saw either four or five bottles, I think the latter number, charged after that period, of which two were for wine, the rest for spirits. Mr. —, therefore, must have continued to conceal these from his sister, either in the house or by drinking them elsewhere.

"Now what is my object? It is to place this poor man in a position of surveillance, so that he may have a chance of leaving off this habit and redeeming his character by the time I have proposed.

"In my present state of health it would be presumptuous in me to look forward to filling this See at the time when that period arrives, but I trust that my successor would act as I shall myself if I should be spared so long. That is, I shall see in the first place that the testimonial be signed by three clergymen whose respectability I can depend upon as a security against those careless and indiscriminate signatures which are too often applied to such documents. In the next place I shall make my own inquiries, for the signers of the testimonial may themselves be deceived. And, lastly, if I should live to see Mr. — restored to character and his functions, I shall endeavour to see that he is not placed in a situation where he may be again exposed to temptation. A man educated and connected as he has been should be placed in contact with a better class of society than he seems of later years to have associated with.

"You will see from my letter the kind of situation I should think good for him at present. But I should wish it to be near some clergyman of character and good feeling, who might at once console, advise, and superintend him, seeing him so often as to be able to bear testimony to his habits. I should also say that it would be very desirable he should be within reach of you, who have shown him so much kindness, and are by his account so much more nearly connected with him than I was aware of, though I understood there was some family connection between you. If you are aware of any clergyman such as I describe in a situation which you think eligible, I would with great pleasure give my assistance in writing to recommend

Mr. — to his care. I remain, dear Sir, your obedient, faithful servant,
"S. LICHFIELD."

Dr. Butler lived to witness the reformation towards which he was so anxious to contribute. See letter of 17th February 1839, in which he permits Mr. — to resume his engagements in the ministry of the Church.

To Henry Hall, Esq., Leeds

Eccleshall Castle, February 27th, 1837.

"SIR, Having received by yesterday's post a letter from Mr. Robert Hall of 8, Dean's Yard, Westminster, stating himself to be one of the trustees of the advowson of the vicarage of Leeds, and requesting me to address to you as senior trustee my opinion of the qualifications of the Rev. Walter Farquhar Hook, Vicar of Trinity Church, Coventry, to supply the present vacancy at Leeds, I feel bound to comply with this request, though I have already performed a similar duty for the Rev. Samuel Hey [1] of Ockbrook, because I do not appear as a partisan or advocate of any person, and feel that I cannot refuse to give testimony to any clergyman of respectability when called upon.

"I have personally known Mr. Hook for many years, and I hold him to be one of the most deeply learned and orthodox divines now living. As a parochial minister he is considered (not only in the district to which he belongs, but far beyond it) an example of what an indefatigable, pious, and strictly conscientious clergyman of the Church of England ought to be. His immense church at Coventry I have witnessed full to overflowing. He has inspired into that large parish under his care, containing about ten thousand inhabitants, quite a new life and existence, and the example has widely spread through the city, which is becoming full of attachment to the Church, though previously remarkable for Dissent.

[1] The Rev. Samuel Hey of Queens' College, Cambridge, B.A. 1809, M.A. 1812, Vicar of Ockbrook, 1816, died 14th April 1852 at the house of his son the Rev. Robt. Hey of Belper (*Gent. Mag.*, 1852, i, 529).

"His benevolence and liberality, manifested by his ceaseless attention to the spiritual and temporal wants of the poor, are unbounded, and I had once the pleasure of being present when he gave a Christmas dinner to five hundred children in the schools, which he has founded or superintended and improved. In private life he is a gentleman of most agreeable and polished manners, as well as of the highest honour and integrity.

"I may appear to have written strongly, but I am quite sure I have written only the truth; and I ought to say that in political opinions Mr. Hook and I do not perfectly agree: you may therefore feel assured that I have not been influenced in my testimony by any party feeling.

"I have the honour to be, Sir, your very obedient servant,
"S. LICHFIELD.

"You are aware, I presume, that Mr. Hook is not now in my diocese, Coventry having been transferred during the last month from me to the Bishop of Worcester."

To W. Evans, Esq., and the Secretaries for the New Church of the Holy Trinity at Derby

Eccleshall Castle, March 11th, 1837.

"DEAR SIR, Never having seen the Deed of Endowment of Trinity Church, I find I have been led into an entire misconception of the actual point in question. It is now stated in brief to me by Mr. Hawarth, and I wish I could say it made the case easier. In fact it seems to place me under greater difficulties.

"It appears that the patronage is intended to be vested in Mr. Thomas West of Brighton for forty years, and afterwards in trustees appointed by the deed, who have power to appoint new trustees in case of vacancy, but nothing is said in the deed about approbation of the Bishop. Now as the actual right of presentation is vested in an individual for the next forty years, a period which neither myself nor my immediate successor are likely to see the end of, of course there can be nothing personally offensive to me, and any idea of that kind must be abandoned. But then comes the important question, what right or power have they or I to set aside the provisions of the Act of Parliament 1 & 2 Will. IV, C. 37, 2, P. 315, where the approbation of the Bishop is expressly required? or how dare I, having sworn to maintain to my successors all the rights and privileges of the See, abandon one of them? I am the farthest person in the world from wishing to throw difficulties in the way of a good work, but I see no way of escape; if you can show me one which I can fairly adopt I am sure I shall thank you. What further increases the difficulty in the case is that it is impossible the Bishop could have signified his consent to the trustees when actually in possession of the church, but can only have expressed his intentions or wishes vaguely, and as I may have done, under ignorance or forgetfulness of the Act above referred to. For the Bishop left the diocese in the end of 1835, and the church was not, and could not be, vested till it was purchased with the help of a grant of £600 only voted by the Diocesan Society on March 23rd, but a few days before the Bishop's death. I furthermore find that he was most exact and particular in asserting the right on all other similar occasions.

"I conceive, therefore, that the parties who fancy themselves aggrieved have nothing to complain of but the Act of Parliament, which has not been altered from the moment the church was first thought of, on a particular clause of which they act, but modify it to suit their own pleasure, which they cannot do. There are no new terms imposed on them by me, or conditions which they were not and could not be aware of. The Act of Parliament was before them then as it is now, and neither they nor I can alter it.

"I am, dear Sir, very truly yours,
"S. LICHFIELD."

At a meeting of the Committee of Trinity Church held at Mr. Bemrose's house on the 18th day of March 1837 it was resolved:

"That the thanks of this Committee be given to the Bishop for his letter of the 14th of March, proposing that there shall be a clause inserted in the Deed of Endowment, stating that as often as vacancies shall occur they shall be filled up by the surviving trustees, according to the provisions of the Act 1 & 2 Will. IV, C. 38, Clause 2; and that the Committee willingly concur in his Lordship's desire that the casting vote in cases of equality should be with him.

"WILLIAM EVANS, CHAIRMAN."

From John Webster, Esq.

Derby, March 24th, 1837.

"MY LORD, A section of the Methodist Connexion under the name Arminian Methodists have been very much grieved by the following painful circumstances, which they feel bound to lay before your Lordship as a severe act of persecution.

"At the village of S— in the Derby Circuit and in your Lordship's diocese, John Cousins, a member of the above society and a resident of the said parish, had his infant child publicly baptised in the said society's chapel on the 5th of February last, according to rule and form thereof, and registered according to Act of Parliament. The child died on the 12th instant, and the church bell rang for it. The Rev. —, minister of the church, was properly and regularly informed of the interment, but refused to bury the corpse unless he was compelled so to do. He afterwards said they might put it into the churchyard if they chose so to do without the burial service, declaring that he would not bury any children whose names could not be found in the register of the church. On being asked if he only opposed this section of Methodists, he answered 'he should not make a straw difference' between them and the Wesleyans, who also have a chapel and society in the village; all who were not found in his register would be excluded.

"The trustees of the Arminian Chapel, myself being one, were therefore obliged, although very objectionable, to allow the corpse to be interred within the chapel until we had time and opportunity to acquaint your Lordship and receive an answer, as the child had been deceased three days.

"We are willing to hope it has originated in a want of information on the business on the part of the Rev. gentleman which a few more years in his station would have supplied, rather than ascribe it to an intolerant principle in this enlightened age, so unbecoming the Gospel of our Lord and Saviour Jesus Christ. We therefore solicit your Lordship's authority that it may not be repeated again."

To John Webster, Esq.

Eccleshall Castle, March 25th, 1837.

"SIR, I am much concerned at receiving the account in your letter, and lose not a moment in writing to yourself and Mr. —— on the subject.

"With Mr. —— I have little personal acquaintance, but I know that he is a young man, and, as you very fairly and candidly state, may be labouring under an error of judgement arising from want of experience. I never heard anything to the disadvantage of his character, and I think from his peculiar mode of expressing himself with regard to the register, there must be some feeling of irritation in his mind on that subject arising from the proposed alterations, rather than any uncharitable feeling towards a class of Christians who hold opinions in which he does not concur.

"Be that, however, as it may, I have written to him on the subject, and await his answer.

"One thing I trust I may feel confident of, from the tone of moderation and forbearance that pervades your letter, that should he upon consideration change his mind, and consent to bury the infant according to the customary form, and the parents should wish the body removed from its present resting-place, the funeral may not be attended by any unusual concourse or demonstration of triumph. Your own feelings as a Christian will, I trust, forbid this, and I am quite confident that no good ever did or ever can result to any sect or class of men from a conduct which is not regulated by Christian charity and forbearance.

"Of course at present I pass no judgement on Mr. ——'s conduct, having heard but one side of the question, but I have put him in possession of my views of it, not as an individual case, but as a general subject, and have enclosed your letter

that he may see the complaint, requesting him to return it to me with his answer. I remain, Sir, your obedient humble servant,
"S. LICHFIELD.

" P.S. I may just add that Mr. —, if he should change his former decision, and be ready to bury the corpse, is not obliged to take it *into the church*, and indeed by this time there may be possibly substantial reasons against it.

" He may at once proceed to the grave, omitting the psalms and lesson, and I believe in cases of infants of such tender age this is customary."

To the Clergyman referred to in the Foregoing Letters

Eccleshall Castle, March 26th, 1837.

" REV. SIR, I enclose a letter which I have just received containing a complaint against you, which, if well founded (and from the tone of moderation which pervades it, I am inclined to give it credit), may, I fear, involve you in serious consequences.

" From your dwelling on the name of the person to be interred not being found on your register, I am induced to think that you are under some error, or labouring under some degree of displeasure respecting the lately proposed parliamentary measures on the subject of registration. It would be more satisfactory to find that your refusal arose from this cause than from an indisposition to bestow the rites of sepulture on any class of Christians whose views do not exactly concur with your own; but as I do not know the motive which led to your refusal, I must beg leave to offer a few remarks in either case.

" In the former your ground is not tenable for a moment. Suppose I were to go to S— and die there, you would be bound to bury me though not in your register. If a stranger passing through your parish were to die at an inn, or to be found dead in the road, and a coroner's inquest did not bring in a verdict of *felo de se*, you would be bound to perform the service though the person is not to be found in your register, and you do not so much as know whether he has died unbaptised or not. Again, how many of your actual parishioners who have resided for years in your parish and attended your church may not be found in your register. They may have been born elsewhere, and settled in your parish afterwards. Nay, they may even be regular churchmen born in your parish, and not be entered in your register. A grandfather or grandmother may wish the child brought to their house in a different parish for the christening. Or a child being taken by its parents before baptism on a visit to relatives may be taken ill, and baptised out of your parish. In short, a thousand cases may occur where the names of *bona-fide* parishioners are not to be found in your register, and would you on that account refuse them what is commonly called Christian burial?

"Now in the other case I cannot conceive how your refusal can be justified, unless the party bringing the corpse inform you that they intend to interfere with the service or actually do interfere by *formulae* of prayers and ceremonies of their own. In that case I think you would have a right to refuse. The case of refusal to 'persons who die unbaptised,' according to the Rubrick at the head of the burial service, is more set at rest by the famous judgement of Sir John Nicholl[1] than it used to be, and you cannot now refuse to bury as having died unbaptised any who have received baptism according to their respective sects. This, perhaps, is carrying lay baptism as far as it can go, but I should observe that the Church of England, though it discourages, does not absolutely deny the validity of lay baptism, and that by the last decision of the Archbishops and Bishops, at a Conference held at Lambeth in the year 1712, it was agreed that lay baptism, if with water in the name of the Father, Son, and Holy Ghost, was not to be repeated by a clergyman on the admission of the party as a member of the Church of England.

"If you will permit me to give you my advice upon the subject, it is that you should reconsider the matter, and if you find reason to think that you have acted incautiously or

---

[1] Sir John Nicholl was Dean of Arches, and Judge of the Prerogative Court of Canterbury, High Court of Admiralty, and Vicar-General to the Archbishop of Canterbury. The case referred to by Dr. Butler was Kempe *v.* Wickes, 3, Phillimore, p. 264.

erroneously, I should advise you to tell Mr. Webster that you recall your objection, and are ready to bury the child if the parents wish to remove it. I think you will thereby save yourself much trouble and obloquy, and perhaps much expense, for supposing the enclosed case to be correctly stated, and an action to be brought against you, I greatly fear you would find yourself liable to heavy costs.

"Another consideration which will probably have great weight with you is, that by consenting to bury the child you will do an act of conciliation which may be serviceable to the Church, and will evince a spirit of Christian charity and a mind open to conviction which are highly creditable to a Christian minister.

"In times like these one is particularly anxious to avoid obloquy against the Church for insisting too rigidly on ceremonials. I beg you to return the enclosed to me at your early convenience, and am, Rev. Sir, your obedient faithful servant,

"S. LICHFIELD."

To the same Clergyman

Eccleshall Castle, April 2nd, 1837.

"REV. SIR, I am sorry you have been at the trouble of collecting authorities of which I was well aware, and which are quite unnecessary; I never supposed that you acted from other than conscientious motives.

"Still I advised you, I hope with mildness and courtesy, for the best, and if it will be any relief to your scruples, with that view only, and not for the sake of exercising episcopal authority, I require you to offer to perform the service. I do this because I know that, if law proceedings are taken against you, you will be subject to heavy and great expense, and will assuredly fail in your cause.

"I remain, Rev. Sir, your obedient faithful servant,

"S. LICHFIELD."

The following paragraph was erased from the draft of the letter given above:

"Several of the Rubricks ought to be reformed to suit the

circumstances of the times. They stand now as a snare to tender consciences, when the ecclesiastical law requires one thing, and the civil law which supersedes it, another. But in this case the celebrated decision of Sir John Nicholl, and several others, are clear against you."

To a Clergyman

Eccleshall Castle, April 3rd, 1837.

" REV. SIR, Some days ago I received from the guardians of the Ellesmere Union a letter stating that they had elected you chaplain thereto with a salary of £50 a year, and requesting me to license you accordingly.

" But a short time previously to that I had received a letter stating that the curacy of Hadnall contained more than four hundred souls, and that you reside no less than ten miles from it, which gave much dissatisfaction to the inhabitants—a thing naturally to be expected.

" By inquiry at Lichfield I find you have no licence of non-residence, and I most assuredly shall not grant you one under such circumstances.

" The Act requires that in such a case you should have a resident curate, and that where the value of the living is under £80 he should have the whole proceeds; if you do not appoint such a curate as I may approve within three months, it authorises me to appoint one.

" Now it is impossible that you can fulfil your duties at Ellesmere as Chaplain to the Union if you reside at Hadnall, or at Hadnall if you reside at Ellesmere, unless you keep a resident curate there, and I must therefore call upon you to do this, or to resign Hadnall entirely, or to keep Hadnall, residing in the parish or at most not more than five miles from it, and to give up the appointment at Ellesmere. Under the present circumstances they cannot be held together. I am sorry to give you this information, but I can only act according to the provisions made by the legislature in the performance of my duty.

" I remain, Rev. Sir, your obedient faithful servant,

" S. LICHFIELD."

To Mr. Thomas Simpson, Secretary to the Mechanics' Institute, Lichfield

Eccleshall Castle, April 8th, 1837.

"SIR, I have no objection to my name appearing as one of the patrons of your intended Mechanics' Institute, if you adhere to the plan you propose of making it a purely scientific and literary society unconnected with politics.

"The great benefit which such societies afford in these times arises from their forming a rallying-point in which those whose political opinions may lead them to distrust or dislike each other may meet on neutral ground and on more friendly terms, and learn to exercise mutual forbearance and goodwill.

"You will please therefore to understand that whenever this becomes a political meeting or discusses the political topics of the day, on whichever side, I must claim the liberty of withdrawing my name. If your society is formed you may put me down as a donor of £5 and as a subscriber of £1. I remain, Sir, your obedient humble servant,
"S. LICHFIELD."

To the Rev. W. Fisher

April 22nd, 1837.

"DEAR SIR, I think the Pastoral Aid Society were quite right in not trusting to such a man as Mr. Whinfield to appoint a curate at Heanor, and I hope they will adhere to that principle, but that they will not abandon that destitute and abandoned parish.

"I have no doubt Archdeacon Hodson fully communicated to you my views on the subject; therefore I have nothing to add but that it is one which presses most deeply and seriously on my concern, and that I may truly say that both it and the church at Riddings, near Heanor, are the subjects of my daily and very often of my nightly cares.

"Hoping that you may be able to send me some satisfactory result at least with regard to Heanor, I remain, dear Sir, faithfully yours,
"S. LICHFIELD."

Correspondence

From the Rev. George Matthews

April 21st, 1837.

"MY DEAR BENEFACTOR, By every account I hear of your state of health I cannot but fear that you have been and still continue very dangerously ill. You have been one of the best, if not the very best of my earthly friends, and well may I be sorry. In duty bound am I to pray for your recovery, and may it be daily consolation to you to know that often and earnestly from my soul do I find myself praying for 'Dr. Butler of Shrewsbury,' and this is one reason why I know my prayers are sincere, because as a man rarely dreams and never prays from his heart but in his mother-tongue, so in our prayers do we unconsciously speak of those for whom we pray by the names most natural and familiar and dear to us. God for ever bless and reward you, and I know He will, not only for your own good deed in itself, but because by it you have made me grateful and fervent in my intercessions to Him for you.

"I neither feign nor flatter, for I too much fear the time is coming when no man must be unfeigned and praise beyond suspicion of self-interest. My dear old master, instructor of my youth, and under Providence the support of my life and cause of all the comfort I enjoy, may the peace of God smooth your pillow, and may He 'make all your bed in your sickness.'

"GEORGE MATTHEWS,
"*Vicar of Rudgwick.*"

To a Candidate for Ordination

Suffolk Street, Pall Mall East, April 23rd, 1837.

"SIR, I am very much concerned to say that, as you have not a certificate from the Regius Professor of Divinity that you have attended his lectures, I cannot admit you as a candidate for orders.

"I do not blame you for this defect, nor for your obedience to the mandates, however arbitrary, of those who have the rule over you in your College, and whose authority, if lawfully exercised (a question which you cannot decide, but which I trust will be looked into before a proper tribunal), you are bound to obey. But they cannot and shall not bring me into their measures.

"It is not for one nor for twenty heads of houses to dictate to any Bishop what certificates he shall take or what he shall refuse, or to make him a party to any arbitrary measures they may choose to adopt, or any insults they may choose to offer to any private individual or public functionary whom they may not approve.

"I have not the honour of being known either personally or by correspondence to the Regius Professor or the Margaret Professor of Divinity at Oxford. But this is very clear to me, that I cannot depart from what has hitherto been the constant course, and refuse the certificate of the Regius Professor, requiring in preference that of the Margaret, without offering a gross indignity to the former of these gentlemen (who is also in the superior station), merely in compliance with the mandate of the Principal and Fellows of Brasenose, with whom (except perhaps a few Fellows who have been my pupils) I am equally unknown.

"I remain, Sir, your obedient humble servant,

"S. LICHFIELD."

To the same Candidate

Undated.

"SIR, Having seen in the *Globe* of yesterday evening that the Principal of Brasenose has revoked the regulation which prevented my admitting you as a candidate for orders, I lose not a post to say that I should regret your suffering for a mandate no longer in existence, and that I shall be ready to admit you to examination at my next ordination, which will take place, if it please God, on Sunday, September 17th. I enclose a paper of instructions with regard to books, papers requisite, and time and place of examination.

"Should it be of essential importance to you to be ordained before September 17th, I will give you a private examination any time before June 28th (later I cannot, because I shall then begin my Confirmation tour, which, with some consecrations of churches, will occupy me till my own ordination in September), and letters dimissory to any Bishop who may ordain earlier.

"I shall dispense on this occasion with the production of any certificate of attendance on Divinity lectures, and what I do in your case I shall do in any similar one that may arise.

"I applaud your good sense in not replying to the letter which announced my determination. No benefit could have resulted to you from altercation with your diocesan, and you have insured yourself a willing reception by your acquiescence. I remain, Sir, your sincere friend and well-wisher,

"S. LICHFIELD."

From Mrs. Bather (Dr. Butler's Elder Daughter)

May 10th, 1837.

*

"I must tell you a droll story about Mr. Drury. When in London he went to a hat shop and bought a characteristic hat. All his friends agreed it suited him exactly, and he was extremely pleased with his purchase, which he carried in a blue bandbox on his knee from London to Salisbury, and from Salisbury to Newbury, and from Newbury to Oxford, and finally to Pontesbury. When it came to be unpacked he heard a great 'lack-a-day-ing' in the kitchen, and found his housekeeper and Samuel examining, not his hat, but a beautiful bride's cap trimmed with white ribbons and heaps of blond lace, and in the box were tippets and collars and cuffs *en suite*, to the great astonishment of not only Mrs. Webster and Samuel, but himself also. He now recollects that at Newbury there got into the coach a very nice bridal-looking lady, who had also a blue bandbox, which she nursed on her knee as tenderly as Mr. Drury did his. Of course by some jolt or oversight the boxes were changed at Oxford, and all the poor bride has to console herself with is a very queer hat, which, being perfectly characteristic of Mr. Drury, is by no means likely to be of any use except to the owner. The blond cap, etc., at present remain as trophies at the vicarage. Some people have suggested they should be sent to one of the numerous bazaars in the neighbourhood; some are fervently hoping the Rector will, and others that he will not, keep them till the cap fits somebody who shall be part and parcel of himself, while I really believe he would honestly restore them to their lawful owner if it were possible to do so, which unhappily it is not."

*

The Mr. Drury above referred to was the Rev. Charles Drury of Pontesbury, near Shrewsbury, not the Rev. H. Drury of Harrow, who was his brother.

To the Rev. Charles Cameron, Spedhill

16, Suffolk Street, June 3rd, 1837.

" REV. SIR, I cannot accept titles from the Pastoral Aid Society, whose grants, being only temporary or at most annual, though renewed, are not a sufficiently permanent security to ordain on. Another objection has arisen in my mind of late, from finding that in all cases, except two, a stipulation has been made, not only for ordination, but for immediate or very early ordination by letters dimissory—thus making a kind of stepping-stone into the Church, which I do not approve.

" I expect the candidates to be graduates of one of our English Universities, and it is much more satisfactory to have them before me at the usual time than to grant letters dimissory. I cannot ordain before September on account of my Confirmations and consecrations. I am ready to admit a curate whose character and testimonials I may approve, who is *already* in orders. I remain, Rev. Sir, your obedient faithful servant,

" S. LICHFIELD."

To W. L. Newton, Esq., Leylands, Derby

16, Suffolk Street, June 7th, 1837.

" MY DEAR SIR, Highly as I respect and esteem you, I am sorry that I can never support Sir A. Agnew's Bill. I adhere to the opinion I expressed in one of my late charges as Archdeacon of Derby on that subject, and though I have suffered much obloquy and misrepresentation on that subject, I see no cause to change it. I am as sincere a friend to the due observance of the

Sabbath as any man can be, but I prefer the voluntary principle to penal enactments.

"Nothing, I find by inquiry at the fountain-head, can work better than the Association at Brentford, the plan of which I send you, and the details of which I have had from Mr. Rhodes. Of course it will be my duty to present, or cause to be presented (for I am still unable to attend in person), to the House of Lords, any petitions I may receive in favour of such a Bill as Sir A. Agnew's, but I had much rather they were placed in the first instance in the hands of some member of that House who is more inclined to support the measure than I am. I have sent copies of the enclosed to the archdeacons of the diocese. I remain, dear Sir, very truly yours, "S. LICHFIELD."

From the Rev. Walter Metcalfe

Tamworth, June 8th, 1837.

"MY LORD, I take the liberty of applying to your Lordship for direction under the following circumstances. A few days ago, while visiting the different houses in the chapelry under my care, to ascertain who were of age to be admitted as candidates for Confirmation, a young woman applied to me to be so admitted. She stated that in her infancy she had only been privately baptised, and never afterwards publicly received into the Church. This she wished now to be done. On looking over the different baptismal services I could find none which could be used in such a case, none at least which I thought could properly be used in the public reception of an already baptised adult. I therefore write to ask your Lordship what I ought to do—whether it is necessary that she should be publicly received into the Church, except by Confirmation, and if so what service should be used."

To the Rev. Walter Metcalfe

Suffolk Street, June 9th, 1837.

"DEAR SIR, The circumstances of the case on which you have so properly written to me must occur, I have no doubt, very often at every Confirmation, but the parties concerned are probably for the most part ignorant or careless. It is certainly a *casus omissus* in the Rubrick.

"I have consulted one of the most able and experienced of my episcopal brethren, who agrees with me that it is impossible to avoid some irregularity, but we both think that the rite of Confirmation would be a clear admission of the person receiving it into the Church, although the expressions respecting godfathers and godmothers, etc. (which presuppose a reception into the Church), in the Confirmation office will not apply.

"But the Private Baptism of Infants will not apply, for the Gospel, and exhortation on it, will not do. Nor will the office for Baptism of those of Riper Years, for that supposes the Sacrament of Baptism not to have been previously administered, which in this case it has.

"I should therefore incline to admit the person to Confirmation at once, if duly qualified with regard to the previous preparation. But if she have any scruples or be very anxious to be received into the Church before Confirmation, you can only do so by an irregularity of another kind—that is, by combining the private baptismal office and that for persons of riper years into one, omitting parts of both.

"For instance, having ascertained to your satisfaction that the rite of private baptism was duly administered, you may begin 'I certify you' down to 'heirs of everlasting life,' substituting the word 'person' for 'child' in the expression 'baptising of this child.' Then omit the rest of this address, and the Gospel and exhortation following, till you come to 'Doubt ye not therefore,' and (substituting wherever it may be requisite throughout the service the word 'person' for 'child') proceed to the office of Baptism for those of Riper Years, beginning with the address to the person to be baptised, the first words of which must be thus altered, 'Well-beloved, who hast come hither desiring to be received into the congregation of Church flocks, you have heard how the congregation have prayed,' etc., down to 'All this I steadfastly believe.' Then omit the question 'Wilt thou be baptised?' and go on to that 'Wilt thou then obediently?' Then omit to 'We receive this person,' and so continue; and so to the end of the service, except that instead of saying 'have now by baptism put on Christ' say 'are now received into the congregation of Christ's flock.'"

From Sir Henry Halford

(Original in possession of Mrs. G. L. Bridges and Miss Butler)

June 19th, 1837.

"MY DEAR LORD BISHOP, I found the King a little easier on my return to Windsor Castle last night. His Majesty had done some of the public business with Sir H. Taylor previous to the introduction of the Archbishop, and then went through the solemn ceremony with great attention and apparent comfort. We have thought it proper to state this in the public bulletin to-day. His Majesty sent for the Archbishop again in the afternoon to have the evening prayers. The King, whom I left an hour ago, is very weak to-day, and I fear cannot live long; his Majesty has requested the Archbishop to remain at Windsor. He took pleasure in seeing the Waterloo flag, when it was presented according to annual custom, and expressed a hope that he might live to see the sun set on this most interesting anniversary. Adieu, my dear kind friend. I write this on the road, and am with equal respect and affection, my dear Lord Bishop, your faithful servant,

"HENRY HALFORD."

To the Rev. J. Boyle, Collegiate Church, Wolverhampton

Eccleshall Castle, June 21st, 1837.

"REV. SIR, I endeavoured while in London to get the best information in my power relative to the Marriage and Registration Acts, but could learn nothing very satisfactory. It seemed to me as if their operation was to be learned by practical experience. I discussed them, however, with two very sensible and experienced members of the Episcopal Bench, who agreed with me in regard to the interpretation to be put upon the words of the Marriage Act, § 1, where it is stated in the opening 'that all the rules presented by the rubric,' etc., to the end of the section. The question arises upon the words 'Such marriage may be solemnised in like manner on production of the registrar's certificate, as hereinafter provided'—the doubt being whether the word 'may' is in this case compulsory or merely permissive. Some of the clergy consider it permissive, and, as in the case of the printed paper you have sent me, intend to refuse marrying on the production of the registrar's certificate. I fear they are wrong, and that they will find themselves bound to accept it. But, as I have before said, it seems as if the operation of the Bill was only to be learned by experience. I will just add, on the subject of the Confirmation, that I thought it right to ask the permission of the official of the Collegiate Church before using it.

"I remain, Rev. Sir, your very obedient and faithful servant
"S. LICHFIELD.

"P.S. With regard to the licensing the new churches for marriage, there are points which require some consideration.

"It is very important on account of the Dissenters' competition to give every facility for licensing. On the other hand, I should be very sorry to diminish the income of the mother-church. But we must also consider that this will be the case even if the new churches are not licensed, in consequence of the Dissenters' chapels being licensed nearer to the residence of the parties. I think, therefore, that at least many of the outlying churches will require licences, and may have them without real injury to the Collegiate Church."

To a Clergyman

Eccleshall Castle, June 22nd, 1837.

"REV. SIR, Mr. Bainbrigge was here this morning, to say that the parishioners of — have complained to himself and Mr. Davies, trustees of the Brand estate, that you have fenced out one half of the churchyard by a strong fence, and have turned it into your own pleasure-grounds, having also sunk it considerably to suit their level.

"If this statement be correct, I am afraid you will be found to have exceeded your powers as vicar, the ground having been previously consecrated, and therefore set apart from common uses; and howsoever much this may appear an improvement in the eye of taste, which I can easily suppose it is, still I fear it can only be considered as an encroachment in that of the law, and I would recommend you to remove the strong fence, and separate the consecrated from the unconsecrated ground by a light iron railing, or such other boundary as you may approve.

"I have the honour to be, Rev. Sir, your obedient faithful servant,
"S. LICHFIELD."

To the same Clergyman

Eccleshall Castle, June 30th, 1837.

"REV. SIR, I cannot interfere in any dispute between Mr. Bainbrigge and yourself, or look to the motives by which he may be actuated. The whole question is reduced to the simple inquiry whether you have put up a fence which is an encroachment on the churchyard.

"I shall have this duly investigated, but would rather it were done in your presence than when you were absent. At present, on your own statement, I cannot understand why a fence which protects your grounds from the intrusion of pigs by being placed in the churchyard would not equally do so if placed upon your own land.

"I remain, Rev. Sir, your obedient humble servant,
"S. LICHFIELD."

CHAPTER THIRTY-THREE: CORRESPONDENCE, 4TH JULY 1837–24TH DECEMBER 1837

From the Bishop of Durham
Curzon Street, July 4th, 1837.

*

"I AM VERY SORRY THAT YOU LEFT TOWN WITHout being presented to our young Queen, who received us with the most becoming grace and modesty. I am also very sorry that you have felt it necessary to engage in so much Confirmation this year; and if I had not a prospect of quite as much as I think my strength will enable me to encounter, I should have been glad to have relieved you of a part at least of your duties.

"Nothing, of course, is talked of but the poor King's funeral, the dissolution of Parliament, and the young Queen. Everything one hears of her is eminently favourable, but she keeps very quiet, and most properly so, until after the funeral. The Ministers and their friends appear to be in excellent spirits, more so indeed than some of our brethren."

*

From J. J. Peele, Esq.
(Original in Shrewsbury Museum)
July 15th, 1837.

"MY LORD, I have the pleasure of assuring your Lordship that the trustees appointed by the Master of the Court of Chancery for the Corporation livings are:

1. Your Lordship.
2. Lord Clive.
3. Sir A. V. Corbet.
4. J. A. Lloyd, Esq.
5. R. A. Slaney, Esq.

"The counsel and agent of the Town Council struggled hard to have Messrs. Lecaite and Yardley named, but your Lordship's letter was so strong an authority against clergymen being appointed that the opposition to them was successful."

Correspondence

To Mrs. Bather (Dr. Butler's Elder Daughter)
(Original in possession of Mrs. G. L. Bridges and Miss Butler)

Colwich Abbey, July 16th, 1837.

" MY DEAREST MARY, All is quite well, but for fear you should see some absurd account in the papers of an accident which happened yesterday and might have had bad consequences I send you a line by way of precaution.

" I had ascended with a large party of ladies and gentlemen, and clergy in their gowns, to a hill near Wirksworth called Middleton, there to lay the foundation-stone of a new church, when all at once came on one of the most awful thunderstorms I ever saw—close to us—the thunder following the lightning instantly.

" As we had no sort of shelter but a few umbrellas, and were all wet to the skin in an instant, I thought the best way would be to proceed as if it were quite fair, but abridge the ceremony by only singing the 100th Psalm (it had a fine effect in the storm), saying a prayer, and then retiring home. This we did, in such a storm of thunder, hail, and rain as I scarcely ever witnessed.

" The workmen then began to raise the heavy stone by ropes and pulleys, when all at once the scaffolding gave way, and, intended as it was to hold half a dozen people at most, came down with a score of us at a fall of about twelve feet in the middle of the stones. None of us on the scaffolding was injured in the slightest degree. Two of the many persons underneath it who there sought some unavailing protection from the storm were a little hurt, but not materially—one with a cut near the eye, the other in his leg. Mr. Harward has promised me that he will send a proper account to the Derby papers, but before we had ourselves returned to Wirksworth news had arrived there that the scaffold had been struck by lightning, dreadful injury received, etc., etc. As it was, the escape was general, and a great mercy that it was so, for the danger was considerable. I am not sensible this morning of the slightest bruise, nor even of any cold or inconvenience from the wetting.

" I know nothing of the Bishop of Durham. I hope that

Mr. Bather is better, and am, dear Mary, your very affectionate father, "S. LICHFIELD."

To a Clergyman

Beaumaris, August 4th, 1837.

"REV. SIR, I have just received your letter, and am sorry to say that I can give you no further answer than that I must adhere to my decision without entering into further discussion on that point.

"But as there is one in which you imply want of fair dealing in Mr. Harward from his not mentioning my decision to you till after I had left Wirksworth, I feel it my duty to clear him of this. The unfortunate accident which interrupted our interesting ceremonial obliged me to return wet and more hurt than I chose to confess, or indeed was aware. I have not yet recovered. I had fifteen miles to travel, part very hilly, and was beyond my time, and was not in a state to see any one on business even had I remained at Wirksworth; there is therefore no ground to charge Mr. Harward with want of fair dealing. I most highly esteem him as an upright, honourable man, an excellent and attentive parish priest, and a sound divine untainted with fanaticism. I wish all my clergy resembled him. He preached the best visitation sermon for me at Derby, when I was Archdeacon, that I have yet heard. I have asked him if he wishes you to continue at Wirksworth; he replies he does not. I cannot therefore allow your continuance, but am, Rev. Sir, your sincere well-wisher, "S. LICHFIELD."

To Archdeacon Bather

September 5th, 1837.

"MY DEAR ARCHDEACON, My expectations at — have in no respect been disappointed. Upon my arrival at the church porch Mr. — came out to meet me. We went into the vestry, and while there he said, 'I hope your Lordship will dine with me to-day.' An invitation so given was not to be accepted, and I told him I was engaged, having ordered dinner for myself at the inn. Mr. —, it is true, had on a gown, no cassock, and a pair of striped Oxford grey trousers—not exactly the dress in which to meet his Bishop, who was to confirm in his church.

"When the surplices were brought to Mr. Evans, one was so absolutely filthy that he refused it; the other was merely a degree better, and indeed so dirty that I could not help saying, 'I wish, Mr. Evans, I could see you in a cleaner surplice.'

"Though it might be supposed that I had driven from Condover, there was neither wine nor biscuit—no, nor a glass of cold water—on the table. On going to the altar, no chair was provided for the Bishop, and I was forced to send to the vestry for a common rush-bottomed armchair. Mrs. C— came into the vestry after the Confirmation to apologise for Mr. C—'s being unable to receive me, which I told her I well knew to be the case. Then Mr. —, turning to Mrs. C—, said, 'Mrs. — is ill with the exertion of the bazaar.'

"Finding I did not look like sugar-candy when I saw all these instances of disrespectful neglect both in the vestry and church, he made a most unfortunate explanation to Mr. Evans, which he desired him to tell me, saying he was sorry he could not invite me to dinner, as his house was in great confusion, being full of toys from the bazaar. He seemed to have forgotten that he had invited me at a time when he was quite sure I would not accept it, but forgot to invite me (which no clergyman throughout my diocese except himself has done) a fortnight before the Confirmation, when he could have done so with grace; and with equal propriety, and without the possibility of giving offence, might have said to-day, or have written to me yesterday or the day before to say, that he was afraid he could not give me so comfortable a reception as he wished, owing to Mrs. —'s illness and the confusion of the bazaar; and then he added, 'Surely the Bishop cannot think I meant to slight him.' I care not sixpence as to myself individually, but when I appear in my public character I like things to be done with attention and decency, which they were not to-day. The negligence was great, and if this is not a slight I know not what is. I put you in possession of these facts, and if he says anything to you on the subject you may make what use you please of them."

Life and Letters of Dr. Butler

From H.R.H. the Duke of Sussex
(Published by permission of Her Majesty)

Kinmel Park, St. Asaph, September 19th, 1837.

"MY DEAR LORD, I have long intended to address you a letter, and anxiously to inquire after the state of your health, but from a variety of circumstances have been prevented from so doing. Returned again to this hospitable mansion at Kinmel, I feel myself more at liberty, and will therefore not refuse myself that pleasure of which I have been hitherto so continually deprived. But first let me congratulate your Lordship on the favourable accounts which I received at Shrewsbury as to the improved state of your health. God grant that it may long continue so, for the satisfaction of your friends as likewise for the benefit of society. On passing by the old school, I could not refrain from stopping and calling upon the young master, with whom I passed a very pleasant hour. We conversed together about your Lordship, and I was most happy to learn from him that you had successfully performed the arduous duty of confirming sixty-six of his pupils. The scene must have been one highly interesting to your Lordship, as it must have brought back to your recollection many events of a nature to have put your kind and affectionate feelings to the test. The very circumstance of returning to the old foundation in a new character, to admit into our Community a set of young lads who, thanks to your own exertions, owe their education and residence to your exertions for so many years in the sacred cause, as likewise finding the seminary presided over by one of your own most distinguished and favourite pupils, must have caused you emotions of a very exalted nature. Indeed I can hardly conceive any event more gratifying, or one more likely to excite feelings which, however delightful, must be in your present state somewhat controlled not to injure your health.

"Dr. Kennedy satisfied my curiosity upon all these points. We then conversed about the school, and I was happy to learn that it was keeping up its character, the importance of which I endeavoured to impress most strongly upon his mind. The more Eton, Westminster, and the Charterhouse are neglected, the greater the necessity that Shrewsbury, Harrow, and Winchester, as likewise Rugby, should prove to the world that advantageous alterations may be introduced into our public seminaries consonant with the opinions and the intellectual improvements going on daily in society.

"Dr. Kennedy told me that he had provided a German master for the school, which I think very judicious, in consequence of the connections of our language with the German, as likewise on account of the astonishing advance that sober and diligent nation is making in all the departments of science. We conversed over various matters, of passing events, of the state of things, of the Universities, and of men, and I certainly left the worthy master with feelings of respect and delight at the thoughts that your own wishes must be gratified on knowing that your place is so ably filled by so faithful a follower and so affectionate a disciple as Dr. Kennedy.

"As yet I cannot say much of this neighbourhood, having been but little out, in consequence of suffering slightly from my exertions in London during the last three months. Our excellent friend Lord Dinorben is pretty well, although under some affliction in consequence of the recent death of his favourite sister Lady Williams, who I believe is to be buried this week. She was a very amiable person, to whom he was most fondly attached, and at his time of life, when friends and relations drop off, one cannot help reflecting that their loss is not to be replaced. This, of course, is a source of affliction, but I have no doubt it has its good likewise, as it is a warning to ourselves and prepares us for the hour when we shall be called away to a better and, I believe, a more happy existence.

"My stay will not be long, I fear, in this part of the world, as the business of a new Parliament will necessarily call me back to town earlier than otherwise would be the case; but I think in the course of the winter I shall come down into your neighbourhood for a few days' shooting with my friend the Earl of Lichfield, and if I can get away for one morning I will endeavour then to make your Lordship a visit, should you be at that time at your residence. Lord Dinorben, who is aware that I am writing to your Lordship, requests to be most kindly remem-

bered to you. Except myself and Mr. Whateley, there are no other inmates but members of his own family. Lord and Lady Gordon arrived here on Saturday, and I found Lieutenant-Colonel and Mrs. Gray and family settled at Kinmel House. I fear I have trespassed too long upon your Lordship's valuable time, and therefore will conclude with subscribing myself, with affectionate regards, your Lordship's attached and obliged
"AUGUSTUS FREDERICK.

"P.S. Has your Lordship perused Macaulay's review of Basil Montagu's work upon Lord Bacon? I do not think I have for a long time perused an article of such interest, or written with greater power and ability."

To a Parent

Eccleshall Castle, September 24th, 1837.

"SIR, I beg to assure you I am the last person who would take offence at a parent's anxiety to advance his son's interests, but I am sorry to say that you write under a great apparent misapprehension of my ability to serve him. The Bishop of Lichfield is one of the poorest patrons on the Bench; he not only has but little to give for a Bishop, but the value of that little is small. Almost the only important living in his gift is transferred to Worcester, and he will probably have but one stall in his Cathedral at his free disposal. I have but three livings in Cheshire—the only good one I gave away immediately on my coming into the See. It is double the value of a living not in my own gift held by my son, whose merits I appreciate as you do those of yours, but I would not give it him that I might not appear selfish. Your son I have always heard highly spoken of, but so, I thank God, are many of the seven or eight hundred clergy in my diocese, among whom I have to dispose of about thirty pieces of preferment, many not equal in value even to Coseley, supposing I live to present to all in my gift, but as I cannot value my life at three months' purchase, you see how little chance I have of giving any.

"I have made no promise to any one, and I probably never

shall, but though I have clergy in view who I think would do honour to any appointment I could make, I cannot see till vacancies arise what may be the fittest course for me to pursue. I shall probably dissatisfy many on every occasion, even though I may be anxious to do right. I cannot but wish your son all success, but from some more efficient patron, for I certainly will hold out no expectation where there is so little chance of its being fulfilled. I remain, Sir, your very obedient humble servant,

"S. LICHFIELD."

From Mr. N— (a Schoolmaster)

September 23rd, 1837.

"MAY IT PLEASE YOUR LORDSHIP, It is with the deepest regret I have to complain to your Lordship of the very disgraceful conduct of the Rev. Mr. —, minister of the parish of —, in which I reside. For thirty years or more I believe he has been the minister of this parish, and during the greater part of that period his conduct has been anything rather than what it ought to be, but more particularly of late years he is grown so very drunken, and has exhibited such an utter disregard for the welfare of himself, for the flock over which he presides, and for religion in general, that it has become absolutely necessary your Lordship should be made acquainted with it, in order that something may be done to recall him to a sense of his duty as a man, but more especially as a minister of Jesus Christ.

"I have a considerable school in the parish, and I have observed with sorrow that all the instructions I can instil into the minds of my pupils are rendered abortive by the wicked example of he who ought to be their guide to a better world. I have also a family of six children, and, with the best wishes to bring them up in a proper manner, I fear they also may be infected with the contagion of so bad an example in their minister. On attending the Sacrament, which is very rarely administered in this parish, I was sorry to observe that neither the minister nor his clerk received it; and it would be endless and tiresome for your Lordship to peruse or for me to state the many acts of wickedness and drunkenness committed by this person. I would therefore only crave your Lordship's attention and patience while I relate a few particulars that have come to my knowledge within the last twelve months, during which time he has grown worse and worse, and is never sober when he can get at liquor.

"Is there a juggler, mountebank, or showman enters the village, he is the first to give them encouragement and to wish them success, and the first to witness such sights, and by his example to encourage others. Is there a dog-fight, a bull to be baited, or a fight between two of his parishioners, he is the first to witness and encourage it, and I have known him prevented for a month together doing duty, from black eyes which he had received when drunk and fighting with his own son. Not long ago a fight happened at one of the public-houses, and he must needs get on a wall to see it, when one of the bystanders pushed him down, and, being drunk, it so enraged him that he drew a knife, and swore that if he knew who did it, he would stab him to the heart. At Whitsuntide this year he was drunk before service time, and because the club-men did not come to church just at the moment he wanted them, he got into a violent rage, and swore he had prepared a good sermon for them, and says he, 'What the devil do you want?' At night he dined as usual with them and got beastly drunk, but this is an almost daily occurrence. A short time since he was out till after midnight, and because the man who has the care of him did not at once get up to let him in, he went and borrowed an axe and cut the door to pieces to make an entrance. I have known him, when in this beastly state, put into a small cart by the boys of the village, and exhibited through the streets like some wild beast, and at every turn a shout would be set up that I have heard at the distance of half a mile. At all weddings, christenings, and funerals he is in liquor, and if he has not money to procure it, he makes a practice of demeaning himself by asking his clerk for some, and he curses and swears and makes use of language that would disgrace the mouth of the most abandoned reprobate. He was so drunk the other day at the funeral of one Mrs. Hill that he could scarcely get through the service, and afterwards went to the house of deceased and got so drunk that he was obliged to be conveyed home in a chair. Some days after, a little girl died suddenly, and on pretence of his love for the child, he said he wished to see her after death, to which the father consented. On returning downstairs, he seated himself in a chair, and would not leave the house until he had obliged the poor man to send for a quart of ale for him to drink, which he did much against his will.

"But not to tire your Lordship with more details, I beg to state that I have waited five years for an alteration for the better, but finding the state of the parish daily getting worse, and that no one attempts to inform your Lordship of it, I could no longer hold my peace, and I do hope I need not apologise for so doing, since my only aim is the honour of God, the benefit of my fellow-creatures, and the ultimate good of him of whom I now complain. In consequence of such conduct two sets of Dissenters have meetings here, and as very few attend the church, I fear that in a short time the parishioners in general will be induced to forsake it altogether. I trust I love God, and I love my Church, and I humbly trust and hope that your Lordship will be pleased to take such steps in this affair as may redeem our holy religion from the degraded state into which it is sunk in this parish by the culpable neglect and bad conduct of its wicked minister. And may God of His infinite mercy turn this man from the error of his ways, and bring him out of darkness into His marvellous light, before the day of grace be for ever fled. And may we all unite in our endeavour to establish the religion of the Blessed Jesus here on earth, that we, through grace, may have an inheritance in Heaven, where our Blessed Saviour stands as our Mediator and Intercessor at the right hand of God. Amen.

"N.B. I beg to refer your Lordship for his general character to the Rev. —, Vicar of —, and to the Rev. Mr. —, Minister of —, two adjoining parishes. These reverend gentlemen know his conduct in general, although they may not be aware of many particulars. Some years ago I begged the Rev. Mr. — to speak to him touching his conduct and to try to do him good in a brotherly Christian way, but our minister is of so violent a disposition that the reverend gentleman declined to hold any correspondence with him."

Note in Dr. Butler's handwriting:

"Will be inquired into as soon as the Bishop can see the Archdeacon next week. Meanwhile Bishop wants to know the names and characters of the churchwardens, and whether Mr. N— is ready to substantiate his charges upon oath, and can bring other witnesses in confirmation of them.—S.L."

From Mr. N— (a Schoolmaster)

October 3rd, 1837.

"MY LORD, In obedience to your Lordship's commands of the 28th ult. I hasten to inform you that Mr. Christopher C—, an Irishman and a man of wicked life and bad principles, a farmer, and whose house stands near to the parsonage, has been chosen churchwarden by the minister year after year, for many years past, and they were constant Sunday-evening companions in drunkenness until last spring, when Mr. —'s conduct one night was so bad that even his wicked companion grew tired of him and ordered him to quit his house, and since then his visits have been less frequent. Mr. James O— is the other churchwarden chosen by the parishioners for the current year, and I am not aware of any irregular conduct on his part; but I am convinced that if your Lordship should be pleased to authorise an inquiry into the parish affairs, the books which ought to be kept are either not in being, or else in the most confused and disorderly state, as an instance of which I beg to direct your Lordship's attention to this one thing. Sometime in the year 1836, the overseer, Thomas Grant, presented to the magistrates of Wolverhampton a statement of defalcations which had occurred in the parish respecting levies for the poor, among which was one to the amount of £113 and upwards against the Rev. Mr. —, upon suing which the magistrates declared that no levy should be granted until the whole of those arrears were made good. The result is that no levy for the poor has since been collected, and all those donations left by charitably disposed persons (and of which there hangs a table in the church to a great amount), which should have been distributed among the orderly and deserving poor as an encouragement to maintain their families without parish assistance, have been paid (I am informed) to the Union instead of levies, and the original intentions of the donors have been by these means entirely set aside, and for which there seems to be no redress except by the generous interference of your Lordship.

"In addition to the details in my last letter I beg to state to your Lordship that in 1834 Mrs. Hilton, an elderly lady in the parish, was taken ill, and apprehensive that her end was approaching. Mr. — attended her in his capacity as minister; but instead of affording the least spiritual consolation, his conduct and conversation proved so very disgusting to her (being constantly on the topics of dog-fights, bull-baiting, and language to the same effect), that she was under the necessity of dispensing with his attendance, and of quitting this life without the comfort of the Sacrament of the Lord's Supper.

"And some time afterwards at the same house, in the presence of the Rev. J. W. W— and Miss Anslow, the niece of Mr. Hilton, when he was drinking himself drunk, Miss Anslow, being grieved to see him in such a state, observed to him that the duty of the Church was by him so much neglected that it ought to be made known to the Bishop, upon which he flew in a passion, cursed the Bishop, the King, and all concerned, and swore he knew those present were endeavouring to get him out; but, says he, with an oath, 'It shall cost you something to do it.' Miss Anslow can substantiate the former occurrence, and she and the Rev. J. W. W—, the latter upon oath. His conduct, indeed, on this occasion was so very wicked that Mr. W— was under the necessity of threatening to report it to the then Bishop of the Diocese. And when a sick person requires to receive the Sacrament, he is in the habit of going from house to house begging wine for the purpose; two instances of this sort have occurred within the last six weeks, to the great disgrace of religion in general and of this parish in particular. Yet, notwithstanding all that has been or may be said against the morals and behaviour of the Rev. Mr. —, I should much rather rejoice at his conversion than his conviction, but I do fear that desirable object, after so long a course of wickedness, will not be easily brought about.

"I have stated below the several charges against the Rev. —, and against each the names of those persons who were present on each disgraceful occasion, as far as I have been enabled to ascertain; but in a few days more I trust I shall be enabled to add considerably to the list of witnesses, when I will write your Lordship again.

"Fighting with his own son and receiving black eyes, and stabbing his son with a knife. Drunkenness and cursing and swearing at Whitsuntide. John Furber, the parish clerk, told me last night that he remembers the whole affair, though five or six years ago, and that he was the person who fetched the Rev. Mr. F— to do the duty, who officiated five or six Sundays on this occasion.

"Cutting the parsonage door to pieces with an axe. Drunkenness at Miss Fitzpatrick's funeral, and being conveyed home in a donkey-cart. Jane Richards, who lent him the axe; Mr. Charles Brown, who stood by; and John Furber, the clerk; and Thomas Thorpe, who repaired the door; besides Mr. Savage and his wife, who were inside.

"Drunkenness at Mrs. Hill's funeral, and conveyance home in a chair. Mr. Thomas Thorpe, William Hollis, and Mr. Savage.

"Ill-conduct at the death of James Harper's daughter. James Harper, of whom he demanded drink, and Mrs. Mary Harper, his wife, who fetched it.

"Ill-conduct when attending the late Mrs. Hilton in sickness. Miss Mary Coats Anslow.

"Disgraceful scene at Mrs. Hilton's in cursing the Bishop and the King. Miss Mary Coats Anslow and the Rev. J. W. W—, Minister, W—.

"Witnessing a battle, and shocking language used by him at the 'Pigot's Arms' public-house.

"Your Lordship will perceive that I have not been able to collect the whole evidence, but I am doing all I can."[1]

[1] Cf. letter on pp. 351, 352.

Correspondence

To the Rev. Matthew Tunstall, Belper, Derbyshire

Eccleshall Castle, October 6th, 1837.

"REV. SIR, I am sorry to tell you I cannot admit the Rev. — as your curate at Belper and Turnditch. I regret that previously to sending him the nomination (which I have returned to him) you did not think it proper to acquaint me with your intentions, for it is the duty of every clergyman to give his diocesan due notice in this respect, that he may make the requisite inquiries, not only as to moral character and fitness of capacity, but also as to the soundness of doctrine and religious opinions of the party about to be appointed.

"I must therefore request you to look out for some other assistant, whose name, reference for inquiries, and present residence you will have the kindness to make known to me. With regard to Mr. — you do not so much as state whether he was selected by yourself, recommended by a friend, or proposed by the Pastoral Aid Society, all which are points which I hold it very desirable to know. I cannot admit a curate on a title who has not received an education at Cambridge, Oxford, or Durham, and in any other case I must have an Englishman who, though only a literate person, may bring me satisfactory testimonials on the points above mentioned. I remain, Rev. Sir, your affectionate brother,

"S. LICHFIELD."

To the Curate referred to in the preceding Letter

Eccleshall Castle, October 6th, 1837.

"REV. SIR, On my return from Lichfield I found your letter and papers, and I can assure you it is with great pain that I feel bound to tell you, in as kind and little offensive a manner as possible, that the same reasons that prevent me from admitting you as a candidate for the order of priesthood in this diocese necessarily oblige me to decline the offer of your services as a deacon. I return your nomination and testimonials, though I might retain them as addressed to myself, as a proof of my being influenced in my decision by no personal motive whatever, but merely by a sense of duty, for the sincerity of which declaration

I trust you will give me the same credit as I am perfectly willing to allow to you.

"Of the first three signatures Mr. Gell's is a name for which, though we may differ in some of our theological opinions, I have recently given a proof of my esteem by an appointment to a confidential office. For Mr. Shirley I have long entertained a very high respect, and should certainly have fixed on him for a similar appointment had he been resident in the county. With Mr. Greville I have not the honour of being so well acquainted personally, but I make not the slightest question of his respectability. But there is a fourth name—an unusual thing—subjoined at which I was startled for the moment, till I recollected the invariable kindness with which he spoke of you even when lamenting the differences which existed between you. May I hope that you were led from motives of pure respect and regard for him, and not from any more mixed feeling, to ask his signature? I should much rejoice if it has been the means of establishing a good understanding between you, and mean to write to him on the subject. I remain, Rev. Sir, your affectionate brother, "S. LICHFIELD."

To the Rev. J. Harward, Wirksworth

Eccleshall Castle, October 6th, 1837.

"MY DEAR SIR, Most distressing as it is to me to say a word which may give pain to a man whom I esteem so much as I do you, I must confess to you that in the signature you have given to Mr. ——'s testimonials you have suffered your kindness of heart much to outrun your prudence. After having stated to me that he told his congregation in an extempore sermon that he was now teaching under the influence of the Spirit, the scales having fallen from his eyes, and that he lamented the darkness prevailing in the parish; after having told you that he felt a change wrought in his heart instantaneously, and power imparted to him to explain and understand in a way he dared not deviate from, and much more that I need not repeat; and after his gross and indecent violations of the discipline of the Church of England, as well as the utter inconsistency with her doctrines on the grounds above mentioned,—how can I, my dear sir, be anything but astounded at finding your name to a testimonial which states that he hath not at any time, as far as you know or believe, held, written, or taught anything contrary to the doctrine or discipline of the United Church of England and Ireland, and moreover that you believe him to be a person worthy to be licensed to the curacy of Belper (containing ten thousand souls)? It is true your letter to me explains that you have a reservation as to discipline, but this does not appear in the testimonial, which is the document he has to produce to the public, and I have no doubt will produce, for I have refused to license him. But in what a predicament am I placed, and in what a predicament may I be obliged to place you, if he or his party get some one to attack me in the House of Lords or Commons, which I fully expect, or before the Archbishop, and I am obliged to produce in self-defence your letter of August 7th, containing what is above stated and much more. I am greatly afraid his application was only made to entangle you, for it was already signed by three beneficed clergymen—and your name was certainly written fourth and last, as is evident from inspection of the document. Now it is very unusual to have more than three signatures, and yours was certainly not requisite. I enclose a copy of what I have said to him on the subject, for it seemed to me necessary to notice it, as affording me some ground for defending you from the apparent inconsistency between the testimonial and former charges.

"I have said this much with pain, from the fear that it may give you uneasiness; but I beseech you to consider that, though I am grieved at what you have done from too great feelings of kindness, nothing relating to it can for a moment disturb the deep and friendly regard with which I remain, dear Sir, very truly yours,

"S. LICHFIELD."

From Mr. N— (a Schoolmaster)

October 8th, 1837.

"MY LORD, When I first wrote your Lordship to complain of the conduct of the Rev. Mr. —, I did so, not with any particular desire that he should be brought to trial, but under the idea that your Lordship, being made acquainted with his ill-behaviour, might be induced to reprove him in such manner as your Lordship may deem most effectual to restrain him in future from his wicked courses. I was most certainly not aware of the difficulties that seem to lie in your Lordship's way as respects this affair, otherwise I think I should not have troubled your Lordship with a narration which must prove so very disagreeable to you. It is much to be lamented that cases of this nature do not come within the scope of your Lordship's authority, or I do believe they would not be long unredressed.

"There appears, moreover, to be more difficulty in procuring evidence than I at first apprehended, for though the facts stated by me are manifest as the sun at noon, yet upon calling on those who ought to speak out there appears a certain reluctance to come forward, such as I should not have expected, but it seems, these scenes being constantly occurring, the people are in general become indifferent to them.

"I am very sorry that it will be out of my power to meet your Lordship's secretary, Mr. Mott, at Newport on the 18th instant, as my school being three times a day—that is to say, morning, afternoon, and evening—it takes up the whole of my time, and having a wife and six children all at home to maintain, it is quite as much as I can do and use my utmost exertions to provide them a subsistence. But should your Lordship still determine to pursue this affair, and to depute some one to this neighbourhood to investigate the matter more fully, I will give all the assistance I can, and will not flinch from speaking all I know when called upon.

"I am sorry to have to say that Mr. —, since I first wrote to your Lordship, was, on Tuesday night the 26th ult., found drunk by a female named Ann Peplow, lying on his back in the street in the middle of the village."

To the Rev. Matthew Tunstall

Eccleshall Castle, October 13th, 1837.

"REV. SIR, The conclusion of your letter, which assures me it was written without Mr. —'s knowledge or concurrence,

is very satisfactory to me as far as that gentleman is concerned, but I regret to say that I have very strong reasons for being obliged to withhold my concurrence in your proposal; nor, indeed, to deal plainly, can I consent to his officiating at Belper for a single Sunday. I am told the living is exceedingly too small for its very onerous duties, and the curacy in like manner, and for that among other reasons I should be glad to show the curate every indulgence and attention in my power. But the present case is one in which, with every disposition to oblige you, weightier considerations make it impossible. If you can provide any other person whom I may approve I shall not hesitate to accede to your wishes. I remain, Rev. Sir, your obedient humble servant,
" S. LICHFIELD."

To the Ven. Archdeacon Hodson

Eccleshall Castle, October 13th, 1837.

" MY DEAR ARCHDEACON, I have really an unpleasant business on which to write to you, but I must beg you to tell your groom, who accompanied you here, that if he does not restore me or tell you at once where I may recover my dog which he took from this house, I must send a summons for him on Monday morning. I value the dog exceedingly as having been given me by Robert Evans. He is a black terrier puppy about five months old (I have had him four), with tanned muzzle, a little tan on the breast and down the fore-legs, his ears and tail lately cropped, the latter not quite healed. He would not so much as follow my own servants out of the home grounds, and I have traced your man by a number of witnesses coaxing him along the road all the way to Stone and returning back without him. I daresay he will tell you that the dog followed him against his will, and he could not drive him back and lost him in Stone. I am not fool enough to believe that. The dog would not follow anybody, and so far from attempting to drive him back, he was seen coaxing him on. My coachman has been at his mother's, but could make nothing out there. The man went before our servants' dinner-time, saying that, as his master was out, he should go and see some friends. He is supposed to have returned about six, at least he did not appear here till then, and never opened his lips about the dog. I suppose he has either sold him or given him to the care of some friend in Stone. All that I can say is, if he does not accept the offer of indemnity as far as I am concerned now, he may depend on hearing further from me. I would recommend you not to give him too long time for deliberation, else he will get the dog made away with. Believe me, dear Archdeacon, yours faithfully,

"S. LICHFIELD."

From H.R.H. the Duke of Sussex
(Published by permission of Her Majesty)
October 22nd, 1837.

" MY DEAR LORD, I have to return you my best thanks for two letters which I have received from you,—the first conveying to me your address to your *ci-devant* pupils on the occasion of confirming sixty-six of them, and which I perused with much interest; the second announcing to me the kind intention of Mrs. Johnstone to send me a Memoir of her late husband's life, which she has entrusted to your care. I shall accept with gratitude the gift, as I have no doubt it will contain matter of great interest, and I am gratified by the worthy lady's recollection of me upon the present occasion. Perhaps your Lordship would be so kind as to convey these sentiments to Mrs. Johnstone. In my way up to town I fear I cannot avail myself of your Lordship's kind offer, as I remain here till the latest moment, when I hurry up to town to meet her Majesty's Ministers previous to the 9th of November. In the beginning of December I shall most probably come into your neighbourhood, when I will certainly take advantage of your kind invitation with the greatest pleasure, since I long to see how your Lordship has put your valuable library together, which must be a magnificent collection. Has your Lordship heard anything of your brother of Durham? I would think the Rev. Messrs. Townsend and Greaves must afford him some trouble as well as to the Lord Archbishop of York. What would these men be about? They are certainly agitating points which had much better be left alone, and raising questions to which many would dissent, not to use a stronger expression of their being objectionable.

"The attempt at declaring the Church independent of the State is one which no Englishman who understands the history and laws of his country can allow to be suggested without entering his immediate protest. More I will not say at present, but I fear that the House of Commons will not allow such a document as that which appeared in the *Morning Chronicle* of the 19th, signed G. Townsend, to pass unnoticed.

"Excuse, my dear Lord, this hasty scrawl, and with wishing you health and happiness believe me ever, with esteem and regard, your Lordship's obliged, etc., etc.,

"AUGUSTUS FREDERICK."

From the document above referred to, which appeared in the *Morning Chronicle*, 18th October 1837, I take the following:

"At a meeting of the clergy of the peculiar of the Dean and Chapter of Durham in Allerton and Allertonshire (convened by the Master-Keeper at the request of the clergy), held at Northallerton, September 18th, 1837, the Rev. George Townsend, Master-Keeper, in the chair, it was resolved

"I. 'That the privileges granted by the State to the Episcopal Church in England do neither weaken nor interrupt, much less destroy, its duties as a Church of God.'

"II. 'That our duty to God, as ministers of the Church, is to be preferred to obedience to any human enactments which may clash with our more solemn obligations.'

"III. 'That the mode of our duty to God is prescribed, partly by Scripture, and partly by the written laws and rubric of the Church as a spiritual society.'

"IV. 'That a petition be drawn up and presented to the Archbishop of York, the ecclesiastical head of this province, on the subject of certain specific grievances now pressing upon the clergy with regard—

1. To certain clauses in the new Marriage Act.
2. To certain clauses in the Registration Act.

3. To the law of enclosure of waste lands, as affected by the Tithe Commutation Act.
4. To the law of *praemunire*.
5. To the assembling of Convocation.'

" v. 'That in petitioning for exemption from civil punishment for our religious obedience to the ecclesiastical laws which we, in our consciences, believe to be consistent with Scripture and antiquity—agreed upon in Convocation, and prescribed by the rubric—we pray only for the same privileges as those which are now enjoyed by all Jews, Turks, heretics, and sectarians of every description.'

" vi. 'That a quorum be requested to draw up a petition relating to the five grievances of which this meeting complains; and that the Rev. George Townsend, the Rev. Henry John Duncombe, and the Rev. — Greaves be requested to wait upon the Archbishop when they have ascertained upon what day his Grace will be pleased to receive the same.'"

Then followed the petition embodying the resolutions.

To a Clergyman

Eccleshall Castle, October 20th, 1837.

" REV. SIR, I have repeatedly said that the charge against you is not for any crime, but for conduct which tends to lower a clergyman in the estimation of his brethren—that of demanding money for assistance given occasionally. You admit that you have been in the habit of doing this for four years, and whether you have actually received the money or not from such as could afford it makes, in my view of the case, no difference. If you think you can clear yourself from the imputation which you yourself admit, having before stated that you are ready to declare upon oath that you have never taken duties at another church for remuneration, when you procured your own duty to be served gratuitously, I am ready to give you that opportunity if you choose to meet me at the Crown at Stone on Thursday, November 2nd, at twelve o'clock (my engagements are such that, though I have tried to fix an earlier day, I cannot), accompanied by any three friends you may choose. I shall invite the Archdeacon of Stafford and the Rural Dean of —— to be present *ex officio*; I shall summon Mr. B——, Mr. R——, and Mr. A—— as witnesses, and if I find occasion to summon any others I will let you know; and I shall ask two or three persons of respectability to be present unconnected with ——, in order to prevent any misrepresentation. If you bring any attorney, I shall take care to have one of these two or three persons in the profession of the law, simply that his acquaintance with the laws of evidence may prevent any improper questions being put. The others may be clergy. I remain, Rev. Sir, your obedient humble servant,

"S. LICHFIELD.

"P.S. I beg the favour of an early answer."

To a Clergyman

Eccleshall Castle, October 23rd, 1837.

"REV. SIR, In reply to your letter of the 20th, which I received last night, I beg to say that I cannot deem it expedient that you should accept the offer made you by the Independent Dissenters for the use of their chapel for your expository lectures. I trust, however, that I need not exhort you to decline with courtesy, both on your part and my own, what it is but fair to presume is offered in kindness. Still there would be an anomaly in your acceptance which I cannot by any means approve or admit.

"The population of Stowe in 1831 was 1,283, increased very likely by this time to the number you state, and Hixton appears on the map the most populous township, but not above a mile or a mile and a quarter at most from Stowe, if it is rightly laid down. If the inhabitants will not take the trouble to come so far to hear your sermons, and much more to hear the beautiful prayers of our Liturgy, which are superior to any sermons that were ever written, I am sure they do not deserve to have them brought to their doors. They are like men who would offer sacrifice to the Lord their God of that which doth cost them nothing. If your church is too small, can it not be enlarged by a side-aisle or gallery?

"If nothing but a room at Hixton will serve their turn, are there not sufficient inhabitants to subscribe and rent one, which, if a case of great and sufficient exigence were made out, might be licensed for exposition of the Scriptures and prayer according to the ritual of the Church of England?

"I presume you are curate to Mr. Cave Browne Cave, but I do not recollect signing your licence. I beg you to inform me whether you are licensed, and if not, why so long a time as four months has been allowed to pass without application made to me. I remain, Rev. Sir, your very humble servant,

"S. LICHFIELD."

To the Rev. W. Fisher

Eccleshall Castle, November 4th, 1837.

"REV. SIR, In a letter which I have just received from the Rev. Richard Whinfield of Heanor, he tells me that in a conversation with you respecting the appointment of a curate by the Pastoral Aid Society, you told him that you did not know whether a clergyman recommended by himself or by me would be accepted by them, as he must be an Evangelical man.

"Allow me to ask whether this statement of his is either in words, or at least in substance, correct? and also if there actually does exist any such rule in the society?

"I remain, Rev. Sir, your affectionate brother,

"S. LICHFIELD."

To a Clergyman

Eccleshall Castle, November 9th, 1837.

"REV. SIR, Every application made to me connected with the Pastoral Aid Society has been accompanied with a recommendation of a candidate for orders. Having observed this, I decline receiving such. If you will find me a curate already in orders with whose character upon inquiry I may be satisfied, and who blends discretion with diligence in the discharge of his parochial duties, I shall have no objection to license him. Archdeacon Hodson well knows the sort of curate whom I should approve, and if you will take the trouble to consult him,

it will be very satisfactory to me. I remain, Rev. Sir, your obedient faithful servant,
"S. LICHFIELD."

From Mrs. Butler

November (?), 1837.

"MY DEAREST BISHOP, I received your letter with such delight last night, partly because I thought that it was hardly probable I should hear from you before to-day, for I concluded you would have been too tired to have written from Daventry. I am so very glad that you are so much better and write in such good spirits; it puts me in mind of old times again. I am very glad that Noah drove you so well, and think there is great promise of him. Poor old John[1] gave me a very good report of you from Stafford; he told us you were talking with Mr. Hodson in such good spirits. The poor old man seems so happy here that I have agreed to have him stay his week. To-day it is beautiful weather, and Mr. Moore is taking advantage of it, and is very busy arranging about the trees being thinned where necessary; he is as anxious about them as possible.

"If there is another volume of Girdlestone's Old Testament published perhaps you will send me it, as I shall be very glad to go on with it, and I shall like it bound the same as the others. God grant me understanding to hearken to His word! We yesterday had a letter from my sister Fanny; it was written to Harriet as well as myself; she writes a wonderful hand for so old a woman. We are all very comfortable here; the girls read of an evening, while us elder ones work. Harriet and I have begun the new stair-carpet, which I think will be very pretty, but there is too small a piece worked to judge of it at present. We are going to take a walk, for we find after twelve or one o'clock the beauty of the day goes off, and now we dine at two it is best to go out early. We have not heard from Tom, but hope we shall soon, for I am a little anxious to know how Fanny is at Langar; he did not say much for her in his last letter. We have not had a line from Mary, but we shall hear very soon, I daresay, for she, dear soul, is seldom long without

[1] John Gregory, a former servant at the schools. -ED.

writing. I feel much better than I used to do; I find an astonishing difference in myself since last August, when we were at Beaumaris. With all our love, believe me, dearest Bishop, your affectionate wife,
            " HARRIET BUTLER."

To C. K. Murray, Esq.
  16, Suffolk Street, November 16th, 1837.

" DEAR SIR, May I ask you to call the attention of the Church Commissioners to the case of the residentiary stall of Sawley, in the Cathedral of Lichfield, if they have not already come to a decision about it? You may recollect that it is at present attached by Act of Parliament to the living of St. Philip's at Birmingham, which is taken out of my patronage by the new arrangement of the See and transferred to that of the Bishop of Worcester. The incumbent of St. Philip's is old, infirm, and has had two severe paralytic attacks; his life therefore cannot be reckoned of any probable very long duration, and may possibly be brought to an unexpected termination should fresh attacks of paralysis come on. Now in that case, should the new Rector of St. Philip's appointed by the Bishop of Worcester come to Lichfield and claim from me immediate installation to his stall (in fact I do not know whether he may not even take possession of it as part of his living, without institution under the present Act of Parliament), I should be placed in a very awkward situation were I to refuse him, unless I could show the authority of the Church Commissioners for so doing. If they would be pleased during the present incumbency to make an order for the extinction of the stall on its becoming vacant, and for the appropriation of its revenues in such way as they may think fit, I should then feel justified in refusing institution to a new rector, should he demand it. By the way I may just mention that the income of the stall is very large, and would provide an ample endowment for the Rector of St. Philip's, and also a respectable income for the minister of any new church which might be built in that very populous district. I remain, dear Sir, your obedient faithful servant,   " S. LICHFIELD."

Correspondence

To the Rev. C. Girdlestone

16, Suffolk Street, Pall Mall East, November 25th, 1837

"DEAR SIR, The business of Parliament and Convocation, which I regularly attended, though my name does not appear in the papers, together with a most distressing affair at Lichfield, which you will probably hear of, has so entirely occupied me this week that I could not sooner reply to your letters. I cannot but consider it an honour to have been fixed upon by two such respectable clergymen as Mr. Lewis and yourself to decide a question between you; but I must own that, had I been at Eccleshall, I should have begged you to apply in some other quarter, from a sense of my own inability to do justice to the case when I had no references at hand to whom I might apply in cases of doubt or difficulty. Here, where I can have the very best assistance possible, as often as I require it, and where I can submit my whole judgement to the revision of faithful, experienced, and confidential advisers, I feel that I ought not to shrink from the discharge of the duty required of me, and will therefore undertake it on hearing that you both assent to the conditions following:

"The object being to put an end to a dispute, I propose that you shall agree to my decision being final, and, as it will be carefully revised before it is announced, that it shall not be subject to further revision.

"That if either of you have anything to add to the statement I have already received, this shall be done in the course of next week, so that nothing fresh shall be received by me after Monday, December 4th.

"That I shall not be called upon to assign the reasons of my decision, or to give the names of the parties whom I may have consulted, assuring you now, as I do, that they shall be persons of known honour and experience. On receiving an agreement signed by both of you to this effect, I will use all care and diligence in the matter.

"Meantime, with cordial good wishes to you both, I remain, dear Sir, faithfully yours,

"S. LICHFIELD."

To — (?)

16, Suffolk Street, November 26th, 1837.

"DEAR SIR, I do not well enough recollect the peculiarities of St. John's Chapel to say whether they present any strong obstacle to my acceptance of it as a title, but this I can say, that I shall not look out for any, and shall be anxious to accommodate you to the best of my power. I expect that all candidates should be at least A.B. of one of our English Universities (Durham included), or if of T. C. D. that they shall have been born of English parents. My general rule is to require six months' notice, both for the purpose of making my own inquiries and of giving the candidate time to prepare himself in the subjects required.

"I have also found it necessary to refuse candidates for ordination from the Pastoral Aid Society, because I found none but such were ever sent to me, and I do not choose to be made a stepping-stone in this manner for admission into Holy Orders. Curates who are already ordained I am quite ready to admit from that society (subject, of course, to my approval in other respects), as that is a very different case. If therefore, as I infer, you have any intention of obtaining assistance from thence, may I beg you to recommend to me a curate already in orders?

"I have, however, one exception to the rule I have quoted above, which is when the candidate for orders comes to me on the recommendation of the incumbent, without the recommendation of the society to him in the first instance—because that is, in fact, a transaction between individuals, and not between an individual and a great public body; and if you have such a candidate to offer—you, of course, and not the society (for they cannot do it), becoming responsible, as in all other cases, for the stipend and for his continuance—I shall have no objection to receive him as a candidate, although you may have a grant in aid from the society. My next ordination will be, D.V., on Sunday, January 28th, and though the time presses, yet if you cannot obtain an eligible curate already ordained, I will waive my usual regulations as to previous notice in your favour, if the candidate is one for whom you can personally answer.

"I wish I could say the same respecting the system of trustee patronage. But I am sure it is carried too far already, and the check which I require is also invariably insisted upon by the Incorporated Society for the Building and Enlargement of Churches. I do not think that your worst enemy or mine would venture to accuse either of us of being influenced in this matter by mercenary motives. I remain, dear Sir, faithfully yours,

"S. LICHFIELD."

To the Churchwardens of Stoke-upon-Trent

16, Suffolk Street, Pall Mall, November 30th, 1837.

"GENTLEMEN, I have received within the last two days a document from yourselves and other inhabitants of the parish of Stoke-upon-Trent, bearing testimony to the merits of Sir William Dunbar and asking for preferment for him if I have any to bestow. I hope and trust that I am as deeply sensible of the great worth of Sir William's services as any of the gentlemen who have signed that address, and I should feel sorry if I did not believe that Sir William Dunbar himself knows how highly I esteem him. But you probably are not aware how small in extent and value my patronage is, the only really important piece of preferment being taken from me by the alteration in my diocese under the Church Commissioners, and of the little probability there is of my having any at my disposal, considering how precarious my own life is, and how much older I am than the great majority of the incumbents.

"But, gentlemen, were the contrary the case, you must excuse me if I say that the method you have taken, though often adopted, is the most unlikely, on all occasions, to succeed — because it interferes so entirely with the right of patronage, and so cripples the hands of patrons, who may have many highly deserving clergymen on their lists besides the individual whom you recommend, and may have views and engagements of which you know not and which they cannot put by; I trust therefore you will excuse my sincerity and plain dealing, and not attribute it to any disrespect or want of goodwill, when I say that I must decline holding out any promise or expectation of

that kind whatever. I have the honour to be, gentlemen, your very obedient faithful servant,
"S. LICHFIELD."

From the Ven. Archdeacon Bather

Shrewsbury, St. Julian's Vestry, December 2nd, 1837.

" MY DEAR LORD, I have been requested by a meeting of the clergy of my archdeaconry to inquire of you—Whether, in the opinion of the Episcopal Bench, any revision or amendment is likely to take place, or to be attempted in the present Session of Parliament, of the late Acts of William IV and her present Majesty for 'Marriages in England' and for 'Registration of Births, Deaths, and Marriages.'

" The clergy are not in haste to lay their grievances before Parliament by Petition. In some particulars they may themselves have misapprehended the provisions of Acts so complicated, and possibly may be in some cases mistaken in the view they take of the bearing and probable effects of them, but, as at present advised, they feel aggrieved in several ways: by the imposition of burdens on themselves and the subjecting of them to penalties for the neglect of duties hard to be performed and not heretofore required of them; by the contrariety (as they take it) of the new Statutes to the ancient Rubricks which they are bound to observe; and, above all, by the danger which seems to arise out of the Act—that the people will be led, in spite of the best efforts of their spiritual guides, to neglect the Sacrament of Baptism. Under these views, if no amendment of the Acts takes place speedily, the clergy may think it their duty to petition the Legislature in due time.

" I need not trouble your Lordship with full particulars, but the chief points are these:

I. " The Rubrick requires the publication of banns—the Act requires marriage to be solemnised on production of the registrar's certificate.

II. " The Rubrick in the Burial Service forbids Christian burial to unbaptised persons—the Act requires burial of any corpse on production of certificate that the death has been registered.

III. "By § 27 of Will. IV, Cap. 86, the clergy are required to send notice of the burial of any corpse which they may inter within seven days after burial (if certificate of registration of death has not been delivered), and that at their own cost and responsibility, and under £10 penalty, to registrar of district where deceased died, whatever be the distance from place of burial.

IV. "In Registration Act there are provisions which tend to bring baptism into disesteem and disuse.

"Probably the clergy on examination will see that there is no ground for objecting under the first head, and that they had better not pray that the registrar's certificate may not come into the church. As to the second point, the question is not about persons baptised by Dissenters, but wholly unbaptised, as they are more likely to be now than ever. It would be well that the clergy should have their minds set at rest on this point. The third point is a grievance, I think, chiefly in the case of parties brought to be buried from a distance. As to the last, an examination of the sections relating to it, XVIII, XIX, XX-XXII, XXIII of the Registration Act, I cannot think but a great snare is laid for the people, which it does not become a Christian Government to lay. The ignorant will see no difference between naming a child and baptising it, and others, having secured the civil privileges to their children by registration, will not care about baptism. This will not happen necessarily, but yet will come to pass in fact. And let the clergy do their duty as they may, they will not be able to prevent it in large towns. The provision that the baptismal name may be added only on payment of a fee many think should be repealed, by abolition of the fee. But this will not do much, though perhaps something.

"The clergy will be thankful for any information your Lordship can give them, either as to the likelihood of any amendment taking place, or in a way of explanation of the case as it stands."

On the envelope the Archdeacon adds, "There is a most remarkable falling off in the baptisms this year in the town of Shrewsbury."

From the Rev. T. W. Peile

Durham, December 14th, 1837.

"MY DEAR LORD, A hint that was given me to-day tempts me to break through the restraint that I have for some time past imposed upon myself, through fear of trespassing upon your Lordship's valuable time, engrossed as I have reason to know it has been with an arrear of business, unhappily entailed upon a state of health which I could wish to be still better, though I have from time to time had the satisfaction of hearing that it is improving.

"Mr. Steel, a Fellow of Trinity and one of the Masters at Harrow, passing through Durham, called upon me and intimated that, if I chose to offer myself, I might without much difficulty be elected High-Master of St. Paul's School. I heard a few weeks ago that Sleath was about to retire, and never doubted that some Pauline, and most probably my old competitor Lee of Rugby, would succeed him. Lee, however, is not about to stir, whether because he loves St. Paul's less, or Rugby more, I cannot tell; or whether, as is more probable, he is looking to be first where he now confessedly is second. Perhaps it does not say much for the vacant chair, that none of the many distinguished men that this school (by good luck, I believe, more than by good management) has sent out of late seems very anxious to fill it. Of this, however, your Lordship will know much more than I do, and therefore ask you in confidence, as one whose judgement and advice I value more than that of any friend I have, *would St. Paul's do for a friend and pupil of yours*—for one who, through your Lordship's kind exertions, was all but elected Head of Harrow? I await your Lordship's opinion on this head, before I can even think further of the matter.

*

"I have but one thing more to trouble your Lordship with, and I have done. I have been very busily employing my spare moments during the past year in preparing an improved edition of the *Agamemnon*, with copious English notes, critical, ex-

1837] *Correspondence*

planatory, and philological, and now that I have nearly completed a thousand lines, I was looking forward to the pleasure of requesting your Lordship to permit me to inscribe my volume to you, and this (though, as it happens, prematurely mentioned) I hope your Lordship will do, when first I have satisfied you, as I trust I shall, that the work shall not be unworthy of yourself and pupil. I hope to have it ready for the press in June, when (if not before) I may find your Lordship in town, and in this, as in all other scholastic matters, I shall beg the favour of your advice and introduction."

From a Clergyman

December 18th, 1837.

"MY LORD, I am sorry that I am compelled to trouble your Lordship respecting my parish clerk, whose misconduct at various times has been a subject of complaint to our late diocesan and to Mr. Mott.

"My present ground of complaint is that he takes away for his own use part of the unconsecrated wine that remains after the celebration of the Lord's Supper. I and the churchwardens have remonstrated with him, and to our faces he said that he had been accustomed so to do, and that he should continue his custom, and did take the wine from the church, and has said that he shall again do so on Christmas Day next when the Eucharist is administered. Whether my father allowed the clerk to have any of the wine for his own use I am not aware, but I have written to ascertain the fact; but at any rate I do not intend that he should for the future. But as he resists my authority I am compelled to appeal to your Lordship,—and the second ground of complaint is that he refuses to pay my fees which are owing for weekly duties. In short the man puts us all to defiance. Happily we have come to no open rupture, as I have thought it more prudent to submit to his insolence, until I know whether he or I am to be master. I wait your Lordship's reply, which several of my brother-clergymen are also desirous to see."

Answer to the Foregoing

Eccleshall Castle, December 21st, 1837.

"Rev. Sir, The clerk of your parish has no more right to any part of the bread and wine which remains unconsecrated than the most entire stranger, unless he can show immemorial custom or some special donation in his behalf. Otherwise I imagine your redress is very easy by summoning him before a magistrate, for to me it appears an absolute appropriation to his own use of that which is not his, without consent of the owner, for which it is not difficult to find a proper term.

"If he refuses to pay you your fees, he is, I apprehend, amenable to a similar tribunal, and this is the course which I would recommend as the more summary of the two.

"If, on the other hand, you decide on a presentment against him in the Spiritual Court, the process will indeed be longer, but the costs, if he is convicted, will fall very heavily upon him. And if you carry the matter further, and should convict him of canonical disobedience, he will be liable, not only to the heavy costs, but to suspension or privation of his office. I remain, Rev. Sir, your very faithful and obedient servant,

"S. LICHFIELD."

From the Rev. T. W. Peile

Durham, December 19th, 1837.

"My dear Lord, Many thanks for your Lordship's kind and considerate letter. I fully admit the truth of what you say on the subject of income, and when I think of it, I fear your Lordship must have been tempted to think me grasping. But it was of my children, not of myself, that I was thinking, when I for one evening entertained the ill-advised notion of another change; and before the receipt of your Lordship's ready answer to my letter, I had decided upon the very grounds which are therein stated not to think again of St. Paul's, unless it were actually offered to me, or, which was hardly less improbable, unless your Lordship should recommend it, or put it in a new and more attractive light.

"As it is, I have done, and cordially wish *our* candidate Massie may succeed. Kempe, a Pauline, I hear, and Donaldson, Fellow of Trinity, are in the field.

"On the subject of my *Agamemnon*, my dear Lord, you have given me fresh hopes by your encouraging notice of it, and by your kind compliance with my request to send it forth under the auspicious sanction of your Lordship's name. With no little pride and pleasure, be assured, I catch at the unexpected advantage of consulting your Lordship's notes and enriching my work from thence. If Sleath & Co. have done me no other service, I at least owe them something for this. Pray let me have them at your Lordship's earliest convenience, and I will promise to take every care of so precious a deposit. I have a quiet month before me now, and another at Easter, and by help of these, and what other spare moments I can find, hope to make a finish before the end of June.

"With your Lordship's permission I would then like, if all be well, to meet you in town (or if at Eccleshall, to see you on my way) to show you my papers, and to obtain the benefit of your Lordship's advice as to the best mode of putting them to press. I fear you will think my notes too lengthy, and indeed I often wish I had had my thoughts to express, as I best might, in pithy Porsonian Latin. Still there are many advantages on the side of English translations and notes, and my object is to make, not only the noble and difficult play which forms my text, but a sound knowledge of Greek as familiar as possible to our English youth, whose preparatory studies are apt at the present day to be too much dilated and diluted, and who sometimes strike me as degenerating from what we used to be, and as not possessing energy enough to deal with classical annotations in any other than their mother-tongue.

"I have derived great assistance from Klausen, the last German editor of Aeschylus, without, however, making him such a 'Magnus Apollo' as Professor Scholefield has made of Wellauer.

"If the *Agamemnon* succeeds, I hope to follow it up with the *Chöephorae*, *Eumenides*, and *Supplices*. I gave a public course of philological lectures on these four plays last year.

"'John Young'[1] called this morning, with an Infirmary Sermon from Kennedy, and good tidings of Shrewsbury.

"I am rambling on, and trespassing upon your Lordship's time and patience, but a host of old associations and feelings crowd upon me as I write. I will cut them short, however, by requesting only that I may hear something of Mrs. Butler, and of my friend Tom and his family, when you have occasion to write again. Meanwhile believe me, my dear Lord,

"Your Lordship's obliged and very faithful friend,
"THOMAS W. PEILE."

To — (?)

Eccleshall Castle, December 22nd, 1837.

"MY DEAR SIR, Belper is a place which at the census of 1831 contained 7,890 inhabitants, now increased, I believe, to more than 9,000. It is a curacy itself attached to Duffield, and is held in conjunction with the curacy of Turnditch, containing in 1831 926, now considerably above 1000 inhabitants. When the present incumbent of both these curacies came to Belper, where no clergyman had ever before resided, Belper was £37 17s. 6d. and Turnditch was £41 16s. per annum. This was in 1807. Belper is now £158, subject to a deduction of £50 for a curate's salary, and Turnditch £63 per annum. The incumbent of Belper, who has resided there since 1807, is now become infirm, is seventy-two years of age, feeble in voice and powers (while the church holds a congregation of 1,800), and some twelve years ago underwent the severe operation of lithotomy.

"He had a parliamentary grant of £1,200 for Belper; he also collected £200, and challenged Queen Anne's Bounty therewith for £300 more. He has built a comfortable and substantial parsonage house, and expended thereon £300 out of his own pocket, and now feeling his infirmities and the expenses consequent upon them pressing on him, he wishes to have from the Assistant Curates' Fund an allowance for a curate. He informs me he has five services every Sunday, three I presume at D. . . ."

(Rest of letter not drafted.—ED.)

[1] An assistant master at Shrewsbury.

Correspondence

To a Clergyman

Eccleshall Castle, December 24th, 1837.

"REV. SIR, I have received the enclosed from the Governors of the Clerical Charities in Bloomsbury Place to send you. But I must add that they express their surprise and think that there must be negligence on your part to stir yourself, or something wrong somewhere, that you have been so long a petitioner for their bounty. You appear to have much too high an opinion of your claims. In your letter of December 9th you speak of various kindnesses you have received as a pleasing testimony of regard for a clergyman who will, without doubt, be considered as having paramount claims elsewhere than on the kindness of private friends.

"Sir, this is not the language a petitioner ought to use who receives constant kindness from public charity, and whose case is not at all harder than that of many deserving brethren.

"In your letter of December 14th you tell me that you think if I applied to the two Archbishops they would do something for you. I have no right nor ground for applying to the two Archbishops for you. I do not believe that any such application was ever made by any Bishop for any distressed clergyman, however great his merits or however long his services.

"I see clearly you think I take no pains to do you service. This is an utterly groundless supposition. I have taken more pains than you dream of—not because of your importunity, not because of any opinion I entertain of your excessive merits or extraordinary claims, but because I believe you to be in want, and am sorry for you, and think you hardly used in the Ellesmere Workhouse business. I remain, Sir, your obedient humble servant,

"S. LICHFIELD."

CHAPTER THIRTY-FOUR: CORRESPONDENCE, (?) JANUARY 1838– 16TH JUNE 1838

From Lord Berwick

January (?), 1838.

"MY DEAR FRIEND, I DID NOT ANSWER your melancholy but most kind letter of the end of last month because I waited till I could hear from other good authority that your health was better. This I ascertained at last with great satisfaction, but soon after became ill myself, and am now only recovering from the severity of the attack, which I trust, however, may do me good, as it has carried away the gout which had been lingering in my feet for several months. I had not time nor room in my last long scrawl to tell you all I wished about church-building, *i.e.* what I had done or personally intended to do, nor will I plague you at length upon the subject. Suffice it to say, before I called at Eccleshall, having precisely anticipated not only the very sum you named as proper for me to subscribe, but that in all probability the money would not be called for immediately, I wrote to Mr. —, mentioning my anxiety, yet present poverty, and begged the question as to what I ought to subscribe. Although he writes and answers almost all points of my other letters, he made no reply to that, which I thought very ominous, nor has he noticed it to this day. I was the more struck and the more dissuaded from a repetition of my question from a similar circumstance having once occurred in regard to a church in Shrewsbury, when he himself said the money would not be wanted directly, and yet placed it against me in his very first account. I will say no more until we meet, but will contrive this subscription shall appear on the first favourable opportunity. You will believe me when I tell you that I received your most kind and religious advice most thankfully. I hope also in the properest mind to receive it, having lately lost many friends and relations, and not being in very strong health myself; at the time too I had the afflicting account of the real situation of poor Edward Owen, who had been reported better, the father of eleven children.

"I will certainly get the book you name; I think I have

heard of it. I travelled to York with a Prayer-Book and my Rugby Bible, in which I found my name in stronger characters than I write now. I brought them here, and they are now before me. My Bibles, and I have many, have not, I think, the marginal references, and I will endeavour to get one that possesses them; but, alas! to use a French expression, I must 'begin with the beginning,' and want to have some grammar, if I may use such an expression, some explanation or interpretation or introduction as to the composition of Bible, Prayer-Book, and Testament, to go more resolutely to their contents. Something of the sort we had at school, but the hurried life I have led has obliterated all traces, though I believe the Bible should speak for itself, yet taking chapters at random would not have adequate effect. I must not finish this without returning to something more worldly.

"I have had the hard task imposed upon me of asking you if you can ordain without a title. I have said No, but have been begged to put the question. I am possibly the only person who knows you in this neighbourhood, and the man who asks me must be acquainted with twenty people who know the Bishop of the Diocese; it is most unfair. The fact is, Mr. C—, the former candidate for Coventry School, has a son who is a private tutor with emoluments in a gentleman's family, and must lose these if he takes a curacy. He has excellent testimonials. Give yourself no trouble about this or any other subject in this scrawl. I passed through Rugby on my way here; I will not tell you all I felt, but the 'momentary bliss' was not so great as formerly.

"I thought of you as I passed the Avon from Brownsoever, and fancied your then little figure stepping up to me to see if I had caught the pike in the shallow backwater running up by the Newbold Road, but there are now grand arches there for railroads and canals, etc. Enough of this,

"So affectionately yours,
"B."

From Edward T. Coke, Esq.

Brimmington Hall, Chesterfield, January 8th, 1838.

"MY LORD, May I beg your Lordship's advice on the following points? Brimmington is one of the hamlets in Chesterfield parish; it has its own minister and its own chapel, but has not the power of raising a church rate to defray the unavoidable and customary expenses of the chapel.

"At a most numerously attended meeting held in the chancel of Chesterfield Church on July 14th, 1837, and called by the churchwardens for the purpose of proposing a church-rate, the amendment that 'the consideration of the original question should be adjourned to that day twelvemonth' was carried by a vast majority.

"I am free to confess that this majority was principally created by the 'church-going people' (if I may use such a term) of Brimmington and the other hamlets. They do not object to a church-rate so that the amount is applied to their own church, but contend that the hardship is great, when they have been compelled for a long period of years to defray the expenses of two churches, one of which is situate two miles distant and in the midst of a populous and wealthy town. In taking such a step, however, they appear to have overlooked the fact of their having deprived their own churchwardens of the power of defraying the expenses of the church situated in their own village. Thus, my Lord, we have not the means of discharging our last year's bills; our parish and vestry clerk too have not yet received their salaries for 1837, and I feel that we cannot call on the inhabitants for a voluntary subscription, as we have already raised in that manner during the past year £19 for painting the church, in addition to which all the principal landowners have subscribed very largely towards the erection of a parsonage house in the village, which it is hoped will be completed this year, and also towards a new church in Chesterfield.

"I can only see one method by which we can raise the requisite sum of money, but it is a method on which I anticipate an unfavourable opinion from your Lordship. If, however, it should not be illegal, it will relieve us from a great dilemma.

The proposed method is this. There are five (5) vacant pews in the church, for all of which I have applications, and all the applicants are willing to have the appropriation made to them for life, and voluntarily offer to give a larger sum of money into the hands of the churchwardens than will liquidate the debt against the church. The churchwardens do not offer for sale or rent the above pews, deeming any such step to be illegal, nor will they close with the offer that has been made them until they have received your Lordship's opinion on the subject.

" If this method is either illegal or objectionable on other accounts, will your Lordship have the kindness to point out some means of discharging those debts for which the churchwardens appear to be held responsible? "

The note on the foregoing letter indicating the lines of Dr. Butler's answer ran:

" Can *sanction* nothing. If the parties are unseated, and the churchwarden seats them in a private arrangement, I neither advise nor know of the measure."

From Mr. James Wood

Eccleshall, January 9th, 1838.

" MY LORD, In reference to the interview with your Lordship on Saturday, and presuming that some information might be desired respecting the parties who, with Barrow, have been applied to by Mr. Seckerson, I beg leave to state to your Lordship the following particulars:

" 1st. Henry Brown, Jail Butts, who was proceeded against, and whose expenses were foregone by your Lordship, again refuses to pay his amerciaments; he, with Barnett, was at the head of the late party, and was the means of disaffection in many others; he is a man well-to-do, amerced very moderately, and a fit person for an example to be made of.

" 2nd. Samuel Emery, Elford Heath, now in arrear £1 3s. 7d., but not before proceeded against, strongly suspected of breaking windows—another fit object.

"3rd. John Shirley, Jail Butts, a young man without wife or family, an obstinate abusive person three years in arrear.

"4th. James Hitchin, jun., Offley Hay, has lately built a cottage on his father's garden (who is an amerced cottager), but will not pay the amerciaments laid on him, say four courts.

"5th. Robert Evans, Jail Butts, an old man amerced for two cottages, one of which his son lives in, one of the oldest refusers, but not before proceeded against on account of his age.

"To-day is the latest time given them by Mr. Seckerson, and none have yet noticed the applications except Barrow. Some twenty others or more are, I have reason to believe, deferring payment till they know what will be done, and I feel quite convinced that steps must be promptly adopted, of such a nature as to convince them of your Lordship's authority, before any order can be restored.

"Mr. Seckerson desired me to let him have the results of his applications to-morrow, but having made this statement to your Lordship I shall of course await your Lordship's directions."

To the Rector of an Important Parish

Eccleshall Castle, February 2nd, 1838.

"REV. SIR, I lose not a post in telling you that I am more than pleased, I am gratified and even affected by your candid and judicious letter. It shows a return of right feeling, of which I willingly anticipate the permanent restoration, and I can but think that if you would allow me to make a cautious and discreet use of it, I might thereby be of material service to you, in gaining you many friends and disarming hostility. I shall, however, do nothing of that kind without your consent. Still I think it would be a beneficial step, especially considered with regard to your residence, which I readily consent to leave as you propose, only wishing you to give me as much notice as possible; certainly three clear months would be requisite to Sir William Dunbar that he may look out for a house. The prejudices of people are strong, and at any rate it will be necessary that you should win your way by degrees. Some will never be satisfied, but the kinder and better part of those who have the opportunity of witnessing your conduct by degrees will be gained—and on that account I think your residence would be advantageous to you and desirable. I shall write to the two curates to say that you wish them to remain; but I shall tell Sir William that I think it probable you will reside without taking any part of the duty till I think it advisable to open it to you by degrees—of all which both you and they shall have due notice. I am anxious to promote your comfort and interest, but I must look at the feelings, and in some points even at the prejudices, of so populous a parish. I remain, Rev. Sir, your sincere well-wisher,

" S. LICHFIELD."

To a Clergyman

7, Hyde Park Place, February 15th, 1838.

" REV. SIR, On reading your letter, which I received yesterday, I find that it presented far more important difficulties than you appeared to apprehend. I felt also that it was impossible for me to take any step in the House of Lords without previous communication with the Archbishop of Canterbury and the Bishop of London, and without seeing the Bill now pending in the Lords. I therefore ordered my carriage immediately to go to Lambeth, but finding on my way that the Archbishop could see nobody, owing to the loss of a friend and connection, I made the best of my way to the Bishop of London. He also was absent at a Commissioners' meeting, and I then drove to my town secretary, Mr. Burder, one of the best men of business in London, and thoroughly versed in the business of the House of Lords, having attended almost daily during the session for nearly thirty years. He confirmed all my views of the subject, and told me it was utterly useless, either now or at any future period, to propose relief in a case like yours, but especially in an urgent case like the present, when Government are impatient of delay, being anxious to pass the Bill without loss of time.

" This morning I have seen the Indemnity Bill, and have consulted not only the Archbishop and Bishop of London, but nearly all the Bishops yet in town. The Bill does not apply at all to your case, being confined to joint-stock companies of *more than six* partners.

"I am sorry to tell you that there is an unanimous opinion against the possibility of obtaining relief in your case, a private bank and a public joint-stock company being so widely different. There is but one point in which there may be somewhat in your favour, which is, if you have never appeared publicly either in the banking-house or on the bills as a partner. But this, I fear, would not make the proceedings of yourself and your co-partners legal. Ever since the time of Henry VIII, and in every enactment for the residence or government of spiritual persons, all who hold any dignity or benefice are expressly excluded from anything like traffic; and if you and your partners did not know this, the law says you ought to have known it and *ignorantia juris non excusat*. You may be a partner if you are not beneficed in any way. I knew the late Mr. Rocke well, and know that he struggled in vain to keep the living of Clungunford, and was at last obliged to resign it that he might remain at the bank. His name is still in it under his will. Last Monday an action was set down, but was withdrawn under some compromise, against a most respectable neighbour of mine at Eccleshall, who has a living near me, on similar grounds. I know a third case in which it would have been very desirable to place a young clergyman in his father's banking-house, but on taking the first legal advice that could be obtained he was obliged to desist. The only counsel, therefore, which I can venture to offer you under present circumstances, when many needy knaves are on the look-out, is either to resign your preferment or to withdraw from the bank on the best terms you can: unless you venture to risk the wording of the Plurality Bill, which is likely to pass this session, and which may possibly contain some modification of the present unmitigated law of Henry VIII—that is, provided the sharp-set Radicals in the House of Commons permit it to pass, which I do not think they will, nor do I even know that any such clause will be introduced. I remain, Rev. Sir, your obedient faithful servant,

"S. LICHFIELD."

Correspondence

To the Rev. Robert Scott
(Then proposing to stand for the Greek Professorship at Glasgow.—ED.)

7, Hyde Park Place, February 16th, 1838.

"DEAR SCOTT, I was detained so long at the Bounty Board yesterday as to make it impossible for me to get through my letters, which happened to be very urgent and important. I hope a day will not be of great consequence to you. I thought it right to touch the Principal's *amor patriae* by allusion to Sir Wauter. Och, man! ye're a lucky chiel to bear the name and kith an' kin o' that great man! 'twill be a passport to you through the land o' cakes and a' the world o'er.

"Well, good luck to you, and let me have the result. Think of the impudence of Sister Peg if she dares to refuse an English clergyman.

"You certainly judge right in trying, if your account of the income is at all correct. Truly yours, "S. LICHFIELD."

To the Rev. the Principal of the University, Glasgow

House of Lords, February 16th, 1838.

"SIR, At the request of the Rev. Robert Scott, a former highly distinguished pupil of mine, now Fellow and one of the tutors of Balliol College, Oxford, I am induced to trouble you with this testimonial.

"Mr. Scott was highly distinguished at school and at Oxford, where, while he was an undergraduate at Christ Church, he obtained the highest University honour, an University Scholarship. Having been afterwards elected a Fellow and one of the tutors of Balliol College, he removed there, where he still remains in the discharge of his duties. He has obtained many other high University honours, among them the Latin Essay prize, which he had the honour to read before the Duke of Wellington at his installation as Chancellor.

"I consider Mr. Scott as one of the very best Greek scholars now living, and a work in which he is at present engaged, a translation (with improvements) of Passow's German and Greek Lexicon, is a pledge of his capacity. Besides which he is a most elegant and accomplished scholar in other respects, and a truly amiable and highly valued member of society, having an irreproachable character both for morals and religion. He is, in one word—and what higher can I say of him?—no disgrace to your illustrious countryman whose name he bears, and with whose family he is collaterally connected. I will most confidently pledge myself that, if elected to the Greek Professorship, he will disappoint no pledge that I have given for him, no expectation that has been raised respecting him.

"I have the honour to be, Sir, your very obedient and faithful servant,

"S. LICHFIELD."

From the Rev. Robert Scott

Balliol, Saturday, February 17th, 1838.

" MY DEAR LORD, I can never sufficiently express my gratitude for the flattering and affectionate terms in which you speak of me. I had relied upon your well-known and tried kindness, but even from that I could never have looked for so overwhelming a testimony of your good opinion. It is, indeed, what I have never deserved. But it will be a stimulus to me to go on in the course which has gained it for me, in the hope, however slight, that it may be the means prospectively of verifying itself. Believe me, I will ever cherish it as a proof, not indeed of my possessing all the qualifications which you are willing to ascribe to me, but of my conduct having been such as to win from you that partiality which has never been bestowed wholly unworthily.

" But, alas! Sister Peg is inexorable; and, sooth to say, I cannot blame her. For the puir body is unco sair for feughten the now wi' burghers, an' reliefs, an' seceders, and thae cattle, with whom her battle is the harder in proportion as the line of demarcation between her and them is the less broad.

" I have received a pithy letter from the Very Rev. Duncan MacFarlan—'the gracious Duncan'—which would have relieved you from the trouble of 'testifying,' had it arrived sooner. He quotes the Act of Union, which is precise as to declarations both of doctrine and practice; he states that these must—more especially at a time when, etc., etc.—be rigidly enforced, and he gives his own decided judgement that an English clergyman is not eligible. Farewell then to my hopes of going 'bauck again' to the North (at any time an unnatural notion for a Scot) in search of preferment; farewell to my visions of 'hyperborean felicity'!

Ταῦτα μέν, ὦ παῖ κρείσσονα χρυσοῦ,
μεγάλης δὲ τύχης καὶ Ὑπερβορέου,
μείζονα φωνεῖς·—οὐ δύνασαι γάρ,

as Müller proposes to read it in the *Chöephorae*.

"With kindest regards to Mrs. Butler, believe me, my dear Lord, ever most gratefully and affectionately yours,

"ROBERT SCOTT."

To the Ven. Archdeacon Hodson

7, Hyde Park Place, February 28th, 1838.

"MY DEAR ARCHDEACON, As I never sleep at the longest more than three hours at a time, I may safely say that Stoke and its dependencies have never been out of my thoughts more than six hours ever since I have been in town, and my anxieties about it increase.

"Mr. B— and all the clergy must know that I cannot, if I were ever so disposed, keep the Rector from returning to reside; but I am not so disposed, because to prevent him (though I certainly wish he would not reside) would be in violation of the late Bishop's permission, and of my own word given to him in consequence—he having agreed to the other terms required, and thirdly, because, though non-residence would be more desirable, I cannot make it a penalty after what has passed. With regard to the clergy not admitting him into their society, every man must judge for himself, according to his feelings of Christian charity and his sense of propriety. But any who were so disposed might give him some little degree of notice without being on visiting terms with him. That, however, is their affair. I can do nothing more. Greatly as I respect Mr. B—, I know him to be a man of strong feelings and prejudices, and very apt to be contradictory, and I was always in fear from that quarter. But a thing has lately been rumoured to me about which I have felt anxious to write to you, and was only waiting your communication.

"I have been told that it is suspected some scheme is going on against Kitchen, whom I believe to be a very valuable man, to get him from Stone. Now there is a good house at Stone, and I have been thinking if it were possible for Kitchen and Sir W. Dunbar to exchange curacies, each would be as well off as at present, and many difficulties at Stoke, and perhaps at Stone too, would be got over. Do you think this feasible? As for Sir W. Dunbar remaining at Stoke if he prefers going, I quite differ from Mr. B— in the notion of keeping him—nay, I would go so much further as to say that, knowing what I now do know, I would rather aid him in his removal than prevent it.

"What you say of the Rector's father is very likely to be true, and I have once or more than once already said as much to you. I see little that remains but to ask that you will let Mr. Coldwell and Mr. Atkinson read the letters, if you see fit, and then return them to me. I shall write to the Rector soon after I receive them, and shall represent to him the impolicy and probable uncomfortableness of his return, but can do no more. I think I can succeed if you find there is any prospect of the exchange of curacies between Sir William Dunbar and Mr. Kitchen. Perhaps my greatest difficulty there will be with the Vicar of Stone, who talks of resigning the living whenever he meets with a fit person, and of his interest with the Chancellor to obtain it for whomsoever he pleases, but seems not yet to have taken into account that my consent is necessary to make his resignation valid.

"Well, this subject is all painful, and the rest not less so. I cannot help thinking that your letter has arrived very *à propos* to a day of humiliation and self-reflection. I am sorry to see a party spirit already at work between the two societies. I hope you state my utter disavowal of getting up an opposition to the

P. A. Society. But it is very hard one may not ask for a subscription to another society without being open to this charge. Alas poor human nature, when we see men whom we used to esteem the best among us so wanting in true Christian charity. It proves, however, how much easier both to read and preach the precepts of the Gospel are, than they are to practise.

"Allow me to recommend to your notice some inquiry into the Stone business. I shall be glad to hear when you have any information of consequence. Believe me, my dear Archdeacon, faithfully yours,
"S. LICHFIELD."

From G. A. C. May, Esq., afterwards Chief Justice of Ireland

Magdalene College, Saturday morning, March 3rd, 1838.

"MY DEAR LORD, The Classical Tripos was given out yesterday evening. I think I have every reason to be satisfied with my place—third. Thompson, I am sorry to say, is only seventh, Parkinson eighth, Metcalfe a second class. At Thompson's position I am more grieved than surprised, though confessedly of great talents, or rather genius, yet since he left Shrewsbury he has certainly applied them rather to the pursuit of theoretical speculations than the acquisition of deep scholarship, the consequence of which is that we have now to lament that so many far his inferiors have been placed above him. For my own part I ever have and ever shall consider him my superior in originality and depth of thought, though I think I may say that I have made the most of respectable talents and he the least of very brilliant ones.

"Vaughan and Lord Lyttelton are bracketed for the first. I believe I was thirty marks behind them, and that George Kennedy placed me first. It is scarcely necessary for me to add that I have to thank you, my Lord, for my present as well as my past success, and not only for the advantage I have derived from your talents and learning, or in a word from Shrewsbury, but also for the interest you have ever been kind enough to take in my welfare.

"To Mrs. Butler I desire my most grateful remembrance, and would wish you to believe that few rejoiced more sincerely at

your Lordship's exaltation, or more heartily wish you a long and happy enjoyment of your well-earned honours, than your affectionate pupil,
"GEORGE A. C. MAY."

To the Rector of an important Parish

7, Hyde Park Place, March 9th, 1838.

"DEAR SIR, I wish I was enabled to fulfil my promise of writing to you, when I had anything of importance to inform you of, by sending you a more agreeable communication. I must, however, inform you that, having sounded all the most respectable clergy in your neighbourhood, I find them unanimous in the opinion that your return there would be attended with much mischief, with great unpleasantness to yourself, and with the revival of an evil spirit and much bitterness among your parishioners. Still if you determine on going I shall not oppose; I have pledged myself, and I do not mean to recede; but if I may give you the most friendly advice in my power, I certainly would recommend you not to make the attempt for a year or two. The very yielding will conciliate, and the delay will be all so much gain.

"Having said this in a pure feeling of goodwill, I must leave the decision to your own choice, only requesting you to feel assured that I am anxious both to advise you for the best and to promote your comfort to the best of my power, because I place a full reliance on the sincerity of your professions. I remain, dear Sir, your obedient faithful servant,
"S. LICHFIELD."

I take the following from a small diary of Dr. Butler's kept during his episcopacy, and destroyed by me:

"Wednesday Mar. 14 (1838). Bad night. No sleep whatever; went to court very feeble, and when I attempted to rise having kissed the Queen's hand, could not without staggering and being helped."

A letter from Mr. Commissioner Reynolds refers to this incident.

Correspondence

From James Fraser, Esq., afterwards Bishop of Manchester

Lincoln College, Oxon, March 16th, 1838.

"MY LORD, Flattering myself that you would continue to take the same kind interest in my welfare and success that you always exhibited towards me while I was fortunate enough to be your pupil, I take the liberty of writing a few lines to you, at once to acquaint you with my good fortune, and to return my sincere acknowledgements of the invaluable benefits I received at your hands. I must therefore inform you that this morning I received a message from the Vice-Chancellor requesting my attendance; I immediately obeyed the summons, and was no less gratified than astounded when he conveyed to me the delightful intelligence that I was second for the University Scholarship. He read to me the announcement sent to him by the examiners, which was to the following purport: ' The examiners appointed for Dean Ireland's scholarship beg to announce to the Vice-Chancellor that they have elected Mr. Lingen, Scholar of Trinity, on that foundation; and request that the words " proxime accessit " may be affixed to the name of Mr. Fraser, Scholar of Lincoln College.' Now I believe this is a distinction rarely conferred on the second candidate unless there be but little difference between him and the first, and I therefore fully appreciate what Dr. Jenkins added, ' that, next to gaining the scholarship, it was the highest University honour I could obtain.' The successful man, Lingen, is an old school-fellow of mine. He received his education at your old pupil's the Rev. Thomas Rowley, at Bridgnorth; he was higher there in the school than I was when I left, and was considered exceedingly clever, as he has abundantly verified by getting the University Scholarship in his third term. There were twenty candidates for the honour. The examination commenced on Saturday last, and ended on Thursday evening. We had ten papers, the heads of which I will briefly recapitulate. 1. English into Latin. 2. Greek into English–a passage from Lucian. 3. English Essay: subject–' The Condition, Character, and Influence of Women in the Best Ages of Greece and Rome.' 4. English into Greek–a passage from *Salmonia*. 5. Greek critical paper. 6. Latin Elegiacs, subject 'Palilia.' 7. Aristophanic Iambics: Shakespeare, *Much Ado about Nothing*, Act IV, Scene ii, from speech of the Sexton, 'Master, you go not the right way to examine,' down to Dogberry's speech ending with 'Oh that I had been writ down an ass!' 8. Latin letter: subject —Cicero to Hortensius, in answer to a letter from the latter, requesting his advice as to laying and ornamenting his gardens in Rome. 9. Latin critical paper. 10. A passage of Plautus to be translated into English prose.

"I have now only to return you, my Lord, my most heartfelt thanks for the many favours you have bestowed upon me, and to assure you that I feel deeply the benefit of them."

From the Rev. H. (afterwards Archdeacon) Moore

Vicarage, Eccleshall, March 21st, 1838.

"MY DEAR LORD, I am very much disappointed to hear you are so poorly, because Mrs. Lloyd's kind note to my wife gave us hopes you were getting better and better. I do not wonder at your being overcome at the Levee; it really must be a dreadfully trying business. I hope you did not get any harm at the House the other night when I saw you there—I always tell your Lordship it's a bad place for you, but if you will go, then I seriously advise you, in case of a division, to take care and keep on the side where the largest numbers are, for leaving a crowded house and getting amongst only a few people must subject you to sudden chills, which are very bad.

"Pray, my Lord, ask Sir Henry if this is not good advice. The packages are come, and safe in a dark place on the left, as you enter the housekeeper's room.

"Mudding your pool has not yet begun, but will be the week after next, at which time the masons are coming into the house, and Bromfield to look after them all together.

"I forgot to say in my last that I had been to Colwich, where all were well, the swans inclusive. They have now established themselves on the water, where, after the manner of their progenitors, they bully everything that comes near them. The wild ducks, widgeons, etc., however, were too many for them by virtue of their diving, which puzzled these autocrats of the water sorely.

"I hope you have seen Lord Brougham's description of us Tories, as professing to be for Church and King, by which we mean that we are for the clergy rather than the gospel and for the King than for the Constitution. I'll say masses for him without number for such an excellent piece of fun."

From the Rev. John Young

Shrewsbury, April 9th, 1838.

"MY LORD, Your testimonial in my favour was irresistible, and I have been successful, thereby adding one more to the number of those whom you have first trained to know their duty, and then raised by your influence to an independent station in society. I am deeply indebted to your Lordship's kindness, and will endeavour to do justice to your expressed opinion, by devoting myself entirely to the prosperity of the endowment.

"Houghton is six miles from Sunderland, seven from Durham, eleven from Newcastle. The situation therefore is excellent, and I hope by continual attention to obtain a fair portion of the patronage of those towns. Dr. Kennedy has been exceedingly kind to me, and I hope the electors, as the half-year is so far advanced, will allow me to continue my service here until its close in June."

To Josh. Wilson, Esq., Camfield Hall

(Strictly Confidential.)

7, Hyde Park Place, April 12th, 1838.

"SIR, I kept no copy of my letter to you, but I can safely say that I did not mean to give it so much latitude as you seem to apprehend. I meant to say that I would pay attention to your recommendation, but not so as to preclude my own approval of the person whom you might recommend, nor to preclude myself from looking out for a fit person at the same time, for it is desirable to fill up this vacancy as soon as may be.

"Your letter obliges me to make a strictly confidential communication. I never heard of Mr. C— (he is not licensed to Pinxton, as he ought to have been) till Mr. Ellis Williams spoke to me of him in very high terms, whereupon, being anxious to provide a curate for an important parish in Staffordshire, I requested Archdeacon Hodson of Stafford to see him, and report to me. This was before you wrote to me about S. Normanton. He did see him, but in the interval you had written to me. It was found that the parish for which I intended him would not suit him, but that he had a wish to go to S. Normanton, and papers of recommendation were forwarded to me. In consequence I made my own inquiries, and although I believe he has conducted himself very well and given great satisfaction at Pinxton, it is not my intention to engage his further services at S. Normanton.

"It is a place requiring particular attention, and causing much anxiety to the Bishop. I have every reason to think I have found a suitable person, but am too anxious on the subject to come to a hasty conclusion. I have the honour to be, Sir, your very obedient and faithful servant,
"S. LICHFIELD."

From the Rev. James Hildyard

Christ College, Cambridge, April 21st, 1838.

"MY DEAR LORD, Allow me to return you my most sincere thanks for the extremely handsome and cordial testimonial which I find lying on my table upon my return from Birmingham. The late period at which my offering myself as a candidate commenced, and which you very justly rebuke me for, obliged me to make applications for testimonials before I had taken a personal survey of the establishment itself. My visit to Birmingham has been since made for that purpose, and had I not learnt that your Lordship was in town, I should have proceeded to Eccleshall to thank you for what you had done for me, and at the same time to apologise for having given you so much trouble to no purpose.

"The result of my inquiries on the spot was, that the school was going to be put on such a foundation as would tend materially to swamp classical literature by introducing a kind of commercial system, which, though very useful in a town like Birmingham, would not be quite in accordance with my taste and pursuits.

"It was this alteration in the establishment which was to produce the additional number of pupils, and so raise the master's stipend to the sum named in the advertisement. At present it falls considerably below the mark, and the house, etc., are maintained at a fearful cost. It would require a capital of nearly £2,000 to enter.

"All this I could only learn by a visit to the place itself, and my sole regret is, not that I have to relinquish the scheme altogether, but that by a premature offer my friends should have been unnecessarily troubled on my account.

"Nevertheless it must and ever will be a great satisfaction to me to find, from the numerous and heartily warm letters furnished me on this occasion, that I live not without esteem in the eyes of valued and influential friends, whose goodwill and approbation I have thus an additional inducement to persevere in deserving.

"To yourself, my dear Lord, my obligations are of no ordinary kind, and such as nothing in my power can ever either return or express. I must content myself with remaining your ever grateful and ever I trust faithful servant,

"JAMES HILDYARD."

From the Rev. H. Moore

Vicarage, Eccleshall, April 27th, 1838.

"MY DEAR LORD, I was just about writing to ask how you were going on when Mrs. Lloyd's letter came with an improved account. On it, I need not add, 'there was joy in that city.' The weather, I fear, is still sadly against you. Here it is most wretchedly cold, so that it is quite punishing to go out. Court Granville left us this morning, was rejoiced to hear you were better, and sent his kindest respects and regards to your Lordship and all at Hyde Park Place. We have just got Charlotte Girdlestone come here. She has just entertained me with an account of a man in her brother's parish who belongs to the New Connection (Methodists), who, as he said, were quite different from the Old. Girdlestone asked him in what the difference was; the answer sounded like 'ossire.' It turned out to be 'horse-hire,' and this 'horse-hire' to mean that one Connection paid horse-hire for the preachers and the other did not. This is so new a point of controversy that it seems worthy of your Lordship's consideration and that of the Bench. The plants are all come and are planted. The old swans have bullied their progeny from off the water. Would it not be a good thing to have the young ones pinioned and sent to Copmere? Pray a line from some good member of the family to tell how you are going on."

From the Ven. Archdeacon Bather

May (?), 1838.

*

"I will not enter upon the other part of your letter further than to say that I cannot possibly wonder that you or any right-thinking person should feel oppressed by the thought of the inadequacy of our gratitude and love to God. It is natural that the sense of this should increase daily, as the sense of the vastness of that which calls for love and gratitude increases. Yet you may have such a measure of both these as God will accept, having Himself brought you to them, and as may be continually growing, though it will never be what you could desire.

"I never happened to see the book you speak of, but it is a very consolatory thought to see how marvellously people often agree in the main, who are considering Divine truth simply for practical purposes, to be personally the better for it first, before they proceed to tell others what they have found out."

From Mr. James Wood, Bailiff of the Manor

May 21st, 1838.

"MY LORD, To-day being the day appointed by Messrs. Seckerson & Fowkes for ejecting two cottagers, the sheriff's officers ejected one, who immediately knocked off the lock and re-entered; and from the lateness of the hour, and the little help they could procure in Eccleshall, they have returned to Stafford, intending to-morrow to bring more help. In the meantime I beg leave to represent to your Lordship my exposed situation, and the threats and intimidations I am subject to, whilst in the faithful discharge of my office, your Lordship's agent and Steward of the Manor being so distant from me as to prevent immediate communication. I am apprehensive that to-night will not pass without something unpleasant, or mischief being done, and I therefore most respectfully submit to your Lordship my need of protection."

To — (?)

7, Hyde Park Place, June 4th, 1838.

" SIR, You have gone much out of your way in writing to me respecting Henry Brown, one of the most contumacious, and head of a party who gave great trouble to the late Bishop, and would have been legally called to account by him, had he lived but a few months longer. The duty fell on me (in consequence of his death), which he as well as I are bound to fulfil towards our successors; but so far from oppression, the whole party who were contumacious, and in consequence about to stand an action against me above a year ago, when the Assizes came on, well knowing they had no ground to stand on, I forgave them all, and what is more, I paid the whole costs which they were indebted to me, and the only recompense I obtained was that some of them laughed at me and called me a fool for my pains, to which I do not intend subjecting myself a second time. I have left the whole matter in the hands of the Steward of the Manor, who must act as he thinks fit for the interest of myself and those who come after me into the See. I presume you know that the amerciament is made on oath by a jury, and not fixed arbitrarily by me. As to Brown's excuse for non-payment, I am in possession of facts about that and many other things which perhaps you may not know, but I must beg to drop a subject which I am too ill to write upon. I am, Sir, your humble servant,

" S. LICHFIELD."

From the Rev. C. M. Long

Whitchurch, June 5th, 1838.

"MY LORD, I cannot say how much gratified I feel by your kindness in writing to tell me how you are. I should much have liked to have seen you again before I left London, but was afraid of intruding, and since I returned here I have been suffering from an attack of a complaint which I have every year about this time, which renders me quite incapable of any exertion and consequently very low-spirited.

"I am rejoiced to hear that the Archdeacon's letter has been a comfort to you, and though it may please God for a time to keep from you that assurance of pardon which you desire, and to try you by doubt, your humble resignation to His will, your self-abasement, and your looking so truly to Christ alone, make me confident in thinking that you are a partaker of His salvation now, and will soon rejoice in celebrating the praises of His redeeming love.

"You are constantly in my thoughts and my prayers. May He who is Himself our salvation bless you in the desire of your heart and comfort you."

To a Clergyman

Hyde Park Place, June 16th, 1838.

"SIR, I can assure you I had always understood that your complaint was of a nervous kind, and not arising from the stomach. Whatever be the cause, if it incapacitates you from duty, I do not see how you can undertake a place like W—, where certainly more attention and tact is required than in almost any that I know, and for the management of which I am not prepared by anything I can see in your letters to think you well qualified. There is an insinuation in your letter which I received this morning highly improper, and very little calculated to raise a good opinion of the writer. There is hardly a respectable clergyman in your neighbourhood who does not know that you possessed my good wishes. If I have not always sent you money when you wrote to ask it, I have had good reasons, first because I thought you importunate and knew that you had wearied my predecessor with your correspondence, and next because I am obliged to apportion what I give to the variety and great numbers as well as the merits of the applicants.

"I suppose I shall hear from Mr. H— in due time, but I certainly do not promise to listen to his application, unless I find better reason to do so than my inquiries, which have been numerous and careful, have hitherto given me reason to expect. I remain, Sir, your humble servant,
"S. LICHFIELD."

CHAPTER THIRTY-FIVE: CORRESPONDENCE, (?) 4TH JULY 1838—
THE END OF 1838

To John Tomlinson, Esq.

July 4th (?), 1838.

"SIR, I ARRIVED HERE ON SATURDAY NIGHT, BUT too ill to answer your letter with my own hand.

"I am sorry to say that I totally differ from your view of the clause to which you object in the Plurality Bill. I am sure the Bishops have no intentions of arbitrary encroachments, and I think the clause most important to the interests of the inhabitants of populous places. I have long considered the sale of livings as the greatest of all the evils in our Church Establishment, and heartily wish some checks may be put on it at an early period. I have the honour to be, Sir, your very obedient and humble servant, "S. LICHFIELD."

From the Bishop of Durham (Dr. Maltby)

Oxford, July 14th, 1838.

"MY DEAR BISHOP, I was delighted to hear so good an account of you after your return, both from yourself and Mrs. Lloyd, and I am also delighted to think there is a chance of our meeting once more at Hatton.

"Certainly I had no idea of visiting that place of early and sacred associations this year. But the birth of a first great-grandson to Dr. Parr, and Lynes's exceeding anxiety that we should be present on the occasion, induced me to deviate from the route I had planned, and I have promised to be at Hatton to a latish dinner this day sen'night, and assist at the ceremony next day, Sunday. On Monday morning I must be off for the North, as I have done much and have much to do. Now let me try your geographical learning again, and beg you to put on your considering cap, take rule in hand, and draw a straight line on the map from Hatton to Bishop Auckland. Then point out the best resting-places after a fair day's journey. We think of passing a couple of hours with Mrs. Parr on the Monday, but I do not mind eighty or ninety miles a day.

"Sincerely hoping that there may be no impediment to our

meeting on Saturday, and that you will have eaten your mutton chop or *sausage* before we arrive, and with Mrs. Maltby's and Henry's kindest wishes to you and the ladies, I am, my dear Bishop, yours most truly,
"E. DUNELM."

Dr. Butler went to Hatton, and with Dr. Maltby assisted at the baptism of Dr. Parr's grandson, now Colonel Parr Lynes.

From the Ven. Archdeacon Hodson

Brewood, July 20th, 1838.

"MY DEAR LORD, I write to your Lordship on my way home from my parochial visitation of the district around Wolverhampton, which has occupied the last four days.

"My immediate object is to communicate to your Lordship respecting P—.[1] Nothing can be worse than the state of things as reported to me by the churchwardens, confirmed by neighbouring clergy, and indeed evinced by my own observation. The wretched incumbent was brought home drunk in a cart last Saturday night—is frequently seen lying in the roads in a state of intoxication—lives like a pig, in a poor house, with a pauper as his companion, in one room of a large vicarage house which is sadly out of repairs, and which if not speedily repaired will soon be in a ruinous condition. The parish registers have not been filled up for the last two or three years, and are lying about in all directions.

"Together with P—, which is a vicarage worth between £300 and £400 a year, he holds —, where he does duty at twelve o'clock on Sundays, having besides full morning service and afternoon prayers at P—. Your Lordship will judge *how* these duties are performed by a drunkard of sixty-seven. I had a serious conversation with him, in which I told him that complaints had been made to your Lordship, and repeated to myself, the evidence being unquestionable; referred to the state of the registers, vicarage premises, his own ruined affairs (for he has for many years been on an allowance of £120 per annum, the rest of his income being assigned for the benefit of his

[1] Cf. letters under date September 23rd and October 3rd, 1837.

creditors), as proof of his incompetency to discharge aright the duties of his office; and urged him to avert worse consequences by a retirement from the parish (if your Lordship would allow him to retire), and commit the care of both the parishes to a curate to be nominated by you.

" He has a son curate of a parish at no great distance, but out of the diocese, with whom he could reside.

" He showed at first a disposition to mount the high horse and assert his innocence, but seeing that this did not avail, he withdrew opposition, and will I think submit, if your Lordship will insist on his retiring as the only alternative to your appointing a commission of inquiry to investigate his conduct upon the spot. I apprehend you might, without any undue stretch of power, request three or four neighbouring clergymen to inquire and report to you touching the truth of the statements that have been made as to his conduct, and confirmed by my observation, even if you should hesitate to write to him on my official report only; on that point, however, your Lordship will judge better than I can.

" If you approve the suggestion and the incumbent yield, I think there will be no difficulty in getting a curate to undertake the entire and sole charge of the parishes without calling on him to pay anything."

To Richard Vernon Smith, Esq., House of Commons

Eccleshall Castle, August 12th, 1838.

" Sir, In reply to your letter which I have the honour to receive this morning I beg to say that I have no objection, as far as I am myself concerned, to the printing the return of leases which I sent to Lord John Russell, but I cannot help thinking the lessees to be a party concerned and to be omitted or to be consulted. It is one thing to send information to a committee of the House of Commons, and another to make that public without the consent of parties interested therein. They are numerous, and may consider it in many points as an *exposé* of their private affairs.

" Will you permit me, therefore, to ask you whether this

objection has been started before, or whether the lessors have given their consent without reference to the lessees? In the former case I must join with the parties objecting to the publication without the concurrence of the lessees; in the latter I do not wish to stand as a single objector."

*

From the Rev. R. Scott

Balliol, Oxford, Wednesday [early in September (?), 1838].

" MY DEAR LORD, In the hope that your health is much better than it was when I last troubled you with a letter, I write to beg one more favour in addition to all that you have done me.

" I have been examining the authorities on the subject of the Vote by Ballot at Athens, and by contemporary evidence I think I have made it appear that this did not involve secrecy of voting until after the Thirty Tyrants.

" I am printing at the Clarendon the results of my inquiry, and my request is that you will permit me to dedicate them to you. I would not ask this if I thought there was anything political in my Essay which you would disapprove. But the only modern political question it touches is simply that of the ballot, and that only in reference to the argument from Athenian history. In fact there is very little, though something, of politics in it—none at all except what is directed against some crude theories which Lytton Bulwer has published as historical facts.

" Under these circumstances I shall be very much obliged to you if you will allow me to inscribe it to you as follows:

TO THE RIGHT REVEREND
SAMUEL,
LORD BISHOP OF LICHFIELD,
ETC., ETC.
THE GRATEFUL OFFERING
OF ONE WHO HAS HAD THE HAPPINESS
TO BE HIS PUPIL.

" Pray remember me most kindly to Mrs. Butler and my other

old kind friends, and believe me, my dear Lord, ever gratefully yours, "ROBERT SCOTT."

The pamphlet is entitled *The Athenian Ballot, and Secret Suffrage* (Oxford, 1838), and is dedicated as above.

To — (?)

Eccleshall Castle, September 1st, 1838.

"REV. SIR, I have not been returned half an hour from a consecration tour, and can say little on the subject of your letter, which I have just opened, as it does not afford me sufficient data.

"One thing is quite clear, that the salary offered to the incumbent is not one that I can accept. The value of the living is £300 clear, and the pittance proposed for the curate is £50, but there are sundry other points of importance which you do not state.

"I know not from your letter of what College Mr. R— is a graduate, where he is a resident, or from what persons I am to make my private inquiries respecting him, and, in fact, have not the honour of personal acquaintance with yourself.

"You will see from the paper sent herewith what I expect in these particulars, and I am sorry to say I certainly cannot ordain Mr. R— on so short a notice. Ordination is a very serious and solemn affair. It binds a man for life to a course of holy duties, and is not to be entered upon rashly, unadvisedly, or without due preparation. Should I live, my next ordination after September will probably be held in January, and under any particular urgency, but not else, I might ask some Bishop who ordains between the end of November and Christmas Day to accept of letters dimissory from me. If Mr. W— is willing to advance the curate's stipend to £70 a year, and let him take the cure of Sandiacre with it, where as well as at Kirk Hallam there is only one duty each Sunday, and they may therefore be performed alternately, the two will not be too heavy for one man, and the stipend, though Sandiacre is extremely small in value, may be raised sufficiently to secure his permanent residence. There is no house of residence at either place. I remain, Rev. Sir, your obedient humble servant,

"S. LICHFIELD."

To a Clergyman

Eccleshall Castle, September 3rd, 1838.

"REV. SIR, I am much concerned that I am called upon in the discharge of my duty, in consequence of two complaints that have been laid before me by Mr. Thornburgh, your curate, to write to you respecting them. The one is that the only allowance you make to your two curates is £50 between them, one half of which goes to the curate of Turnditch, the other pittance, only £25 per annum, to himself, for three Sunday duties besides the weekly in the great church of Belper, although Mr. Barber holds your written promise to allow him £50 more, and although you give no assistance yourself at the service except the four quarterly sacraments, and have wholly deprived them of Mr. Leigh's assistance at the third service. The other is that you positively refuse his request—a very proper one, in my opinion—to allow the Holy Communion to be administered more frequently. Surely, sir, you cannot think monthly sacraments too frequent in a population of about ten thousand souls; you cannot intend that such a vast body of people should live without the means of grace offered them oftener than four times a year. And surely, sir, you cannot think the real labourer so unworthy of his hire, that you are to sit still with the profits of your living, and pay him £25 a year for the charge of ten thousand souls. Let me entreat you, sir, to attend to this my earnest remonstrance, without driving me to lay you under sequestration. I have the authority, and it is my duty to God and man that I should use it to rectify this great evil; but I would much rather do it by persuasion than by compulsion, and in the former case I may even hope that I am bringing you to serious reflection on what I can hardly think short of a grievous sin. I remain, Rev. Sir, your affectionate brother,

"S. LICHFIELD."

To a Clergyman

Eccleshall Castle, September 8th, 1838.

"REV. SIR, I never heard of a testimonial, however respectably signed by any three clergymen, being received by a Bishop without the counter-signature of their Diocesan. I must therefore return Mr. C—'s testimonial for counter-signature, though I admit that nothing can be more respectable than the signatures attached to it. On one point let me caution you, and let me request that before your final agreement with Mr. C— you will send me some information on the subject.

"He appears to be a native of Ireland, where party spirit, both in politics and religion, seems very high. The Irish also are of a more quick and ardent temperament than we are in England, and there are many Roman Catholics in Glossop, in which parish Mr. C— will officiate. I therefore think it necessary to look for a man who, without compromising his Protestant principles, may yet have discretion enough not to provoke hostilities by challenging or accepting challenges to disputation, or adopting such other measures as the difference of the classes of Protestants and Papists, coming into near and close hostility with each other in Ireland, renders not unfrequent there, but which I should be very sorry to see introduced here.

"I must beg you to be explicit with Mr. C— on this point. Should his answer be satisfactory, and his testimonial be counter-signed by the Bishop, there will be no difficulty in admitting him. I remain, Rev. Sir, your obedient and faithful servant,

"S. LICHFIELD."

To — (?)

Eccleshall Castle, September 19th, 1838.

"REV. SIR, On considering what is the best way in which effect may be given to the wishes of the sub-committee for inspecting schools in my diocese, established by the aid of public grants, it appears to me that I cannot appoint any one inspector for all the schools, or expect him to take a journey of some hundred miles in the diocese, and a very troublesome office connected therewith, without paying him a proper remuneration both for his trouble and expenses; and I therefore intend to apply to the incumbents of the respective parishes mentioned—if you will send me in a parcel twenty copies of each paper—and desire them to return their answers to you.

"The questions may be necessary and important on this occasion, but I must fear they will be but indifferently filled up if they are often to be repeated.

"Of course I cannot frank and write all the necessary communications at once, but will despatch them as fast as I can.

"We shall then endeavour to establish a good normal school at Lichfield for the instruction of teachers in the diocese..."

From S. Leigh Sotheby, Esq.

Wellington Street, September 22nd, 1838.

"MY LORD BISHOP, I am truly indebted to your Lordship for the permission to re-examine the Commonplace Book of Melanchthon, which, with my portfolio, has arrived at Messrs. Longman's.

"I should have acknowledged the receipt of your Lordship's kind communication earlier, but I was out of town on business.

"The perusal of your Lordship's opinion on the different characters of writing in that extraordinary volume has afforded me the utmost gratification and satisfaction, and your Lordship further granting me permission to state that opinion is an act of the most kind consideration and condescension.

"As I am going into the country for a fortnight to recruit my health, I hope your Lordship will feel satisfied as to the safety of the volume at Messrs. Longman's, on which, as its careful examination will occupy me several days, I shall not proceed to write until my return."

The commonplace book above referred to is now in the MS. department of the British Museum. The number of the MS. is 12059, on writing for which number the book may be seen. It is mainly in Melanchthon's own handwriting, and contains on a blank half-page near the beginning of the volume the opinion, in Dr. Butler's own writing, referred to by Mr. Sotheby.

From the Rev. R. Scott

Balliol, Wednesday, October (?), 1838.

"MY DEAR LORD, I am sorry that my misunderstanding your last letter but one should have given you more trouble.

"I see no reason to doubt that whenever the change of the manner of voting took place (*i.e.* I think after the Thirty) the plan which Pollux and the Scholiasts describe, and which is countenanced by Aristotle and Aeschines, came at once into use. By this a man took two ballots, say a black and white, walked up to the brass and wood urns, and laying one hand on the κημός of each, dropped one into each, taking care that if he meant to condemn the black ball should drop into the brass urn—if to acquit, the white one.

"As from the construction of the κημός only one person could make use of the ballot-box at once, there seems no reason to doubt the real secrecy of this way of voting. And I conceive that this, which certainly was used later, may be supposed (in the absence of evidence) to be what is referred to even in Lysias, who decidedly does speak of the κρύβδην.

"At least this hypothesis is sufficient, by showing what certainly may have been the case, to relieve my scheme from the objection which would necessarily attach to it, if its truth involved the difficulty you pointed out.

"In that case it would prove too much; and however plausible it might appear, one would naturally say that there must be some lurking error or fallacy.

"Believe me, my dear Lord, ever most truly yours,

"ROBERT SCOTT."

Correspondence

To — (?)

October 9th, 1838.

"Nothing can be more striking than the reluctance to give evidence against them [the clergy–ED.]. The laity are often apt to blame Bishops for not correcting this or that offence, without being aware that what is matter of notoriety to themselves, and what may reach the ears of a Bishop by rumour, will not be proved before him, even by the very persons who complain, when he inquires into it. During the nearly twenty years I have been in office as Archdeacon or Bishop, I have constantly remarked this; and when, after enormous expense, the case fails for want of evidence, the Bishop, anxious as he may be to remedy the evil, is blamed for neglect or laxity. I much fear this might have been the case now but for your kind assistance, for nothing can be more base than the conduct of the witnesses at Stone, especially those at the Fountain there, the scene of Mr. —'s last gross misconduct.

"I have the honour to be, with many thanks, Sir, your obliged and faithful servant,

"S. LICHFIELD."

To — (?)

(Original in a book now in possession of the British Museum. See Reading-Room Catalogue under Dr. Butler's name and description.)

Eccleshall Castle, October 9th, 1838.

"DEAR SIR, I am not aware of any particular form of abjuration existing; that which you propose, whether drawn up by yourself or adopted from any formula, appears to me proper and sufficient. After the person has answered this question in the affirmative, I think you should say to the following purport:

"'In the presence of God and of this congregation, I hereby receive and admit you A. B. as a member of the Protestant Church of England and Ireland as by law established, and pray with God that you may continue in the same until your life's end.'

"I would then recommend you to use the whole or some of the under-mentioned collects: Second Sunday in Advent, First Sunday after the Epiphany, Second Collect for Good Friday, Collect for All Saints' Day. I remain, dear Sir, faithfully yours,
"S. LICHFIELD.

"P.S. You have done quite right in writing to me first. I think you may omit the benediction in the Visitation for the Sick at the end of the ceremony, and insert it immediately after the form of admission, as it is addressed to the individual; and then proceed with the collects before mentioned, ending with 'The Grace of our Lord,' etc."

From the Rev. R. Scott

Balliol, October 15th, 1838.

"MY DEAR LORD, I should not have troubled you again so soon, had I not found that you have, since I wrote, conferred another favour upon me by the kind present of your portrait.

"I have long wished for a more satisfactory one than the old print, which has hung over my chimney-piece ever since I have been in Oxford; and I really think that this is a very good and agreeable likeness, as well as a very good specimen of art. But whatever it had been, the certificate of your kindness in the corner would have given the highest value to it. Believe me, I am most grateful for your remembering me so kindly.

"As to the ballot, I cannot say that there was *not* a curtain or case; but there is no hint of such a thing. And as until some proof is brought of it we are entitled, nay bound, to suppose that there was not, it follows, I think, that a mode of voting was adopted which excluded secrecy.

"The phrase κρύβδην ψηφίζειν is *never* used before Lysias (after the Thirty's time) of the voting in courts of justice. Until that time it is only found of the ostracism. No allusion to secrecy occurs until the same time. Soon afterwards we find the plan of voting with a κύρος and an ἄκυρος καδίσκος (which necessarily implies secrecy) in use. Granting, then, the secrecy of the vote from Lysias downwards, I think we have all the proof of which a negative is capable that it was not in use before.

"It certainly rests with those who believe that the votes were secret originally to produce some one passage from a contemporary which is inconsistent with open voting.

"Remember me most kindly to the ladies, and believe me, my dear Lord, very gratefully yours, "ROBERT SCOTT."

The portrait above referred to is the one by Thomas Phillips, R.A., engraved by Cousins. It was a question with me whether to reproduce this or Kirkby's portrait for my frontispiece, but I believe I have done rightly in preferring Kirkby's.

To Messrs. Wise and Le Hunt, Ashborne, for the use of the Governors and Assistants of Ashborne Grammar School

Eccleshall Castle, October 17th, 1838.

"GENTLEMEN, Having carefully considered the documents that you have laid before me, I must say that, with regard to the exercises of the two boys Chambers and Bamford, they show most decidedly both as regards the good Latin, which is corrected by Mr. Gibbs into bad, and the bad Latin, which is not corrected by him into good, but especially by the former, his manifest incapacity, as a second master of a grammar school; and I wonder how he ever became elected, for his testimonials are the weakest I ever saw as to his abilities and attainments, though good as to his moral character.

"On considering Mr. Gepp's letter, I am of opinion that his complaint is well founded, and I lament to say that I must pronounce Mr. Gibbs *grossly* incompetent.

"Still it is fair to add that I have some doubts, not as to the propriety of his removal, but as to your power of now removing him. The passage quoted by Mr. Gepp from the charter is decidedly against the election of such a man, but provision is not there made for his subsequent removal on the same ground. It stands to common sense that he ought to be removed; but the law, though said to be the perfection of wisdom, does not always agree with common sense, and I should be afraid to remove Mr. Gibbs without an able counsel's opinion. Neither do I find in the charter any passage which appears to me to bear out assertion that the second master is to be the head-master's assistant as well as deputy when need may require. The English rules have been evidently formed upon the charter, and therefore do not assume a greater power; and the charter having provided that a fit and learned person should be chosen, seems to have considered this a sufficient security for his competence, and not to have taken into the account any possible subsequent discovery of incapacity. Another reason why I doubt your power of removal is that you have borne with him twenty years without making the discovery of his unfitness, which is a point, I think, not to be overlooked, for in this case the former head-master and indeed the trustees may be said to have neglected their duty, and to have lost their remedy by so long a delay.

"Whether the following clause at the end of the charter may help to sanction the removal of an incompetent master, I cannot say; I think not, as it is confined to *ordinationes et statuta*. (I am so ill that I cannot go on, but must resign to an amanuensis.)

"'Et quod quilibet, sub-paedagogus, gubernator, et assistens scholae praedictae pro tempore existente sit et erit remoturus et remoturi, et de tempore in tempus amoveri possint secundum ordinationes et statuta ut permittitur fiendum et faciendum.'* If Mr. Gibbs denies that the corrections are his, I would recommend the trustees to call the boys whose exercises I have seen into the room in their presence, and to set them an exercise which they have not done before, three or four pages forward in the book from the place which they are now doing in the school. The boys may be allowed before the exercise is set to go for their dictionaries and grammars, if they are used to have that help. Mr. Gibbs should then be called, and be requested to correct the exercises in the presence of the trustees before the boys leave the room, and should not be allowed to leave the room himself till he has corrected them. The boys, whether two or five in number, should each have a separate exercise, and not the same piece. I remain, Gentlemen, your obedient faithful servant,

"S. LICHFIELD."

Correspondence

To a Clergyman

Eccleshall Castle, October 18th, 1838.

"REV. SIR, Whatever may be the feelings of the adverse party towards you, I am much afraid that they are right in their opinion, and that you will find yourself involved in great difficulty.

"I am exceedingly surprised that your attorney, having heard the report, after signing of the contract, and before the completion of the purchase, should have suffered you to complete it. I am also surprised that you did not mention to me the report, however slight, or however discredited by yourself, which you knew on the 22nd of August, especially as you knew before institution that a strong party was forming against you in the parish. I recollect that when I advised you to write to Mr. H— as a courtesy due to him in a case somewhat unusual, there seemed a hesitation on your part to do so.

"Whether you wrote or not I have not learnt. My impression was, when you first applied to me, that you had purchased the advowsons long before Mr. H— was appointed to his second living, and that you took advantage of an undoubted right upon or soon after his second presentation, for reasons best known to yourself and which it was not my province to inquire into. I thought you were urgent for institution that you might the sooner put an end to hostility in the parish by making the appointment irrevocable, and therefore, feeling I had no right to cause vexatious delay, I complied with your wishes as well as I could. I certainly do not mean to say that you were at all aware of the consequences of your contract, but wish you had been more frankly communicative, as I might have saved you from consequences of which I am painfully apprehensive, as I should have certainly recommended delay till all doubt could be removed. I have ordered a case to be drawn up and the opinion of an eminent civilian taken as to the course I ought to pursue, and I have requested the earliest answer. Till that arrives, by which of course I must be entirely guided, I can come to no decision; but I cannot and ought not to conceal from you that I apprehend you are by no means in

a safe position, though I assure you I wish it may turn out differently from my expectation. I am, Rev. Sir, your obedient faithful servant,
"S. LICHFIELD."

To the Ven. Archdeacon Hodson

Eccleshall Castle, October 20th, 1838.

"MY DEAR ARCHDEACON, I was far too ill and fatigued yesterday to enter into the Matlock question, and can now only state my objections shortly, but I hope intelligibly; and though I most sincerely wish I may do it without giving offence to any one, I shall do it at the risk of consequences in all sincerity and truth.

"The church is proposed to be built under a clause in the Building Act which if not acted upon with the greatest care might become one of the most oppressive and obnoxious to patrons, incumbents, and Bishops that I know of, and in many cases might create or perpetuate party spirit and party feuds where every sober man would wish to establish goodwill and unanimity.

"I dislike the very increasing patronage of small livings among trustees over whom the Bishop has no control and in whose election he has no voice; and though he has the power of a refusal to the erection of a church in the first instance, yet it is one that it is painful to exercise, subjects him to much misinterpretation, and requires, if I may venture to say so, some courage to make use of.

"I object again because I think the sum provided for the establishment of such livings far too small, a subject which I have partly entered upon at our diocesan district meeting in September, and shall more largely pursue on another occasion. It places the Bishop in awkward collision with trustees whom he may respect for their private worth, though he cannot concur in all their religious sentiments; nor do I think that when they are once named to him, his own feelings of the courtesy due from one gentleman to another will allow him to make individual objections. I recollect that on the last application made to me for a building of this nature I expressed my reluctance to consent, and was told that the plans had been drawn and money collected, if I mistake not with the view of paying honour to my predecessor, and upon that of course I yielded; but you will see how easy it is on all occasions to collect the money, draw the plan, and then appeal to the Bishop, and say, 'A great many people here have subscribed, and it will be very hard upon them if you refuse your consent.'

"I have also considerable doubt whether Matlock Bath is a place where such a church is needed. The season is not long, nor the company, I believe, numerous at any one period. There is Bonsall within a mile on one side and Cromford within a mile on the other, while the parish church can, I think, hardly be two miles distant by the road. The living also of Matlock itself at the present moment is vacant, and I cannot therefore take any steps in the business. But my present general view is, I confess, adverse to a plan which I cannot conceive calculated to promote that spirit of kind and charitable feeling that I wish to see others practise as well as adhere to most strictly myself. If the patronage was given up to the Bishop instead of being placed in trustees, many of the difficulties would be obviated.

"I am too much exhausted to add more now, but write this because you are about to leave home on Monday. I am truly yours,
"S. LICHFIELD."

From E. S. Chandos-Pole, Esq.

Radborne, near Derby, November 6th, 1838.

"MY LORD, The application which I enclose is not the first of the kind I have received. Some years ago I could not make up my mind that I was acting right in being an obstacle to any kind of religious instruction, which these people seemed anxious to afford, in a populous neighbourhood, where there was not much church room or much church service. I named the matter to the late Bishop Ryder, and promised him I would wait and see what was possible to be done. I don't like to let them have the ground, for fear of encouraging dissent and schism, and I am not sure I am doing as I ought in being a bar to their getting what information a set of well-intentioned persons would otherwise afford them. I take the liberty therefore of requesting your Lordship will give me your sanction for either granting or refusing what is asked of me."

To E. S. Chandos-Pole, Esq.

(Private and confidential.)

Eccleshall Castle, November 8th, 1838.

"SIR, I sensibly feel the honour you are pleased to confer upon me by consulting me with respect to the grant of land to the Wesleyan Methodists for building a chapel in the parish of Killamarsh, and, as I infer, in the direct road to the parish church. But I must beg your indulgence when I state that it is a case in which it would be most highly improper in me to express an opinion, because I cannot avoid being liable either way to great misinterpretation, and because in these times every act of persons in any public station is most narrowly looked after and most severely criticised. I could not therefore give my opinion without being placed on the horns of a dilemma, either as withholding instruction from a class of persons who stand in need of it, or encouraging schism by promoting the views of a party not in direct union with the Church. I find by looking into the ecclesiastical returns that the population of Killamarsh at the last census is 774, and the accommodation in the church sufficient for 400, more than half the parish, and more than is usually found sufficient anywhere. I merely give you this information, as the parliamentary document from which I take it is a very bulky volume and not easily accessible. But this would certainly be a reason with me against granting any allowance to the Church people themselves should they apply for the means of enlarging their church from the diocesan fund."

Dr. Butler wrote to the Bishop of Durham asking advice, and received an answer dated 29th November, in which the Bishop, after admitting the difficulty of the case, concluded by saying, "If there be no church within a mile and a half of the Methodists, it seems reasonable that they should have one."

Correspondence

From Mr. Commissioner Reynolds

Newmarket, November 8th, 1838.

"MY VERY DEAR BISHOP AND FRIEND, News for you;—Caravan has beaten Grey Momus by three lengths—started at full speed—kept it up the whole two miles—Robinson rode the victor beautifully—all the knowing ones taken in—Day chopfallen! What is Lord Durham to this, or *pace tua dixerim*, the Bishops of Durham and Norwich and poor old Mr. Turner, or Newman and Pusey? To write from Newmarket and not send word of this would be unpardonable; and let the tidings reconcile, or rather conciliate, you to the announcement that some time about the hour of five on Wednesday, November 21st, we, H. R. R. and A. R., purpose to attack Eccleshall Castle and find a lodgement for the night; on Tuesday, the 20th, we Trenthamise: thus far we extend our courtesy, that if on Friday, the 15th, we shall find at the post office at Nottingham that the Castle gates will be shut against us, we shall forbear to approach them.

"Didn't your ears tingle on Tuesday, the 30th of October? They ought, for friend Watkinson and we remembered you in our cups at Earl's Colne: there too was No. 42's bridal daughter, looking very sweet and gentle and Eve-like—*vide* Fourth Book of *Paradise Lost*.

"To-morrow we go to Cambridge; and having nothing to do at my two places in succession, Huntingdon and Peterborough, shall bide there two or three days. With what mingled feelings and deep interest must the old man whose affections are not worn out ever revisit that spot where you and I passed so many a day since which—

"'There's many a lad we loved gone dead,
And many a lass grown old'!

"Well, now, my dear Lord, I do so very much long to see you. I shall 'in good truth and sincere verity' be most cruelly vexed if I cannot get a peep at you, so pray let me find a line from the Castle when I reach Nottingham on the 15th. My work on the whole will be diminished, but it happens most provokingly that I have my full share at Stafford."

To the Rev. W. B. Sleath, D.D.

Date about November 4th, 1838.

"DEAR DR. SLEATH, Is the Rev. Hugh Ker Cokburne still Vicar of Etwall, and does he reside there? It seems to me as if that is not the name exactly, and I have some recollection of directing to him elsewhere.

"Of course I must hear what he has to say, yet if you have sent him an absolute notice of resignation, and he accepts it, you may, I fear, have placed both yourself and me in an awkward position as to your continuance.

"I am ready to write to him and to inquire into the causes of his dissatisfaction as soon as you supply me with the address and information I have asked for in the first paragraph. And also I should wish to know what sort of objections were taken by him to the curates whom you provided, and any instances of improper language held by him towards you. But as I should be very desirous of promoting, if not actual friendship, at least mutual forbearance between you, I should be very glad to use my exertions rather in a merely amicable than a judicial capacity.

"I must confess I am not surprised that, after your long public services and at your age, you should choose rather to resign than to submit to indignities either of action or language; the difficulty is in the resumption of your office if you have actually gave notice of your resignation, compatibly with what you owe to yourself and the station which you occupy. I am, dear Dr. Sleath, yours faithfully,

"S. L."

To the Rev. H. Ker Cokburne

Eccleshall Castle, November 9th, 1838.

"REV. SIR, Dr. Sleath, the curate of Etwall, has written to me stating that he entered upon that curacy on condition of taking an assistant curate who was to give satisfaction to the parish at large—a condition so vague and indefinite that I fear the most zealous curate must despair of fulfilling it; that nevertheless he three times tried to fulfil his engagement, but that what he calls frivolous objections were made before you by certain individuals to him unknown, and particularly of late against Mr. Dickenson, upon which you acted, and have peremptorily forbidden Mr. Dickenson to come into the church; and that ultimately you have begged him (Dr. Sleath), when he offered to resign the curacy, to reconsider the matter, and to acquaint you with his final decision, either to quit the curacy on giving you three months' notice, or to fulfil the terms on which he accepted the curacy—that is, to find a sub-curate who shall give satisfaction to the parish at large.

"What I wish to inquire of you, sir, is whether Mr. Dickenson is guilty of any offence against morals, or holding or teaching any heterodox doctrines, or neglect of duty in any respect. Dr. Sleath professes not to know the cause for which you have required the removal of Mr. Dickenson or his predecessors, except that some individuals to him unknown have made to you some unfavourable representations against them. It seems to me hard that they should suffer without a hearing, and my request to you is that you will be so good as to put me in possession of the charges alleged against them by their accusers, and the names of the parties accusing them. I remain, Rev. Sir, your very obedient and humble servant,
"S. LICHFIELD."

To the Rev. H. Ker Cokburne

Eccleshall Castle, November 16th, 1838.

"REV. SIR, Though I cannot but feel concerned at your having had the trouble to write to me so fully at length when you were yourself indisposed, yet I am the more obliged to you for the valuable information you have given me, and the candid manner in which you have supplied it, and not least of all is the testimonial in favour of Dr. Sleath, which you have with so great fairness sent me this morning, and which, with your permission, I will retain a few days before I return it to you. The fact is, I am so ill myself that I can hardly dictate, and not without the greatest difficulty write a letter; and having at this moment much troublesome business before me, I should wish to defer the consideration of that testimonial a few days longer.

"My first knowledge of Dr. Sleath began fifty-six years ago, when I found him an Assistant Master at Rugby School, and though I was put in the form above that which he taught, yet he was kind to me, became acquainted with some of my friends, and I have kept up my acquaintance with him ever since. He is a man of great benevolence and simplicity of character, and remarkable ardour of disposition, considering his age. This leads him to jump too hastily sometimes to his conclusions, and I doubt not he has done so on the present occasion, else there could not be so great a difference between his statement as to the removal of the curates and your own, or his assumption that I have in any way prejudged the case in his favour, when in fact I have stated in every letter that, before coming to any conclusion, it is necessary that I should hear both sides of this question, and I took great pains in one of my early letters to set him right as to Mr. Dickenson being a curate to him, which I believe in law cannot be, whatever private understanding there may be between the Dr. and yourself as to the employment of that gentleman's services. Now with regard to Mr. Dickenson and his impediment, I must beg to say that I think it must have been greatly exaggerated, though it is very possible he may at first have hesitated from nervousness, but I have heard that is wearing, if not worn off quite. Had there been anything striking in it when he appeared before me for examination, I must have noticed it, and would not have ordained him if I had perceived any objectionable impediment. It is true I did not examine him *viva voce*, because I am unable to hold conversations of any extent, and therefore confined my share of the examination to the looking over of written papers; but Mr. Evans, my Chaplain, was here and did examine him, and reported him as having done remarkably well, but said not a word about the impediment, which I am quite sure he would have noticed had it appeared important.

"I think it is clear that the majority of the parish are in favour of Dr. Sleath, but it is impossible to expect perfect unanimity. The person you speak of as being of the class commonly called Evangelical is very likely to be prejudiced against Dr. Sleath—first of all, because persons of that description, especially in humbler life, are apt to be led away by their feelings, and to sacrifice Christian charity upon the altar of spiritual pride. I do not say this of all, but as a not unfrequent occurrence, especially in the condition of life alluded to. In the next place, Dr. Sleath is himself unfriendly to that class, and very much wants discretion and forbearance in speaking of and to them, as I myself once witnessed at Repton many years ago. You state that you have not heard Mr. Dickenson yourself, and I really think it would be hard upon the young man to remove him, until it is ascertained that there is real ground for complaint, not from one, nor half a dozen individuals, but from a considerable number of the parishioners. I should like, if you have no objection, to get a friend upon whose judgement I can rely to attend the church for one or two Sundays to hear Mr. Dickenson, unknown to any of the parties in the parish, and to make his report to me. This, I think, will ensure an impartial account, and I would communicate it to you as soon as I received it. In the meantime I would write to Dr. Sleath to request him to accept my good offices in recommending him to conciliate any persons whom he conceives to be adverse to him, and to cultivate a good understanding between you and himself, suspending any opinion about Mr. Dickenson for the present, beyond what I have already given him, that he cannot legally be considered as his curate. I remain, Rev. Sir, your very obedient and faithful servant,

"S. LICHFIELD."

To the Ven. Archdeacon Hodson

Eccleshall Castle, November 10th, 1838.

"MY DEAR ARCHDEACON, I have received the enclosed, which causes me some uneasiness, this morning. If I recollect right, the Bishop stipulated that when Mr. — did return he should undertake no duty in the church without his licence to that effect. On such a supposition I propose to write to him a letter of which I send you a copy, begging you to suggest any alterations or additions which may occur to you. Believe me truly yours,

"S. LICHFIELD."

The enclosure ran:

"REV. SIR, While I admit at once your right to return, having fulfilled the full term of absence agreed upon between the late Bishop and yourself, I am afraid I must remind you of a clause in that agreement that you should undertake no duty in the church till fully sanctioned by his authority, and I must also earnestly beg you to believe that I retain precisely the same friendly interest for your welfare and kind reception in your parish as when I wrote last to you. And these feelings induced me to approve of your continuing absent on licence renewed to you, but the condition for which you stipulate compels me to add very reluctantly that I cannot consent to accept such terms.

"In the first place, I am sure it is expedient that you should not think of resuming your official duties in any degree till your parishioners have again become familiarised to you, and have satisfied themselves, by observing the propriety of your conduct, of your steadiness of purpose to live suitably to your sacred calling. In the next place, you have reduced me, however unwillingly, to mention what it may distress you to hear, and what I had hoped to have been spared the pain of mentioning to you, which is totally independent of the reason already assigned. I mean a personal infirmity of voice, gesture, and delivery, which must operate as a bar against the utility of any man in his profession as far as the public services of the Church are concerned, however good may be his purposes and however sound his doctrines. This has often struck me in the interviews I have had with you. My advice therefore which I give to you is what I should give to my own son were he in a similar state of nervousness and incapacity, for were you to attempt to officiate I am sure you would only lose ground and do yourself harm. If you make your resumption of duty whenever you do return a *sine qua non* for the condition of your absence now, I must say that I would rather see you return now, taking no duty, than resuming it whenever you do return as a matter of course. It should be done gradually and cautiously at any time, and not till your present nervous attacks have been subdued. This

Correspondence

advice is given from none but the best and kindest motives, and it is what I would give in such a state of nervous affection to the most exemplary clergyman in my diocese. I wish you to consider it, and let me know the result; and believe me your sincere friend and well-wisher,

"S. LICHFIELD."

To E. S. Chandos-Pole, Esq.

Eccleshall Castle, November 12th, 1838.

"SIR, It has occurred to me that I can answer your letter without waiting to collect information by fresh inquiries from the Archdeacon and Rural Deans, by the help of my own observations, which I made when I visited Killamarsh as Archdeacon some sixteen years ago; for the same Mr. Mountain was then curate who is just about now to quit the curacy, and whose removal may enable me to make some important improvements, with the assistance of the parishioners and landholders, without admitting the Wesleyan Methodists into the parish.

"I must freely confess to you that your inquiry placed me in a dilemma of some difficulty, for at a time when the actions of Bishops are scrutinised with no common severity, and motives assigned to those actions which are not remarkable for charity towards the Bench, I felt that if I recommended you not to grant the favour required I should be called a bigoted, unchristian-like opposer of true religion, or if I advised the granting of the favour sought I should be called an enemy of that Church of which I was nominated an unworthy head. I have resolved, however, to lay before you facts which may assist you in forming your own judgement, and to add a very few words from myself, of which I would request you would consider yourself the sole depositary, without communicating them elsewhere. The church of Killamarsh is an ancient stone building which will contain perhaps three hundred, exclusive of charity children. The only accommodation for the poor are three seats, which may hold fifteen or eighteen persons. Cleanliness is much neglected, the damp great. The service is once a day, and arranged so that there shall be one morning service at ten, and then two successive afternoon services for the two next

Sundays. There is no glebe house. There is a small endowed school for English, and a Sunday School containing about seventy boys and girls. The population of Killamarsh in 1831 was 774. From these data, sir, you will observe that the church will afford accommodation for more than a third of the inhabitants of the parish; but as there is so very little provision of sittings for the poor, I should strongly recommend the erection of a gallery to contain a small number of free sittings, but the principal part of the sittings to be let at very low rates. Experience has taught me that the poor will come much more thankfully to church when they have a seat which they can *bona fide* call their own, than when they are accommodated with entirely free ones. If room could be provided for from sixty to a hundred persons, two-thirds of these sittings being charged at a shilling or two shillings per annum, and only one-third left free, enough would be done for their accommodation. Then, I apprehend, the little endowed school might be augmented and enlarged; and if a house could be provided for the resident curate, to which there are great facilities now given by Boards in London, the parish would soon be in a condition not to require the assistance of the Wesleyan Methodists. I must own their proposed site for their chapel looks very much as if it was intended to convey a reproach to the Church, in the chief road to which it would be a prominent feature, and the language used respecting the neglected state of the parish, though it may be true, and perhaps must be so in part till a residence house is provided, is not particularly decorous. I have the honour to be, Sir, your very obedient and faithful servant,

"S. LICHFIELD."

To the Foreman of a Jury impanelled at the Bishop's Court, 22nd October 1838

Eccleshall Castle, November 21st, 1838.

" SIR, It is only this morning that I received a letter containing a petition of Henry Brown and John Shirley to be reinstated in their cottages, which is recommended to me by the last jury of the Manor Court held on October 22nd. I mention this that the gentlemen who formed the jury, of which you were the foreman, may understand that there has been no neglect on my part, but that I had not the least knowledge of the subject till this morning, exactly a month since the recommendation of the jury was given, and I shall feel much obliged to you if you will make this known to them, and also my regret at not being able to comply with their request for the reasons following, which I hope they will approve. In the first place Brown and Shirley have been most decidedly the most violent opposers of my right, but they, as well as all those who were misled by them, were freely forgiven by me and were allowed to continue in their cottages, and more than that, I took upon myself all those costs which they had agreed to pay, and which were not inconsiderable. No sooner was the intended day of trial over than the people were again misled. I was called a fool for my weak indulgence, and every act of defiance was used towards me. In particular Shirley proceeded to such acts of violence that I was obliged to send to Stafford for police support. Now I hope I am of a forgiving disposition, and most especially so towards the poor, but it is necessary to make examples, and the man who yields continually to his feelings of good-nature will only be doing a real public injury and be laughed at for his pains. The men had full notice that if, after the forgiveness they had received, they again trespassed, they would most assuredly lose their cottages, and that they must not fancy I should be weak enough to recall that determination and be laughed at as a fool a second time. Besides this, Wood, who is the bailiff under Seckerson, received continual annoyance, if not from these two persons themselves, I have no doubt at their instigation, and I am determined to protect and support my officers in the lawful exercise of their authority. Furthermore, I have placed in the cottages men of whose character I took pains to be well informed before I placed them there, and I trust that yourself and brother-jurymen will think it would be unfair in me to displace such tenants, who have given me no ground to do so. For these as well as for some other reasons which I might detail if I had not written at such length already, I am sorry to say I cannot restore these men. Their application comes too late;

they had their warning of what was to happen, and they would not abide by it. Will you be kind enough to explain this to your brother-jurymen? and believe me to be, Sir, your and their sincere well-wisher and obedient servant,

"S. LICHFIELD."

From the Rev. James Hildyard

Christ's College, November 30th, 1838.

"MY DEAR LORD, I fear the half-sheet I sent you on Wednesday last would throw very little light on the manner in which I purpose editing the present play. And as my design was to elicit any hints that you might throw out for the conduct of future plays, or even the remainder of this, I was sorry not to be able to send you more at once.

"The present half-sheet will in some measure supply the deficiency, and you will, I hope, be able to spare some half-hour for its perusal, in order that if any material improvement should occur to you I may avail myself of it as I did with the *Menaechmi*.

"We hope to get the play out early in January.

"You would be glad to see that three of your former pupils are at the same time examiners for the Classical Tripos—namely, Shilleto, G. Kennedy, and myself."

From the Rev. James Hildyard

Christ's College, December 2nd, 1838.

"MY DEAR LORD, I hasten to thank you for your very kind letter received this morning. I was not at all aware of there being three more MSS. of Plautus in England; much less did I guess they were in the possession of one who takes such an interest in him and his humble editor. Had I known this fact earlier, I should certainly have petitioned for that favour which I am now proud to accept agreeably to your kind offer. But do you not fear I am too far advanced in the present play to introduce the collation of your MSS. into it? You see we are struck off to the 160th line, and two more half-sheets are in type. Nevertheless I would gladly suspend operations (and shall do so for a day or two in the hope of hearing your opinion), if you thought it advisable. The *Aululara* is only in two of your MSS., and I think I could collate them in a couple (or three) days. Could I bring my unstruck-off sheets with me, and insert the few remarks that might be necessary in them, and then explain in the Preface that it was not till such a line (the 160th) that I was made aware of your treasure?

"Nothing prevents my leaving Cambridge at a day's notice, and the railroad, I remember, goes near or through Eccleshall.

"But pray advise me, my dear Lord, and above all don't let my coming under your roof be the cause of any excitement to yourself in your present delicate state.

"I reprint the *Menaechmi* as soon as the *Aululara* is off my hands, and I am glad to see it is in your first MS. That must be a curious volume, as only one out of eleven in the British Museum contains these ten plays, and one, of the three I saw at Vienna. The Cambridge MS. has only the eight *first*, as they are called.

"With many thanks for this proof of your kindness, believe me ever, my dear Lord, your much attached servant,

"JAMES HILDYARD."

From the Same

Christ's College, December 8th, 1838.

"MY DEAR LORD, I am happy in being able to announce the safe arrival of your MSS., which I received soon after despatching my letter of yesterday. They seem in very good condition, and, curiously enough, in no way resemble any of the other sixteen MSS. which I have already seen.

"The little dumpy one seems to be particularly original, and I certainly shall not depise it for its apparent insignificance. Another business has engaged my leisure all this day or I would have made some test of them, which might give me some insight into their relative value; when I have done so I will inform you of the result of my observations.

"It is my present intention to introduce the various readings they may furnish into my text and Critt. Nott. from the place I am at present, noticing that they then first came to my hand,

and in the Preface to give a more full account of them, which, with submission, I should like you to see before printed. The *Menaechmi* I shall be too glad to collate in them, as it is only in one of the Museum MSS., and not in our Cambridge one. With repeated thanks for this kind favour, believe me, my dear Lord, yours ever sincerely, "JAMES HILDYARD."

From the Rev. T. W. Peile

Durham, December 19th, 1838.

"MY DEAR LORD, When I received your Lordship's *letter of credit* in London, the benefit of which I did not fail to experience, although I am thus late in acknowledging it, I feared you were suffering from the fatigues of a recent ordination and other episcopal duties, and therefore forbore to write, and in the nine or ten weeks that have since elapsed I have been so incessantly occupied with the business of Term as hardly to find time to report progress.

"Mr. Murray, thanks to your Lordship, and to his friend Mitchell's report of my MS., which was submitted to him in confidence, at once agreed to undertake the whole cost of publication, and to divide with me the whole profits (if any) of an edition of my play. These are his usual terms, and I think them liberal, and certainly they suit my circumstances very well. The work is now passing through the Clarendon Press – a Cambridge editor printing in Oxford and correcting the proofs in Durham! – and I hope it will be out before the end of January. Meanwhile, as in private duty bound – *ne cum scriptore tuo* – I spare you the recital. I send you what I have set down for my Preface, on which I invite your Lordship's friendly criticism, and in which, if you will have the goodness to return it, I will endeavour to amend anything that your Lordship may think objectionable. There is much in it, I know, in which I cannot expect your Lordship to go along with me. I feel that this new style of editing, for which I have endeavoured to make the best apology I could, is in fact a concession to 'the spirit of the age,' in which, even if with Lord J. Russell I were to admit that the light of general information is more widely diffused, I cannot but think it is, at the same time, less vigorously reflected back than it was wont to be. We have no ' shining lights,' no literary ' giants in these days.' The education of our young men, I think, is too much diluted, and from this and other conspiring causes their best energies are enfeebled, and it will be well if we who have seen and known the men of old time can, even by meeting them on their own ground, succeed in putting them through the bracing exercises of the old *régime*.

"I am somewhat bold in speaking of ' new theories,' but dare think my references will make my words good. They relate chiefly to some peculiar uses of τε (!), and of that ill-named and worse understood mood the Optative, in particular the use of the Optative and Subjunctive after ὅπως, its kindred particles accompanied with ἄν, where Matthiae is deficient. All this, however, your Lordship must take on credit for the present."

I did not find the conclusion of this letter.

From the Rev. W. H. Wayne

Hill Cottage, Derby, December 29th, 1838.

" MY LORD BISHOP, Having been obliged by the complaint in my throat to give up all duty requiring even the slightest exertion of the voice, I am again resident in the parish of Duffield, and my attention has been a good deal turned to the state of my parish of Heage, and the men employed in that chapelry, and in Belper and Duffield on the railroad.

" On the former subject I have had some conversation with my curate, Mr. Leigh, on the latter with Mr. Barber, and beg to trouble your Lordship with the result.

" Your Lordship is aware that the whole proceeds of Heage (excepting a sum appropriated to the building a parsonage house) are less than £80 a year, for which Mr. Leigh gives one Sunday service, taking a few pupils, and any clerical services which the neighbourhood may offer as a means of livelihood, for he is a married man.

" The great evil of this system is the almost total neglect of the Heage Sunday and other schools, and the very defective visiting of the poor. Under these circumstances I have proposed to Mr. Leigh to make application to the Society for the Supply of Additional Curates for £50 a year, on condition that Mr. Leigh give an additional service, keep no school, but devote his whole time to Heage. To this he would agree, and I earnestly hope your Lordship will forward my request.

"You are aware that Heage contains about two thousand inhabitants, all poor, and for the most part colliers and ironstone getters, who must be visited late and early, or they are hardly ever met with. I could say much more, my Lord, in favour of this my application, but your Lordship's acquaintance with the great deficiency of clerical labourers in that neighbourhood will, I am sure, plead powerfully in my poor people's favour.

"The labourers on the railroad present another object of much interest. In the parish of Duffield, including the townships of Duffield, Milford, Belper, and Heage, there are supposed to be about two thousand labourers, not a few of whom have their wives and families settled in little turf cabins on the line of railroad.

"Such an influx of strangers, many not of the best character, in a parish already far too populous to admit of any adequate superintendence from the clergy already in the district, cannot be but attended with much evil. Many of these men, even if disposed to go to church, would be ashamed to appear in their working dress, the only one they have, and Mr. Barber agrees with me in thinking that, could a clergyman be found of some experience and readiness in expressing himself, whose whole time and energies should be devoted to the railway labourers and their families on the line above mentioned, namely, throughout the whole parish of Duffield, incalculable good might be done. I have not spoken on the subject to Mr. Tunstall, but [do not (?) – ED.] doubt of obtaining his sanction to anything which your Lordship may be pleased to suggest for the purpose of meeting the present extraordinary though temporary demand on the clergy of the district.

"Your Lordship is probably aware that the Bishop of Bath and Wells has given a title to a 'railroad missionary' on the Great Western line, who receives £150 a year from one of the societies; they allow this large sum in consideration of his being obliged to keep a horse, on account of the extent of the line. We think of confining ourselves to the parish of Duffield, including its chapelries, and the reason of my writing on the subject rather than Mr. Barber is that, should your Lordship wish either of us to give a title, he thinks I should do it rather than he, as by far the greater number of labourers are towards the Heage end of his parish, but this he would leave entirely to your Lordship's discretion. Possibly your Lordship might prefer the more general term of railroad missionary, but we think this parish of Duffield offers an abundant field of usefulness.

"Is your Lordship acquainted with any one whom you can recommend for this important and difficult sphere? We know not any one; and though we are informed that such a man would most easily be found in Ireland, we feel some reluctance to looking to that quarter, and should feel truly grateful could your Lordship recommend a proper person to the Society for supplying Additional Curates who might speedily enter on his work. I need not remind your Lordship that many who might acquit themselves well in a quiet parish would be quite unequal to so difficult and delicate an undertaking. Strength of body, hardihood, strong good sense, and a temper imperturbably good must be united to the most self-denying zeal and activity.

"Having ventured to say thus much, I must apologise for the trouble I am giving, but confidently hope that the importance of the subject will be accepted as sufficient excuse. Earnestly hoping that your Lordship is in better health, I gladly leave the matter in your hands, and have the honour to be, my Lord Bishop, your faithful and obedient servant,

"W. H. WAYNE."

To the Rev. W. H. Wayne

End of December, 1838 (?); January, 1839 (?).

"DEAR SIR, I quite agree with you that it would be very desirable if Mr. Leigh would devote his whole time to Heage, and shall be very ready to recommend your application to the

Additional Curates' Society as one well worthy of their attention. In the present state of my health, being obliged to send to the Bishop of Hereford to come here and take my ordination for me on the 12th of January, and indeed not having left the house since the beginning of November, it is quite impossible that I can be present myself; but whatever assistance my recommendation can give you certainly shall have. Still I would advise you not to be very sanguine. I was regular in my attendance on the meetings of the Society as long as my health permitted, and the cases were then so numerous, and in many instances so remarkably urgent, that it seemed essential to defer the claims of less populous parishes, however urgent they might appear, till those of denser population were examined and attended to. How far Heage, with its two thousand inhabitants, may come within the scope of the Society's grants, I cannot say. At the last meeting I attended it seemed to be the general opinion that we had not then funds sufficient to relieve populations under three thousand. With regard to your next question about a railway missionary, the intention I am sure is good (possibly the effect might be good also); but it seems to me an institution not recognised in any way by the Church of England, and such as I should be very sorry to enter upon as an individual Bishop *meo periculo*. There is indeed this difference between the case of Mr. Barber and yourself and a more general one—that you merely speak for yourselves through your own parishes, and give your consent to the measure, but other clergymen may think differently, and hold themselves aggrieved by any such interference within the limits of their own engagements. Can you show me any regulation in the Canons or Articles of the Church of England authorising any such appointment? It seems to me directly adverse to the spirit and constitution of our Church, and would soon, I believe, introduce the itinerant conventicle system, of which I do not believe you would approve any more than Mr. Barber or myself. I am sure I have no right to accept such an appointment as a title, and if I had I would never ordain or even license an Irishman thereto. A great many of these labourers are Irish, and the greatest portion of them Irish Roman Catholics, and the formation of such an institution would only lead to inevitable collision between the Catholic and Protestant part of the workmen, which would hardly fail to end in riot and bloodshed. Add to this, that if two thousand workmen are employed upon the railroad through the parish of Duffield they cannot be many months before they complete it, when they will be out of your jurisdiction. If you and Mr. Barber choose to give a weekly lecture in your churches to such of the workmen as may please to attend, I have no objection, but I think for things to be done well they must be done ' according to order.' I remain, dear Sir, yours faithfully,

" S. LICHFIELD."

CHAPTER THIRTY-SIX: CORRESPONDENCE, 22ND JANUARY 1839– 8TH JUNE 1839

To a Clergyman

Eccleshall Castle, January 22nd, 1839.

" DEAR SIR, I HAVE RECEIVED A LETTER from a Mr. G—, who says he has been nominated by you to the curacy of Stoke-upon-Trent when it becomes vacant on the 14th of next March, and he wishes to know whether I shall object to him, as being an Irishman. I suppose you mean him to supply the place of Sir William Dunbar, who I thought was not to leave till midsummer. That, however, is of little consequence. Mr. G— states that he has been a pupil of Dr. Durney, and has till lately principally lived in England, and has been educated at an English University.

" These matters are all in favour of his admission, which I never could have consented to without them; but I must own, my dear Sir, in so very important an appointment as that of principal curate at a place like Stoke, I should have been glad if you and I had had a little previous correspondence, so as to ascertain Mr. G—'s qualifications without exposing him to the risk of a painful refusal on my part, should they on inquiry turn out insufficient. I need not remind you, I am sure, how much activity and zeal are requisite in one who undertakes the arduous office of principal curate in so very populous a place. I am glad to see that Mr. G— writes much like a gentleman; but much more is required, and a strict inquiry must be made into his general habits from reference to persons of known respectability. I hope you have been careful to do this already; but I must have my own references also, and it will be desirable to be informed whether Mr. G— has already had much experience in a populous parish. In a word, though I am also writing to him, I should be obliged to you for such information as you may have yourself collected on this head.

" I remain, dear Sir, your obedient, faithful servant,

" S. LICHFIELD."

Correspondence

To the Rector of a Populous Mining Parish

Eccleshall Castle, January 25th, 1839.

"REV. SIR, I should wish to know before entering into the subject of a new curate for — what salary you intend to offer, and whether you intend to retain the services of Mr. Boyle. It is quite certain that the duties of that immense parish cannot be performed efficiently by one man; and though I believe Mr. Boyle to be a very laborious and diligent minister, it is impossible that he can go through the whole of the duties there without either suffering himself or neglecting something. I have been requested by several parties for various reasons to issue commissions of inquiry into the revenues of the church, but have not yet decided what proceedings to adopt; except either to have a resident incumbent and one curate at least resident, or two resident curates under the Residence Act—assigning in any case the largest stipend that the Residence Act allows. This in my opinion is but just to the curate or curates of so important a benefice. I remain, Rev. Sir, your very faithful servant,

"S. LICHFIELD."

To — (?)

Eccleshall Castle, January 27th, 1839.

"DEAR SIR, Neither Mr. Mott nor your son, and perhaps I may add not even yourself, appear to me to understand the point upon which I ground my dissatisfaction with him. Admitting, on your assurance and his own, that he forgot on Thursday, Friday, and Saturday mornings to bring up the letters of yourself and Mr. Malcolm, he first said to me that he forgot it even from Saturday to Sunday night; but on my urging that it was impossible he could forget after Saturday morning, when I told him I should expect him to reside, he admitted then that that circumstance did bring the matter to his mind; and on my then asking him why he did not immediately bring up the letters, or send them up under cover to me with a note to say he was sorry he had forgotten them so long, he replied he did not think it signified. Now I put it to yourself, my dear sir, as a gentleman to say whether that was a fit answer for a young man to make to his Bishop, in any case to tell his Diocesan that it did not signify whether he delivered to him letters which he well knew he had or not; and putting the point of civility and attention out of the question, I submit it to you further, whether he knowing he had letters for me in his possession, and being in my house that day at dinner, I am not justified in saying that it appears very disingenuous not to have delivered them to me till at the moment of his final departure he took them out of his pocket and gave them to my servant to give me. If we acquit him of disrespect, if we acquit him of disingenuousness, what are we to say of him in point of common sense? Can we look upon him as qualified to take the charge of a parish?—unless at least he is first tutored into it, if I may say so, and led by a more experienced hand till he is able to walk alone. My opinion on the subject was not, I assure you, rashly formed or acted on. I consulted the Bishop of Hereford and his Archdeacon and my own examining chaplain, who were staying in the house. They all entirely concurred in my view of the case and of the necessity of noticing it as I did, and I am still of opinion, whatever may be his actual exemption from disingenuous design, that the appearance of it is unfavourable to him, and would justify any man in drawing the conclusions which I did. I have not yet heard from Mr. Malcolm or from Mr. Ricketts, to whom as incumbent I felt it my duty to write in the first instance. If Mr. Malcolm declines the curacy, should Mr. Ricketts offer it him, or if Mr. Ricketts does not wish to offer it him, and still adheres to his nomination of your son on condition of his residing in the parish, as the petitioners have required, should proper lodgings be obtained for him, or if that cannot be, on condition of their providing a house for him, he residing in the interval with you, and going over to his sitting-room at Killamarsh frequently in the week, and performing the duty there to the satisfaction of the inhabitants, I will order his licence made out, though I must confess not without reluctance at present. I own I think the plan which I proposed of his learning his duties under you would be more to his advantage.

"I remain, dear Sir, yours faithfully,

"S. LICHFIELD."

Correspondence

To the Churchwardens of St. Werburgh's, Derby

Eccleshall Castle, January 28th, 1839.

"GENTLEMEN, I cannot but lament to have received your inquiry, though it is one which I am bound by duty as well as by inclination to answer to the best of my power. You are temporary officers appointed for a year only, and your selection may be counteracted next year by your successors. The disturbance of the Bishop's award, which was itself attended with so much difficulty and ill-will, cannot fail to excite again the same evil spirit, and I should extremely deprecate your doing so, even if I were satisfied (which I am not) that the case would be in your favour if it came before a legal tribunal. What is done in London, and I think in some other populous cities, would be a much safer proceeding, and one which you may legally adopt, as I believe. It is this: to order the pews to be reserved for their owners till the service has been begun five minutes, or till the clergyman has advanced as far as the Psalms, and then to permit them to be opened to any respectable individuals who are unseated. I am aware that your case is somewhat different from that of London, inasmuch as you probably speak of allotting seats to unprovided parishioners. This only makes your case the stronger. There may possibly also be a question as to your having a right to put persons into any seats except those in the body of the church, but it is really one of those legal intricacies which I cannot answer. I think the Bishop's award was printed. I have no doubt it was drawn up with care and upon the best advice that could be obtained, and I am sure the best advice I can give for the maintenance of harmony in the parish is to abide by it. I remain, gentlemen, your faithful humble servant,
"S. LICHFIELD."

From the Ven. Archdeacon Hodson

Rectory, Newcastle (probably January, 1839).

"MY DEAR LORD, After a lengthy discussion, in which Mr. Blunt of Lilleshall, Mr. Aitkins of Hanley, and ten other clergymen, including Mr. Leigh, took part, it has been resolved to submit to your Lordship the following outline of a plan for relieving the spiritual destitution of the Potteries.

"1. That measures be taken for erecting in the first instance five additional churches within the limits of the Potteries.

"2. That each church contain from 600 to 1,000 sittings, according to the wants present and prospective of the district for which it shall be provided.

"3. That, with the requisite consents, a district, with cure of souls, be attached to each church.

"4. That an endowment of £1,000, together with a parsonage house, be provided for each in addition to the repairs' fund required by the 1st and 2nd Wm. IV.

"5. That the patronage of each church so built and endowed be, with the Bishop's consent, vested as follows:

"(1) In any single individual (being a member of the Church of England) who shall be willing to contribute the sums required for endowment, parsonage house, and repairs' fund, as prescribed in Art. 4.

"(2) In all other cases either in the Bishop singly, or conjointly in trustees elected according to the Act, as shall be decided in each case by the majority of the subscribers.

"6. That the above scheme, if approved by the Lord Bishop, be submitted to the patrons and incumbents of the respective parishes within which it is proposed to build, for their concurrence.

"It would take me too long (and it is now midnight) to tell your Lordship the reasons which led to the adoption of the preceding resolutions—some of them, as your Lordship will perceive, varying from the proposition which I laid before you this morning. It was thought undesirable to insist on £2,000 as the minimum, when the Act allows £1,000, and many objected to mixing the Bishop's name up with other trustees. As to the former, I hope that £1,000 with a house will appear to your Lordship nearly, if not quite, equivalent to £2,000. On the latter, the feeling was that it would be placing the Bishop in an awkward position, if he should be called upon as a Bishop to license a clergyman to whom as trustee he had objected.

"Will your Lordship kindly communicate your views on the

preceding propositions, either to Mr. Leigh or myself, as may be most agreeable to you? If equally agreeable, the former will be more direct."

To a Clergyman

Eccleshall Castle, February 17th, 1839.

"REV. SIR, The accounts which I have uniformly received of you having been on all occasions satisfactory, I am induced to believe that you have conquered a habit injurious to your health, your character, and your means of support, and may be safely allowed to resume that occupation which becomes your very superior education and connections. Believe me it was with regret that I was obliged to suspend for a time your engagements in the ministry of the Church, and it is therefore with no common pleasure, under a conviction of your future steadiness, that I allow you to resume them. Wishing for your welfare, and that you may have strength given you from above to resist temptation for the future, I remain, Rev. Sir, your faithful humble servant,
"S. LICHFIELD."

To T. Wise, Esq., Ashborne

Eccleshall Castle, February 18th, 1839.

"SIR, I considered the questions contained in your letter of the 9th inst. so important that I determined to go through the examination of the exercises sent to me as well as my own eyes would permit me, and not to trust to the reading of another.

"I beg now to say that, having done this very carefully, although there is an improvement for the better, which in two or three instances rather surprises me, in Mr. Gibbs's corrections, I most certainly do not think that the exercises as corrected, or omitted to be corrected, by Mr. Gibbs show that he is competent to discharge the duties of under-master so far as relates to teaching the Latin grammar, mentioned in the seventh rule of the statutes sent with your letter—and I am further of opinion that a book of exercises, such as that which you have sent me, or some similar one, is absolutely essential for the exemplification of the Latin grammar and for properly teaching it.

"The two most important exercises sent me by far are those of Greaves and Chambers—Greaves' being remarkable for the number of right corrections made by the master, and Chambers' for the number omitted to have been made; but with regard to Greaves' I must remark that his whole number of faults are fifteen, of which the master has corrected fourteen, but then six of these depend upon the same word, which the boy has made masculine and the master neuter.

"In another case four of the faults depend upon one word, which the boy has made masculine and the master has rightly corrected neuter. This, in fact, therefore reduces the apparent number of faults and corrections very considerably; but the fault which the master has overlooked is of a very gross kind, and far out-balances all the corrections in the two cases above alluded to.

"With regard to Chambers' exercise, it contains, strictly speaking, eighteen faults (but we may perhaps reduce them to seventeen), of which only six are rightly corrected by the master. Of the remainder two are wrongly corrected and nine are overlooked. There is one case also more in which the boy's Latin is corrected, though it is more elegant than the master's. Greaves' exercise, I should say, is so easy that it is almost impossible to miss correcting it rightly. Chambers' requires some knowledge of Latin to correct it, and is a fair test of a man's acquirements. With my best respects to the trustees, I remain, Sir, your obedient and humble servant,

"S. LICHFIELD."

To the Rev. J. B—

Eccleshall Castle, February 23rd, 1839.

"DEAR SIR, Your Rector has been here consulting me upon two proposals. One is that he would give to one of his curates £100 certain and the fees arising from the search of the registers. Another, that he would give the other curate £100 per annum certain and the fees of the surrogateship. He states that the register fees, I think, will amount to about £70 per annum, and the surrogate fees to between £20 and £30. Or he proposes for the second curate giving you £70 per annum, and leaving you to provide him according to your own judgement. Then, as I understand, this is to comprehend the second duty or lectureship which the parish paid for. If the parish wish a third duty, he will leave it to them to subscribe for that as they did for the lectureship.

"Will you be so good as to write to me without loss of time, and to inform me how far these proposals are agreeable to you? It seems to me that if you could obtain the nomination of the second curate with the £70 towards the stipend, it would be more desirable than any arrangement that could be made. Believe me, dear Sir, yours faithfully,
"S. LICHFIELD."

To the Rev. J. B—

Eccleshall Castle, February 25th, 1839.

"DEAR SIR, It was not my intention to write to you as actually negotiating between yourself and your Rector, but as wishing to learn from yourself which of the proposals made by him to me was likely to be most agreeable to you. You have chosen as I thought you would, and as I am persuaded you will find most for your comfort. I now give you this advice. Let your agreement be put down in plain, clear terms in black and white, stating the sources from which your own income, and also the £70 allowed you towards a curate, are to arise. There should be nothing vague nor questionable between you and the incumbent. Let it be put down on paper, and a copy possessed by each of you, and signed by each. This is what I propose *ad minuendas controversias*, and this will settle the point about the surrogate fees, to which the Rector appears to have strong attachment. I remain, dear Sir, your faithful humble servant,
"S. LICHFIELD."

From a Clergyman

February 23rd, 1839.

"MY LORD, I take the liberty of writing to your Lordship to inform you that I received the enclosed tract by post, and as it was written by one of your clergy I beg to call your Lord ship's attention to it. Had there been no name to the tract, I should have thought it had been written by a Dissenter, and not by one bearing the name of a minister of the Establishment.

"I beg to call your Lordship's attention particularly as to what is said of the Prayer-Book: 'I know its defects but too well; they have been the plague of my life.'

"I beg to apologise for intruding upon the time of your Lordship, but the nature of the tract appeared to me so monstrous I felt it my duty to send it you."

Answer to the Foregoing

Eccleshall Castle, February 26th, 1839.

"REV. SIR, Mr. Price having addressed his letter to the Bishop of Exeter, I shall leave it to his Lordship to take what notice of it he thinks fit. You will therefore, I trust, excuse my taking any steps respecting it before I hear from his Lordship. I remain, Rev. Sir, your faithful humble servant,

"S. LICHFIELD."

I cannot find that any correspondence passed between the Bishops of Exeter and Lichfield with regard to Mr. Price's tract.

To G. Durant, Esq., Tong Castle

Eccleshall Castle, February 25th, 1839.

"SIR, Most certainly I have not the power of giving you permission to pay the income for Tong Church due to Dr. Muckleston to any poor clergyman who will undertake the duty there without his consent or my licence. Nor will my licence be granted to any one who does not bring me testimonials to his religious and moral character properly signed. I do not see therefore any further step that I can take till Dr. Muckleston appoints a curate, or till three months shall have elapsed without appointing one, when I may do it myself, unless I think that there is a good reason for granting delay on account of an approaching ordination, when I may admit a candidate whom he may recommend and whom I on examination may find worthy. Allow me to assure you that it is much more difficult to obtain a curate, especially on a short notice, in which state Mr. Robinson has left Dr. Muckleston, than you appear to apprehend; but your appeal to the Archbishop, who I am quite sure will feel most anxious to do justice to all parties, will probably be the means of satisfying you that I have not overstated the difficulties of the case. I have the honour to be, Sir, your very obedient humble servant,

"S. LICHFIELD."

To the Rector of a Populous Mining Parish

Eccleshall Castle, February 27th, 1839.

"DEAR SIR, I never understood that you were called upon to pay more than £200 a year to your curates between them, and I am quite sure that I never told you you were. I considered it a very inadequate payment for the very heavy duty they had to perform, and I considered your proposed voluntary addition as no very extraordinary sacrifice, or in fact as anything but what might be expected from any liberally disposed clergyman who leaves the whole onus of the duty of an enormous parish on his curates, and receives the larger share of the income to himself. I am therefore not a little surprised that in so short an interval as has elapsed between Saturday and this morning you have changed your mind, and make a very different offer from that you made to me.

"Your offer to me was then specific—either to give each of your curates £100 in money, and to give Mr. B— £70 a year more out of the register fees and the other curate £20 a year more out of the surrogate fees (perhaps I may have stated this wrongly in so far as I may have interchanged the sources from which this addition to the £100 to each was to come), or to give Mr. B— £100 in money and £70 in fees from one or other of these sources, and to allow him £70 a year more to find a second curate who might be agreeable to himself.

*

"The arrangement that appears to me most desirable is that which you proposed of giving Mr. B— £170 a year, and £70 to provide a curate to his own satisfaction—or of giving the two curates the sums you named on Saturday last, and leaving the parishioners to add a third as a lecturer by their own subscription if they think fit. But it certainly appears to me that if you pay, as I think I understand you now do, £200 a year to Mr. B— alone, and instead thereof offer to pay him no more than £120 a year and the second curate £80 — they giving an evening lecture — it is only being liberal to the parish at the expense of Mr. B—, and not your own. I remain, Rev. Sir, your faithful humble servant,

"S. LICHFIELD."

To the Ecclesiastical Commissioners

End of February, 1839.

" MY LORDS AND GENTLEMEN, Before your final adoption of measures relative to the Cathedral Church of Lichfield, I humbly beg leave to represent its present case to you, and that of the preferment in the gift of the Bishop. With regard to the latter, it is not extensive nor valuable in proportion to the number of clergy whose meritorious services give them a claim to episcopal encouragement. It consists of — livings, two of which only are above £500 and under £600 a year, the remainder for the most part under £250 and not averaging £200. The only preferment of value was the six residentiaryships, now proposed to be reduced to four, though I humbly and anxiously hope to be raised to five; the sixth, which is much the most valuable of all the stalls, is so connected with Birmingham that I do not venture to ask for it, unless you should see cause to spare £400 a year out of its large revenue, amounting, as I have been told, in the whole to little short of £3,000, for the maintenance of the sixth canon, if you should ultimately resolve on retaining the original number. There are in the diocese at present — churches and chapels, and many more are preparing, so that the numbers of the clergy are necessarily great, while the means that the Bishop has of providing for the most deserving of them are becoming less and less.

" There are sinecure prebendal stalls, the occupiers of which ultimately become the patrons of certain livings attached to them, almost all very small in value; and it would, I think, be an essential benefit to the clergy if these sinecure stalls, of which the Bishop had the disposal, were to continue in his patronage, but annexed to the churches in such manner that the stall and church falling together the Bishop who bestows the one should at the same time confer the other. Thus the livings, which at present are not necessarily held with the stalls, would always go with them, and the income would materially be improved, and that objection would be completely obviated which has been often urged of bestowing the income which arises from certain preferment away from the place of its local interest.

" I will not urge the present great inconvenience which the Cathedral of Lichfield will suffer by reducing its residentiaries to four. They are at present five in number, but of those five two from ill-health, that is to say Dr. Gardner and Mr. Ryder, are perfectly unable to attend to keep residence."

(No more of draft found. The blanks were no doubt filled up by Dr. Butler after he had ascertained what the figures should be. – ED.)

From James Fraser, Esq., afterwards Bishop of Manchester

Lincoln College, Oxon, March 8th, 1839.

" MY LORD, With the warmest feelings of gratitude and satisfaction, I am enabled to communicate an event which has realised my fondest hopes, and has made me feel doubly thankful to those friends who were the means of my enjoying the inestimable advantages of your advice and instruction. I was last night informed by Dr. Jenkins, the pro-Vice-Chancellor, that the examiners appointed for the Dean Ireland Scholarship had declared their election to have fallen upon myself, and that consequently I was one of the happiest of mortals.

" We had rather a hard examination for five days, and there were seventeen competitors for the honour. The papers set were as follows: No. 1. English to be translated into Latin Prose. No. 2. Greek into English, a passage from the oration of Lysias against Andocides. No. 3. An English Essay, on the convivial entertainments of the Greeks and Romans historically and philosophically considered. No. 4. To be translated into Greek Prose, a passage from Jeremy Taylor, chap. i, sec. 3. No. 5. A piece from *Cymbeline*, to be rendered into a Greek idyll in the style of Theocritus. No. 6. Greek passages and critical questions. No. 7. To write a scene after the manner and in the metre of Terence, the *dramatis personae* being: (1) an old gentleman of Attica in pursuit of his son, who has gone without leave to Athens; (2) a slave, the counsellor and companion of the son's flight. Scene: Athens. No. 8. Latin passages and critical questions. No. 9. Four different pieces of English poetry to be rendered into Latin Elegiacs. And 10thly, a passage from Quinctilian, I believe, to be translated into English.

"I must confess the result was totally unexpected by me, as I have been suffering for the last four months from rather severe inflammation of the eyes, which has materially impeded my reading, but I am rejoiced to say that I have at last deserved that my name should have a place among the many honours inscribed on the Shrewsbury Boards. I sincerely trust that this may find your Lordship and Mrs. Butler in good health, and that you may long live to fill the station you now so deservedly adorn will be ever the heartfelt wish of your Lordship's ever most grateful and obliged pupil,   "JAMES FRASER."

To a Clergyman

Eccleshall Castle, March 10th, 1839.

"REV. SIR, I am sorry to return your testimonial not countersigned, because I do not think that the living of X— is vacant. With regard to the opinion you have sent me, the opinion of the first lawyer in England is of no value unless one sees the case that is laid before him. This I have not done; therefore it is no disrespect to your legal adviser that I do not yield to it. There are circumstances in the case which are very important and very delicate; and if it has been moved by you in the first instance, I cannot but think you had better have rested in quiet. With regard to the strong language which you use by the advice of a common friend, as you say, about urging me, you will, I hope, always find me ready to do my duty without urging, and never willing to overstep it for all the urging that may be applied. I remain, Rev. Sir, your very faithful humble servant,

"S. LICHFIELD."

From the Bishop of Durham (Dr. Maltby)

(Private.)

Curzon Street, March 15th, 1839 (?).

"MY DEAR BISHOP, Your answer [1] is excellent, and I wish some of our brethren who have been appointed under the present Government had half your caution and sagacity.

"I was let into the secret of the proposed address the night I came to town, and perceived immediately that, however it might be disguised, it was only part and parcel of that antipathy to all changes which has been the main cause of our present confusion. However, I had an answer at once ready, that I had been in communication with the Home Office upon those points in the Report upon which I differed from the Commissioners in regard to the Chapter and University of Durham; that my representations were received with the utmost respect and attention; and that I could not join what had the appearance of a secret cabal while I was engaged in open and straightforward negotiations.

"I have never disguised my disapprobation of the Procrustes system of reducing all Chapters great or small to a Dean and four Canons. It has always appeared to me both pedantic and democratic—and there is nothing, I believe, in the whole scheme that has excited so much disgust as this. I have intimated this very strongly to Lord John, and through him to the Commissioners, and strongly advised that, instead of clauses 1 and 2 of the Report, they should adopt the following:

"1. Cathedral Churches of Canterbury, Durham, and Winchester, with Christchurch, Westminster, and Windsor, shall consist of a Dean and six Canons.

---

[1] The "answer" is probably the letter to the Ecclesiastical Commissioners on p. 394, but Bishop Maltby has not dated his letter fully, nor has Dr. Butler dated the one he wrote to the Commissioners.—ED.

" 2. Ely and Worcester of a Dean and five Canons; the rest in England of a Dean and four.

" This would be a concession to the popular opinions, and remove the pedantry of uniformity of numbers, yet would not greatly impair the efficiency of the scheme.

" It might appease the wrath of malcontents. It would, I think, satisfy reasonable men, and prevent that serious opposition which in our House more especially threatens destruction to the Bill, if the Commissioners remain unyielding in all respects.

" These are the views I wish to impress on my parliamentary friends; and if some reasonable care be taken that what is drawn from any one diocese should be applied to the benefit of that diocese, I anticipate no evil, but rather good, from the measure.

*

" I do not think that Sir Henry intended to write gloomily about your case. He may have written doubtingly, because he does not appear to know exactly what is your present condition. But he seems anxious to have you in town, that he may judge about you with his own eyes.

" I am not sorry to have been absent from the House during these debates on the Corn Laws. My notion is that an alteration would neither be so injurious to the agriculturist nor so beneficial to the manufacturer as is hastily contended, and some modifications might very safely be admitted. It must, however, be a very perplexing question to Government, because while it is treated as an open question in the House of Commons, Ministers send out their summonses as if it were a Ministerial one with us. I have told Lord Melbourne very frankly my own imperfect views upon the subject. I am always, my dear Bishop, yours most truly,
"E. DUNELM."

From the Ven. Archdeacon Bather

Meole, March 28th, 1839.

" MY DEAR BISHOP, What I wanted was some such sanction of our proceedings as you sent to Lichfield, which might be read at the meeting either by the chairman or myself, as you saw good.

" Expressing, as you have done, regret at your absence, and also your general approbation of the diocesan plan for religious education; your conviction that the establishment of 'Commercial' or 'Middle Schools' in the several districts is desirable (which might be done by getting up new schools or helping old ones under proper regulations); your concurrence particularly in the necessity of District Boards or Associations, such as the Diocesan Board has recommended; and your wish to bring the whole diocese to act together.

" Of course I only mean these for hints. I think there is no need to enter much into detail, which might subject us to be asked more questions than we could answer. One Normal School for training masters will, I think, be enough, at least at present—namely, the one at Lichfield. But it is said there is a feeling in favour of Church of England Middle Schools on the part of many tradesmen and farmers, who are now almost obliged to send their sons to academies conducted by Dissenters.

" What you say of course will be pretty much my text. I shall take much the same general ground as I did at Lichfield, only I must be more statistical.

" There is a cry for education or knowledge. It must be based on religion. Religious instruction can only be given under some specific form. Existing plans want both extension and amendment. The Church has means, if properly called out, and ought to act as a body. The higher orders are provided for, the lower also in some measure. The middle have been overlooked. They do not want Charity Schools, would not accept them, but means of getting what they are ready to pay for—an education suitable to their wants and agreeable to their principles.

" In order to improve the condition of the country with reference to education, we want to train masters, provide these Middle Schools of which the middle ranks may avail themselves at their discretion—to bring existing Charity Schools into union and under a well-digested system of inspection, which would do good under any circumstances, and is become absolutely necessary now, when projectors complain so much of the want of it, and allege that as a reason for establishing Boards and Inspectors after their own fashion.

"The Cathedral strength being properly directed and set to work, Archdeacons, Rural Deans, and Clergy all acting in their several places, the Church might carry out the intentions of the compilers of our Liturgy, etc., etc., and ought to do so.

"There need be no interference with Dissenters, who might educate their own in their own way, and have good right to do so, and what we believe, and believe to be necessary, we ought to impart.

"I shall try to work out something of this sort, and to put it as plainly as I can without offensiveness.

"I send you Lord Liverpool's letter, who seems anxious to take pains. You might address your letter to him, having understood that he takes the chair, if you thought proper. You will see that I have advertised. I shall also issue circulars, and will send you a copy, and use my private influence, such as it is. We must make a demonstration, and not have a failure if we can help it."

*

To a Clergyman
Eccleshall Castle, March 30th, 1839.

"REV. SIR, Mr. C— has been with me in consequence of the reprimand I gave him for altering the Lessons at his pleasure, for absenting himself from his parish without your concurrence, and for refusing to give cottage lectures, according to his agreement with you. He has shown me your letter asking his occasional aid now and then (and nothing more) in a cottage lecture, to which he says he did attend, when able, out of his proper parish of W—, where he constantly gave a second service, which had not before been given. He says that you told him, if he would help you constantly in the cottage lectures, it would enable him to get an allowance from the Pastoral Aid Society, upon which he might be able to have his salary increased by you, and he told you he would have his salary increased by no society whatever.

"But, sir, my surprise is that you have nothing to do with him as your curate; you are your father's curate, and so is he; and there are no deputy curates that I ever heard of over whom there is any other control than that of the incumbent or principal. Another circumstance which surprises me is that I find that you, who accuse Mr. C— of violating his duty, wrongfully I admit, by altering the Lessons on particular occasions, are yourself guilty of a much more serious offence, by neglecting a solemn prayer of the Liturgy which yet you have sworn to conform to, and have never prayed for the Parliament, because, as I have it stated to me, not from Mr. C—, but from very credible authority, you think them such a wicked unchristian set that they ought not to be prayed for. Now, sir, I should say that the more wicked and unchristian we are, the more we need the prayers of good men; but not to go into that matter, I hereby enjoin you to read the prayer for the Parliament at such times as it is appointed by the Rubrick. I shall inquire if you do, and if you do not you must thank yourself for the consequences.

"I find from Mr. C— that he has given you notice to quit on some day in July, at the expiration, however, of half a year from some day in January. He is under no obligation to quit at an earlier period, for your notice for the 28th of April is quite nugatory; I shall therefore let him take his choice in that matter. I expect both you and him to observe a placable and Christian spirit towards each other for the time during which you act together, which at all events cannot be long, and am, Rev. Sir, your very humble servant,

"S. LICHFIELD."

To the same Clergyman

Eccleshall Castle, April 11th, 1839.

"REV. SIR, Your ill-judged and in some points disrespectful letter requires no further answer than an assurance that I shall not 'set any spy over you,' nor yet be deterred from inquiring into your compliance with my injunctions to read the Prayer for the High Court of Parliament, both at morning and evening

service during their session. I remain, Rev. Sir, your very humble servant,
"S. LICHFIELD."

To — Mott, Esq. (?)
Eccleshall Castle, April 5th, 1839.

"MY DEAR SIR, I am truly sorry to hear that the two misguided men, Shirley and Brown, to whom I was willing to show so much indulgence on your intercession, have again refused to submit to the terms you proposed. However, I am not surprised, for I am aware that they are made the tools of persons more crafty and designing than themselves; and though I am really sorry for them, yet they must thank themselves for their own obstinacy, and when they find themselves the victims of ill advisers will repent, though too late.

"I have at present a somewhat indistinct though not unimportant clue to their advisers, and some prospect of the motives of self-interest which have excited them to make these men their dupes. When I am in London I shall follow it up diligently, and perhaps it may lead to unexpected consequences.

"My determination is taken. The two men have had their choice, and they have refused the offers made them by you, perhaps having been told that you made them without my authority, which is not true. I can act but one way, and I wish you to tell them so. Tell them I am not a man easily alarmed, nor yet inclined to encroach on the rights of others. Tell them also I am bound by my oath not to diminish or suffer the rights of income of this See to be invaded or diminished. Unless therefore they agree to submit to the terms you have proposed to them within twelve hours from the time of your communicating this notice to them, and sign the paper to that purport, tell them that they will be too late, and the case must go on; but if either of them, considering the risk he runs, and the disgrace of being made a dupe of by a more designing person than himself (that person not being an attorney), should be induced to give his name up to me, and to bear witness against him in court or elsewhere whenever called upon, he shall upon conviction of the party receive £10 reward. I remain, dear Sir, truly yours,

"S. LICHFIELD.

"In order to avoid mistakes in the minds of the two men, I hereby declare that whatever you undertake (provided it is set down in writing to avoid mistakes) I will abide by."

From a Clergyman
April 8th, 1839.

*

"As Mr. Bernard had expended during his short incumbency twice the gross receipts of the living upon the glebe house, it was unreasonable for his successor to expect dilapidations. But I have found it necessary to increase the accommodation of the house, and to rebuild some parts of the offices. I have added a nursery over the new kitchen, a new bedroom at the top of the house, and a new porch. The particulars of my improvements are stated in the accompanying paper, and the aggregate expense of what is permanent and additional has been £231 9s. 10d., whilst the painting and papering these additions, together with casual and current repairs, gates, fences, etc., have cost a further sum of £133 12s. 11d. It is in respect of the former of these sums only that I solicited assistance from the Bounty Board.

"The inadequacy of an income of £99 10s. in a poor parish of six hundred inhabitants has often occasioned me considerable embarrassment; for however the parishioners, themselves heavily burdened, have kindly assisted me, the deficiency of my subscriptions and collections, to meet the expenses of schools, clothing clubs, friendly societies and lending libraries, of Bibles and books for emigrants, of the celebration of the Coronation, and of the numerous nameless expenses of a parish, has in nine years amounted to a considerable sum. And I also felt it my duty, when the parish at my suggestion undertook any heavy repairs or improvements on the church, to meet their liberality by a corresponding effort on some other important though less indispensable improvement on the sacred edifice. I have altogether expended parochially £196 11s. 10d., and I believe few clergymen could have done much otherwise, nor do I regret the outlay, although the want of private property has frequently made it inconvenient, and this year extremely so."

*

From the Ven. Archdeacon Bather

Meole Brace, April 17th, 1839.

"MY DEAR BISHOP, You will see an account of our meeting in Eddowes'. It went off very well, and I think we made an impression on all ranks, but especially where it seems most desirable—namely, on the tradesmen and farmers. I am more and more impressed the more I consider it with the necessity and policy of attempting to do something in order to connect the education of those classes with the Church. And if we behave ourselves discreetly I think it may be done, at least in Shrewsbury, and that now is the time to make the attempt. I have a letter from Lord Clive very hearty upon the subject. I had written him an exposition of our plans. He speaks strongly in favour, and says he will do what I did not ask—read my letter himself to Lord Powis. Dugard tells me the scheme of a Commercial School in Shrewsbury used to be a favourite one with the old Peer. Lord Liverpool was exceedingly kind, and says he will do anything in his power to aid the working out of our scheme. I was zealously supported by Smythe Owen, to whom I wrote and from whom I expected nothing. The squirearchy were all very friendly. At Shrewsbury there is an opening for a good Commercial School—Parkes and Case, who had it between them, being both gone, and a great complaint that the article is not to be got. The farmers generally are not very well disposed to subscribe to the parish Charity Schools; mine all do it for me, but most of them would rather do anything else. I fully believe it to be that they are jealous of the poor getting a better education than they can procure for their own children. I have seen in those who are a fair representation of the body a surprising zeal and alacrity about this plan of ours, and think, to use the expression of Mr. Eddowes respecting our meeting, that we are hitting the right nail on the head. I shall try to work the matter out. I must endeavour to make my Rural Deans available and helpful to me wherever I can. When we have settled with Lichfield about the proportion they are to have, and statistics have been got, something may be done, possibly after the manner of Bridgnorth, where they have got under weigh on a self-supporting principle. I believe I made an impression in Shrewsbury by two sermons at St. Julian's to parents. However, I will not wear you further on this topic. Only if there is anything I should do, or anything that I should beware of, that occurs to you, you can say it in a few words.

" I am truly thankful to have heard of your safe arrival in town, and I hope you may be quietly mending. I can say with truth also, that you have long had my daily prayers that God would grant you, if He sees good, a longer continuance among us, and that, to use our Church's expressions which are so natural, you may spend the residue of your life in His faith and fear and to His glory. I believe the aspiration to be that of very many with whom you are officially connected, and that you may calculate upon the affectionate support of a large body of those you have to do with, if their wishes for your restoration are realised.

" You know I do not say these things till they run over in spite of me."

From John Burder, Esq., to — (?)

27, Parliament Street, May 4th, 1839.

" MY DEAR SIR, The Bishop referred your letter, with those from Mr. Kitchen and others, to me. I have taken advice upon the subject, and have consulted several persons who were able and willing to afford me every assistance in their power, and it appears that all the clergyman can do is to require the churchwardens to be present, and to keep the peace by their means, and, if those means fail, to libel the parties in the Ecclesiastical Court.

" If the parties brawl, then I apprehend the churchwardens, by the aid of the constable, may remove the offenders. But I advise the clergyman to avail himself of the churchwardens' assistance, and direct them to be the persons to prevent any obstruction or interference with him in the discharge of his duty, and not by any act of his own give the disturbers the least advantage over him. This appears to me to be all that can be done or said by me in the matter."

To the Ven. Archdeacon Hodson

May 5th (?), 1839.

"MY DEAR ARCHDEACON, I hoped from my experience of Burder's accuracy to have been able to send you more satisfactory advice.

"You see that in fact there is nothing that can be called remedy to be applied. I am sure Burder has taken much pains, and it is something to know that there is no proper remedy. Still I think the proper course would be for the Protestant clergyman to bury the body, though deserted by the Catholics, and on no account to suffer their minister to officiate over the body in the Protestant churchyard. Truly yours,

" S. LICHFIELD."

To Thomas Wise, Esq., Ashborne

2, Portland Place, May 21st, 1839.

" DEAR SIR, Among the things chiefly to attend to with regard to the rules for Ashborne School, I consider one—the keeping as close to the charter as may be most expedient—to be nearly the most important, especially not encroaching by new enactments on the privileges of the head-master. You have now got a competent and able master, a thing difficult to find, and I would recommend you to endeavour to keep him by the best means in your power.

" Your rules divide themselves into two parts, one of which relates to the governors and assistants, and the other to the school at large. We will therefore consider them, if you please, apart from each other. With regard to the fifth rule, respecting the governors, as to keeping a secret book, it seems to me that the visitor of the school ought to have the same liberty of access to it as the governors and assistants, otherwise it may be difficult for him to administer justice when called upon in intricate cases. With regard to the eighth rule, which first enacts that two-thirds of the receipts of the estates shall be paid to the head-master, and one-third to the second master, subject nevertheless to certain deductions for repairs, for expenses attending the trust, and for the rent of a playground for the scholars, I see no objection; but the close of this rule, which makes the income subject to such further regulations as may be thought necessary by the said governors and assistants, appears to me to call loudly for an addition to this effect—*with the consent of the Bishop of Lichfield.*

"With regard to the rules concerning the school, there seems a vagueness in the expression *of improper treatment of the boys under his charge.*

"To be sure this is qualified by the subsequent provision made for investigation of the case.

"I think after the words 'fourteen days after the then preceding meeting,' the following clause should be added—*and provided also that such order shall be confirmed and approved by the visitor under his hand and seal.* In the rule for admission of free scholars, it is certainly proper to add—*that no such certificate of admission be valid unless the boy recommended shall be able to read fluently the History of England and to repeat the Catechism set forth in the Book of Common Prayer.*

"With regard to the school hours, I should think it might be sufficient to make the afternoon school from September to October 31st from two to four, and from October 31st to Christmas from two to half-past three; afterwards from Christmas to Lady Day from two to four,—all distant free scholars to come at eight all the year.

"A much more important and delicate question for consideration is that respecting expulsion, in which the rights and privileges of the free scholar and the master are concerned. Cases certainly may occur where the scholar should have a right of appeal, but it is very tender ground, and a master should be very cautious how he inflicts absolute expulsion.

"I think in cases of gross insubordination, or absolute

rebellion, or remarkable immorality, such as a repeated instance of theft or drunkenness, the trustees ought never to interfere. Anything like counteraction between them and the master cannot fail to be injurious to the school. I should also say that, unless the schoolrooms are perfectly detached from the master's houses, the day scholars ought not to have access to them out of school hours, because the master's comfort will be much interfered with thereby. These are the principal topics to which I would beg leave to call your consideration, except that I should think the teaching Mathematics might very well fall to the share of the second master, and be limited to the six first books of Euclid and Quadratic Equations. I remain, dear Sir, your obedient and faithful servant, " S. LICHFIELD."

From the Ven. Archdeacon Hodson

Cheadle, Wednesday morning, May 29th, 1839.

" MY DEAR LORD, I cannot proceed onwards a stage further from Stafford without thanking your Lordship, which I do most cordially and affectionately, for the testimony of your Lordship's esteem and kindly feeling towards me, so unexpectedly brought forward yesterday by my kind friend Mr. Moore. The whole occasion indeed, as your Lordship will readily imagine, was peculiarly gratifying to me; and if anything had been wanting in the matter of the present so handsomely procured for me to make me sensible how much I am indebted to the kindness of my Church brethren, the manner in which it was presented by Mr. Moore would abundantly have compensated for the deficiency.

" But your Lordship's concurrence in this tribute of fraternal regard, and the addition of your kind expression of feeling on the occasion, were quite overpowering to me, and I can only say that I ought to be much humbled in my own estimation for receiving from your Lordship and others so much more kindness than I deserve.

" I was glad to learn from Mr. Moore that you were somewhat better.

"With every dutiful and grateful sentiment, I remain, my dear Lord, your truly obliged and faithful

"G. HODSON."

To the Rev. T. S. Evans

May, 1839.

"DEAR EVANS, I first heard of your Greek verses on the Birth of Mathematics from the Bishop of Durham, who agrees with me that they are decidedly the very best Greek verses either of us has ever read, and I take it that the Bishop is one of the very best judges on such a subject that Europe can produce. The good people at Burton may well be content with this splendid specimen of your attainments as a scholar, but if they wish more I can bear most ample testimony to your proficiency in classical literature, as well as to your moral and religious character. With all good wishes for your prosperity, I remain, dear Evans, truly yours,

"S. LICHFIELD."

From the Rev. T. S. Evans

May 30th, 1839.

*

"My conscience bids me observe that the Greek poem you so highly extolled derives its excellence in great measure from your Lordship, who first imbued me with a love for classical literature. I shall assuredly never forget the impressions of my early days; for, to speak what I think in common with others, so beautifully solemn was your Lordship's manner of unfolding the properties of the ancient writers that those who heard could not choose but learn; nor is it strange if in me, among many of your pupils, was kindled a flame which I hope will never be extinguished."

*

From the Rev. B. H. Kennedy

Shrewsbury, June 8th, 1839.

"MY DEAR LORD, Cope left us for College in October 1837.
"As long as the constitution of the school remains unaltered,

myself and all the masters who succeed to your system will, I hope, refer to your Lordship as its founder, and therein as the true author of all its successful results. We shall all, I trust, be a Butlerian dynasty as long as we last under the present Act of Parliament.

"I have therefore made no distinction of the Boards, nor should I propose to make any between our pupils. Dates, were it needed, would be sufficiently explanatory.

"The prospect for our common pupils and for the school is, at Cambridge, very good. I should even say there is every probability of our heading the Classical Tripos for the four next years—France, Cope, Munro, and Gifford (a boy whom I shall send up this year with strong confidence of his success).

"It grieves us to learn that you still suffer so much.

"I will take care to send all your books, which I have collected, to Eccleshall, with many thanks for the valuable loan of them.

"With our united regards to Mrs. Butler and Mrs. Lloyd, and thanking the latter for her kind note, I remain ever, my dear Lord, your most faithful and affectionate

"BENJ. H. KENNEDY."

Dr. Kennedy's forecast was hardly as brilliant as the actual success of the Shrewsbury men proved to be. France headed the Classical Tripos in 1840, Cope in 1841. Munro was indeed only second in the Tripos, but was Senior Chancellor's Medallist in 1842. Gifford was bracketed head of the Tripos in 1843 in conjunction with another of Dr. Kennedy's pupils, the late G. Druce, whose distinguished career at the Bar was cut short by a fatal fall from his horse some five-and-twenty or thirty years ago.

CHAPTER THIRTY-SEVEN: CORRESPONDENCE, 12TH JUNE 1839—19TH NOVEMBER 1839

From the Rev. T. W. Peile

Durham, June 12th, 1839.

*

"I DESIRED MR. MURRAY TO SEND YOU A PRE-sentation copy of my *Agamemnon*, and though I cannot expect your Lordship to have much leisure to bestow upon it, I should be delighted to know that you thought well of it and could encourage me to proceed. Proceeding, indeed, I am, though necessarily at a slow pace. I have worked my way —and uphill work it is—through nearly a hundred lines of the *Chöephorae*; but I regret to find that, whereas I thought I had brought away all, I have in fact little more than one-third of your Lordship's notes upon it. Some opportunity will, I hope, present itself during the summer of returning with my best thanks the valuable assistance you have given me on the *Agamemnon*, and securing a continuance of the same for my present work. If better may not be I must even trouble you with my presence on this behalf."

*

From the Hon. R. Curzon (Author of " Monasteries of the Levant ")

Parham, Petworth, Sussex, July 14th, 1839.

"MY DEAR LORD, I was grievously troubled a few days ago with a report, that, if it had been true, would have prevented my having the pleasure of seeing you again, but as I find to-day that there was no foundation for it, I cannot resist boring you with an epistle, to tell you how sincerely glad I am to hear you are in as good health as usual, and that you are likely to continue so for many a day yet; so I hope I shall see you again shortly, as I shall be passing through town early in next month, on my way to Bala, where I am going to shoot at the grouse.

"I received a box of manuscripts a few days ago from Abyssinia, and a grimmer set of tomes you never saw: two of them contain the apocryphal Book of Enoch, and one is illuminated in such a manner as to give very unfavourable notions

of the outward appearance of the saints of those regions. Though I fear their doctrines would hardly have so much effect, yet their smell is so strong that it brings the tears into one's eyes—in short they are painfully curious altogether; I wish you could see them. I am thinking of putting one in a bag, and hunting him by the scent, with a pack of hounds: what a glorious day's sport it would be for the Roxborough [*sic*] Club! I must beg pardon for sending you so much nonsense, but as I only send you this letter as a sort of vicarious shake by the hand, I hope you will excuse it from yours very sincerely,
"R. CURZON."

From the Bishop of Durham (Dr. Maltby)
Whitburns, August 11th, 1839 (?).
*

" Yesterday as I was walking very smart by the seaside with new hat by — [name illegible—ED.] which did not fit very tight, an unlucky elf of the air blew this redoubtable hat towards the sea. I flew eager to recover it and was twice knocked down by the surge, to the infinite affright of Mrs. Maltby, who also got very wet in the vain endeavour to rescue me. However, as I was no chicken though nearly a septuagenarian, I walked briskly home, covered as to the head with a white handkerchief and blue something which Mrs. Maltby's anxiety led her to put on my head instead of the drowned hat; and in order to convince the world that I was not only not drowned, but had not even lost my voice, I have been preaching to-day for the church-building society—with some effect, *quoad* a country congregation.

"I do not think you are right about the inscription. I punctuate thus:

Somnio praemonitus miles hanc ponere jussit
Aram. Quae Fabio nupta est, nymphis venerandis.

I suppose Fabius to have been the name of this soldier, who in a dream, perhaps in a fit of illness, wished to erect the altar. His wife, or widow, accomplished his intentions. I need not remind you how constantly the verb implying erecting, dedicating, etc., etc., is omitted in such cases.

"Adieu. We shall rejoice to hear a more favourable account of you by a line addressed to me towards the end of the week, at A. Urquhart's, Esq., St. Colme Street, Edinburgh."

From Sir Henry Halford

Wiston Hall, Leicester (August 1st, or thereabouts, 1839).

"MY DEAR KIND LORD,

*

"Pray let me hear again soon. I am living an uncertain life, being under a constant expectation of a summons to the Duchess of Gloucester, who is ill, and next week are our races, when I am to entertain for three days the Duke of Rutland and his family, and the American Webster and his.

"I wish your Lordship would permit me to ask you whether the enclosed inscription be correct. I can find nothing in your kind present of Morcellus's book to assist me. I should tell your Lordship that when Dr. Baillie was dying, he sent for me into Gloucestershire, where, on my return, after his death, I stopped at Lord Bathurst's. Sir Thos. Lawrence had just arrived to put up a magnificent picture of the Duke of Wellington on horseback; and having, in answer to my inquiries, been assured by Sir Thomas that the clothes, housings, double stirrup leathers, etc., etc., were all portraits, I insisted upon it that this should be recorded at the back of the picture. Lord Bathurst has called upon me to write an inscription in Latin, and I propose the enclosed.[1] Will it do? Pray excuse me, and believe me, my dear kind Lord, always your much attached friend and faithful servant."

*

From a Clergyman

Plymouth, August 6th, 1839.

"MY LORD, I arrived at this place a few days since to find my mother a corpse after four hours' illness, and my father from mental and bodily weakness incapable of managing his own

[1] I did not find the inscription here referred to. —ED.

affairs. His intellect has been for some time on the wane, and this recent loss has tended still further to impair it. His late incompetence to take care of pecuniary matters has led to most disastrous results; designing persons have made a prey of him and involved him in pecuniary difficulties to a serious amount. It was impossible that his family could witness these embarrassments without straining every nerve for the removal of them. My brother (a Fellow and Tutor of Worcester College, Oxford) has given up nearly the whole of his little property in order to effect his father's liberation, and upon myself and my sister will devolve the arrangement of his other debts. I trust that none of us have any other feeling than that of gratitude to God that it is yet in our power at whatever sacrifice to extricate him. Among my father's unsettled accounts is one of £115 for dilapidations at —. Now as the resignation of this living is likely to be very advantageous to Mr. —, who has, I understand, presented his son for it, I cannot but think that my father has been hardly dealt with in the exaction of so large a sum, and the claim, if insisted on, must indeed be liquidated, but the payment of it will ultimately fall upon my brother and myself, whose incomes for the ensuing year are already mortgaged in our parent's favour. If your Lordship can in anywise mediate in this untoward business, it will confer a deep debt of gratitude upon two sons who have already made extreme personal sacrifices that their surviving parent may pass his few remaining days in comfort and respectability.

"If your Lordship would have the kindness to address your answer to me at Lichfield (my father is, I am sorry to say, incapable of the slightest mental exertion), I shall esteem it a favour.

"I propose returning to my Cathedral duties in a few days."

Dr. Butler immediately wrote to R. A. Slaney, Esq., M.P., in a letter of which I found no draft, and received the following answer. All the parties to the transaction, so honourable to those concerned in it, have long since passed away. I venture therefore, though not without great hesitation, to make it public.

Correspondence

From R. A. Slaney, Esq., M.P.

(Confidential.)

Walford Manor, August 16th, 1839.

"MY LORD, Your letter dated the 10th only reached me the day before yesterday on my excursion through North Wales. I hasten to reply to it. With Mr. — I am slightly acquainted. I have never, however, met either of his sons or any other part of his family, but this by no means prevents my feeling sympathy with the gentleman who has written to you, and who appears, with his brother, to be acting in a most disinterested and kind manner towards their surviving parent. With regard to an application to the patron of the living, I should fear it would be fruitless, though the case certainly appears a hard one, especially as it will bear entirely on those who have never been in fault—if fault there was at all. I am very happy, under these circumstances, to be able to give my humble assistance to extricate Mr. — and his brother from their difficulty, but I think it will take away every unpleasant feeling of obligation if they remain ignorant from whom the aid comes; and should they at a future time rise (as I hope they may) into easy circumstances, they can repay me by giving a lift to some one else whom they may judge worthy of a little help, and who is struggling honourably against adverse circumstances.

"I have therefore enclosed to you a cheque for £200, which perhaps you will be good enough to get cashed at your banker's and transmit the amount to Mr. — as a trifling aid from a friend to two dutiful sons.

*

"I return the letter as you desire. It does the writer great honour. I shall be glad at a future day to become known to him and his brother."

From a Clergyman

August (?), 1839.

"MY LORD, When the first notice of my father's embarrassment reached his family, we saw it would be impossible to meet them unless ample time were conceded us. The means that we could jointly muster were scarce sufficient to liquidate such debts as were most pressing, and there yet remained behindhand a considerable balance against him at the Lichfield Bank. Under these circumstances it was of paramount importance to us that we should not be pressed, and the letter which I addressed to your Lordship from Torquay was for the purpose of engaging your mediation on our behalf to this effect.

" The Lichfield Bank, with their customary liberality, have consented to accept as security for their debt a policy of insurance on my father's life, and I am happy to say that money has been procured sufficient to liquidate every outstanding claim upon him, and among them the dilapidations at —. Before, however, the account is settled a close inquiry will be instituted into every circumstance connected with the business, nor will your Lordship's valuable hints be thrown away.

" Although some temporary pressure may be felt, yet surely the assistance rendered to a parent will not be permitted to bear very heavily upon us, and with a full appreciation of that generous offer that is made us we would prefer to meet our present difficulties without aid.

" But not the less are we indebted to that friend who seeks no praise from men. I trust that in my name, and that of every member of the family he would have assisted, our best acknowledgements may wait upon him. His name indeed must still remain a mystery, but never will the recollection of his kindness be effaced.

" We beg your Lordship to accept our grateful thanks. The sympathy that we have met with in our trials has tended much to rob them of their bitterness, and by God's blessing we shall now, I trust, win through them."

From Sir Henry Halford

(Original in possession of Mrs. G. L. Bridges and Miss Butler)

Curzon Street, August 17th, 1839.

" MY DEAR KIND LORD BISHOP, I found your Lordship's letter on my arrival in town this afternoon, and can hardly express the sorrow I feel in reading of your late attack. I believe the digitalis to be quite capable of producing that debility of the nervous system that might give rise to the suffering which your Lordship describes. Its effects will continue a few days after the remedy has been left off, and I am pleased to hear that Dr. Dugard has had recourse to the Huxham's tincture of bark and elixir of vitriol. Pray take courage—all will be well still. Your Lordship has never expressed impatience, never has given advantage to your disease, and the native powers of your constitution have manifested themselves by an unusual energy.

"Pray let me hear again in a few days. I return to Wiston to dinner on Wednesday next, the 21st, and perhaps my amiable friend Mrs. Lloyd will let me hear, if your Lordship find it too fatiguing to write, on Thursday morning. Heaven bless and preserve you, my dear kind Lord Bishop, and do continue to believe me your faithful and affectionate friend,

"HENRY HALFORD."

From the Bishop of Durham (Dr. Maltby)

Auckland Castle, September 15th, 1839 (?).

"MY DEAR BISHOP, It seems the nymphs of Severn or Trent must have been as angry as those who persecuted Aristaeus, being not content with submerging me in the seas, but driving me so violently against a form in the boys' school at Morpeth as to occasion me a month's confinement. I must say the place was very appropriate as the scene of punishment for an affront offered to *you*.

"However, I trust they have relented, as the quiet of home has healed the wound, though the leg is still weak, I suppose from the almost total disuse.

"Next week I am to leave home for a few days, in which I am to combine duty at Barnard Castle and its neighbourhood with the view of some fine and bold scenery on the Tees, if the weather will favour the attempt. My headquarters will be the house of a benevolent and enlightened Catholic, whom, I believe, I have already mentioned to you—Mr. Witham of Lartington. What do you think the Bishop of Exeter or Sir

Robert Inglis would say, if they heard of such a domicile for a Protestant Bishop on a tour of duty?

"I have to consecrate a burial-ground and preach in the morning, partake of a luncheon to which the inhabitants of Barnard Castle have invited me at half-past one, then at half-past two return to church for a Confirmation.

"I admire the zeal of your Wolverhampton folks, and hope they do not annoy you about the patronage of their new churches. I have a high Calvinistic, ultra Evangelical set of gentlemen at Newcastle that will lay down money to build and endow a church, if I will let them build against the wishes of the clergy and have their own way as to the patronage. I ask them what objection to leaving the patronage to the Bishop or some ecclesiastical authority? If they say they distrust him, has he not much more reason not to confide in them? I have continual battles to fight with clergy and non-clergy, but I take care not to lose my temper, and rather laugh at than quarrel with them.

"I am glad to hear of any improvement in your state, though I would rather have it more likely to be permanent, and, as you say, radical—the only application of the word which I can endure."

*

From the Ven. Archdeacon Hodson to Dr. Butler's Daughter

Colwich, Saturday, October 12th (1839).

"DEAR MRS. LLOYD, Can you at a favourable moment ask the Bishop whether he thinks *the clergy* ought to apply for any part of the £30,000 voted for education? The regulations under which it is to be appropriated appear in the last page of to-day's *Staffordshire Advertiser*. Is there anything in those regulations, does the Bishop think, inconsistent with Church principles, and with the spirit of our own Diocesan Institution of which he is President?

"The question has been asked me by more than one of the clergy, and will probably be so again. I do not quite like in a matter of this kind to act on my own judgement, but I will do so if you think it better not to trouble the Bishop."

Correspondence

To the Ven. Archdeacon Hodson

About October 13th, 1839.

"MY DEAR ARCHDEACON, Your question is so far a puzzling one that I cannot understand why the clergy should take such great alarm.

"It is expressly stipulated that the inspectors are to have nothing to do with the religious part of the instruction, and I do not see why it is unreasonable that, while one-half the sum voted for educational purposes is appropriated to the Established Church, the remaining half should be divided among all the various classes of Dissenters, who are equally British subjects with ourselves, and whom it must be a benefit to ourselves to see brought up as moral and intelligent beings.

"Still I know that many of the clergy have strong fears and strong apprehensions on this subject, and it seems to me that the only advice I can properly give is that each man shall judge for himself on the propriety of the application. I have not heard a word from London. Believe me, my dear Archdeacon, truly yours,

"S. LICHFIELD."

To — (?)

Eccleshall Castle, October 14th, 1839.

"SIR, I have received your letter of the 12th inst., and am grieved and shocked at its contents. It is very natural that the parishioners of such a parish as yours should look to the Bishop to correct any misconduct in its minister, but I am sorry to say that we have no power for compelling witnesses to give their testimony.

"A salutary, and I am sure a necessary, power was proposed to be vested in the Bishops by a Bill brought into the House in the last session; but the Commons, jealous of what they supposed was entrusting power to Bishops, who, as they were pleased to think, are always ready to abuse it, threw out the Bill, and we are helpless; and after having spent three or four hundred pounds (scarcely ever less) on endeavouring to bring a disreputable clergyman to a better sense of his duty, the

Bishop is baffled and the offender escapes. This was very near happening to me only last year, and it has twice happened to me that the very men who have brought their complaints before me have refused to substantiate them in the court.

"If three parishioners attend they make a congregation, and I can enforce Mr. ——'s attendance to read prayers to them. I might also order a sermon; but in such a case, or one approaching to it, this would be called an unusual stretch of power, which I should not like to exercise.

"I regret to say that I am still too ill to be able to walk across a room without support, so that it is impossible for me to see Mr. —— in person, but I will write to the Archdeacon of Stafford about him, who I daresay will soon have some further communication with you. I hear there was a report that Mr. —— was about to leave Alton for some distant place. Do you know anything of this or think it likely? Can you give me any evidences of drunkenness which you can swear to in a court, and which any person who has seen them with you will come forward as a witness to confirm? I remain, Sir, your faithful humble servant,
"S. LICHFIELD."

To the Rev. T. Butler

(Original in possession of Mrs. G. L. Bridges and Miss Butler)

October 22nd, 1839.

"MY DEAR TOM, There is nothing in the world that could give me greater pleasure than seeing all your children, and I will take care that their journey shall be no expense to you. Much as I had longed for this, I thought it presumptuous to ask it while so many months remained before your probable arrivals; but now the time begins to approach, and though in a precarious state I may not unreasonably hope to see yourself and Fanny, I do hope also to see the children with you. I vary a good deal, but am suffering principally from severe attacks of asthma, and I do not know whether these are secondary symptoms of a worse disease or simple attacks of that complaint. If the latter, though very painful and distressing, they are much less dangerous than the former are. I presume you will hardly come to us before the duties of Christmas Day are over, but come as early as you can."

From the Ven. Archdeacon Hodson to Dr. Butler's Daughter

Colwich Vicarage, Friday, October 25th, 1839.

"DEAR MRS. LLOYD, At a preliminary meeting held this morning in Stafford to consider the propriety of forming a County Protestant Association, I was asked whether the Bishop would sanction and patronise such an institution? I replied that I thought in the present state of his health any application of that kind would be unreasonable. Ought I to have given any different answer? I wish to do that which is most respectful and delicate to the Bishop's feelings, and therefore, if you think it would be more agreeable to him not to be applied to for his patronage than to withhold it, the matter can rest where it now does, on the ground of health. I am too covetous, however, of his concurrence and sanction to forego them for want of asking, and still less do I like even the appearance of concealing anything from my Bishop. May I therefore ask you kindly to act for me in this matter as you judge best, and either to read this note to him or burn it, as you think most proper?

"I have hitherto stood quite aloof from every public anti-Catholic movement, from a doubt as to the utility and a dislike to many of the proceedings of certain Protestant societies which have been formed of late years. When, however, Roman Catholic associations are circulating Popish tracts *from house to house*, as is the case at Stafford at this moment, and partially in my own parish also—and when, as at Tixell [?], Roman Catholic priests are claiming *a right* to our churchyards—it seems time that Protestants should combine in self-defence.

"Many are waiting with much anxiety to know what will be done, or whether anything can be done, to punish the insolence of Mr. Green; and there is a strong impression that if this recent attempt to throw down the barriers of our Church pass unnoticed, it will be regarded as the signal for other similar encroachments from other classes of Dissenters as well as Romanists.

"You will excuse my troubling you with a communication of this nature, but I am applied and appealed to from many quarters, and I am unwilling to take too much or too little on myself in a state of things so full of public interest, not to say danger, as the present."

*

To the Ven. Archdeacon Hodson

Eccleshall Castle, October 27th, 1839.

"MY DEAR ARCHDEACON, I greatly appreciate the kindness and delicacy which led you to write to Mrs. Lloyd respecting the projected Protestant Association. Liable as I may be to misconception on the part of some of our brethren, I feel confident that you will acquit me of any want of proper feeling towards the Church of England from any attachment to the Church of Rome. I firmly believe the Church of England to be built on one of the soundest and purest systems of faith that ever Church relied on, and the Church of Rome to be full of errors and corrupted with false doctrines, to which I grieve to see its members in very many instances pertinaciously adhere.

"On my first receiving the account of Green's conduct, I lost not a moment in acting thereon, and by the very same day's post I sent it up to London, and desired Burder to lay it before the Archbishop and inquire if his Grace had any directions to give. I have written to Burder several times since on that subject, but have only heard from him once, saying I should hear soon, but that is now a week or ten days ago, so that in fact it would not be proper for me to act on the present occasion. But in the present state of my health I should be quite unequal to doing so, and I only wish the clergy in general to judge for themselves, hoping that whatever measures they may adopt will be taken with care and consideration, for the preservation of Christian charity. With regard to transgressions of the law by forbidden intrusions, penalties are provided which, if the laws have any force, will soon put a stop to the threatened abuse. Will you say this, respectfully and delicately, and especially stating my firm attachment to the Church of England?

They will, I doubt not, choose an abler and more efficient president than I should make. I remain, dear Archdeacon, very truly yours,
"S. LICHFIELD."

From the Bishop of Durham (Dr. Maltby)

Auckland Castle, November 6th, 1839.

" MY DEAR BISHOP, Your letter is truly gratifying to me, for certainly there cannot be a better judge of what is orthodoxy and what propriety of conduct in a Bishop.

" A very curious fact has come to light in the controversy this has excited in the provincial papers, but you shall have it in the very words of the article, and accordingly it is enclosed.[1]

" If I had not witnessed it and been exposed to all the buffetings of it, I could not have believed that such a very trivial circumstance could have been so commented upon, and that men otherwise sensible and well disposed should have swallowed instead of rejecting with disgust the sophistry and malignity of the *Times*.

" I was not aware that Hardy was an Unitarian. I have used the book all my life, having had a copy interleaved when I was reading for orders, and have been in the habit of using it more or less all my life. I cannot say that I have studied the notes very deeply, for I looked to other sources of information; but I saw enough to know that it was a sort of a compilation from Poole's *Synopsis*; but I never recollect to have seen anything of a Unitarian tendency, which shows at least how innocent a book such a man may write or edit, even so nearly connected with religion. I believe I have seen Harwood's Greek Testament, and think I had a copy once, but of its contents I know nothing.

" Singular it is that in our early days there was no edition of the Greek Testament – none at all accessible to general readers – but Hardy's. Since that we have had Rosenmüller, *cum plurimis aliis e Germania*, Elsley's and Slade's annotations, Valpy and Bloomfield's editions – all the helps, in short, to make us understand the book better – yet how little is it better

---

[1] I did not find the article here referred to, and have been unable to discover its subject. – ED.

and how much less practised, for I protest we are gone back in liberality more than a century. We must go back to the times of Clarke, Whiston and the good old convocation to find a parallel, if parallel can be found, to what has been passing lately.

"My secretary is just come over from Durham on business, and I must only add that three brace of grouse were despatched to you *via* Liverpool two days ago, and I hope they arrived in good order.

"What does Archdeacon Bather say to this unchristian hubbub?"

From Mr. Commissioner Reynolds

Neath, November 13th, 1839.

"MY DEAR LORD BISHOP, I have been thinking of you many a time and oft since I have been upon my travels, and yesterday I lighted upon a Staffordshire paper at Carmarthen, in which I saw mention of your name, and in such a guise that I was resolved to write a bit of nonsense to you, thinking it might cheer your kind heart to see that my wounded heart can admit such fooleries; but the paper, the *Globe*, I have just seen forbids this jesting. I read the death of the brother of your beloved son-in-law. I remember him well, and his wife; and have I not heard he had a large family? I am sure this event will afflict you; and who that knows you will not think of you the more when sorrow comes upon you? So this makes me write to beg you will let me hear of you, how you are and all belonging to you. I have been away now nearly three weeks, and, thank God, my poor wife and I are much better and calmer; yet, alas! often do we feel the loss of her who was, aye, and most deservedly, the gem and pride of our lives. But no more of ourselves.

"Do, pray do, send me an account of yourself and Mrs. Butler and your dear daughters. Oh what a blessed thing it is to talk of such as living! And tell me too how the Archdeacon is.

"I am moving through the region of Chartism, and hope to escape so as to be at Gloucester on the 20th; there I shall look for tidings from you.

"How are our dear friends at Trentham? Should you see any of the womankind, give my love to them, and tell them I mean some day to write to them.

"God bless you, my dear and most kind friend, and preserve you to your family and your friends! My wife is part of myself in all this prayer, and in sincere regards to all around you, ever, ever yours most heartfully,
"H. R. REYNOLDS."

To the Rev. A. W. Cawston

("The Fortunate Youth." See vol. i, pp. 152-164)

Eccleshall Castle, November 19th, 1839.

"REV. SIR, It is so many years since I have had any intercourse or communication with you, that I must beg to be excused after such an interval from undertaking any recommendation.

"If you succeed, you will see the importance of attention and regularity, and I have not the least wish or intention to throw any difficulties in your way. I remain, Rev. Sir, your faithful humble servant,
"S. LICHFIELD."

CHAPTER THIRTY-EIGHT: DEATH, AND FUNERAL SERMONS

Dr. Butler's Death and Funeral, Epitaph, Sermons by Archdeacon Bather and the Rev. H. Moore, Sale of Antiquities, Library, and MSS., Letter from the Rev. R. W. Evans to Dr. Butler's Son

AND NOW MY TASK, IF WHAT HAS BEEN SO long a labour of love may be so called, draws very near to its end. Ill, with but occasional intervals of relief, as Dr. Butler had been during the whole of his episcopacy, no trace of it appears in his handwriting until about the last three months of his life. Till then it is always the same firm, scholarly, and most beautifully legible script, with an *n* for an *n* and a *u* for a *u*, no matter how rapidly he was writing. In July and the beginning of August he rallied more hopefully than perhaps at any time since he had left Shrewsbury, and his friends began to be almost sanguine about his recovery; but early in August he relapsed, and though even as late as the end of October his doctors still maintained that he might very possibly recover, he became weaker and more suffering continually. The body of the later letters in his letter-book is written by my aunt Mrs. Lloyd, the signature being alone his—sadly pathetic in its feebleness, but with the same uncompromising clearness to the very end.

On the 3rd December 1839, late in the evening, a sudden and marked change for the worse came over him, but he lingered, now free from pain, till one o'clock in the morning of the 4th. I have been told by an old servant then in the Castle that after midnight he said to the doctor who was attending on him, "Doctor; shall I rally, or shall I send for my son?" The answer was that it might be safer to send for my father. "Thank you," said Dr. Butler, "you are a sensible man." After which he became unconscious, and presently expired, still apparently sleeping. The messenger who was despatched at daybreak reached my father's house at Langar in the forenoon of 4th December, and I well remember his arrival. It was my fourth birthday, and a woman of the village who used to come and do sewing at the Rectory had brought me a little pot of honey and a string of birds' eggs as a birthday present. My father came into the nursery and told us that grandpapa was dead;

whereon the honey and the birds' eggs were for a time, to my sorrow, taken from me—doubtless to impress the event upon my memory.

I have been told by my father that Dr. Butler desired a *post-mortem* examination to be made, so that his doctors might possibly be guided in any similar case, but he asked that they should not examine his head, inasmuch as he was sure there was no brain mischief. It was ascertained that he had been suffering from *cardiascites*, which I understand is water on the heart.

The funeral took place on 12th December at St. Mary's, Shrewsbury. The vault and the stone to cover it had been prepared by Dr. Butler while still at the schools. My father, writing to my mother two days afterwards, said:

"Every house, shop, private house, or cottage in sight of the line of procession, *i.e.* up Wyle Cop, High Street, Pride Hill, to St. Mary's, was shut as if it was midnight, all the way from the Column, and I believe all over the town. Business was entirely suspended; and though the mass of the people were in contact as thick as the footways would admit—in fact almost the entire population—yet there was no noise, no crowding forward or pushing, and scarce any one beyond the kerbstone. All the bells in the town muffled, and St. Mary's as full as on a Sunday morning—probably more so. About sixty or seventy clergy, Mayor, Corporation, tradesmen, etc., all in mourning, and with hatbands, etc., at their own expense. Some few of the boys, who stayed on purpose. The paper will give you the names of the people there, but it is impossible to conceive anything like the real feeling that seemed to accompany it throughout high and low. Willis was very kind and nice about it, and came from Ludlow on purpose.

"Kennedy came to me next day at the Raven and took me home. He and Rowland and some six or seven more are resolved into a committee for a public monument in St. Mary's on a splendid scale. Everybody most kind everywhere."

*

No unworthy tribute to him who had taught the town's householders twice over. I cannot think that any such funeral has since been seen in Shrewsbury.

The stone which covers him in St. Mary's churchyard bears the following inscription:

> LOCUS-SEPULTURAE
> QUEM . SIBI . ET . SUIS . VIVUS . NUNCUPAVIT
> SAMUEL . BUTLER . S . T . P
> EPISCOPUS . LICHFIELDIENSIS

This was the inscription which Dr. Butler desired should be set over him, and set over him it accordingly was. But it is one thing to write and another to make sure that well-meaning friends shall not improve. After the words above given there is a thin line drawn, and beneath this, apparently forming part of the inscription, are the words:

> CONCESSA . FACULTATE . ADSIGNATUS . EST

This used to puzzle me when I was at school, and various were the explanations which reached me from others who were hardly less puzzled than myself. Some said it was a rendering (taken perhaps from the Vulgate) of one of the obscurer texts in the Old or New Testament. One boy, I remember, held forth learnedly about it as an admirable example alike of the terseness of the Latin language and of the obscurity which that terseness sometimes caused. " Adsignatus est," he exclaimed, " *i.e.* ' he was assigned,' that is to say ' appointed.' To what? Obviously to the See of Lichfield—the whole passage being only a gloss or explanation of the words *Episcopus Lichfieldiensis* which have immediately preceded. The meaning of *concessa facultate* is transparent. The line, therefore, amplified agreeably to the more redundant genius of the English language, informs us that Dr. Butler's great faculties or abilities having been now generally conceded, he was appointed by Lord Melbourne to the See of Lichfield and Coventry."

Never fully satisfied with the explanation, but too constitutionally indolent to worry further, I was haunted occasionally for some forty years by a latent curiosity as to the meaning of this line, till at last, hardly more than ten years since, it occurred to me to ask my father. "Oh," said he, "it was not my doing; — feared that questions might arise as to whether or no a faculty for the interment had been obtained from the Dean of Arches. He urged that this ought to be made clear on the face of the tomb itself, and I yielded." I doubt whether the added line will make this "clear" to the general reader.

Two sermons were preached on the occasion of Dr. Butler's death. The first at Eccleshall by the Rev. Henry Moore, then vicar; the second was preached at St. Mary's, Shrewsbury, by Archdeacon Bather. Both were preached on 15th December 1839.

Mr. Moore took for his text Job ii, part of verse 10: "What? shall we receive good at the hand of God, and shall we not receive evil? In all this did not Job sin with his lips."

After telling the story of Job the preacher continued:

"How vividly would all this bring before your minds, if you had known and watched him as I have done, that great and upright man whose loss, in common with so many sad hearts, I have this day to deplore. Like Job, he was one of the greatest of all the men of his times, displaying in his character gifts and graces and acquirements of rare excellence in themselves, and rarer still in their combination. He was a man of exceeding quickness, yet of most patient application; of vast compass of learning and knowledge, but the extent of his acquirements was quite equalled by his clearness and accuracy. Whatever he had to do he did with zeal and diligence; yet with such perfect ease, that he would pause in the midst of his work, speak of subjects on which others happened at the moment to be interested, and give the information which he saw they needed. He was too earnest in his purposes not to be sometimes moved by the folly, or ignorance, or wickedness, which alas! all men, especially men in high station, must encounter in their passage through the world; but his mind was soon calm again, and he would try by gentle persuasion to turn them from their wrongdoings — pity and endeavour to excuse their folly, and not unfrequently pass it by with a quiet smile. Malice he never bore; vengeance he never sought; but was at peace with all men, as he desired all men to be at peace with him. With the warmest benevolence, that led him to be doing deeds of the noblest generosity, and many of them in so secret a manner that ' his left hand knew not what his right hand did'; with a love of literature and research which displayed itself in an almost princely collection of choice books, beautiful works of art, and rarest antiquities, so that his house at its very threshold told tales of other times,—he yet joined so watchful a prudence that he has left no room even for the most captious to say that he gratified himself at the cost of his family. Against this indeed the integrity and uprightness of his mind was a sure safeguard. For upright he was in thought, word, and deed; and that simplicity of manner which charmed all who knew him was the offspring of the guileless simplicity of his mind, turning almost instinctively and always decidedly from whatever duty and conscience forbade. The root too of this integrity was constantly visible in his intense love of truth for truth's sake. From prejudice, heat, party spirit, and all that could darken and mislead his understanding, he seemed cautiously to free himself; admirable was the candour with which he weighed the arguments of men immeasurably his inferiors, and either showed them their mistakes or yielded to their reasoning.

"It would be to leave out what was the brightest part of his nature if I did not add that the affections of his heart were equal to the powers and accomplishments of his mind. He loved the meanest thing that breathes; of every animal, nay every insect, he had some tale to tell which spoke of the interest he took in them; and most truly can it be said he thought nothing that was human unworthy his regard; he would 'rejoice with those that rejoiced, and weep with those that wept.' In one word, the brother-man was to be seen in every act and deed of his daily life. In his family it is difficult to speak of him, for delicacy draws a veil over that hallowed place. Yet it ought to be said that there was nothing but gentleness and affection, with now and then bursts of feeling and kindness discovering the depth of love that was in his heart, and all cheered and enlivened by that pleasant wit which, as a halo, surrounded his mind, and constantly broke out like a bright sun sparkling upon the waters. Thus, like Job, though after a somewhat different sort and manner, he was a man of great possessions: rich in graces of heart and mind; rich in gifts of children and children's children; rich also in the fame acquired through the numerous distinctions of those whom he had trained up in soundest learning; rich at last in the highest dignity and emolument which his Church and country could bestow."

*

After referring to Dr. Butler's protracted sufferings, Mr. Moore continued:

"Steadily and calmly, as though he had been in the full bloom of health and vigour of manhood, he applied himself to the duties of his office. With a spirit that was well described as indomitable, he travelled over miles of country, and underwent bodily labour that might have tried even a strong man; with unwearying exactness and promptitude he carried on a various, and in many cases most anxious, correspondence on the important affairs of his diocese; he saw, from time to time, those of his clergy who desired to consult him on matters connected with their cures; and he did all so clearly, so wisely, and so kindly, that none had to complain of negligence or delay, and none ever took counsel of or saw him without being impressed with the strength of his understanding, the fairness of his mind, the correctness of his views, and the kindness of his nature. So that no Bishop ever left the world more sincerely regretted or who was more affectionately looked up to by his clergy as a friend and father.

*

"He 'humbled himself under the mighty hand of God,' and no word of complaint ever escaped from his lips; but he exhibited a noble example of the creature submitting himself to his Creator. It was visible to all that he looked not upon his sickness as a chance or accident, but received it as an ordinance of God to him for good; and he would not unfrequently praise God for it, and declare it had been the greatest blessing of his life. His mourning was not for his present suffering, but for the want of what he thought a sufficient measure of gratitude for lovingkindnesses of old. Once, before receiving the blessed Sacrament of our Lord's body and blood, he said, ' I do not feel as I would wish to feel; my whole life has been a life of mercies, and I am not ungrateful for them; but I do not feel that glow and flame of gratitude and love that I could desire.' And his almost dying words were, ' I can never recover again; but let Him do what seemeth Him best—only may I have grace to bear it."

*

The other sermon was preached at St. Mary's, Shrewsbury, 15th December 1839, by Dr. Butler's son-in-law, Archdeacon Bather, who took for his text 2 Peter iii, 18: " Grow in grace, and in the knowledge of our Lord and Saviour Jesus Christ."

*

" The basis of his character from the time he began to show himself was simplicity, integrity, love of truth, and plain-dealing. If he spoke precipitately, it was to say what he thought, and whatsoever he did it was without studying how in the doing of it he might appear to men. He never wore a stage dress. He did what he thought right in itself and expedient under the circumstances, and left men's construction of him to take its course. And he ever possessed that quality of a great mind, a clear apprehension of his own deficiencies. He had the humility which could seek and take advice, as well as the wisdom which made him capable of bestowing it; he was a learner as well as a teacher all his life, and willing and anxious to be so to his dying day.

" As to his intercourse with men, he had ' put on charity, which is the bond of perfectness.' He had that real liberality of judgement which gives honour where honour is due in every case. Though he had a peculiar hatred of ostentation, and would never willingly let his left hand know what his right hand did, it could not be hidden that to his power, and beyond it, he was ever ' ready to distribute and willing to communicate.' Neither was it of his substance and wealth alone. Full as he was of occupation, few men ever worked more than he for others beside and beyond his own proper calling. He never neglected that for anything; but his habits were so punctual, and his proceedings so well arranged, that he had always had at command that which idle people never possess—I mean leisure to bestow upon his friends.

*

"But we shall do well to recognize and mark, as far as we may, the secret of his great success. It arose, I believe, quite as much from his moral as from his intellectual qualifications. He had no doubt, together with his learning, that which does not always accompany it—a great talent for imparting what he knew to others, and making plain to them what he so exactly saw himself. But he would not have succeeded in exciting the desire of knowledge so generally, in blowing up the little spark into a blaze so often, in comforting the feeble-minded, and supporting the weak, and setting at ease the bashful and the timid, and making all exert themselves, and rendering study popular, and gaining the confidence and the affections of his pupils, had mere learning and mere skill in teaching been all that he brought with him to the work. He loved his pupils, took a real and lively interest in their welfare, proceeded with manly openness and candour in all his dealings with them, pretended to nothing himself which did not belong to him, took no unfair advantages, cherished no unfair suspicions respecting any of them, did equal justice among them inflexibly, and made them fully sensible that he did so. Hence they entirely trusted him and looked up to him; and his influence over them was answerable to his patience, industry, and zeal on their behalf.

"Doubtless all this did not come at once. If it was a work of time to make the school, it was a work of time also to make the master. No man comes thoroughly furnished in the outset to such a business as this. But as he wrestled manfully for many years against many outward difficulties, so he wrestled likewise, and by God's grace prevailed, against his own natural infirmities. He laboured to improve in the art of self-government, he profited by experience and by reflection on his own mistakes, till at length his profiting appeared unto all men and obstacles gave way before him.

*

"Standing where I do, I must add that no man within our memory has been so great a benefactor to this town as he was whilst he lived in it; and this not only accidentally and indirectly whilst pursuing another object; he was ever a zealous and munificent contributor to all useful undertakings, and ever ready to co-operate actively in doing good for the advantage of the place.

"Here his career might have ended; and if it had, I should at least have been justified in saying that he was worthy to be held in grateful remembrance by yourselves.

*

"But his career did not so close. He was elevated to the Episcopal Bench. Had he foreknown when he was called to it what his bodily state was about to be, he would not have accepted the dignity or incurred the responsibility of office. But happily —I use the word advisedly—he was in ignorance of this. Though not strong, it seemed at the time that he might have rallied and have held on usefully for many years. He took the office; and who may blame him?

"Now it is said commonly that honours and advancement are wont to change men's manners.

*

"And thus it was in his case. He had that in him, hidden as it were under a bushel, which was now set upon a candlestick, and has given light to all within the house. He occupied his new position with easy dignity, and rose to it, as it should seem at once, without an effort. He more than justified the high opinion of those who had most confidence in him; and if any stood in doubt, he happily disappointed them. He soon gained the respect of all fair and candid observers, and secured quickly the affections also of all whom courtesy and kind attention might suffice to win.

"Notwithstanding the early failure of his strength, and the very severe sufferings which he had to undergo, it was speedily evident that he was qualified by God's grace effectually to take the oversight where he was placed. He was humbled by the responsibility, not elated by the eminence of his station; and he showed–more clearly indeed than under other circumstances he could have done–of how much a great mind is capable, and what talent and industry can do, and high principle will do, in spite of obstacles.

"The business of the diocese, I will say first, has not suffered. His qualifications for the conduct of affairs were sterling. He did not mistake mere bustle and activity for real despatch, or look upon things as done when they were but entered upon. He was very quick, but he was at the same time ever self-possessed and quiet. He was never hurried; for he did not suffer himself to be over-excited, nor by undue exertion at one time unfit himself for the next coming duties. He went ever calmly on, never procrastinating, but doing a fair day's work every day. And as to what was to be done by correspondence, his letters were patterns of simplicity and clearness. He did not weigh syllables or look out for phrases; but, seizing the point at once, set forth his meaning in the plainest words–briefly, but without any affectation of pithiness, or offensive point, or shortness. He kept nobody waiting for a reply; and he was as kind and considerate as he was perspicuous. He trampled long upon difficulties with an unbroken spirit. He did not spare himself a moment whilst labour was possible. He not only contributed munificently to all schemes of piety and charity; he attended public meetings, and actively promoted public objects. And during his very protracted and very painful illness he has hardly ever excused himself so far from exertion as not to have dictated replies to all communications of importance, and taken oversight to a considerable extent of all urgent matters, though in some instances of episcopal duty he has been constrained to cast himself upon his brethren for assistance.

"I shall not bear testimony as to particulars where I have not had opportunities of observation. But I am sure he loved his clergy, and I should do the general body of them great injustice if I did not say that they loved him. He demeaned himself wisely towards them as well as faithfully. He was 'given,' as a Bishop ought to be, 'to hospitality.' He was at all times easy of access and ready to give advice and help in difficulties, and he was not punctilious in trifles or rigid in anything, though he firmly required whatsoever was important, and was not soon shaken in his decisions when he had once formed his judgement. Further than this, he paid due attention to everybody under him. He was a lover of good men, but he held those with whom he was concerned to be so simply in proportion to his knowledge of them that they honestly and industriously did their duty. He neither took up nor opposed any set or section, but he respected and cherished whatsoever right thing he saw in any, and by his mild and truly paternal deportment he endeared himself to all. So that, if he is lamented—as he so surely is—by his pupils and his personal friends, his clergy as a body will assuredly be fellow-sharers with them.

"I now come to another view of him. Home is the situation in which character is best tested, and everyday behaviour and the everyday charities of social life are the most important things of all. But at home he was seen particularly to advantage. Here especially his light shone brightly and steadily to the glory of God. His filial piety was remarkable. He was eminently a kind master to his domestics, and his demeanour towards his wife and children was such as it was not easy to behold without edifying. Here was that mutual confidence which is so delightful; that 'perfect love which casteth out fear' completely; that bearing of one another's burdens, and dwelling together in unity, which cannot be where the head of the family has not possessed himself of the affections of all beneath him. This kept him alive, I do believe, so long; he could not have borne the wear and tear of eight-and-thirty years of continual trial of his patience and his temper had he not had such a haven of peace to retire to from day to day, when his spirits were exhausted and his day's work done. But at the same time this was a privilege to be won. He must have earned it, or he had not possessed it.

*

" He had more than three years of illness and great suffering: what he did in spite of it I have shown you; how he bore the trial itself, resigned himself to God's sovereign pleasure in it, gave thanks for it, and gained spiritual advantage from it, is another thing. I shall not expose the privacy of a sick-chamber to inform you, or quote sayings uttered in simplicity, and meant only for the ears which heard them. But his patience, I will say, was as remarkable as his sufferings. His kind consideration for those who ministered to him was unvarying; and he still manifested the humility, and, I may add, the teachableness of a child. He gave himself day and night to the word of God and to prayer. He was thankful for the counsels of any who would converse with him, and for the prayers of any who would pray for him. And none could well fail to see that he 'worshipped God in the spirit,' and 'rejoiced' only 'in Christ Jesus,' and had quite ceased from all 'confidence in the flesh.' He was continually praising God for His goodness, and for the mercy which he testified had followed him all the days of his life, in despite of his own unworthiness; but, for his weeks, and months, and, at length, years of suffering—in these especially he saw and recognised the good hand of his God upon him, acknowledged his need of them, 'accepted' in them 'the punishment of his iniquity,' and declared ever with the holy Psalmist, 'It is good for me that I have been afflicted, that I might learn Thy statutes.'"

*

My old friend and tutor the late Rev. Richard Shilleto told me that Archdeacon Bather had himself been among those who had strongly disapproved of Dr. Butler's appointment, but ere long admitted that he had had small cause for apprehension. I have observed that archdeacons almost invariably suspect their new Bishop at first, and afterwards come to like him. The sermons from which I have taken the foregoing extracts must have been written independently, yet it is remarkable how closely they coincide in their estimate of the character they are portraying. Both carry with them an impression of genuineness; both, however, err in representing Dr. Butler's health as having broken down after and not before he became Bishop, and both exaggerate the continuousness of his sufferings. Terrible as they were—so much so that I destroyed the diary in which the narrative was briefly told by Dr. Butler himself—there were occasional periods of a week or two together during which he was fairly well, and many letters from friends congratulate him upon his improved health. The most hopeful of all these short breaks was, as I have already said, in July 1839 — but it was the last.

The same mistake, coupled with the same general estimate of Dr. Butler's character, was made in the *Gentleman's Magazine* for February 1840. The following extract must suffice:

"In Bishop Butler we have to lament the loss of a man of varied acquirements, playful wit, profound learning, unbending integrity, and profound religion; all accompanied by a benevolence of heart, candour of mind, and simplicity of manner that were the graces and adornments of his whole nature. . . . Placed when he had scarcely reached manhood at the head of Shrewsbury School, he raised it from the lowest grade of depression to the highest pitch of distinction, sending forth from her venerable walls an intellectual progeny who have filled both Universities with his and their fame. Laden with the honours flowing in upon him as the fruit of thirty-eight years' successful labour, he was raised in 1836 to the Episcopate. From that moment to the day of his death he knew no day of health, scarcely an hour free from suffering. Yet this has been the noblest part of his life; for his patient, uncomplaining submission to the hand of God has been an example to all around him, and his indefatigable attention, 'to his power and beyond his power,' to the great trust committed to him, combined with the mildness of his manner and the fatherliness of his conduct, has gained a hold on the respect and affection of his clergy which no common man, amid such seclusion as his has necessarily been, could possibly have acquired."

A committee was appointed, over which Lord Powis presided, for the purpose of erecting a life-sized statue of Dr. Butler in St. Mary's Church. Eight hundred pounds were subscribed, and the work was entrusted to Chantrey, whose failing health prevented him, I believe, from even beginning it. Eventually he surrendered the commission to E. H. Baily, who exhibited the clay model in the Royal Academy Exhibition of 1843. Photography was not invented till some months after Dr. Butler's death, and Mr. Baily, who had never seen Dr.

Butler, worked almost entirely from Cousins's engraving of Phillips's picture. My cousin Archdeacon Lloyd tells me that the model was a very graceful figure, widely different from that ultimately executed. The committee found fault both with the likeness and the arrangement of the lower part of the figure; the result was that the likeness and attitude were made worse, not better. It was erected in the Trinity Chapel of St. Mary's Church in the autumn of 1843, and stood there for many years, till it was found desirable to erect an altar on the site occupied by the statue, which was then moved to its present place under the tower of the church. I am afraid I must own that I consider it one of the least satisfactory pieces of sculpture that I know anywhere.

Of the various portraits painted of Dr. Butler I have always understood that Kirkby's, now in the head-master's house on Kingsland, is the best likeness; but Phillips's picture was so like my father that I should think there must have been a good deal of likeness to Dr. Butler.

Of the collections formed by Dr. Butler during his lifetime, the coins and various other Greek, Roman, and Etruscan antiquities were sold by Messrs. Christie & Manson 12th February 1840, and realized £885.

The first part of the library was sold by the same firm on Monday 23rd March (and five following days) 1840, and realized £1,352 5s.

The second part, consisting of the Aldine Collection, which I am told was the most complete that has ever been got together, was sold 1st June (and eight following days) 1840. It realized £2,614 9s. 6d. The late Mr. Panizzi was anxious that it should be bought *en bloc* for the British Museum, but the trustees would not sanction the purchase. Mr. Fortescue, of the British Museum, tells me that the rage for Aldines, now quite extinct, was already by 1840 in full decline. If I was asked what was the greatest mistake made by Dr. Butler during his whole life, I should not be able to find another so serious as the having allowed himself to collect Aldines. It is the only one that I could plausibly sustain—unless perhaps his having permitted himself to share in the translation of *Charlemagne*.

The third part, consisting of early books and MSS. (which last were largely bought by the British Museum), was sold by Messrs. Christie & Manson some time later in the same season, and realized £5,272 3s. The three collections, therefore, of antiquities, printed books, and MSS. realized over £10,000.

In the catalogue of the MSS. I see repeated allusion to Bishop Butler's Manuscript Catalogue. I have never seen this, and do not know what became of it. The priced catalogue, from which the foregoing figures are derived, is in the British Museum, the press mark being 011900. ee. 18(2). London, 1840, 8vo.

Of the letters from friends to my father upon Dr. Butler's death I will only give the following, from perhaps the best loved of all his pupils, the Rev. R. W. Evans:

From the Rev. (afterwards Archdeacon) R. W. Evans to the Rev. T. Butler

(Original in possession of Mrs. G. L. Bridges and Miss Butler)

Tarvin, December 16th, 1839.

"MY DEAR BUTLER, Though I have seen you so very lately I cannot refrain from writing a few lines to you, for while I was with you I had no good opportunity, and had I found it should have been unable to express what I wished. I do not write to console, for of that none of you have need; never was a bereaved family left so rich in all those things which form the matter of Christian consolation. A life spent in active usefulness, and latterly, in spite of ill-health, given up with the devotion of a true and primitive Christian Bishop to the administration of his diocese in such a way as to excite the astonishment and admiration of all that saw the infirm state of his body, and so employed to the last dregs of his strength that it may be said to have been concluded on the field of battle—this alone should be sufficient to draw the sting from all sorrow, and to cause you to submit in thankfulness to the hand which has taken him away to his rest. But I write for the selfish purpose of relieving my own feelings. Your dear and venerated father has been to me, under God, the instrument of many and great blessings.

How much I received from him beyond the measure which is commonly dealt out in instruction, you yourself know, with whom I have shared in this respect his paternal care. He was not one who was content with inculcating mere critical accuracy, and with informing us with the mere body of ancient literature, but he also infused a lively spirit, a delicate taste, which I have been able to trace distinctly in all that made the proper advantage of his instructions. And to this peculiar excellence of his I can clearly refer all the literary success (whatever that may be) which I have enjoyed. I can at this moment in memory place myself before him as he was explaining the author whom we had construed. Nor did he lose sight of us when we had left his immediate inspection, but on every occasion on which he could counsel or befriend he was at hand. None experienced his kindness to the degree that I have done. I am now writing in a place that I owe to him. Here he posted me in the best piece of preferment that was in his gift, and gave me an opportunity of exercising my profession which I might have looked for in vain from any other hand. Blessed be his memory! To have been his chaplain is indeed an honour, and that he should have chosen me for that office will be to me a source of gratification to my life's end.

" Can my services be available to you in any way? Most gladly will they be afforded. How little at best can I repay from that large store of kindness and benefit which I have received! God comfort you and bless you, my dear friend, and all your family.

" I trust that Mrs. Butler and Mrs. Lloyd still feel support to their admirable fortitude, and that you have all experienced, in the alleviation to the sharpness of sorrow, that though sorrow endureth for a night, joy cometh in the morning.

" Believe me, remembering me kindly to them,
" Ever yours most truly,
" R. W. EVANS.

" I do hope that now that you will be less tied down you will be able to come and see me here."

CHAPTER THIRTY-NINE: CONCLUSION

IF THE CHARACTER DISPLAYED IN THE FOREgoing pages through Dr. Butler's own letters and those of his friends has not been already found acceptable by the reader, nothing that I can add by way of peroration is likely to make it more so. It will be much if I do not rather mar than make. There are, however, certain points on which I would say a few words before I leave my subject.

In the first place as regards examinations. The late Professor Kennedy, in a passage quoted on an earlier page, said that it was Dr. Butler's system of examinations that made his school so great. I cannot think that this, serviceable though it no doubt was in Dr. Butler's hands, had much to do with the matter. He knew how each boy was doing quite well enough to be able to place him equitably, and his boys would have trusted him sufficiently whether they had been examined or no. The moving the boys within the sixth form so that each one of them knew that if he would keep his place he must work for it, and all except the head boy might hope to rise if he could beat one who was above him, while the head boy might fear to fall—this revolution, first introduced by Dr. Butler, was the most important thing. Examinations gave sanction and circumstance to the moving: they stimulated a boy who had been idle during the early part of a half-year to make up leeway, if he could, before the time of trial came; they served as milestones, and perhaps showed the boys themselves better wherein they were most deficient; moreover they familiarized them with the nature of the ordeals through which they must pass at the Universities; but examinations do not make scholars—they only test them, and that, do what the master can, often very imperfectly. No doubt Dr. Butler's experience taught him that on the whole they were useful stimulants to exertion; but long after the other great schools had followed his lead in this respect as in many others, Shrewsbury still retained its preeminence as the foremost classical school in England. It was not the examinations, but the good sense that prompted their introduction, the confidence with which Dr. Butler inspired his boys that no pains were too great for him to take as regards giving each neither more nor less than his due, the enthusiasm

Conclusion

with which he filled them, his warm affection for them, the amiability and self-control that never failed him no matter how much they might provoke him, the untiring energy, sagacity, modesty (for no man was more patient of correction), in a word the uprightness of his character—the attractiveness of his own strong and genial personality—this it was, and not his system of examinations, that made his school so great.

Another point which struck me in many a letter which I have been unable to give, lest, to use Mr. Murray's words to myself, I should "smother Dr. Butler under his own monument," was his immunity from a vice which I am afraid I consider to be a growing one—I mean, the fear of giving himself away. Those who indulge themselves in this fear are probably quite unaware that he who shrinks from expressing an opinion which may be reasonably asked will ere long shrink from forming one that he should reasonably form. Nothing conduces to indolence and timidity of thought like indolence and timidity of expression. Expression is to the mind what action is to the bodily organ, and he who would be vigorous in thought must be prompt and fearless in expression also, for expression helps to model the thought itself that is to be expressed. But let this pass. Whoever appealed for advice, encouragement, or correction was sure of obtaining the fullest, frankest, and most prompt consideration that Dr. Butler could give him, no matter how busy nor how ill (and from his childhood he was never well for long together) he might be. Would indeed that he were living, for I know no man of his eminence to whom I can appeal with like prospect of consideration and assistance.

Nevertheless I doubt whether he was ever in his element either as a scholar or as a divine. The natural bent of his mind was towards jurisprudence and statesmanship. Admirably, again, as he often wrote, he does not appear to have greatly cared about making his mark on literature or philosophy. I do not think he thought about making his mark upon anything. He would do what he had to do, mark or no mark; and the work he did, though pregnant with invaluable and enduring benefit to the education of the higher classes, was as prohibitive of personal literary achievement as it was far-reaching in its effect on the literary achievements of other people. What he might have done if he had given no pledges in early manhood, if he had then had means and leisure, or again if his fatally cumbrous Aeschylus had not hung like a millstone about his neck during the years when the school was so small as to give him time that he might call his own—this it is idle to inquire. He was contemplative as well as active; nevertheless practical questions attracted him more than speculative ones, and what leisure he had was given to Catholic emancipation and to University and Church reform rather than to philosophical inquiry. As soon as it became obvious that his path of least resistance lay in the direction of a scholastic, and hence in those days necessarily of a clerical career, he shut the doors leading to many great fields of inquiry in his own face; and this done there must be little or no philosophy. His path once marked out for him, he became a soldier fighting upon a certain side, and on that side he would fight—chivalrous always to his opponents.

How to do his best by his pupils—this came first. Second—after he became Archdeacon hardly second, and on his elevation to the Bench all in all—was his desire to serve the truest interests of the Church of England. Those truest interests he believed to lie in the avoidance of extreme opinions, however logical, and in greater adaptability to changing circumstances hereafter.

I asked Dr. Welldon, the last survivor of those who were masters under Dr. Butler, as I had asked Professor Kennedy, to what party in the Church I ought to say that Dr. Butler more particularly belonged. "Certainly Broad," was his reply, but he cannot have meant "Broad" in the sense which the word now commonly bears. "Broad" of a Churchman now means rationalistic, or at any rate leaning towards rationalism, and I have never been able to detect a trace of such leaning in anything written by Dr. Butler either published or unpublished. Dr. Parr, in a letter given vol. i, p. 284, writing of Dr. Butler's mother, said that her whole life was a preparation for everything which was "intelligible and credible" in a future state. No such words could have been penned by Dr. Butler, and I imagine they must have shocked him even when coming from one for whom his reverence was as unbounded as it was for

Conclusion

Dr. Parr. What had intelligibility and credibility to do with one another? He would not have attempted to define what was meant by a future state—he would take it as he found it in the creeds and in the New Testament, accepting it as a fundamental article of faith, and shrinking with awe from all attempt to bring it within the domain of human reason. And so with all the essential doctrines of Christianity. He did not pretend to nor think it his duty to even try to comprehend them, but he believed them as a son believes the teaching of a father while yet he cannot understand it.

Writing to my mother, for example, who came of a Unitarian family, but joined the Church of England, Dr. Butler said:

"I understand your chief objection is to the creed which goes by the name of Athanasian, derived from a man who did not draw it up. Now though I most firmly believe the main doctrine which that creed intends to inculcate (that of the Trinity), I concur with many abler and better members of our Church in wishing it were not a part of our Liturgy. The doctrine which it attempts to explain is one of revelation, and one that human capacity cannot comprehend. It is just as impossible for us to understand it as it is for us to understand the joys of heaven or the pains of hell. We must receive it as we do them, in the humble trust that we shall know more of it when this mortal shall have put on immortality. On this account therefore, as well as on account of its damnatory clauses, which many construe in their severest sense, I wish, as many of our greatest and wisest divines have wished before me, that it did not form part of our Liturgy."

In doctrine therefore it is plain that Dr. Butler had no more sympathy with what is now called the Broad Church party than with the Oxford Movement; but if by Broad is meant sober, tolerant, anxious to avoid all occasion of stumbling to weaker brethren, ready to make all charitable allowances for others who differed widely from himself, convinced that all extremes of opinion, in whatever direction, do harm to those who hold them—that they are dangerous to the peace of both Church and State, have no good effect on conduct, and are foreign to the genius of Christianity, or of any other faith that can be called Religion—if this is what is meant by Broad, no man could well be broader.

Above all things he deprecated the effort so strenuously made by some of his most valued friends to resist all change in the practice and Liturgy of the Church of England. He has not, that I know of, said so in express words, but it is easy to see that he recognized the fatuousness of the attempt to stereotype once and for ever the creed of any nation whose intellectual and political life is not also stereotyped. Science is a mode of revelation, and so far as we can see the only mode that is now vouchsafed to us. Slowly and very cautiously a Church that is to be the Church of a nation must adapt itself to the growing intelligence and moral sense of the nation to whose spiritual well-being it is to minister; change must come, and the aim of right-minded persons must be in the direction, not of resisting modifications which the enlarged perceptions of any age may render from time to time expedient, but of softening them, of helping them to come in whatever manner shall cause least shock to those who will be pained by them. A large measure of compromise and inconsistency is required of all who are well-wishers to their country, and hence to the Church of their country, to whatever school of thought they may individually belong. I dare not trust myself to say more on this head, lest I should father on Dr. Butler opinions that were not his; but that his inner mind was as I have above portrayed it, I no more question than I do his full and devout acceptance of every doctrine which he understood the Church of England to maintain.

The temptation is strong to pursue this question of change in the doctrines and practices of our Church. What have been the manifest changes in the average practice of the Church of England since the death of him whose life I have been endeavouring to record? Any man whose memory extends over half a century must admit that they have been neither few nor small. Neither can any observant onlooker question in which direction they have mainly been. It is tempting to inquire how far they are in harmony with the instincts of laymen generally who bear no ill-will to the Church, and how far many of such men look

Conclusion

askance upon them, however much they may acquiesce in them for the sake of peace. The Church is so potent a factor of the well-being of the nation, that the direction in which she is tending, the use she is making of her power, and the effects of that use upon her future hold, or loss of hold, on the masses in whom, whether we like it or no, all power is now ultimately vested, are questions which one who has so long been dealing with the life of a high dignitary of the Church must feel sorely tempted, not only to ask, but according to his lights to answer —nevertheless I imagine that I shall do most wisely by leaving the reader to ask and answer them for himself.

One passage, however, of Dr. Butler's own I venture to repeat, from page 76 of my first volume; for I know of none in either volume that I believe the reader may more serviceably carry away with him. It is this:

"No man who views the daily increase of Puritanism (which in its root and branches, in its tenets and effects, resembles the Pharisaical system of the Jews), no man who compares its late and present progress with events which the history of our own nation has recorded in dark and blood-stained characters, no man who has remarked the subtlety, restlessness, and impetuosity of spiritual pride, when united by opportunities favourable for action with the inordinate and insatiable lust of temporal power, can look without alarm and dismay to consequences which not only exercise the sagacity of the philosopher, but in truth force themselves upon the most common observer of human nature, as unfolded in the events of daily life.

"If the great and characteristic blessing of the Reformation was the removal of needless and burthensome ceremonies, of an usurped dominion over the minds and consciences of men, of authority bearing down right, and of dogmatism putting reason to silence and setting at defiance the clearest and most salutary suggestions of common-sense, let us beware that we are not again entangled in a yoke of bondage not less galling than that from which we have been set free. Let us look well to ourselves and our posterity, and let us be careful to preserve that liberty which our ancestors obtained for us by their wisdom, and sealed to us by their blood."

Life and Letters of Dr. Butler [xxxix

Here then I leave my work, not without regret, not without compunction, and yet not without a hope that those readers whom I would most wish to satisfy may on the whole vouchsafe it their approval.

APPENDIX

NOTE

Butler was extremely jealous for his grandfather's honour, both as a scholar and in every other respect. In a letter to Mr. Phillips of Shrewsbury (13th April 1897), printed in *Samuel Butler: a Memoir*, by H. F. Jones, (ii, 266), he says: " I was much shocked that Munro should have written that Dr. B. left the school in a very poor state as regards Greek scholarship, and that Kennedy should have held his peace; but, after consultation with Mr. Moss, I passed it over. . . ." Among the Miscellaneous Papers in the Butler Collection at St. John's College, Cambridge, is a manuscript of nine leaves quarto entitled: " A reply to certain aspersions on Dr. Butler [by H. A. J. Munro] in the preface to Sandys's edition of Cope's *Rhetorick* of Aristotle. With a copy of Dr. Kennedy's first Greek verse examination paper [1836]. And a few notes on John Gregory—alias John Dandy." Butler contends that the examination paper shows that the standard expected was very high, and that Dr. Kennedy, who had been at Shrewsbury under Dr. Butler both as boy and assistant-master, and whom he succeeded in the head mastership in 1836, must have known that Munro's statement was unjust and ought to have said so. In the course of his remarks Butler says: " When I wrote my *Life and Letters of Dr. Butler*, I knew what Munro had said, and bearing in mind the glamour of Munro's name was much tempted to call attention to it; yielding, however, to the advice of a friend, I contented myself with reprinting the Honour Boards of Shrewsbury School, and with showing what an unusually large proportion of the boys whom Dr. Butler left at the head of the school distinguished themselves in after life."

The John Gregory referred to above was Dr. Butler's eccentric manservant at Shrewsbury.

The Editors have to thank the Rev. the Head Master of Shrewsbury and the Rev. J. E. Auden for kindly correcting Butler's transcript of the Honour Boards.

H.F.J.
A.T.B.

Appendix

THE HONOUR BOARDS OF SHREWSBURY SCHOOL

From 1806 *to* 1882, *the date of the removal of the Schools to their new site on Kingsland*

1806 Thomas Smart Hughes, St. John's College, Cambridge,
     Browne Medal for Latin Ode.
1807 Thomas Smart Hughes, St. John's College, Cambridge,
     Browne Medal for Greek Ode.
  „ John Turner, St. John's College, Cambridge,
     Second Bachelor's Prize.
1808 William Henry Parry, St. John's College, Cambridge,
     16th Wrangler.
1809 John Evans, Clare Hall, Cambridge,
     6th Wrangler.
  „ W. R. Gilby, Trinity College, Cambridge,
     7th Wrangler.
  „ Thomas Smart Hughes, St. John's College, Cambridge,
     First Bachelor's Prize.
1810 Thomas Smart Hughes, St. John's College, Cambridge,
     First Bachelor's Prize.
  „ William Henry Parry, St. John's College, Cambridge,
     Third Bachelor's Prize.
1811 Robert Wilson Evans, Trinity College, Cambridge,
     7th Wrangler.
  „ Robert Wilson Evans, Trinity College, Cambridge,
     JUNIOR CHANCELLOR'S MEDALLIST.
1812 Marmaduke Lawson, St. John's College, Cambridge,
     Browne Medal for Latin Ode.
  „ Robert Wilson Evans, Trinity College, Cambridge,
     First Bachelor's Prize.
1813 William Henry Parry, St. John's College, Cambridge,
     Norrisian Prize.
  „ Robert Wilson Evans, Trinity College, Cambridge,
     First Bachelor's Prize.
1814 Marmaduke Lawson, St. John's College, Cambridge,
     PITT UNIVERSITY SCHOLAR. The first elected on that foundation.

Life and Letters of Dr. Butler

1816 Marmaduke Lawson, Magdalene College, Cambridge,
CHANCELLOR'S MEDALLIST (AEQU.).

„ Richard P. Thursfield, St. John's College, Cambridge,
Second Bell's Scholar.

1817 Rev. Thomas Smart Hughes, Fellow of Emmanuel College, Cambridge, and Proctor of the University,
The Seatonian Prize.

1819 Spencer Wilde, St. John's College, Cambridge,
Recorded equal to Bell's Scholar.

1821 Edward Baines, Christ's College, Cambridge,
Second Bell's Scholar.

„ Edward Baines, Christ's College, Cambridge,
Browne Medal for Epigrams.

1823 John Price, St. John's College, Cambridge,
Recorded equal to Bell's Scholar.

„ Benjamin Hall Kennedy, St. John's College, Cambridge,
THE PORSON PRIZE, WHILE YET IN THE SIXTH FORM OF SHREWSBURY SCHOOL.

„ Benjamin Hall Kennedy, St. John's College, Cambridge,
Adjudged the Browne Medal for Latin Ode.

1824 Edward Baines, Christ's College, Cambridge,
4th in First Class of the Classical Tripos.

„ W. Crawley, Magdalene College, Cambridge,
27th Wrangler.

„ Benjamin Hall Kennedy, St. John's College, Cambridge,
PITT UNIVERSITY SCHOLAR.

„ Benjamin Hall Kennedy, St. John's College, Cambridge,
Browne Medal for Greek Ode.

„ Benjamin Hall Kennedy, St. John's College, Cambridge,
Browne Medal for Latin Ode.

„ Benjamin Hall Kennedy, St. John's College, Cambridge,
THE PORSON PRIZE.

1825 Thomas Williamson Peile, Trinity College, Cambridge,
DAVIES UNIVERSITY SCHOLAR.

„ John Hodgson, Trinity College, Cambridge,
THE PORSON PRIZE.

Appendix

1825 Benjamin Hall Kennedy, St. John's College, Cambridge,
  Browne Medal for Epigrams.
1826 John Hodgson, Trinity College, Cambridge,
  16th Wrangler.
  „ John Price, St. John's College, Cambridge,
  3RD IN FIRST CLASS OF THE CLASSICAL TRIPOS.
  „ John Hodgson, Trinity College, Cambridge,
  5th in First Class of Classical Tripos.
  „ Frederick Gretton, St. John's College, Cambridge,
  7th in First Class of the Classical Tripos.
  „ John Hodgson, Trinity College, Cambridge,
  JUNIOR CHANCELLOR'S MEDALLIST.
  „ Horatio Hildyard, St. Peter's College, Cambridge,
  First Bell's Scholar.
  „ Thomas Butler, St. John's College, Cambridge,
  Recorded equal to Bell's Scholar.
  „ Benjamin Hall Kennedy, St. John's College, Cambridge,
  THE PORSON PRIZE.
1827 George Butterton, St. John's College, Cambridge,
  8th Wrangler.
  „ Benjamin Hall Kennedy, St. John's College, Cambridge,
  SENIOR CLASSIC.
  „ George Butterton, St. John's College, Cambridge,
  3RD IN FIRST CLASS OF THE CLASSICAL TRIPOS.
  „ Benjamin Hall Kennedy, St. John's College, Cambridge,
  SENIOR CHANCELLOR'S MEDALLIST.
  „ George H. Johnson, Queen's College, Oxford,
  IRELAND UNIVERSITY SCHOLAR.
  „ Thomas Williamson Peile, Trinity College, Cambridge,
  Second Undergraduate's Latin Essay.
1828 Thomas Williamson Peile, Trinity College, Cambridge,
  18th Wrangler.
  „ Thomas Williamson Peile, Trinity College, Cambridge,
  2ND IN FIRST CLASS OF THE CLASSICAL TRIPOS.
  „ Thomas Williamson Peile, Trinity College, Cambridge,
  JUNIOR CHANCELLOR'S MEDALLIST.
  „ Charles R. Kennedy, Trinity College, Cambridge,
  First Bell's Scholar.

1828 Edward Massie, Wadham College, Oxford,
   IRELAND UNIVERSITY SCHOLAR.
,, Benjamin Hall Kennedy, St. John's College, Cambridge,
   First Bachelor's Prize.
,, George H. Johnson, Queen's College, Oxford,
   DOUBLE FIRST CLASS.
1829 Horatio Hildyard, St. Peter's College, Cambridge,
   5th in First Class of the Classical Tripos.
,, Robert Smith, St. John's College, Cambridge,
   6th in First Class of the Classical Tripos.
,, Thomas Butler, St. John's College, Cambridge,
   7th in First Class of the Classical Tripos.
,, Charles Borrett, Magdalen College, Oxford,
   IRELAND UNIVERSITY SCHOLAR.
,, John Thomas, Wadham College, Oxford,
   CRAVEN UNIVERSITY SCHOLAR.
,, Charles R. Kennedy, Trinity College, Cambridge,
   Browne Medal for Greek Ode.
,, Charles R. Kennedy, Trinity College, Cambridge,
   THE PORSON PRIZE.
,, Herbert Johnson, Wadham College, Oxford,
   FIRST CLASS, LIT. HUM.
1830 Charles Whitley, St. John's College, Cambridge,
   SENIOR WRANGLER.
,, Edward Yardley, Magdalene College, Cambridge,
   40th Wrangler.
,, Charles R. Kennedy, Trinity College, Cambridge,
   PITT UNIVERSITY SCHOLAR.
,, Peter S. Payne, Balliol College, Oxford,
   IRELAND UNIVERSITY SCHOLAR.
,, James Hildyard, Christ's College, Cambridge,
   Browne Medal for Greek Ode.
,, Charles R. Kennedy, Trinity College, Cambridge,
   Browne Medal for Latin Ode.
,, Robert Scott, Christ Church, Oxford,
   CRAVEN UNIVERSITY SCHOLAR.
,, Charles R. Kennedy, Trinity College, Cambridge,
   THE PORSON PRIZE.

Appendix

1831 Charles R. Kennedy, Trinity College, Cambridge,
   SENIOR CLASSIC.
„ Charles Johnstone, Caius College, Cambridge,
   4th in First Class of the Classical Tripos.
„ James Hildyard, Christ's College, Cambridge,
   BATTIE UNIVERSITY SCHOLAR.
„ Thomas Brancker, admitted of Wadham College, Oxford,
   but not yet resident, elected IRELAND UNIVERSITY
      SCHOLAR WHILE YET IN THE SIXTH FORM OF
      SHREWSBURY SCHOOL.
„ George J. Kennedy, St. John's College, Cambridge,
   First Bell's Scholar.
„ George H. Johnson, Queen's College, Oxford,
   Mathematical University Scholar. The first
   elected on that foundation.
„ James Hildyard, Christ's College, Cambridge,
   Browne Medal for Greek Ode.
„ James Hildyard, Christ's College, Cambridge,
   Browne Medal for Latin Ode.
„ James Hildyard, Christ's College, Cambridge,
   Browne Medal for Epigrams.
„ George J. Kennedy, St. John's College, Cambridge,
   THE PORSON PRIZE.
„ Peter S. Payne, Balliol College, Oxford,
   FIRST CLASS, LIT. HUM.
1832 Richard Shilleto, Trinity College, Cambridge,
   2ND IN FIRST CLASS OF THE CLASSICAL TRIPOS.
„ Edward Broadhurst, Magdalene College, Cambridge,
   7th in First Class of the Classical Tripos.
„ George J. Kennedy, St. John's College, Cambridge,
   DAVIES UNIVERSITY SCHOLAR.
„ Peter S. Payne, B.A., Scholar of Balliol College, Oxford,
   Open Fellowship at Balliol College.
„ Horatio Hildyard, St. Peter's College, Cambridge,
   Second Bachelor's Prize.
„ John Thomas, Trinity College, Oxford,
   Latin Verse Prize.

1832 James Hildyard, Christ's College, Cambridge,
  Browne Medal for Greek Ode.
,, James Hildyard, Christ's College, Cambridge,
  Browne Medal for Latin Ode.
,, James Hildyard, Christ's College, Cambridge,
  Members' Prize for Latin Essay.
1833 James Hildyard, Christ's College, Cambridge,
  2ND IN FIRST CLASS OF THE CLASSICAL TRIPOS.
,, Robert Scott, Christ Church, Oxford,
  IRELAND UNIVERSITY SCHOLAR.
,, James Hildyard, Christ's College, Cambridge,
  CHANCELLOR'S JUNIOR MEDALLIST.
,, George H. Marsh, St. John's College, Cambridge,
  Bell's Scholar.
,, John Gibbons Longueville, Wadham College, Oxford,
  FIRST CLASS, LIT. HUM.
,, Robert Scott, Student of Christ Church, Oxford,
  FIRST CLASS, LIT. HUM.
,, Thomas F. Henney, Pembroke College, Oxford,
  FIRST CLASS, LIT. HUM.
,, William Fletcher, Trinity College, Oxford,
  FIRST CLASS, LIT. HUM.
,, James Hildyard, A.B., Christ's College, Cambridge,
  First Bachelor's Prize.
1834 William Henry Trentham, St. John's College, Cambridge,
  13th Wrangler.
,, George J. Kennedy, St. John's College, Cambridge,
  SENIOR CLASSIC.
,, Edward Warter, Magdalene College, Cambridge,
  4th in First Class of Classical Tripos.
,, Alexander G. Hildyard, Pembroke College, Cambridge,
  Second Bell's Scholar.
,, Robert Scott, B.A., Student of Christ Church, Oxford,
  Bachelor's Prize for Latin Essay.
,, Robert Scott, B.A., Student of Christ Church, Oxford,
  Open Fellowship at Balliol College.
1835 Francis Procter, Catherine Hall, Cambridge,
  30th Wrangler.

Appendix

1835 John Cooper, Trinity College, Cambridge,
33rd Wrangler.
„ George F. Harris, Trinity College, Cambridge,
3RD IN FIRST CLASS OF THE CLASSICAL TRIPOS.
„ John Cooper, Trinity College, Cambridge,
7th in First Class of the Classical Tripos.
„ William G. Humphry, Trinity College, Cambridge,
PITT UNIVERSITY SCHOLAR.
„ George A. Chichester May, Magdalene College, Cambridge.
Bell's Scholar.
„ Edward J. Edwards, B.A., Balliol College, Oxford,
Kennicott Hebrew Scholar.
1836 William Twiss Turner, Trinity College, Cambridge,
15th Wrangler.
„ Thomas Headlam, Trinity College, Cambridge,
17th Wrangler.
„ George Henry Marsh, St. John's College, Cambridge,
2ND IN FIRST CLASS OF THE CLASSICAL TRIPOS.
„ William Henry Bateson, St. John's College, Cambridge,
3RD IN FIRST CLASS OF THE CLASSICAL TRIPOS.
„ Richard Edward Turner, Trinity College, Cambridge,
6th in First Class of the Classical Tripos.
„ William Dickenson, Trinity College, Oxford,
Latin Verse Prize.
„ W. G. Humphry, Trinity College, Cambridge,
Undergraduate's Latin Essay.
1837 Alex. J. Ellis, Trinity College, Cambridge,
5th Wrangler.
„ W. G. Humphry, Trinity College, Cambridge,
27th Wrangler.
„ W. G. Humphry, Trinity College, Cambridge,
SENIOR CLASSIC.
„ W. G. Humphry, Trinity College, Cambridge,
CHANCELLOR'S JUNIOR MEDALLIST.
„ Henry Holden, Balliol College, Oxford,
FIRST CLASS, LIT. HUM.
1838 H. J. Hodgson, Trinity College, Cambridge,
24th Wrangler.

Life and Letters of Dr. Butler

1838 G. A. C. May, Magdalene College, Cambridge,
    36th Wrangler.
,, G. A. C. May, Magdalene College, Cambridge,
    3RD IN FIRST CLASS OF THE CLASSICAL TRIPOS.
,, Henry Thompson, St. John's College, Cambridge,
    7th in First Class of the Classical Tripos.
,, William Parkinson, St. John's College, Cambridge,
    8th in First Class of the Classical Tripos.
,, James Fraser, Lincoln College, Oxford,
    RECORDED 2ND TO IRELAND UNIVERSITY SCHOLAR WITH THE WORDS "PROXIME ACCESSIT."
,, Rev. Robert Scott, M.A., Fellow of Balliol College, Oxford,
    Denyer's Theological Essay.
,, Robert Middleton Dukes, Lincoln College, Oxford,
    FIRST CLASS, LIT. HUM.
,, Thomas S. Evans, St. John's College, Cambridge,
    THE PORSON PRIZE.
,, William Dickenson, B.A., Trinity College, Oxford,
    Latin Essay.
1839 A. M. Hopper, Trinity College, Cambridge,
    6th in First Class of the Classical Tripos.
,, James Fraser, Lincoln College, Oxford,
    IRELAND UNIVERSITY SCHOLAR.
,, Edward M. Cope, Trinity College, Cambridge,
    THE PORSON PRIZE.
,, James Fraser, Lincoln College, Oxford,
    FIRST CLASS, LIT. HUM.
1840 H. C. Rothery, St. John's College, Cambridge,
    10th Wrangler.
,, Francis France, St. John's College, Cambridge,
    SENIOR CLASSIC (AEQU.).
,, Edward Bather, Merton College, Oxford,
    FIRST CLASS, LIT. HUM.
,, J. Bather, St. John's College, Cambridge,
    Re-examined with Craven University Scholar.
,, James Fraser, B.A., Scholar of Lincoln College, Oxford,
    Open Fellowship at Oriel College.
1841 E. M. Cope, Trinity College, Cambridge,
    SENIOR CLASSIC.

Appendix

1841 John Bather, St. John's College, Cambridge,
        2ND IN FIRST CLASS OF THE CLASSICAL TRIPOS.
,, Henry Thring, Magdalene College, Cambridge,
        3RD IN FIRST CLASS OF THE CLASSICAL TRIPOS.
,, Hugh Andrew Johnstone Munro, Trinity College, Cambridge,
        CRAVEN UNIVERSITY SCHOLAR.
,, G. Druce, St. Peter's College, Cambridge,
        THE PORSON PRIZE.
,, G. Nugee, Trinity College, Cambridge,
        Latin Essay.
1842 H. A. J. Munro, Trinity College, Cambridge,
        2ND IN FIRST CLASS OF THE CLASSICAL TRIPOS.
,, Francis Morse, St. John's College, Cambridge,
        7th in First Class of the Classical Tripos.
,, E. H. Gifford, St. John's College, Cambridge,
        PITT UNIVERSITY SCHOLAR.
,, G. Druce, St. Peter's College, Cambridge,
        SECOND TO PITT SCHOLAR.
,, H. A. J. Munro, Trinity College, Cambridge,
        SENIOR CHANCELLOR'S MEDALLIST.
,, G. Druce, St. Peter's College, Cambridge,
        THE PORSON PRIZE.
,, W. G. Clark, Trinity College, Cambridge,
        Browne Medal for Greek Ode.
,, W. G. Clark, Trinity College, Cambridge,
        Browne Medal for Epigrams.
,, Thomas Ramsbotham, Christ's College, Cambridge,
        Latin Essay.
,, W. Basil T. Jones, Trinity College, Oxford,
        IRELAND UNIVERSITY SCHOLAR.
,, M. Bright, Magdalene College, Cambridge,
        Hebrew Prize.
1843 E. H. Gifford, St. John's College, Cambridge,
        15th Wrangler.
,, { George Druce, St. Peter's College, Cambridge, and
    E. H. Gifford, St. John's College, Cambridge,
        SENIOR CLASSICS (AEQU.).

1843 E. H. Gifford, St. John's College, Cambridge,
  SENIOR CHANCELLOR'S MEDALLIST.
 ,, G. Druce, St. Peter's College, Cambridge,
  JUNIOR CHANCELLOR'S MEDALLIST.
 ,, W. G. Clark, Trinity College, Cambridge,
  Browne Medal for Greek Ode.
 ,, W. G. Clark, Trinity College, Cambridge,
  THE PORSON PRIZE.
 ,, Rev. M. Bright, Magdalene College, Cambridge,
  Tyrwhitt's Hebrew Scholar.
 ,, G. Nugee, Trinity College, Cambridge,
  Latin Essay.
1844 W. G. Clark, Trinity College, Cambridge,
  2ND IN FIRST CLASS OF THE CLASSICAL TRIPOS.
 ,, W. G. Clark, Trinity College, Cambridge,
  JUNIOR CHANCELLOR'S MEDALLIST.
 ,, G. O. Morgan, Balliol College, Oxford,
  CRAVEN UNIVERSITY SCHOLAR.
 ,, J. G. C. Fussell, Trinity College, Cambridge,
  Browne Medal for Epigrams.
 ,, J. G. C. Fussell, Trinity College, Cambridge,
  Re-examined with Browne's University Scholar.
 ,, J. G. C. Fussell, Trinity College, Cambridge,
  Prize for Latin Essay.
1845 H. De Winton, Trinity College, Cambridge,
  Browne Medal for Greek Ode.
 ,, G. Nugee, Trinity College, Cambridge,
  Sir P. Maitland's English Essay.
 ,, James Riddell, Scholar of Balliol College, Oxford,
  FIRST CLASS, LIT. HUM.
1846 H. De Winton, Trinity College, Cambridge,
  3RD IN FIRST CLASS OF THE CLASSICAL TRIPOS.
 ,, G. O. Morgan, Balliol College, Oxford,
  Newdigate Prize for English Poem.
 ,, James Riddell, B.A., Scholar of Balliol College, Oxford,
  Open Fellowship at Balliol College.
 ,, Robert Trimmer, Wadham College, Oxford,
  English Essay.

Appendix

1847 G. O. Morgan, Scholar of Worcester College, Oxford,
    FIRST CLASS, LIT. HUM.
1848 J. E. B. Mayor, St. John's College, Cambridge,
    3RD IN FIRST CLASS OF THE CLASSICAL TRIPOS.
„   H. C. A. Tayler, Trinity College, Cambridge,
    Browne Medal for Epigrams.
1849 H. C. A. Tayler, Trinity College, Cambridge,
    4th in First Class of the Classical Tripos.
„   W. Owen, St. John's College, Cambridge,
    PROXIME ACCESSIT TO CRAVEN SCHOLAR.
„   W. Owen, St. John's College, Cambridge,
    Camden Medal for Latin Heroic Poem.
„   F. Kewley, St. John's College, Cambridge,
    THE PORSON PRIZE.
1850 T. Clayton, Trinity College, Oxford,
    HERTFORD UNIVERSITY SCHOLAR.
„   G. O. Morgan, B.A., Scholar of Worcester College, Oxford,
    Stowell Civil Law Fellowship at University College.
„   G. O. Morgan, Worcester College, Oxford,
    Prize for English Essay.
„   W. Owen, St. John's College, Cambridge,
    THE PORSON PRIZE.
„   P. Perring, Trinity College, Cambridge,
    Browne Medal for Greek Ode.
1851 J. S. Clarke, St. John's College, Cambridge,
    11th Wrangler.
„   J. W. Taylor, St. Peter's College, Cambridge,
    12th in First Class of the Classical Tripos.
„   Henry Parker, B.A., University College, Oxford,
    Open Fellowship at Oriel College.
„   G. O. Morgan, Worcester College, Oxford,
    Eldon Law Scholar.
„   H. C. A. Tayler, Trinity College, Cambridge,
    Latin Essay.
„   G. B. Morley, St. John's College, Cambridge,
    THE PORSON PRIZE.

Life and Letters of Dr. Butler

1852 Robert Burn, Trinity College, Cambridge,
    SENIOR CLASSIC (AEQU.).
,, Philip Perring, Trinity College, Cambridge,
    4th in First Class of the Classical Tripos.
,, W. Chandless, Trinity College, Cambridge,
    5th in First Class of the Classical Tripos.
,, Arthur White, Magdalene College, Cambridge,
    16th in First Class of the Classical Tripos.
,, S. H. Burbury, St. John's College, Cambridge,
    THE PORSON PRIZE.
,, D. Trinder, Exeter College, Oxford,
    Ellerton's Theological Essay.
,, J. L. Balfour, Queen's College, Oxford,
    Denyer's Theological Essay.
,, Henry Parker, Fellow of Oriel College, Oxford,
    Latin Essay.
,, W. Basil Jones, M.A., Fellow of Queen's College, Oxford,
    Open Fellowship at University College.
,, W. Inge, Worcester College, Oxford,
    First Class in Moderations.
1853 A. B. Rocke, Christ Church, Oxford,
    First Class in Moderations.
,, H. A. Morgan, Jesus College, Cambridge,
    25th Wrangler.
,, Edw. L. Brown, Trinity College, Cambridge,
    First Bell's Scholar.
,, W. Inge, Scholar of Worcester College, Oxford,
    FIRST CLASS, LIT. HUM.
,, S. H. Burbury, St. John's College, Cambridge,
    CRAVEN UNIVERSITY SCHOLAR.
,, S. H. Burbury, St. John's College, Cambridge,
    THE PORSON PRIZE.
1854 Benjamin Worthy Horne, St. John's College, Cambridge,
    4th Wrangler.
,, H. G. Day, St. John's College, Cambridge,
    5th Wrangler.
,, H. G. Day, St. John's College, Cambridge,
    9th in First Class of the Classical Tripos.

Appendix

1854 S. H. Burbury, St. John's College, Cambridge,
   15th Wrangler.
„ S. H. Burbury, St. John's College, Cambridge,
    2ND IN FIRST CLASS OF THE CLASSICAL TRIPOS.
„ S. H. Burbury, St. John's College, Cambridge,
    JUNIOR CHANCELLOR'S MEDALLIST.
„ G. P. M. Campbell, Magdalene College, Cambridge,
   7th in First Class of the Classical Tripos.
„ E. L. Fox, Balliol College, Oxford,
   First Class Natural Sciences.
1855 T. Clayton, Scholar of Trinity College, Oxford,
   English Essay.
„ E. L. Brown, Trinity College, Cambridge,
    PROXIME ACCESSIT TO CRAVEN SCHOLAR.
„ E. L. Brown, Trinity College, Cambridge,
    THE PORSON PRIZE.
1856 E. L. Brown, Trinity College, Cambridge,
    SENIOR CLASSIC.
„ E. L. Brown, Trinity College, Cambridge,
    SENIOR CHANCELLOR'S MEDALLIST.
„ Arthur Holmes, St. John's College, Cambridge,
    CRAVEN UNIVERSITY SCHOLAR.
„ Arthur Holmes, St. John's College, Cambridge,
   First Bell's Scholar.
„ W. P. James, Oriel College, Oxford,
   Newdigate English Poem.
„ Arthur Holmes, St. John's College, Cambridge,
    THE PORSON PRIZE.
„ E. C. Clark, Trinity College, Cambridge,
   Browne Medal for Epigrams.
1857 J. R. Lee, Magdalene College, Cambridge,
   5th in First Class of the Classical Tripos.
„ R. Whiting, Trinity College, Cambridge,
   Second Bell's Scholar.
„ Arthur Holmes, St. John's College, Cambridge,
    THE PORSON PRIZE.
„ R. Whiting, Trinity College, Cambridge,
   Browne Medal for Epigrams.

1857 Arthur Holmes, St. John's College, Cambridge,
    Browne Medal for Greek Ode.
1858 E. L. Horne, Clare College, Cambridge,
    35th Wrangler.
„ E. C. Clark, Trinity College, Cambridge,
    SENIOR CLASSIC.
„ A. W. Potts, St. John's College, Cambridge,
    2ND IN FIRST CLASS OF THE CLASSICAL TRIPOS.
„ S. Butler, St. John's College, Cambridge,
    12th Aequ. in First Class of the Classical Tripos.
„ E. C. Clark, Trinity College, Cambridge,
    SENIOR CHANCELLOR'S MEDALLIST.
„ A. W. Potts, St. John's College, Cambridge,
    JUNIOR CHANCELLOR'S MEDALLIST.
„ Arthur Holmes, St. John's College, Cambridge,
    THE PORSON PRIZE.
„ Arthur Holmes, St. John's College, Cambridge,
    Browne Medal for Greek Ode.
„ Arthur Holmes, St. John's College, Cambridge,
    Chancellor's Medal for English Poem.
„ T. W. Lewis, Jesus College, Oxford,
    First Class, Natural Sciences.
1859 T. G. Vyvyan, Caius College, Cambridge,
    9th Wrangler.
„ Arthur Holmes, St. John's College, Cambridge,
    2ND IN FIRST CLASS OF THE CLASSICAL TRIPOS.
„ Robert Whiting, Trinity College, Cambridge,
    THE PORSON PRIZE.
„ Herbert M. Luckock, Jesus College, Cambridge,
    Latin Essay.
1860 G. Macfarlan, Trinity College, Cambridge,
    14th Wrangler.
„ R. S. Ferguson, St. John's College, Cambridge,
    27th Wrangler.
„ R. Whiting, Trinity College, Cambridge,
    6th in First Class of the Classical Tripos.

Appendix

1860 H. M. Luckock, Jesus College, Cambridge,
    First Class Theological Tripos (distinguished in Hebrew).
,, H. M. Luckock, Jesus College, Cambridge,
    Scholefield Greek Testament Prize.
,, H. M. Luckock, Jesus College, Cambridge,
    Carus Greek Testament Prize.
1861 John Batten, Balliol College, Oxford,
    First Class in Moderations.
,, C. E. Graves, St. John's College, Cambridge,
    THE PORSON PRIZE (AEQU.).
,, H. W. Moss, St. John's College, Cambridge,
    THE PORSON PRIZE (AEQU.).
,, H. M. Luckock, Jesus College, Cambridge,
    Latin Essay.
,, H. M. Luckock, Jesus College, Cambridge,
    Crosse Theological Scholarship.
1862 C. E. Graves, St. John's College, Cambridge,
    2ND IN FIRST CLASS OF THE CLASSICAL TRIPOS.
,, T. Gwatkin, St. John's College, Cambridge,
    10th in First Class of the Classical Tripos.
,, H. W. Moss, St. John's College, Cambridge,
    CRAVEN UNIVERSITY SCHOLAR.
,, J. E. L. Shadwell, Christ Church, Oxford,
    PROXIME ACCESSIT TO HERTFORD UNIVERSITY SCHOLAR.
,, H. W. Moss, St. John's College, Cambridge,
    THE PORSON PRIZE.
,, H. M. Luckock, Jesus College, Cambridge,
    Latin Essay.
,, H. M. Luckock, Jesus College, Cambridge,
    Tyrwhitt's Hebrew Scholar.
1863 J. E. L. Shadwell, Christ Church, Oxford,
    First Class in Moderations.
,, J. D. Lester, Jesus College, Oxford,
    First Class in Moderations.
,, J. E. L. Shadwell, Christ Church, Oxford,
    PROXIME ACCESSIT TO IRELAND UNIVERSITY SCHOLAR.

1863 W. F. Smith, St. John's College, Cambridge,
Second Bell's Scholar.
„ H. W. Moss, St. John's College, Cambridge,
THE PORSON PRIZE.
„ H. W. Moss, St. John's College, Cambridge,
Browne Medal for Greek Elegiacs.
1864 G. S. D. Murray, Wadham College, Oxford,
First Class in Moderations.
„ R. E. Williams, Jesus College, Oxford,
First Class in Moderations.
„ W. Whitworth, Pembroke College, Cambridge,
34th Wrangler.
„ H. W. Moss, St. John's College, Cambridge,
SENIOR CLASSIC.
„ G. Preston, Magdalene College, Cambridge,
16th in First Class of the Classical Tripos.
„ C. W. Cooper, Gonville and Caius College, Cambridge,
4th in First Class Natural Sciences Tripos.
„ J. E. L. Shadwell, Christ Church, Oxford,
IRELAND UNIVERSITY SCHOLAR.
„ T. W. Brogden, St. John's College, Cambridge,
THE PORSON PRIZE.
1865 F. Gunton, Magdalene College, Cambridge,
Browne Medal for Latin Ode.
„ F. Gunton, Magdalene College, Cambridge,
Camden Medal for Latin Heroic Poem.
„ J. E. L. Shadwell, Christ Church, Oxford,
FIRST CLASS, LIT. HUM.
„ J. E. L. Shadwell, Christ Church, Oxford,
CRAVEN UNIVERSITY SCHOLAR (AEQU.).
„ H. M. Gwatkin, St. John's College, Cambridge,
Carus Divinity Prize.
1866 W. F. Smith, St. John's College, Cambridge,
2ND IN FIRST CLASS OF THE CLASSICAL TRIPOS.
„ T. Moss, St. John's College, Cambridge,
CRAVEN UNIVERSITY SCHOLAR.
„ T. Moss, St. John's College, Cambridge,
Browne Medal for Latin Ode.

Appendix

1866 T. Moss, St. John's College, Cambridge,
    Browne Medal for Greek Epigram.
„ F. Gunton, Magdalene College, Cambridge,
    Camden Medal for Latin Heroic Poem.
1867 H. M. Gwatkin, St. John's College, Cambridge,
    35th Wrangler.
„ G. T. Hall, Trinity College, Cambridge,
    38th Wrangler.
„ T. W. Brogden, St. John's College, Cambridge,
    9th Aequ. in First Class of the Classical Tripos.
„ H. M. Gwatkin, St. John's College, Cambridge,
    9th Aequ. in First Class of the Classical Tripos.
„ F. Gunton, Magdalene College, Cambridge,
    16th in First Class of the Classical Tripos.
„ C. Dodd, Merton College, Oxford,
    FIRST CLASS, FINAL MATHEMATICAL SCHOOL.
„ G. H. Whitaker, St. John's College, Cambridge,
    Bell's University Scholar.
„ G. H. Hallam, St. John's College, Cambridge,
    Browne Medal for Greek Ode.
„ G. H. Hallam, St. John's College, Cambridge,
    Browne Medal for Latin Ode.
„ T. Moss, St. John's College, Cambridge,
    Chancellor's Medal for English Poem.
„ T. Moss, St. John's College, Cambridge,
    THE PORSON PRIZE.
1868 C. E. B. Barnwell, Christ Church, Oxford,
    First Class in Moderations.
„ T. Moss, St. John's College, Cambridge,
    4th in First Class of the Classical Tripos.
„ G. H. Hallam, St. John's College, Cambridge,
    CRAVEN UNIVERSITY SCHOLAR.
„ H. M. Gwatkin, St. John's College, Cambridge,
    First Class, Moral Sciences Tripos.
„ G. H. Hallam, St. John's College, Cambridge,
    Browne Medal for Greek Ode.
„ H. M. Gwatkin, St. John's College, Cambridge,
    First Class in Theological Tripos. Scholefield Prize and Hebrew Prize.

1869 J. S. Lewis, Christ Church, Oxford,
    First Class in Moderations.
,, G. H. Hallam, St. John's College, Cambridge,
    SENIOR CLASSIC (AEQU.).
,, W. E. Heitland, St. John's College, Cambridge,
    CRAVEN UNIVERSITY SCHOLAR.
,, H. M. Gwatkin, St. John's College, Cambridge,
    Crosse University Scholar.
,, R. D. Hodgson, Trinity College, Cambridge,
    Browne Medal for Greek Elegiacs.
,, R. D. Hodgson, Trinity College, Cambridge,
    THE PORSON PRIZE.
,, G. S. D. Murray, B.A., Wadham College, Oxford,
    Senior Studentship at Christ Church.
,, H. M. Gwatkin, St. John's College, Cambridge,
    Carus Greek Testament Prize (Aequ.).
1870 A. H. Gilkes, Christ Church, Oxford,
    First Class in Moderations.
,, G. H. Whitaker, St. John's College, Cambridge,
    SENIOR CLASSIC (AEQU.).
,, H. M. Gwatkin, St. John's College, Cambridge,
    Tyrwhitt's Hebrew Scholar.
,, T. E. Page, St. John's College, Cambridge,
    Browne Medal for Latin Ode.
,, C. Dixon, Gonville and Caius College, Cambridge,
    Browne Medal for Greek Epigram.
,, T. E. Page, St. John's College, Cambridge,
    THE PORSON PRIZE (AEQU.).
1871 F. Paget, Christ Church, Oxford,
    First Class in Moderations.
,, W. E. Heitland, St. John's College, Cambridge,
    SENIOR CLASSIC.
,, H. L. Manby, Emmanuel College, Cambridge,
    11th Aequ. in First Class of the Classical Tripos.
,, R. D. Archer-Hind, Trinity College, Cambridge,
    CRAVEN UNIVERSITY SCHOLAR.
,, T. E. Page, St. John's College, Cambridge,
    PORSON UNIVERSITY SCHOLAR.

Appendix

1871 F. Paget, Christ Church, Oxford,
    HERTFORD UNIVERSITY SCHOLAR.
„ C. Dixon, Gonville and Caius College, Cambridge,
    Browne Medal for Greek Elegiacs.
„ T. E. Page, St. John's College, Cambridge,
    Browne Medal for Latin Ode.
„ E. B. Moser, St. John's College, Cambridge,
    Browne Medal for Latin Epigram.
„ F. Paget, Christ Church, Oxford,
    Chancellor's Prize for Latin Verse.
1872 H. A. Powys, St. John's College, Oxford,
    First Class in Moderations.
„ R. D. Archer-Hind, Trinity College, Cambridge,
    3RD AEQU. IN FIRST CLASS OF THE CLASSICAL TRIPOS.
„ R. D. Archer-Hind, Trinity College, Cambridge,
    SENIOR CHANCELLOR'S MEDALLIST.
„ T. E. Page, St. John's College, Cambridge,
    DAVIES UNIVERSITY SCHOLAR.
„ T. E. Page, St. John's College, Cambridge,
    Chancellor's Medal for English Poem.
„ T. E. Page, St. John's College, Cambridge,
    Browne Medal for Latin Ode.
„ E. B. Moser, St. John's College, Cambridge,
    Browne Medal for Greek Epigram.
1873 J. H. Onions, Christ Church, Oxford,
    First Class in Moderations.
„ T. E. Page, St. John's College, Cambridge,
    2ND AEQU. IN FIRST CLASS OF THE CLASSICAL TRIPOS.
„ A. H. Gilkes, Christ Church, Oxford,
    FIRST CLASS IN THE FINAL CLASSICAL SCHOOL.
„ T. E. Page, St. John's College, Cambridge,
    CHANCELLOR'S CLASSICAL MEDALLIST.
„ H. Wace, St. John's College, Cambridge,
    PORSON UNIVERSITY SCHOLAR.
„ J. H. Onions, Christ Church, Oxford,
    Distinguished himself in the Examination for the Hertford University Scholarship.

1873 H. Wace, St. John's College, Cambridge,
    THE PORSON PRIZE.
„ H. Wace, St. John's College, Cambridge,
    The Powis Medal for Latin Heroic Poem.
1874 S. B. Guest, Exeter College, Oxford,
    First Class in Moderations.
„ C. Bramley, Jesus College, Cambridge,
    6th Aequ. in First Class of the Classical Tripos.
„ E. B. Moser, St. John's College, Cambridge,
    11th in First Class of the Classical Tripos.
„ W. G. Williams, St. John's College, Cambridge,
    18th in First Class of the Classical Tripos.
„ F. Paget, Christ Church, Oxford,
    FIRST CLASS IN THE FINAL CLASSICAL SCHOOL.
„ J. H. Onions, Christ Church, Oxford,
    Distinguished himself in the Examination for the Ireland University Scholarship.
„ H. Wace, St. John's College, Cambridge,
    CRAVEN UNIVERSITY SCHOLAR.
„ H. Wace, St. John's College, Cambridge.
    THE PORSON PRIZE.
„ H. Wace, St. John's College, Cambridge,
    The Powis Medal for Latin Heroic Poem.
1875 J. H. Deazley, Merton College, Oxford,
    First Class in Moderations.
„ R. F. Horton, New College, Oxford,
    First Class in Moderations.
„ W. J. F. V. Baker, St. John's College, Cambridge,
    4th in First Class of the Classical Tripos.
„ W. Moss, St. John's College, Cambridge,
    19th Aequ. in First Class of the Classical Tripos.
„ H. A. Powys, St. John's College, Oxford,
    First Class in the Modern History School.
„ W. J. F. V. Baker, St. John's College, Cambridge,
    Highly distinguished in the Examination for the Chancellor's Medals.
„ J. H. Onions, Christ Church, Oxford,
    IRELAND UNIVERSITY SCHOLAR.

Appendix

1875 H. Wace, St. John's College, Cambridge,
  THE PORSON PRIZE (AEQU.).
" J. W. Jeudwine, St. John's College, Cambridge,
  4th in the First Class of the Law Tripos.
1876 H. B. Hodgson, Queen's College, Oxford,
  First Class in Moderations.
" H. Wace, St. John's College, Cambridge,
  SENIOR CLASSIC.
" R. C. Seaton, Jesus College, Cambridge,
  12th Aequ. in First Class of the Classical Tripos.
" T. E. Raven, Caius College, Cambridge,
  14th Aequ. in First Class of the Classical Tripos.
" H. Wace, St. John's College, Cambridge,
  SENIOR CHANCELLOR'S MEDALLIST.
" W. W. English, St. John's College, Cambridge,
  Browne Medal for Greek Epigram.
" J. H. Onions, Christ Church, Oxford,
  CRAVEN UNIVERSITY SCHOLAR.
" H. D. Laffan, FIRST IN THE OPEN COMPETITION for admission to the ROYAL MILITARY ACADEMY, WOOLWICH
1877 C. W. S. Corser, Christ Church, Oxford,
  First Class in Moderations.
" J. P. Cranstoun, Oriel College, Oxford,
  First Class in Moderations.
" W. W. English, St. John's College, Cambridge,
  Honourably mentioned by the Examiners for the Craven University Scholarship.
" A. F. Chance, Trinity College, Cambridge,
  THE PORSON PRIZE.
" H. T. Kemp, St. John's College, Cambridge,
  3rd in the First Class of the Law Tripos.
1878 W. W. English, St. John's College, Cambridge,
  3RD IN FIRST CLASS OF THE CLASSICAL TRIPOS.
" H. B. Hodgson, Queen's College, Oxford,
  FIRST CLASS IN THE FINAL CLASSICAL SCHOOL.
" R. F. Horton, New College, Oxford,
  FIRST CLASS IN THE FINAL CLASSICAL SCHOOL.

1878 W. W. English, St. John's College, Cambridge,
JUNIOR CHANCELLOR'S MEDALLIST.
„ C. H. Garland, St. John's College, Cambridge,
Abbott University Scholar.
„ H. D. Laffan, The Royal Military Academy, Woolwich,
The Pollock Medal for distinguished proficiency.
„ H. D. Laffan, FIRST IN THE EXAMINATION at the ROYAL
MILITARY ACADEMY, WOOLWICH, for Commissions
in the Royal Engineers.
„ H. L. Jones, Gonville and Caius College, Cambridge,
First Class in the Natural Sciences Tripos.
1879 H. B. Hodgson, B.A., Queen's College, Oxford,
Senior Studentship at Christ Church.
„ R. F. Horton, B.A., New College, Oxford,
Winchester Fellowship.
„ J. C. Moss, St. John's College, Cambridge,
PORSON UNIVERSITY SCHOLAR.
„ J. R. Wardale, Clare College, Cambridge,
Bell University Scholar (Aequ.).
„ J. C. Moss, St. John's College, Cambridge,
Browne Medal for Greek Ode.
„ J. C. Moss, St. John's College, Cambridge,
Browne Medal for Latin Ode.
„ J. C. Moss, St. John's College, Cambridge,
Browne Medal for Greek Epigram.
„ A. F. Chance, Trinity College, Cambridge,
THE PORSON PRIZE.
1880 A. F. Chance, Trinity College, Cambridge,
Honourably mentioned by the Examiners for the
Chancellor's Medals.
„ J. C. Moss, St. John's College, Cambridge,
CRAVEN UNIVERSITY SCHOLAR.
„ C. H. Garland, St. John's College, Cambridge,
THE PORSON PRIZE (AEQU.).
„ J. C. Moss, St. John's College, Cambridge,
Browne Medal for Greek Ode.
„ J. C. Moss, St. John's College, Cambridge,
Browne Medal for Latin Ode.

Appendix

1881 G. H. Jones, Jesus College, Oxford,
        First Class in Moderations.
,,   C. H. Garland, St. John's College, Cambridge,
        8th Aequ. in First Class of the Classical Tripos.
,,   C. E. Laurence, Pembroke College, Cambridge,
        10th Aequ. in First Class of the Classical Tripos.
,,   R. F. Horton, B.A., New College, Oxford,
        Highly commended by the Examiners for the Denyer and Johnson Scholarship.
,,   J. R. Wardale, Clare College, Cambridge,
        BATTIE UNIVERSITY SCHOLAR.
,,   J. C. Moss, St. John's College, Cambridge,
        The Powis Medal for Latin Heroic Poem.
,,   J. C. Moss, St. John's College, Cambridge,
        Browne Medal for Greek Ode.
,,   J. C. Moss, St. John's College, Cambridge,
        Browne Medal for Latin Ode.
,,   J. C. Moss, St. John's College, Cambridge,
        Browne Medal for Greek Epigram.
,,   H. C. Clarkson, King's College, Cambridge,
        Browne Medal for Latin Epigram.
1882 J. R. Wardale, Clare College, Cambridge,
        2ND IN FIRST CLASS OF THE CLASSICAL TRIPOS.
,,   J. C. Moss, St. John's College, Cambridge,
        3RD IN FIRST CLASS OF THE CLASSICAL TRIPOS.
,,   A. Appleton, Trinity College, Cambridge,
        First Class in the Theological Tripos.
,,   J. C. Moss, St. John's College, Cambridge,
        "Very nearly equal" to the successful candidates for the Chancellor's Medals.
,,   J. R. Wardale, Clare College, Cambridge,
        "Highly distinguished himself" in the Examination for the Chancellor's Medals.
,,   O. Seaman, Clare College, Cambridge,
        THE PORSON PRIZE.

Life and Letters of Dr. Butler

SUCCESSFUL CANDIDATES AT THE OPEN COMPETITION FOR THE CIVIL SERVICE OF INDIA

		First Examination.	Final Examination.
1856	R. Taylor	18th	18th
1860	F. W. J. Rees		
	E. S. Moseley		
	F. H. McLaughlin		
1861	Arthur Yardley		
	E. Turner		
1863	C. D. Maclean		
1868	S. H. James	22nd	1st
	W. Fiddian		
1869	E. B. Steedman	13th	
1870	C. E. Marindin		
1871	W. R. BARRY	1st	
	G. A. Grierson	28th	
1873	W. R. BARRY		1st
	G. A. Grierson		12th
	B. G. Geidt	17th	
1875	B. G. Geidt		8th
1876	S. W. Edgerley	26th	
1879	S. W. Edgerley		8th
	E. T. Lloyd	18th	
1880	H. P. Todd-Naylor	18th	
1881	E. T. Lloyd		2nd

Index

(For letters written by Dr. Butler see under "Butler, Dr. S.," for letters written to him see under the names of the writers; all "letters from" are addressed to Dr. Butler, unless it is stated otherwise.)

AESCHYLUS, commission to edit	I. 23
first volume of, published	I. 59
APPERLEY, —, Dr. Butler's school-days	I. 9-11
ARCHDEACONRY of Derby, appointment to	I. 235
ARNOLD, Dr., and the monitorial system	I. 8
and the Varese chapels	I. 267
extract from diary	I. 424
proposed counter-declaration	II. 102
letter from	II. 106
ASHBORNE Grammar School	II. 361, 389, 406
ASHTON's ordinances	I. 227, 228
ATCHERLEY, Rev. J.	I. 22
ATWOOD, Rev. H. A. S., letter from	I. 393
BAINES, E., letter from	I. 309
BANNISTER, J., letter from	I. 90
BARSTOW, T. I.	II. 197
BATHER, Archdeacon, letters from	II. 320, 346, 398, 404
funeral sermon on Dr. Butler	II. 432-437
BATHER, E. (afterwards Rev.)	II. 196
BATHER, J., Recorder of Shrewsbury, address to Dr. Butler on the occasion of his final speech-day	II. 188
letter from	II. 181
BATHER, J.	II. 196
BATHER, Mrs. *See* Butler, Mary.	
"BEEF ROW," the	I. 420
BENNET, Hon. H. G., letter from	I. 160
BERWICK, Lord. *See* Hill, Hon. W.	
BLAKEWAY, Rev. J. B.	I. 339
letter from	I. 59
BLAND, G. D.	II. 196
BLOMFIELD, C. J. (afterwards Bishop of London), his review of Dr. Butler's Aeschylus	I. 61
Dr. Butler's published letter to	I. 66
and Dr. Butler's pencil	I. 185
letter from	I. 182
letter to Rev. G. Matthews	II. 50
BLUDGEONS, Dr. Butler's judgment *re* certain	II. 211
BOATING, Dr. Butler and	I. 276
BOOTH, Rev. G., letter from	II. 59
BOYCE, H., letter from, to the editor, with anecdote of Dr. Butler	I. xxviii

BRANCKER, Thomas, junr., takes the Ireland while yet in sixth
    form of Shrewsbury School   I. 296; II. 455
BRANCKER, Thomas, senr., letter from   II. 33
BRIGHT, J. Mynors (afterwards Rev.)   II. 194, 197
BROADHURST, E., letter from   II. 7
BROMEHEAD, Rev. A. C., letter from   I. 456
BROMFIELD, Mrs.   I. 351-353
BROUGHAM, Henry, Esq., M.P., Dr. Butler's published
    letters to   I. 227, etc.
BROWNE, P., of Shrewsbury, on Dr. Butler's knowledge of
    pictures   I. 168, 267
    made drawings of all churches in Archdeaconry of Derby   I. 306
BUONAPARTE, Prince Lucien, his *Charlemagne*   I. 81, 82
    Dr. Butler's visit to   I. 88, 89
    letters from   I. 113, 115
BURDER, J., letter from, to (?)   II. 405
BURNEY, Dr. Charles, Dr. Butler's lines on   I. 431
    letter from   I. 142
BURTON, Dr. E., Regius Professor of Divinity at Oxford, letters
    from   I. 419, 420, 449; II. 83
BUTLER, Harriet, wife to Dr. Butler, letters from   I. 170; II. 202, 315
BUTLER, James, and the island of Joanna   I. 3, 4
BUTLER, Lucy, mother to Dr. Butler, letters from   I. 60, 138, 140
BUTLER, Mary, elder daughter to Dr. Butler (afterwards Mrs.
    Bather), letters from   I. 307; II. 285
    to her brother   I. 351, 356, 400
BUTLER, Dr. S., letters from, to
    Assistant Masters   I. xxii, xxiii, xxvi, 396, 397
    Bather, Archdeacon   II. 294
    Bather, Mrs.   II. 293
    Bennet, Hon. H. G.   I. 231
    Blomfield, Rev. C. J. (afterwards Bishop)   I. 183, 283
    Bloomfield, Sir B.   I. 245
    Booth, Rev. G.   II. 60
    Boyer, Mons. Ch.   I. 117
    Boyle, Rev. J.   II. 289
    Bray, C.   I. 236
    Broome, —   I. 206
    Brougham, Lord   II. 65, 83
    Buckeridge, Rev. G.   II. 78
    Burton, Dr. E.   II. 28, 31
    Butler, T. (afterwards Rev.)   I. 351, 385, 410; II. 177, 420
    Cameron, Rev. C.   II. 286
    Candidates for ordination   II. 250, 283, 284
    Carr, Rev. E.   II. 255
    Cawston, Rev. A. W.   II. 425

Index

BUTLER, Dr. S., letters from, to
  Cawston, J.   I. 161
  Chamberlayne, H. T.   II. 208
  Churchwardens   I. 306 ; II. 319, 387
  Clarendon, Lord   I. 333
  Clergymen, sundry unnamed   II. 21, 46, 200, 203, 205, 215, 219, 220, 227, 228, 231, 234, 238, 239, 241, 268, 278, 280, 281, 290, 291, 294, 305, 312, 313, 314, 318, 324, 327, 332, 333, 340, 348, 354, 355, 356, 359, 363, 384, 385, 389, 390, 391, 392, 393, 396, 400, 401
  Cotton, Rev. C. E.   I. 375
  Crawley, Rev. W. (afterwards Archdeacon)   I. 361
  Darwin, Dr. R. W.   I. 188
  Durant, G.   II. 392
  Ecclesiastical Commissioners   II. 394
  Editor of *Sheffield Independent*   I. 283
  Editor of *Shrewsbury Chronicle*   I. 339, 350
  Editor of *The Analyst*   II. 116
  Elmsley, Rev. P.   I. 71
  Evans, Rev. T. S.   II. 409
  Evans, W.   II. 274
  Factory, Overseer of Shrewsbury   I. 189
  Finch, F.   II. 271
  Fisher, Rev. W.   II. 282, 314
  Gell, Rev. P.   II. 159
  Girdlestone, Rev. C.   II. 317
  Glasgow University, Principal of the   II. 335
  Greenlaw, Rev. H. B.   II. 121
  Hall, H.   II. 273
  Harward, Rev. J.   II. 306
  Herford, J.   II. 111
  Hill, Rev. T.   II. 138, 170
  Hodgson, Rev. F. (afterwards Archdeacon)   I. 337
  Hodson, Archdeacon   II. 265, 309, 337, 364, 371, 406, 419, 422
  Holden, Rev. H.   II. 41
  Hone, W.   I. 315, 329
  Hook, Rev. W. F. (afterwards Dean)   II. 86, 94, 129, 251
  Howley, Dr., Archbishop of Canterbury   II. 216
  Hughes, Rev. T. S.   I, 257, 290, 440 ; II, 16, 56, 57, 58, 100, 166
  Irvine, Rev. A.   II. 131, 168, 186
  Jeudwine, J.   I. 48, 111
  Jobson, —   II. 46
  Johnstone, Dr. J.   II. 6
  Jury, foreman of a   II. 374
  Kennedy, Rev. B. H.   I. 399 ; II. 149
  Ker-Cokburne, Rev. H.   II. 368, 369

Life and Letters of Dr. Butler

BUTLER, Dr. S., letters from, to
- Klaproth, J. H. — I. 409; II. 3
- Maltby, Rev. E., D.D. (afterwards Bishop) — II. 80, 118, 125
- Melbourne, Lord — II. 181
- Merian, Baron — I. 149, 318
- Metcalfe, Rev. W. — II. 287
- Monk, Prof. J. H. (afterwards Bishop) — I. 67, 87, 167
- Mott, — — II. 402
- Murray, C. K. — II. 316
- Neville Grenville, Hon. and Rev. G. — I. 345, 355, 357, 370
- Newton, W. L. — II. 286
- Norman, Rev. A. — I. 415
- Parents, sundry unnamed — I. 186, 225, 253, 283, 347, 388, 417, 439; II. 132, 298
- Parents, circulars to — I. 128, 179
- Parr, Dr. — I. 218
- Pole, E. S. Chandos — II. 366, 373
- Potter, Rev. J. P. — I. 450
- Pupil, a — I. 220
- Radford, E. — II. 249
- Rowley, Rev. T. (afterwards D.D.) — II. 67
- Ryder, Hon. H., D.D., Bishop of Lichfield and Coventry — I. 311, 406
- Scott, Rev. R. (afterwards D.D. and Very Rev.) — II. 52, 135, 149, 335
- Scott-Waring, Major — I. 81
- Seager, Rev. C. — II. 67
- Seckerson, P. — II. 258
- Sedgwick, Prof. A. — II. 101, 105, 110, 112, 142
- Shepherd, Rev. W. — I. 298, 301
- Shirley, Rev. W. A. (afterwards Bishop) — I. 427
- Simpson, T. — II. 282
- Sims, Rev. H. — I. 242
- Sleath, Rev. W. B. — II. 368
- Strutt, E., M.P. — II. 245
- Sussex, H.R.H. the Duke of — I. 418, 456
- Tate, Rev. James — I. 432, 443
- Thorp, Rev. R. A. — I. 460, 466
- Tillbrook, Rev. S. — I. 412
- Tomlinson, J. — II. 350
- Tompkins, — — I. 438
- Tradesman, a Shrewsbury — I. 186
- Trustees of Shrewsbury School — I. 324; II. 141
- Tunstall, Rev. M. — II. 305, 308
- Unknown correspondents — I. 54, 323; II. 98, 326, 347, 359, 385, 419
- Vernon Smith, R. — II. 352
- Walker, Rev. J. — II. 207
- Wayne, Rev. W. H. — II. 381

Index

BUTLER, Dr. S., letters from, to
Webb & Hiern, Messrs.	II. 237
Webster, J.	II. 277
Whateley, J. W.	II. 257
Whately, Archbishop	II. 260
Wilson, Josh.	II. 343
Wise, T.	II. 361, 389, 406
Wood, Rev. James, D.D.	II. 151, 161
Woodfall, G.	I. 96
Worsley, Miss F.	II. 445

BUTLER, S., of Bristol	I. 287
BUTLER, Rev. T., letter from, to his wife	II. 427
BUTLER, W. H., letter from	I. 232
BUTLERS, the three Dr. Butlers who have been Head-Masters	I. xvi
BYRON, Lord, letter from	I. 99
CAMBRIDGE defends her residents from Dr. Butler's boys	I. 296
CAREERS of Dr. Butler's last praepostors	II. 195
CARLISLE, N., letter from	I. 305, 449
CARR, —	II. 197
CASE, W. A.	II. 195
CAWSTON, A. W. (afterwards Rev.), letter from	I. 158
subsequent movements	I. 163
CHAPEL, the School, and the Trustees	I. 91
CHARGES, Dr. Butler's, urging life insurance	I. 333
on education of poorer classes	I. 367
on morbid sentimentality	I. 425
Charlemagne, Prince Lucien Buonaparte's poem, translation of, by Dr. Butler and Rev. F. Hodgson	I. 81, 82
CHARTERHOUSE, monitors at	I. 8
Christian Liberty, sermon on	I. 72; II. 447
Church Dignities, pamphlet on	II. 52
CHURCHYARDS, cattle and horses in	I. 457
CIRCULARS to parents	I. 128, 179
CLARENDON, Lord, letters from	I. 233, 332
CLARKE, Rev. C., his sketch of Dr. Butler	I. xxviii
CLERGYMEN, sundry unnamed, letters from	I. 362; II. 45, 213, 229, 230, 236, 323, 391, 403, 413, 415
CLERICAL Society, the, for the Archdeaconry of Derby	I. 372-384
COINS, letters on certain	I. 340, 350
COKE, Rev. E. T., letter from	II. 330
COLERIDGE, S. T., letter from	I. 22
CONSECRATION, Dr. Butler's	II. 203
COPE, E. M. (afterwards Rev.)	II. 195
COPLEY, Sir J. S. (afterwards Lord Lyndhurst), letter from	I. 346
CORY, Dr., letter from	I. 162

Life and Letters of Dr. Butler

COTTON, Rev. C. E., letter from ... I. 379
"COUGHING in a shady grove," etc. ... I. 322
CURREY, W. W., letter from ... I. 139
CURRICULUM, the Shrewsbury, in 1820 ... I. 229, 230
CURZON, Hon. R., letter from ... II. 411

DARWIN, Charles ... I. 188 ; II. 144
DARWIN, Dr. Robert ... I. 339
DELPHI, memorandum on ... I. 184
"DESAVOUE, je te," ... I. 119
DIBDIN, Rev. T. F., D.D., letter from ... II. 101
DICKINSON, S., letter from ... I. 110
DON, Captain Patrick ... I. 7
DRURY, Rev. C. ... II. 285, 286
DRURY, Rev. H., letters from ... I. xviii, 261, 422, 429, 430, 445 ; II. 158, 170, 244
"DUCKSTEALER, he was a" ... I. 363
DU GARD, Dr., letter from ... I. 123

EDUCATION of the poorer classes, Dr. Butler on ... I. 367
ELLISTON, R. W., letter from ... I. 127
ELMSLEY, Rev. P., letters from ... I. 70, 78, 79, 82, 98, 167
    letter to Rev. C. J. Blomfield ... I. 77, 78
EPITAPH on Dr. Butler's parents ... I. 286
    on Dr. Butler ... II. 428
"Eton Roll, The" ... I. 260
"EUBULUS," Dr. Butler's two pamphlets signed ... I. 246
EVANS, Rev. R. W. (afterwards Archdeacon), letters from I. 292 ; II. 157
    letter to Rev. T. Butler ... II. 440
    his preface to the *Bishopric of Souls* ... II. 174
EVANS, Rev. T. S., letter from ... II. 409
EXAMINATIONS, past and present ... I. xx, xxi
    Dr. Kennedy on Dr. Butler's system of ... I. 296, 297 ; II. 442
EXCISEMAN, Dr. Butler and the ... I. 326

FIRE in School tower ... I. 311
FISHING, Greek, Dr. Butler's notes on ... II. 13
    the Odyssean mode of ... II. 24
FOREIGN tours : to Waterloo ... I. 130
    to Switzerland and N. Italy ... I. 166
    to Rome ... I. 265
    Switzerland and N. Italy ... I. 424
FORESTER, Weld, letter from, to the boys ... I. 239
Forte and *forsitan* ... I. 385
"FORTUNATE YOUTH" ... I. 152-164

Index

FOULKES, E. S. (afterwards Rev.)   II. 196
FRANCE, Francis (afterwards Archdeacon)   II. 195
FRASER, James (afterwards Bishop)   II. 195
    letters from   II. 341, 395

"G'S WORLD"   I. 44
GABELL, Dr., Head-Master of Winchester, letter from   I. 181
GARNETT, Dr. R.   I. 173
Geography, Modern and Antient, Dr. Butler's   I. 94
GILPIN, G.   II. 194, 197
GLADSTONE, Rt. Hon. W. E.   I. 296
GREEK, greater proficiency in, at both Oxford and Cambridge, than in Latin   I. 420
GRENVILLE. *See* Neville Grenville.
GRETTON, Dr. G., Dean of Hereford, letter from   I. 218
GUTHRIE'S *Geographical Grammar*   I. 43

HALFORD, Sir H., Bart., letters from   II. 289, 413, 416
HAMPDEN, Dr. (afterwards Bishop), insult to, at Oxford   II. 243
HAWTREY, Rev. E. C. (afterwards D.D. and Head-Master of Eton), letters from   II. 113, 115
HEATH, T., letter from   II. 209
HEBER, Rev. Reg. (afterwards Bishop), letter from   I. 239
HEMANS, Mrs., letter from   I. 405
HERFORD, J., letter from   II. 201
HIGMAN, J. P. (afterwards Rev.), letter from   I. 323
HILDYARD, James (afterwards Rev.), letters from   II. 1, 344, 376, 377
HILDYARD, Rev. W., letter from   II. 1
HILL, Lord   I. 124, 307
    inscriptions on his column at Shrewsbury   I. 213, 214
HILL, Rev. T., letters from   II. 6, 137, 169
HILL, Hon. W. (afterwards Lord Berwick), letters from   I. 56, 271; II. 131, 185, 328
HODGSON, Rev. F. (afterwards Archdeacon and Provost of Eton), translates *Charlemagne* with Dr. Butler   I. 82
    letters from   I. 119, 125; II. 264
HODSON, Archdeacon, letters from   II. 351, 387, 408
    letters to Mrs. Lloyd   II. 418, 421
HOLIDAYS, mischief done by boys going home for   I. 110, 139, 402
HOLYOAKE-GOODRICKE, Sir F., Bart., letter from   II. 179
HOMER, and Shakespeare   I. 82, 217
    a real person   I. 94
HONE, W., letters from   I. 314, 330
HOOK, Rev. W. F. (afterwards D.D. and Dean), letters from   II. 18, 81, 84, 89, 96, 128, 177, 221, 250, 253, 262, 263
HOWLEY, Archbishop, letter from   II. 218

Life and Letters of Dr. Butler

HUGHES, Rev. T. S., sketch of his career — I. 58
    letters from   I. 59, 65, 69, 142, 158, 232, 256, 262, 289, 311, 312, 354; II. 27, 109
    letter to Mr. William Upcott *re* Porson — I. 63
HUMPHRY, Canon W. G., on Dr. Butler — I. 247
    verses on the Princess Victoria going out hunting — II. 41
    taking the Pitt Scholarship — II. 130
HUSTLER, Rev. J. D., letter from — II. 145

" I " and " me," and Greek verbs in ω and ΜΙ — II. 75
ILIAD, written in Asia Minor, by one man – its dialect — I. 94, 95
INFLUENZA in 1833 — II. 58
INSCRIPTIONS, to the Emperor of Russia — I. 150
    notes on Greek, found by Mr. Hughes — I. 173, etc.
    on Lord Hill's column at Shrewsbury — I. 213, 214
    for Mr. Hawkes's monument — I. 298, 301, 303
    on the Burgonian Vase, reading of — I. 440
    Dr. Parr on — I. 300
    a few rules concerning — I. 302
IRELAND Scholarship taken by Shrewsbury men in 1827, 1828, 1829, 1830, 1831, and 1833 — II. 62

JACKSON, E., letter from — I. 117
JAMES, Dr., recreated Rugby — I. 7
    account of the Rugby curriculum — I. 25-44
    Dr. Butler's inscription for his monument — I. 242
    letters from — I. 12, 13, 14, 16, 20, 51
JENKINSON, Hon. C. (afterwards Lord Liverpool), letters from — I. 181; II. 33, 38, 41
JENKYNS, Dr., Master of Balliol, letter from — I. 446
JEUDWINE, J., relations between him and Dr. Butler — I. 45, etc.
    his death — I. 50
    Mr. Willis's memorandum *re* the unruliness of his boys — II. 39
JUBILEE of King George III at Kenilworth — I. 60
" JUDGEMENT," spelling of — I. 246
JUNIUS, Dr. Butler on — I. 97

KEATE, Dr., Head-Master of Eton, letters from — I. 180, 437, 447
KENILWORTH, appointment to living of — I. 52
    evening sermon at — I. 333
KENNEDY, B. H. (afterwards Rev., D.D., and Greek Professor at Cambridge) — I. xx, xxvi, 45, 77, 242; II. 147, 198, 223
    letters from — I. 294, 304, 308, 391; II. 160, 163, 164, 165, 267, 409
    letter to Rev. G. Sandford — I. 296
KIRKBY, Thomas — I. 313
KLAPROTH, J. H., letter from — I. 408

Index

KNOTT, Rev. J. M., circular *re* Mr. Walker's bludgeons   II. 208
LADY, a, letter from   II. 136
LANDOR, W. S., at Rugby   I. 8, 9
LAWSON, Marmaduke, sketch of his career   I. 84
    letters from   I. 85, 95, 115, 119, 171
LAWSUIT, the School   I. 288, 310, 343, 344, 386
LEIGH, Chandos, on Dr. Butler's being asked to stand for Rugby
    in 1827   I. 393
LEIGHTON, Col., letter from   I. 87
LEVIEN, E.   II. 197
LICHFIELD and Coventry, severance of the diocese of   II. 271
LIVERPOOL, Lord. *See* Jenkinson, Hon. C.
LLOYD, Archdeacon   I. xvi ; II. 197, 217, 439
LONG, Rev. C. M., letter from   II. 348
LONGLEY, Dr. (afterwards Archbishop of Canterbury), visit to
    Shrewsbury   I. xviii, 423
    letters from   I. 432 ; II. 171
LONSDALE, J. G. (afterwards Rev.)   II. 196
LYNES, Rev. J., letter from   I. 327

MACNAB, —   II. 195
MADDOCK, Rev. G. A.   I. 386
MAGDALENE, treatment of Dr. Butler's pupils at   I. 233, 234, 236, 345, 355, 361, 370
MALTBY, Dr. E. (afterwards Bishop), letters from   I. 339, 392 ; II. 64, 86, 103, 117, 120, 125, 202, 227, 243, 248, 292, 350, 397, 412, 417, 423
MARKS, Dr. Butler and   I. xxii, xxiii
MARSH, H. A. (afterwards Rev.), address to Dr. Butler on
    occasion of his last speech-day   II. 190
    his career   II. 195
MASKELL, Rev. W., his pamphlet on Owen Parfitt   I. 101, 102
    letter from   I. 108, 109
MASSIE, E. (afterwards Rev.), letter from   I. 407
MATTHEWS, Rev. G., letters from   II. 47, 51, 63, 67, 136, 283
MAY, G. A. C., letter from   II. 339
MAYOR, Prof. J. E. B.   I. xv, xvii
" ME " and " I," and Greek verbs in μι and ω   II. 75
" MELANCHOLY truth," the   I. xxviii
MELANCHTHON'S Commonplace Book   II. 357
MELBOURNE, Lord, letters from   II. 176, 179, 184, 205
MERIAN, Baron Andreas   I. 15
    sketch of his career   I. 135
    letters from   I. 137, 147, 189, 207, 209, 210, 212, 214, 215, 216, 236, 244, 253, 260, 290, 291, 293, 295, 303, 316, 317, 332, 341, 346, 357, 389, 390, 394

Life and Letters of Dr. Butler

MERIAN, Baron Andreas, his death — I. 396, 408
MERIT money, monthly — I. xxiv
METCALFE, Rev. W., letter from — II. 287
MONEY, Miss (afterwards Mrs. St. Barbe), letters from — I. 127, 243, 263; II. 43
MONK, Rev. J. H. (afterwards Bishop) — I. 59, 253
    letters from — I. xviii; II. 156
MONTAGU, E. W. (afterwards Rev.) — II. 196
MOORE, Rev. H. (afterwards Archdeacon), his funeral sermon on Dr. Butler — II. 429
    letters from — II. 342, 345
MORSE, F. (afterwards Rev.) — II. 196
MOSS, Rev. H. W., Head-Master of Shrewsbury School — I. xv.
MUNRO, H. A. J. (afterwards Rev.) — II. 195, 450
MURRAY, John — I. xv; II. 443

N——, Mr., a schoolmaster, letters from — II. 299, 302, 307
NASEBY, night before the battle of — I. 2
NATIONAL anthem, words of, not familiar in 1809 — I. 61
NEVILLE GRENVILLE, Hon. and Rev. George, Master of Magdalene, letter from — I. 370
NORMAN, Rev. A., letters from — I. 277, 381, 414
NOUNS and verbs — I. 321

ODYSSEAN mode of fishing still practised off Sicily — II. 24
ODYSSEY, Porson on the geography of — I. 61
    written by a woman — I. 82
    sooner understood if harder to understand — I. 95
OXFORD defends her residents from Dr. Butler's boys — I. 296

PARDOE, J., letter from — I. 402
PARENT, letter from a — I. 122
PARFITT, Owen, mystery of — I. 101
PARR, Dr. — I. xix, 56, 61-63, 69, 138, 140, 173, 300, 327, 330, 331
    letters from — I. 164, 284
PARR-LYNES, Col., baptised by Bishops Maltby and Butler — II. 351
PARTRIDGES shot flying, the first in Warwickshire — I. 3
PAYNE, P. S., letter from — I. 446
PEACOCK, Rev. G., letter from — II. 130
PEELE, J. J., letter from — II. 292
PEILE, Rev. T. W. (afterwards D.D. and Head-Master of Repton School) — I. 24
    letters from — II. 322, 324, 378, 411
PLATE presented to Dr. Butler — II. 179, 192, 222
POCKET-MONEY, circular *re* — I. 128
POLE, E. S. Chandos, letter from — II. 365

Index

PORSON, Prof.	I. 59, 62, 65, 169
PORTRAITS of Dr. Butler	I. 313; II. 361, 439
PRAEPOSTORS, their duties, and spelling of word	I. 241, 242
Praxis on Latin Prepositions	I. 287
PRAYERS " excused "	I. 353
PRICE, Sir Uvedale, Bart. (?), letter from, to Dr. Parr	I. 321
PUNCH " *aux quatre fleuves* "	I. 425
RAMPINGEST-SCAMPINGEST, etc.	I. 353
RECTOR, letter from a	II. 20
REYNOLDS, Mr. Commissioner, letters from	II. 367, 424
ROME, Dr. Butler at	I. 266-268
ROSCOE, W., M.P., letter from	I. 79
ROTHERY, H. C.	II. 195
ROUTH, Dr., President of Magdalen, letter from	II. 160
ROWLEY, Rev. T. (afterwards D.D.), Head-Master of Bridgnorth School, letter from	II. 66
ROYAL visit to Shrewsbury	II. 33-38
RUGBY School	I. 7-11, 25-44, 53, 283, 392, 393; II. 148
RYDER, Hon. H., Bishop of Lichfield and Coventry, letter from	I. 404
ST. BARBE, Mrs. *See* Money, Miss.	
SALE, C. J. (afterwards Rev.)	II. 196
SALES of Dr. Butler's collections	II. 439
SANDFORD, Rev. G.	I. xx, 296
SCOTT, Rev. Alex., letter from	I. 434
SCOTT, R. (afterwards Master of Balliol and Dean of Rochester)	I. xvii, 434, 435
letters from	I. 450, 458; II. 5, 21, 75, 134, 183 336, 353, 358, 360
SEDGWICK, Prof. Adam, letters from	II. 109, 143
SERMON on *Christian Liberty*, Dr. Butler's	I. 72; II. 447
SERRES, Mrs. Olivia Wilmot	I. 5
SHAKESPEARE and Homer the only two poets	I. 82, 217
SHEEPSHANKS, Rev. T.	I. 163, 276
letter to Mrs. Butler	I. 224
SHELLEY, the storm in which he was lost, and Dr. Butler	I. 270
SHEPHERD, Rev. W., letters from	I. 297, 300
SHILLETO, R. (afterwards Rev.)	I. 185, 277, 352; II. 437
letter from	I. 445
SHIRLEY, Rev. W. A. (afterwards Bishop), letter from	I. 426
SLANEY, R. A., M.P., letters from	II. 18, 415
SOTHEBY, S. Leigh, letter from	II. 357
SPEECH-DAY, Dr. Butler's final	II. 186, etc.
SPENCER, Lord, letter from	I. 240
SPENCER, P.	II. 4

STATUE of Dr. Butler II. 438
STOWELL, Lord, letter from I. 378
STUDIES, School I. 42, 92, 93
SUSSEX, H.R.H. the Duke of, letters from (published by permission of Her Majesty) I. 417, 421; II. 38, 114, 124, 236, 296, 310
SUTTON, Mrs. I. 307
SYMONS, Rev. B. P. (afterwards Master of Wadham), letters from II. 1, 172

TALFOURD, Serjeant, letter from II. 144
TATE, Rev. James, Head-Master of Richmond School, letters from I. 261, 364, 393; II. 8
TAYLOR, R. I. 326
TEA-URN, the first in Kenilworth I. 4
TERMS, Dr. Butler's II. 127
THOMAS, M. (afterwards Bishop) II. 196
THORP, Rev. R. A., letters from I. 448, 459, 463
THRING, H. (afterwards Lord Thring) II. 195
TILLBROOK, Rev. S. I. 125; II. 145
    letters from I. 126, 128, 140, 143, 145, 146, 185, 206, 210, 223, 237, 309, 313, 328, 336, 342, 354, 366, 387, 409, 411, 412
    II. 3, 11, 22, 25, 26, 75, 103
TOURNAY, Rev. W., letter from I. 435
TOWNSEND, Rev. G., letter to the *Morning Chronicle*, October 19th, 1837 II. 311
TRINITY men, their aversion for St. John's I. 67
TRUSTEES of Shrewsbury School I. 53, 91, 310, 371
TURBULENCE, an epidemic of I. 179

UMBRELLA, the first in Kenilworth I. 4
"UTIS, Old" I. 212

VASE, Burgonian, inscription on I. 442
VAUGHAN, Dr., Dean of Llandaff I. xxiv; II. 164
VERBS and nouns I. 321
VYSE, N., letter from I. 442

WARTER, Rev. J. Wood, letter from II. 77
WATERLOO, rejoicings after I. 123
    the field of, in 1816 I. 130, etc.
WATKINSON, Rev. R., letter from II. 180
WAYNE, Rev. W. H., letter from II. 379
WEBB, "Young General," and Georgius Rex apples I. 6
WEBSTER, J., letter from II. 276
WELLDON, Dr. (formerly Head-Master of Tonbridge School) I. xx, 45, 69; II. 197, 444
WHITER, Rev. W., letters from I. 274, 278

Index

"WIG, Wear a" I. 69
WILLIAMS, Bulkeley, letter from I. 233
WILLIAMS, Rev. James, letter from II. 27
WILLIAMS, Rev. P., letter from I. 234
WILLIS, Rev. A. II. 168, 169
    memorandum *re* the unruliness of Mr. Jeudwine's boys II. 39
WILMOT, Dr. I. 5
WINE, boys stealing Dr. Butler's I. 122
WOLVEY, appointment to Prebendal Stall of I. 55
WOOD, Rev. James (afterwards D.D. and Master of St. John's,
    Cambridge), letters from I. 67, 187, 217, 327; II. 167
WOOD, James, bailiff of the Manor of Eccleshall II. 267, 331, 346
WOOD, Rev. John, letters from I. 372, 373, 380, 382, 415
WOOLL, Dr., Head-Master of Rugby I. 283, 392
WORDSWORTH, Dr. C., Master of Trinity, on Dr. Butler's visits
    to Cambridge I. xxiv, xxv
WORDSWORTH, W., Poet, letter from II. 2
WYNNE, Mrs., letter from I. 57

YOUNG, Rev. J., letter from II. 343